Solutions Guide for

CALCULUS AND ANALYTIC GEOMETRY

VOLUME 2

Philip Gillett
University of Wisconsin

Complete solutions by the author
of all problems in Chapters 8 through 14

Published simultaneously in Canada.

Printed in the United States of America.

International Standard Book Number: 0-669-03212-3

PREFACE

This solutions guide is primarily for students. Instructors may find it useful as an aid in selection of problems to assign, but there are no comments suggesting how the textbook should be used. The needs of instructors vary so widely that any advice of that sort would by too vague to be of much help.

Students, on the other hand, can benefit enormously from the judicious use of a solutions manual. Naturally they should be warned not to consult it before tackling the problem assignment on their own. But a conscientious student, willing to resist the temptation of looking up solutions too soon, can learn a great deal by comparing notes with somebody else's work.

In this case the "somebody else" is the author of the textbook, which guarantees that the solutions mesh with the book in style and substance. That does not mean these solutions are the only ones possible, but at least there is a unity between book and solutions manual that should make life easier for the student.

I tried hard to avoid errors and misprints. If any are found, I will appreciate a note about them.

Philip Gillett

CONTENTS

CHAPTER 8   EXPONENTIAL AND LOGARITHMIC FUNCTIONS

Section 8.1   THE NATURAL LOGARITHM

1.(a) $\ln 2 = \int_1^2 \dfrac{dt}{t}$

(b) The partition is $\{1, 5/4, 3/2, 7/4, 2\}$, with $\Delta t = 1/4$ and midpoints 9/8, 11/8, 13/8, 15/8. Hence

$$\int_1^2 \frac{dt}{t} \approx \frac{1}{4}\left(\frac{8}{9}+\frac{8}{11}+\frac{8}{13}+\frac{8}{15}\right) = 2\left(\frac{1}{9}+\frac{1}{11}+\frac{1}{13}+\frac{1}{15}\right) \approx 0.691$$

2.(a) $\ln 3 = \int_1^3 \dfrac{dt}{t}$

(b) The partition is $\{1, 4/3, 5/3, 2, 7/3, 8/3, 3\}$, with $\Delta t = 1/3$ and midpoints 7/6, 9/6, 11/6, 13/6, 15/6, 17/6. Hence

$$\int_1^3 \frac{dt}{t} \approx \frac{1}{3}\left(\frac{6}{7}+\frac{6}{9}+\frac{6}{11}+\frac{6}{13}+\frac{6}{15}+\frac{6}{17}\right) = 2\left(\frac{1}{7}+\frac{1}{9}+\frac{1}{11}+\frac{1}{13}+\frac{1}{15}+\frac{1}{17}\right) \approx 1.095$$

3. $\ln 18 = \ln (2)(3^2) = \ln 2 + \ln (3^2) = \ln 2 + 2\ln 3 \approx 0.69 + 2(1.10) = 2.89$

4. $\ln 1.5 = \ln \dfrac{3}{2} = \ln 3 - \ln 2 \approx 1.10 - 0.69 = 0.41$

5. $\ln \dfrac{1}{9} = \ln 1 - \ln (3^2) = 0 - 2\ln 3 \approx -2(1.10) = -2.2$

6. $\ln (4\sqrt[3]{2}) = \ln (2^2 \cdot 2^{1/3}) = \ln (2^{7/3}) = \dfrac{7}{3}\ln 2 \approx \dfrac{7}{3}(0.69) = 1.61$

7. $\ln 0$ is undefined.

8. $y = \ln x + \ln 2 \approx \ln x + 0.69$, so the graph is the graph of $y = \ln x$ shifted 0.69 units upward. (See Figure 1.)

9. $y = \ln x - \ln 2 \approx \ln x - 0.69$, so the graph is the graph of $y = \ln x$ shifted 0.69 units downward. (See Figure 1.)

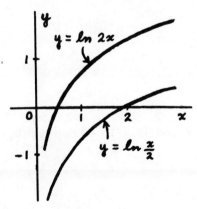

Figure 1

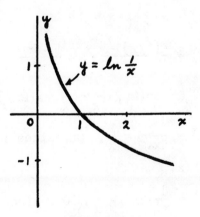

Figure 2

10. $y = -\ln x$, so the graph is the graph of $y = \ln x$ reflected in the x axis. (See Figure 2.)

1

11. $y = \ln x$ if $x > 0$ and $y = \ln(-x)$ if $x < 0$. The graph is the union of the graph of $y = \ln x$ and its reflection in the y axis. (See Figure 3.)

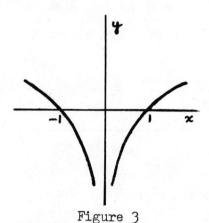

Figure 3

12. If x and y are positive, $\ln x + \ln y = 0 \iff \ln xy = 0 \iff xy = 1$, so the graph is the first-quadrant branch of the hyperbola $xy = 1$.

13. $f'(x) = \dfrac{1}{2x-5} \cdot 2 = \dfrac{2}{2x-5}$

14. $f'(x) = \dfrac{1}{x^3-1} \cdot 3x^2 = \dfrac{3x^2}{x^3-1}$

15. $f'(x) = \dfrac{1}{\cos x} \cdot (-\sin x) = -\tan x$

16. $f'(x) = \dfrac{1}{\sec x} \cdot \sec x \tan x = \tan x$. This is the negative of the result in Problem 15 because $\ln \sec x = \ln(1/\cos x) = -\ln \cos x$.

17. $f'(x) = 2(\ln x) \cdot \dfrac{1}{x} = \dfrac{2}{x} \ln x$

18. $f'(x) = x \cdot \dfrac{1}{x} + \ln x = 1 + \ln x$

19. $f'(x) = \dfrac{x(1/x) - \ln x}{x^2} = \dfrac{1 - \ln x}{x^2}$

20. $f'(x) = \cos(\ln x) \cdot \dfrac{1}{x} = \dfrac{1}{x} \cos(\ln x)$

21. $f'(x) = \dfrac{1}{5x} \cdot 5 = \dfrac{1}{x}$. Or, since $f(x) = \ln 5 + \ln x$ and $\ln 5$ is a constant, $f'(x) = 1/x$.

22. $f'(x) = \dfrac{1}{x^3} \cdot 3x^2 = \dfrac{3}{x}$. Or, since $f(x) = 3 \ln x$, $f'(x) = 3/x$.

23. $f'(x) = \dfrac{1}{x \sin x}(x \cos x + \sin x) = \cot x + \dfrac{1}{x}$. Or, since $f(x) = \ln x + \ln \sin x$, $f'(x) = \dfrac{1}{x} + \dfrac{1}{\sin x} \cdot \cos x = \dfrac{1}{x} + \cot x$.

24. $f'(x) = \frac{1}{\sqrt{x^2+1}} \cdot \frac{x}{\sqrt{x^2+1}} = \frac{x}{x^2+1}$. Or, since $f(x) = \frac{1}{2} \ln(x^2+1)$, $f'(x) =$

$\frac{1}{2} \cdot \frac{1}{x^2+1} \cdot 2x = \frac{x}{x^2+1}$.

25. Since $f(x) = \ln(x^2+1)^{-1}$, $f'(x) = \frac{1}{(x^2+1)^{-1}} \cdot (-1)(x^2+1)^{-2}(2x) = \frac{-2x}{x^2+1}$.

Or, since $f(x) = -\ln(x^2+1)$, $f'(x) = \frac{-1}{x^2+1} \cdot 2x = \frac{-2x}{x^2+1}$.

26. (a) $f'(x) = \frac{1}{\tan x} \cdot \sec^2 x + \frac{1}{\cot x} \cdot (-\csc^2 x) = \frac{1}{\sin x \cos x} - \frac{1}{\sin x \cos x} = 0$ (for

all x for which $\tan x$ and $\cot x$ are positive). Thus $f(x)$ is constant in the

interval $(0, \pi/2)$. Since the period of tan and cot is π, $f(x)$ is the same

constant in $(\pi, 3\pi/2)$, $(-\pi, -\pi/2)$, and so on. To discover the constant, put

$x = \pi/4$ to find $f(x) = \ln 1 + \ln 1 = 0$. Thus $f(x) = 0$ in its domain. The graph

is shown in Figure 4.

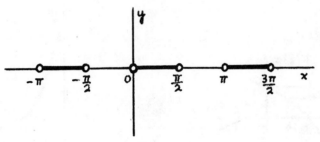

Figure 4

(b) $f(x) = \ln(\tan x \cot x) = \ln 1 = 0$ in the domain.

(c) See Figure 4.

27. (a) $D_x \ln |x| = \frac{1}{|x|} \cdot \frac{|x|}{x} = \frac{1}{x}$

(b) If $x > 0$, $D_x \ln |x| = D_x \ln x = \frac{1}{x}$, while if $x < 0$, $D_x \ln |x| = D_x \ln(-x) =$

$\frac{1}{-x} \cdot (-1) = \frac{1}{x}$.

28. Since $x^2 = |x|^2$, $\ln x^2 = \ln |x|^2 = 2\ln |x|$. If $f(x) = \ln x^2$, then $f'(x) =$

$\frac{1}{x^2} \cdot 2x = \frac{2}{x}$. Or, since $f(x) = 2\ln |x|$, $f'(x) = 2 \cdot \frac{1}{x} = \frac{2}{x}$ (from Problem 27). The

formula $\ln x^2 = 2\ln x$ is valid only if $x > 0$; the formula $\ln x^2 = 2\ln |x|$ holds

for all $x \neq 0$. On the other hand, the left side of $\ln x^3 = 3\ln x$ is defined

only for $x > 0$ in the first place (unlike the left side of $\ln x^2 = 2\ln x$).

29. Using Problem 27 and the Chain Rule, we find $f'(x) = \frac{1}{\sin 2x} \cdot 2\cos 2x =$

$2\cot 2x$. Or, since $f(x) = \ln |2\sin x \cos x| = \ln 2 + \ln |\sin x| + \ln |\cos x|$,

3

$$f'(x) = 0 + \frac{1}{\sin x} \cdot \cos x + \frac{1}{\cos x}(-\sin x) = \frac{\cos^2 x - \sin^2 x}{\sin x \cos x} = \frac{2(\cos^2 x - \sin^2 x)}{2 \sin x \cos x}$$

$$= \frac{2 \cos 2x}{\sin 2x} = 2 \cot 2x$$

30. $\ln xy - 2x - y = 5 \implies \frac{1}{xy}(xy' + y) - 2 - y' = 0 \implies xy' + y - 2xy - xyy' = 0 \implies$

$(x - xy)y' = 2xy - y \implies y' = \dfrac{y(2x - 1)}{x(1 - y)}$

31. $\ln y = x \implies \dfrac{1}{y}\dfrac{dy}{dx} = 1 \implies \dfrac{dy}{dx} = y$

32. Figure 5 shows the graph of F, which is a strictly increasing function because $F'(x) = 1/x > 0$ for all $x > 0$. It follows that $a \neq b \implies \ln a \neq \ln b$, which is equivalent to the implication $\ln a = \ln b \implies a = b$. Not every function has this property. If $f(x) = x^2$, for example, then $f(-1) = f(1)$, but $-1 \neq 1$.

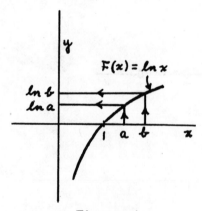

Figure 5

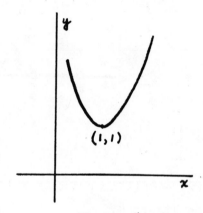

Figure 6

33. The domain is $x > 0$. We have $f'(x) = 2x^2 \cdot \frac{1}{x} + 4x \ln x - 2x = 4x \ln x = 0 \iff$ $\ln x = 0 \iff x = 1$. ($x = 0$ is not in the domain.) Since $f'(x)$ changes from minus to plus at $x = 1$, $f(1) = -1$ is a local minimum.

34.(a) The domain is $x > 0$.

(b) When $x \to 0$, $y \approx -2 \ln x \to \infty$.

(c) $y' = 2x - \frac{2}{x} = \frac{2(x^2 - 1)}{x} = 0$ when $x = 1$. ($x = -1$ is not in the domain.) Since y' changes from minus to plus at $x = 1$, $f(1) = 1$ is a local minimum.

(d) $y'' = 2 + 2/x^2 > 0$, so the curve is always concave up. See Figure 6.

35. The domain requires $\frac{1 + x^2}{1 - x^2} > 0 \iff 1 - x^2 > 0$ (because $1 + x^2$ is always positive) $\iff -1 < x < 1$. When $x \uparrow 1$ or $x \downarrow -1$, $\frac{1 + x^2}{1 - x^2} \to \infty$ and hence $y \to \infty$. Thus $x = \pm 1$ are vertical asymptotes. To find y', write

4

$$y = \ln(1+x^2) - \ln(1-x^2) \implies y' = \frac{2x}{1+x^2} + \frac{2x}{1-x^2} = \frac{4x}{(1+x^2)(1-x^2)}$$

Since $y' = 0$ when $x = 0$ (and changes from minus to plus at $x = 0$), we have a maximum ($y = 0$ at $x = 0$). See Figure 7.

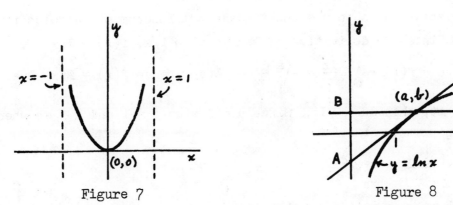

Figure 7   Figure 8

36. See Figure 8. Since $y' = 1/x$, the slope of the tangent at (a,b) is $1/a$. An equation of the tangent is $y - b = \frac{1}{a}(x-a)$. When $x = 0$ we have $y = b-1$, that is, $A = (0, b-1)$. Since $B = (0,b)$, we find $AB = b - (b-1) = 1$.

37. The graphs intersect when $\ln x = -x$, that is, when $x + \ln x = 0$. Figure 9 shows that the root is about $x_0 = 0.6$. Letting $f(x) = x + \ln x$, we have $f'(x) = 1 + 1/x$, so Newton's Method gives

$$x_1 = x_0 - f(x_0)/f'(x_0) = 0.6 - \frac{0.6 + \ln 0.6}{1 + 1/0.6} \approx 0.57$$

Another application gives

$$x_2 = 0.57 - \frac{0.57 + \ln 0.57}{1 + 1/0.57} \approx 0.5671$$

so $x_1 = 0.57$ appears to be accurate to two places.

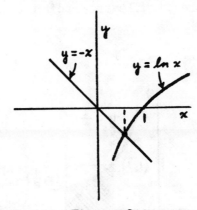

Figure 9

38. The quickest way to do this is to observe that $\ln t$ is an antiderivative

of $1/t$. Hence

$$f(x) = \int_a^x \frac{dt}{t} = \ell n\, t \Big|_a^x = \ell n\, x - \ell n\, a$$

An alternative solution is to use the definition of $\ell n\, x$, writing

$$f(x) = \int_a^1 \frac{dt}{t} + \int_1^x \frac{dt}{t} = \int_1^x \frac{dt}{t} - \int_1^a \frac{dt}{t} = \ell n\, x - \ell n\, a$$

Still another solution is to use the Fundamental Theorem of Calculus to find $f'(x) = 1/x$. Since the derivative of $\ell n\, x$ is also $1/x$, $f(x) = \ell n\, x + C$. Put $x = 1$ to find $C = f(1) = \int_a^1 \frac{dt}{t} = -\int_1^a \frac{dt}{t} = -\ell n\, a$. Hence $f(x) = \ell n\, x - \ell n\, a$.

39.(a) If $u = at$, then $du = a\,dt$. Since $u = a$ when $t = 1$ and $u = ab$ when $t = b$, we have

$$\int_1^b \frac{dt}{t} = \int_1^b \frac{a\,dt}{at} = \int_a^{ab} \frac{du}{u}$$

(b) Since $\ell n\, u$ is an antiderivative of $1/u$,

$$\int_a^{ab} \frac{du}{u} = \ell n\, u \Big|_a^{ab} = \ell n\, ab - \ell n\, a$$

Hence $\int_1^b \frac{dt}{t} = \ell n\, b = \ell n\, ab - \ell n\, a$, or $\ell n\, ab = \ell n\, a + \ell n\, b$.

40. $\ell n\, (a/b) = \ell n\, (ab^{-1}) = \ell n\, a + \ell n\, (b^{-1}) = \ell n\, a + (-1)\ell n\, b = \ell n\, a - \ell n\, b$

41. F is differentiable (with derivative $1/x$). A differentiable function is automatically continuous.

42. The Composite Function Theorem (Sec. 2.5) says that

$$\lim_{x \to 0} \ell n\, \frac{\sin x}{x} = \ell n\, \left(\lim_{x \to 0} \frac{\sin x}{x}\right) = \ell n\, 1 = 0$$

43. $\ell n\, x$ is the shaded area in Figure 10. The rectangle with base $x - 1$ and altitude $1/x$ has smaller area, while the rectangle with base $x - 1$ and altitude 1 has larger area. Hence

$$\frac{1}{x}(x - 1) < \ell n\, x < 1(x - 1), \text{ or } 1 - \frac{1}{x} < \ell n\, x < x - 1$$

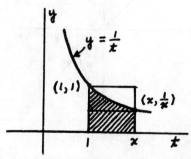

Figure 10

Section 8.2   INVERSE FUNCTIONS

1. f^{-1} exists because no horizontal line intersects the graph of $f(x) = 2x$ more than once. See Figure 1.

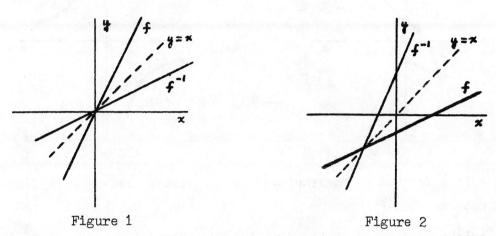

Figure 1   Figure 2

2. f^{-1} exists because no horizontal line intersects the graph of $f(x) = \frac{1}{2}x - 1$ more than once. See Figure 2.

3. f^{-1} exists because no horizontal line intersects the graph of $f(x) = \sqrt{x - 1}$ more than once. See Figure 3.

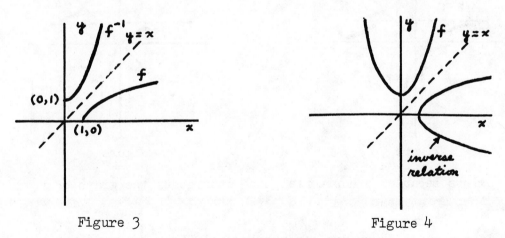

Figure 3   Figure 4

4. f^{-1} does not exist because some horizontal lines intersect the graph of $f(x) = x^2 + 1$ twice. See Figure 4.

5. The graphs are as in Figure 3, with f and f^{-1} interchanged. f^{-1} exists because no horizontal line intersects the graph of $f(x) = x^2 + 1$, $x \geq 0$, more than once.

6. f^{-1} exists because no horizontal line intersects the graph of $f(x) = x^3 + 1$ more than once. See Figure 5.

7

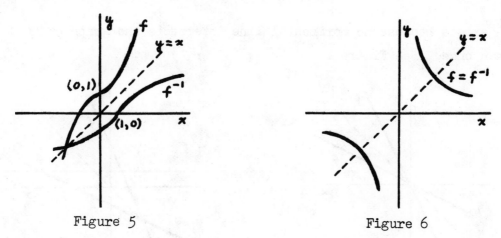

Figure 5   Figure 6

7. f^{-1} exists because no horizontal line intersects the graph of $f(x) = 1/x$ more than once.   See Figure 6.

8. f^{-1} exists because no horizontal line intersects the graph of $f(x) = \dfrac{1}{x-1}$ more than once.   See Figure 7.

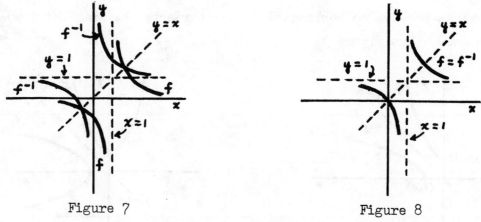

Figure 7   Figure 8

9. f^{-1} exists because no horizontal line intersects the graph of $f(x) = \dfrac{x}{x-1}$ more than once.   See Figure 8.

10. f^{-1} does not exist because some horizontal lines intersect the graph of $f(x) = 1/(x^2+1)$ twice.   See Figure 9.

11. The graphs are the same as in the first-quadrant part of Figure 9. f^{-1} exists because no horizontal line intersects the graph of $f(x) = 1/(x^2+1)$, $x \geq 0$, more than once.

12. f^{-1} does not exist because some horizontal lines intersect the graph of $f(x) = \sin x$, $0 \leq x \leq 2\pi$, twice.   See Figure 10.

8

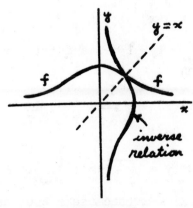

Figure 9

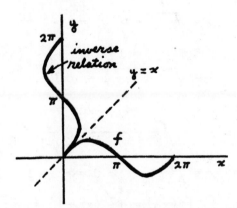

Figure 10

13. f^{-1} exists because no horizontal line intersects the graph of $f(x) = \sin x$, $-\pi/2 \le x \le \pi/2$, more than once. See Figure 11.

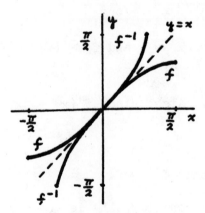

Figure 11

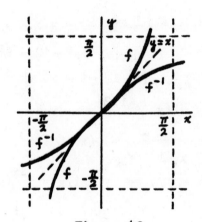

Figure 12

14. f^{-1} exists because no horizontal line intersects the graph of $f(x) = \tan x$, $-\pi/2 < x < \pi/2$, more than once. See Figure 12.

Note: In each of the following (Problems 15-23) we find $y = f^{-1}(x)$ by interchanging x and y in $y = f(x)$ and then solving for y. The same results may be obtained by solving $y = f(x)$ for x and then interchanging x and y.

15.(a) $x = 2y \implies y = \frac{1}{2}x = f^{-1}(x)$

(b) $f^{-1}[f(x)] = f^{-1}(2x) = \frac{1}{2}(2x) = x$ and $f[f^{-1}(x)] = f(\frac{1}{2}x) = 2(\frac{1}{2}x) = x$.

(c) $y = \frac{1}{2}x \implies dy/dx = \frac{1}{2}$. Also, since $f'(x) = 2$, $dy/dx = 1/f'(y) = \frac{1}{2}$.

16.(a) $x = \frac{1}{2}y - 1 \implies 2x = y - 2 \implies y = 2x + 2 = f^{-1}(x)$

(b) $f^{-1}[f(x)] = f^{-1}(\frac{1}{2}x - 1) = 2(\frac{1}{2}x - 1) + 2 = (x - 2) + 2 = x$ and $f[f^{-1}(x)] = f(2x + 2) = \frac{1}{2}(2x + 2) - 1 = (x + 1) - 1 = x$.

9

(c) $y = 2x + 2 \implies dy/dx = 2$. Also, since $f'(x) = \frac{1}{2}$, $dy/dx = 1/f'(y) = 2$.

17.(a) $x = \sqrt{y - 1} \implies x^2 = y - 1 \implies y = x^2 + 1 = f^{-1}(x)$, $x \geq 0$.

(b) $f^{-1}[f(x)] = f^{-1}(\sqrt{x - 1}) = (\sqrt{x - 1})^2 + 1 = (x - 1) + 1 = x$ and $f[f^{-1}(x)] = f(x^2 + 1) = \sqrt{(x^2 + 1) - 1} = \sqrt{x^2} = x$ (because $x \geq 0$).

(c) $y = x^2 + 1 \implies dy/dx = 2x$. Also, since $f'(x) = \dfrac{1}{2\sqrt{x - 1}}$, $dy/dx = 1/f'(y)$ $= 2\sqrt{y - 1} = 2\sqrt{(x^2 + 1) - 1} = 2\sqrt{x^2} = 2x$ (because $x \geq 0$).

18.(a) $x = y^2 + 1$, $y \geq 0 \implies x - 1 = y^2$, $y \geq 0 \implies y = \sqrt{x - 1} = f^{-1}(x)$

(b) $f^{-1}[f(x)] = f^{-1}(x^2 + 1) = \sqrt{(x^2 + 1) - 1} = \sqrt{x^2} = x$ (because $x \geq 0$) and $f[f^{-1}(x)] = f(\sqrt{x - 1}) = (\sqrt{x - 1})^2 + 1 = (x - 1) + 1 = x$.

(c) $y = \sqrt{x - 1} \implies \dfrac{dy}{dx} = \dfrac{1}{2\sqrt{x - 1}}$. Also, since $f'(x) = 2x$, $\dfrac{dy}{dx} = \dfrac{1}{2y} = \dfrac{1}{2\sqrt{x - 1}}$.

19.(a) $x = y^3 + 1 \implies x - 1 = y^3 \implies y = (x - 1)^{1/3} = f^{-1}(x)$

(b) $f^{-1}[f(x)] = f^{-1}(x^3 + 1) = \sqrt[3]{(x^3 + 1) - 1} = \sqrt[3]{x^3} = x$ and $f[f^{-1}(x)] = f(\sqrt[3]{x - 1})$ $(\sqrt[3]{x - 1})^3 + 1 = (x - 1) + 1 = x$.

(c) $y = (x - 1)^{1/3} \implies dy/dx = \frac{1}{3}(x - 1)^{-2/3}$. Also, since $f'(x) = 3x^2$, $\dfrac{dy}{dx} =$ $\dfrac{1}{3y^2} = \dfrac{1}{3(x - 1)^{2/3}} = \frac{1}{3}(x - 1)^{-2/3}$.

20.(a) $x = 1/y \implies y = 1/x = f^{-1}(x)$. (Note that $f^{-1} = f$.)

(b) $f^{-1}[f(x)] = f^{-1}(1/x) = \dfrac{1}{1/x} = x$. The second identity is the same.

(c) $y = 1/x \implies dy/dx = -1/x^2$. Also, since $f'(x) = -1/x^2$, $dy/dx = -y^2 = -1/x^2$.

21.(a) $x = 1/(y - 1) \implies xy - x = 1 \implies xy = x + 1 \implies y = (x + 1)/x = f^{-1}(x)$

(b) $f^{-1}[f(x)] = f^{-1}\left(\dfrac{1}{x - 1}\right) = \dfrac{1/(x - 1) + 1}{1/(x - 1)} = 1 + (x - 1) = x$ and $f[f^{-1}(x)] =$ $f\left(\dfrac{x + 1}{x}\right) = \dfrac{1}{(x + 1)/x - 1} = \dfrac{x}{(x + 1) - x} = x$.

(c) $y = \dfrac{x + 1}{x} = 1 + \dfrac{1}{x} \implies dy/dx = -1/x^2$. Also, since $f'(x) = -1/(x - 1)^2$, $dy/dx = -(y - 1)^2 = -(1 + \dfrac{1}{x} - 1)^2 = -1/x^2$.

22.(a) $x = y/(y - 1) \implies xy - x = y \implies xy - y = x \implies (x - 1)y = x \implies y = \dfrac{x}{x - 1}$ $= f^{-1}(x)$. (Note that $f^{-1} = f$.)

(b) $f^{-1}[f(x)] = f^{-1}\left(\dfrac{x}{x - 1}\right) = \dfrac{x/(x - 1)}{x/(x - 1) - 1} = \dfrac{x}{x - (x - 1)} = x$. The second identity is the same.

(c) $y = \dfrac{x}{x-1} \Rightarrow \dfrac{dy}{dx} = \dfrac{(x-1)-x}{(x-1)^2} = \dfrac{-1}{(x-1)^2}$. Also, since $f'(x) = \dfrac{-1}{(x-1)^2}$,

$$\dfrac{dy}{dx} = -(y-1)^2 = -\left(\dfrac{x}{x-1}-1\right)^2 = -\left(\dfrac{1}{x-1}\right)^2 = \dfrac{-1}{(x-1)^2}.$$

23. (a) $x = 1/(y^2+1)$, $y \geq 0 \Rightarrow xy^2 + x = 1$, $y \geq 0 \Rightarrow xy^2 = 1-x$, $y \geq 0 \Rightarrow$
$y^2 = \dfrac{1-x}{x}$, $y \geq 0 \Rightarrow y = \sqrt{\dfrac{1-x}{x}} = f^{-1}(x)$

(b) $f^{-1}[f(x)] = f^{-1}\left(\dfrac{1}{x^2+1}\right) = \sqrt{\dfrac{1 - 1/(x^2+1)}{1/(x^2+1)}} = \sqrt{(x^2+1)-1} = \sqrt{x^2} = x$

(because $x \geq 0$) and $f[f^{-1}(x)] = f\left(\sqrt{\dfrac{1-x}{x}}\right) = \dfrac{1}{(1-x)/x+1} = \dfrac{x}{(1-x)+x} = x.$

(c) $y = \sqrt{\dfrac{1-x}{x}} \Rightarrow \dfrac{dy}{dx} = \dfrac{1}{2}\left(\dfrac{1-x}{x}\right)^{-1/2}\cdot\dfrac{x(-1)-(1-x)}{x^2} = \dfrac{1}{2}\left(\dfrac{x}{1-x}\right)^{1/2}\cdot\dfrac{-1}{x^2}$. Since

the domain of f^{-1} is $(0,1)$, we can simplify by writing

$$\dfrac{dy}{dx} = \dfrac{-\sqrt{x}}{2x^2\sqrt{1-x}} = \dfrac{-1}{2x^{3/2}\sqrt{1-x}} = \dfrac{-1}{2x\sqrt{x(1-x)}}$$

Also, since $f'(x) = -2x/(x^2+1)^2$,

$$\dfrac{dy}{dx} = -\dfrac{(y^2+1)^2}{2y} = -\dfrac{\left(\dfrac{1-x}{x}+1\right)^2}{2\left(\dfrac{1-x}{x}\right)^{1/2}} = -\dfrac{x^{1/2}(1/x^2)}{2(1-x)^{1/2}} = -\dfrac{1}{2x^{3/2}\sqrt{1-x}} = \dfrac{-1}{2x\sqrt{x(1-x)}}$$

24. Since $f'(x) = 3x^2 + 2 > 0$ for all x, the graph of f is continuous and
rising. Hence no horizontal line intersects it more than once and f^{-1} exists.
Since $f(0) = -1$, the point $(0,-1)$ is on the graph of f, so $(-1,0)$ is on the
graph of f^{-1}. The slope of the graph of $y = f^{-1}(x)$ is

$$\dfrac{dy}{dx} = \dfrac{1}{f'(y)} = \dfrac{1}{3y^2+2} = \dfrac{1}{2} \quad \text{at } (-1,0)$$

The slope of the graph of f is $f'(x) = 3x^2 + 2 = 2$ at $(0,-1)$. These slopes are
reciprocals.

25. If $f(x) = \ell n\, x$, then $f'(x) = 1/x$. Hence the slope of the graph of $y = \ell n^{-1}x$ is $\dfrac{dy}{dx} = \dfrac{1}{f'(y)} = \dfrac{1}{1/y} = y = 1$ at $(0,1)$. The slope of the graph of f is
$f'(x) = 1/x = 1$ at $(1,0)$. These slopes are reciprocals.

26. Since $f(0) = \sin 0 = 0$ and $f(\pi/2) = \sin(\pi/2) = 1$, the points $(0,0)$ and
$(\pi/2,1)$ are on the graph of f. Hence $(0,0)$ and $(1,\pi/2)$ are on the graph of
f^{-1}. Since $f'(x) = \cos x$, the slope of the graph of $y = \sin^{-1}x$ is $dy/dx =$
$1/f'(y) = 1/\cos y$. This is 1 at $(0,0)$ and undefined at $(1,\pi/2)$. The slope of
the graph of f is $f'(x) = \cos x$, which is 1 at $(0,0)$ and 0 at $(\pi/2,1)$. Thus

11

the slopes at $(0,0)$ are reciprocals, while at $(1, \pi/2)$ and $(\pi/2, 1)$ they are undefined and 0, respectively.

27. Since $f(0) = \tan 0 = 0$ and $f(\pi/4) = \tan(\pi/4) = 1$, the points $(0,0)$ and $(\pi/4, 1)$ are on the graph of f. Hence $(0,0)$ and $(1, \pi/4)$ are on the graph of f^{-1}. Since $f'(x) = \sec^2 x$, the slope of the graph of $y = \tan^{-1} x$ is $dy/dx = 1/f'(y) = 1/\sec^2 y$, which is 1 at $(0,0)$ and $\frac{1}{2}$ at $(1, \pi/4)$. The slope of the graph of f is $f'(x) = \sec^2 x$, which is 1 at $(0,0)$ and 2 at $(\pi/4, 1)$.

28. Since some horizontal lines intersect the graph of $f(x) = x^2$ twice, f^{-1} does not exist.

29. The graph of f^{-1} is the reflection of the graph of f in the line $y = x$. If $f^{-1} = f$, this reflection is the same as the graph of f. Hence the graph of f must be symmetric about $y = x$.

30. The graph of g is the reflection of the graph of f in the line $y = x$. When a continuous curve is reflected in a line it remains continuous.

31. If $y = f^{-1}(x)$, then $x = f(y) = y^3$ and $dx/dy = 3y^2$. Thus $dy/dx = 1/(3y^2)$. Since $y = 0$ when $x = 0$, this is undefined at $x = 0$. The geometrical interpretation is that the graph of f has a horizontal tangent at $(0,0)$. Hence the graph of f^{-1} has a vertical tangent at $(0,0)$.

32. $2x\,dx + 2y\,dy = 0$, so $dy/dx = -x/y$ and $dx/dy = -y/x$. These are reciprocals.

33. If $y = f(x) = mx + b$, the inverse may be found by writing

$$x = my + b \implies x - b = my \implies y = \frac{1}{m}(x - b) = f^{-1}(x)$$

The graph of $y = f^{-1}(x)$ is therefore a straight line of slope $1/m$. Its slope by calculus is $dy/dx = 1/f'(y) = 1/m$, since $f'(x) = m$.

34. The domain of $y = \ell n^{-1} x$ is the range of $f(x) = \ell n\, x$, namely $\mathcal{R}$. The range is the domain of f, namely $(0, \infty)$.

35. $y = \ell n^{-1} x$ is the inverse of $f(x) = \ell n\, x$. Since $f'(x) = 1/x$,

$$\frac{dy}{dx} = \frac{1}{f'(y)} = \frac{1}{1/y} = y = \ell n^{-1} x$$

36. Let $x = \ell n^{-1} u$ and $y = \ell n^{-1} v$. Then $\ell n\, x = \ell n(\ell n^{-1} u) = u$ and $\ell n\, y = \ell n(\ell n^{-1} v) = v$. Hence $u + v = \ell n\, x + \ell n\, y = \ell n\, xy$ (by Theorem 1, Sec. 8.1). Take ℓn^{-1} of each side to obtain $\ell n^{-1}(u + v) = \ell n^{-1}(\ell n\, xy) = xy = (\ell n^{-1} u)(\ell n^{-1} v)$.

37. Using the same notation as in Problem 36, we have $u - v = \ell n\, x - \ell n\, y = \ell n(x/y)$ (by Theorem 2, Sec. 8.1). Hence $\ell n^{-1}(u - v) = \ell n^{-1}(\ell n(x/y)) = x/y = (\ell n^{-1} u)/(\ell n^{-1} v)$.

38. Let $y = \ell n^{-1} x$. Then $\ell n\, y = \ell n(\ell n^{-1} x) = x$ and hence $rx = r\ell n\, y = \ell n\, y^r$ (by Theorem 3, Sec. 8.1). It follows that

$$\ell n^{-1}(rx) = \ell n^{-1}(\ell n\, y^r) = y^r = (\ell n^{-1} x)^r$$

Section 8.3   THE NATURAL EXPONENTIAL FUNCTION

1. If x is the number displayed, the e^x key gives e^x. The $\ell n\, x$ key then gives $\ell n\,(e^x) = x$. Similarly, if x is displayed, the $\ell n\, x$ key gives $\ell n\, x$ and the e^x key gives $e^{\ell n\, x} = x$. Hence the original number is returned in both cases.

2. $f_1(x) = x$ for $x > 0$, while $f_2(x) = x$ for all x.

3. $f_1(x) = e^{\ell n\, x^2} = x^2$ for $x > 0$, while $f_2(x) = x^2$ for all x.

4. $f_1(x) = e^{\ell n\, x^3} = x^3$ for $x > 0$, while $f_2(x) = x^3$ for all x.

5. $f_1(x) = e^{\ell n\, 2x} = 2x$ for $x > 0$, while $f_2(x) = 2x$ for all x.

6. $f_1(x) = e^{x}e^{\ell n\, x} = xe^x$ for $x > 0$, while $f_2(x) = xe^x$ for all x.

7. $x = e^{-y} \Longrightarrow \ell n\, x = -y \Longrightarrow y = -\ell n\, x = f^{-1}(x)$

8. $x = \ell n\, 2y \Longrightarrow e^x = 2y \Longrightarrow y = \frac{1}{2}e^x = f^{-1}(x)$

9. $x = e^y - 1 \Longrightarrow x + 1 = e^y \Longrightarrow y = \ell n(x+1) = f^{-1}(x)$

10. $x = \frac{1}{2}\ell n(y+1) \Longrightarrow 2x = \ell n(y+1) \Longrightarrow e^{2x} = y+1 \Longrightarrow y = e^{2x} - 1 = f^{-1}(x)$

11. $x = \dfrac{e^{2y}+1}{e^{2y}-1} \Longrightarrow xe^{2y} - x = e^{2y} + 1 \Longrightarrow (x-1)e^{2y} = x+1 \Longrightarrow e^{2y} = \dfrac{x+1}{x-1} \Longrightarrow$

$2y = \ell n\, \dfrac{x+1}{x-1} \Longrightarrow y = \dfrac{1}{2}\ell n\, \dfrac{x+1}{x-1} = f^{-1}(x)$

12. The given equation reads $\ell n\, x = 1$, from which $x = e$.

13. The graph of $f(x) = e^x$ is rising, so $a < b \Longrightarrow f(a) < f(b)$. Thus

$\ell n\, 2 < 1 < \ell n\, 3 \Longrightarrow e^{\ell n\, 2} < e < e^{\ell n\, 3}$, or $2 < e < 3$

14. From Problem 13 we have $x > 0 \Longrightarrow e^x > e^0$, that is, $e^x > 1$. Similarly, $x < 0 \Longrightarrow e^x < 1$. Since $e^x > 0$ for all x, the second implication actually reads $x < 0 \Longrightarrow 0 < e^x < 1$.

15.(a) The domain of f is the range of $f^{-1}(x) = \ell n\, x$, namely $(-\infty, \infty)$. The range of f is the domain of f^{-1}, namely $(0, \infty)$.

(b) $f'(x) = e^x > 0$ and $f''(x) = e^x > 0$ for all x.

(c) Since $\ell n\, 1 = 0$, the point $(1, 0)$ is on the graph of $f^{-1}(x) = \ell n\, x$. Hence

$(0,1)$ is on the graph of $f(x) = e^x$. Of course it is more direct to observe that $e^0 = 1$.

(d) $y = e^x \to \infty$ when $x \to \infty$ because $x = \ln y \to \infty$ when $y \to \infty$; $y = e^x \to 0$ when $x \to -\infty$ because $x = \ln y \to -\infty$ when $y \to 0$.

16. The graph of $y = e^{2x}$ is similar in shape to the graph of $y = e^x$, but it is steeper when $x > 0$ and approaches the x axis more rapidly when $x < 0$. See Figure 1.

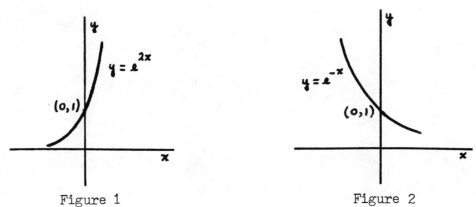

Figure 1   Figure 2

17. The graph of $y = e^{-x}$ is the reflection of the graph of $y = e^x$ in the y axis. See Figure 2.

18. The graph of $y = -e^x$ is the reflection of the graph of $y = e^x$ in the x axis. See Figure 3.

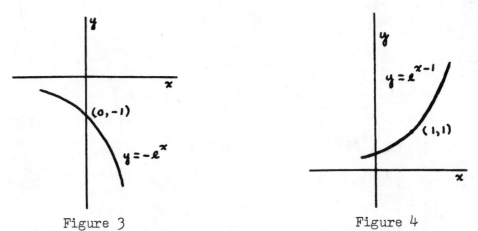

Figure 3   Figure 4

19. The graph of $y = e^{x-1}$ is the graph of $y = e^x$ shifted one unit to the right. See Figure 4.

20. Since e^x and e^{-x} are defined for all x, the domain is $\mathcal{R}$. The equation is unchanged when x and y are replaced by -x and -y, so the graph is symmetric about the origin. Since $y = 0 \iff e^x = e^{-x} \iff e^{2x} = 1 \iff 2x = 0 \iff$

14

$x = 0$, the x and y intercepts are both 0. When $x \to \infty$, $y \approx \frac{1}{2}e^x \to \infty$ and when $x \to -\infty$, $y \approx -\frac{1}{2}e^{-x} \to -\infty$. There are no asymptotes. Since $y' = \frac{1}{2}(e^x + e^{-x}) > 0$ for all x, the curve is always rising. Since $y'' = \frac{1}{2}(e^x - e^{-x})$, the graph is concave up when $x > 0$, down when $x < 0$, with inflection point $(0,0)$. See Figure 5.

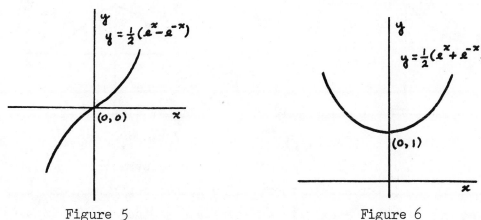

Figure 5   Figure 6

21. Since e^x and e^{-x} are defined for all x, the domain is $\mathcal{R}$. The equation is unchanged when x is replaced by -x, so the graph is symmetric about the y axis. Since $y > 0$ for all x, there is no x intercept; when $x = 0$, $y = 1$. When $x \to \infty$, $y \approx \frac{1}{2}e^x \to \infty$ and when $x \to -\infty$, $y \approx \frac{1}{2}e^{-x} \to \infty$. Since $y' = \frac{1}{2}(e^x - e^{-x})$ $= 0$ when $x = 0$ and since $y'' = \frac{1}{2}(e^x + e^{-x}) > 0$ for all x, the curve is always concave up, with minimum $y = 1$ at $x = 0$. See Figure 6.

22. Since e^x and e^{-x} are defined for all x and $e^x + e^{-x}$ is never 0, the domain is $\mathcal{R}$. The equation is unchanged when x and y are replaced by -x and -y, so the graph is symmetric about the origin. Since $y = 0 \iff x = 0$, the x and y intercepts are both 0. When $x \to \infty$, $y \approx e^x/e^x = 1$ and when $x \to -\infty$, $y \approx$ $-e^{-x}/e^{-x} = -1$, so the lines $y = \pm 1$ are horizontal asymptotes. Since

$$y' = \frac{(e^x + e^{-x})(e^x + e^{-x}) - (e^x - e^{-x})(e^x - e^{-x})}{(e^x + e^{-x})^2}$$

$$= \frac{(e^{2x} + 2 + e^{-2x}) - (e^{2x} - 2 + e^{-2x})}{(e^x + e^{-x})^2} = \frac{4}{(e^x + e^{-x})^2} > 0 \text{ for all } x$$

the curve is always rising. From $y' = 4(e^x + e^{-x})^{-2}$ we have

$$y'' = -8(e^x + e^{-x})^{-3}(e^x - e^{-x}) = \frac{-8(e^x - e^{-x})}{(e^x + e^{-x})^3}$$

This changes from plus to minus at $x = 0$ (where it is 0), so the curve is concave up when $x < 0$, down when $x > 0$, and has inflection point $(0,0)$. See Figure 7.

15

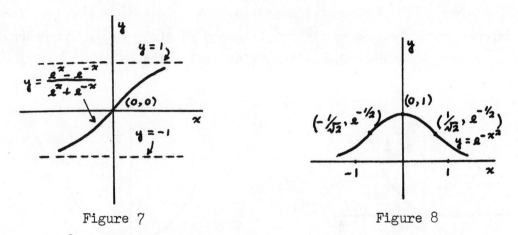

Figure 7   Figure 8

23. Since e^{-x^2} is defined for all x, the domain is $\mathcal{R}$. The equation is unchanged when x is replaced by -x, so the graph is symmetric about the y axis. Since $e^{-x^2} > 0$ for all x, there is no x intercept; when x = 0, y = 1. When $x \to \pm\infty$, $y \to 0$, so the x axis is an asymptote. Since $y' = e^{-x^2}(-2x) = -2xe^{-x^2} = 0$ when x = 0 (and since y' changes from plus to minus at x = 0), we have a maximum at x = 0, namely y = 1. Since $y'' = -2x(-2xe^{-x^2}) - 2e^{-x^2} = 2e^{-x^2}(2x^2 - 1) = 0$ when $x = \pm 1/\sqrt{2}$, the curve is concave up when $|x| > 1/\sqrt{2}$, down when $|x| < 1/\sqrt{2}$, and has inflection points $(\pm 1/\sqrt{2}, e^{-1/2})$. See Figure 8.

24. $y' = xe^x + e^x = (x+1)e^x = 0$ when x = -1. Since y' changes from minus to plus at x = -1, (-1,-1/e) is a low turning point. The graph passes through (0,0) and $y \to \infty$ when $x \to \infty$. It is not clear how y behaves when $x \to -\infty$ (because it is a product of a large negative factor x and a small positive factor e^x). Figure 9 suggests that $y \to 0$; the question is settled in Problem 31, Sec. 11.2. It may also be worthwhile to compute $y'' = (x+1)e^x + e^x = (x+2)e^x$, which yields the inflection point $(-2,-2/e^2)$.

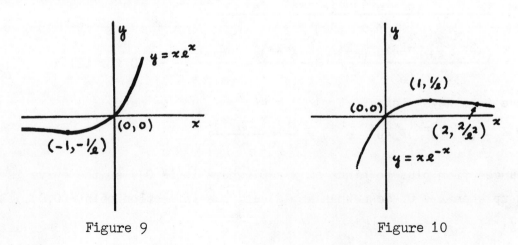

Figure 9   Figure 10

16

25. $y' = x(-e^{-x}) + e^{-x} = (1-x)e^{-x} = 0$ when $x = 1$. Since y' changes from plus to minus at $x = 1$, $(1,1/e)$ is a high turning point. The graph passes through $(0,0)$ and $y \to -\infty$ when $x \to -\infty$. It is not clear how y behaves when $x \to \infty$ (because it is a product of a large number x and a small number e^{-x}). Figure 10 suggests that $y \to 0$; the question is settled in Problem 32, Sec. 11.2. We also have $y'' = (1-x)(-e^{-x}) - e^{-x} = (x-2)e^{-x}$, which yields the inflection point $(2,2/e^2)$.

26. The domain is $x \neq 0$. When $x \downarrow 0$, $y \to \infty$ and when $x \uparrow 0$, $y \to -\infty$, so the y axis is an asymptote. Since

$$y' = \frac{xe^x - e^x}{x^2} = \frac{(x-1)e^x}{x^2} = 0 \text{ when } x = 1$$

(and since y' changes from minus to plus at $x = 1$), $(1,e)$ is a low turning point. When $x \to -\infty$, $y \to 0$, but it is not clear how y behaves when $x \to \infty$ (because it is a quotient of large numbers). Figure 11 suggests that $y \to \infty$; the question is settled in Problem 33, Sec. 11.2.

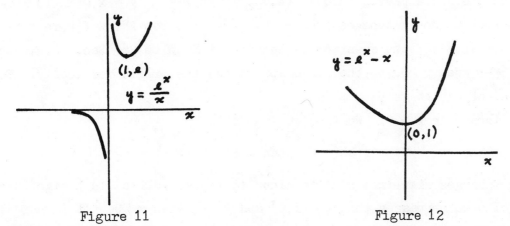

Figure 11   Figure 12

27. $y' = e^x - 1 = 0$ when $e^x = 1$, that is, when $x = 0$. Since $y'' = e^x > 0$ for all x, the curve is always concave up, with low turning point $(0,1)$. When $x \to -\infty$, $y \to \infty$, but it is not clear how y behaves when $x \to \infty$ (because it is a difference of large numbers). Figure 12 suggests that $y \to \infty$; the question is settled in Problem 34, Sec. 11.2.

28. The domain is $x > 0$. We find $y' = x(1/x) + \ln x = 1 + \ln x = 0$ when $\ln x = -1$, or $x = e^{-1}$. Since $y'' = 1/x > 0$ for all $x > 0$, the curve is always concave up, with low turning point $(1/e, -1/e)$. It passes through $(1,0)$ and $y \to \infty$ when $x \to \infty$. It is not clear how y behaves when $x \downarrow 0$ (because it is a product of a small positive factor x and a large negative factor $\ln x$). Figure 13 suggests that $y \to 0$; the question is settled in Problem 35, Sec. 11.2. Note that

$y' \to -\infty$ when $x \downarrow 0$, so the curve becomes more nearly vertical as it approaches the origin. But $(0,0)$ is not on the graph.

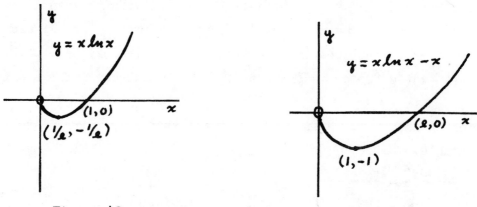

Figure 13   Figure 14

29. The domain is $x > 0$. We find $y' = x(1/x) + \ln x - 1 = \ln x = 0$ when $x = 1$. Since $y'' = 1/x > 0$ for all $x > 0$, the curve is always concave up, with low turning point $(1,-1)$. We find $y = 0 \iff x(\ln x - 1) = 0 \iff \ln x = 1 \iff x = e$, so the curve passes through $(e,0)$. When $x \to \infty$, $y = x(\ln x - 1) \to \infty$, but it is not clear how y behaves when $x \downarrow 0$. (See Problem 28.) Figure 14 suggests that $y \to 0$; the question is settled in Problem 36, Sec. 11.2. Note that $y' \to -\infty$ when $x \downarrow 0$, so the curve approaches the origin vertically. But $(0,0)$ is not on the graph.

30. The domain is $x > 0$. We find

$$y' = \frac{x(1/x) - \ln x}{x^2} = \frac{1 - \ln x}{x^2} = 0 \text{ when } \ln x = 1 \text{ (or } x = e)$$

Since y' changes sign from plus to minus at $x = e$, $(e,1/e)$ is a high turning point. The curve passes through $(1,0)$ and $y \to -\infty$ when $x \downarrow 0$. It is not clear how y behaves when $x \to \infty$ (because it is a quotient of large numbers). Figure 15 suggests that $y \to 0$; the question is settled in Problem 37, Sec. 11.2.

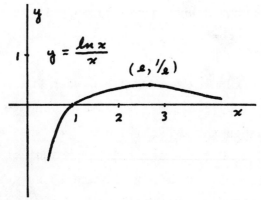

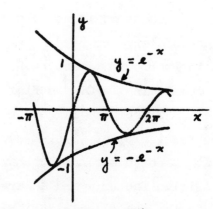

Figure 15   Figure 16

31. (a) Since e^{-x} is positive, $-1 \le \sin x \le 1 \Longrightarrow -e^{-x} \le e^{-x} \sin x \le e^{-x}$. The graphs of $y = e^{-x} \sin x$ and $y = e^{-x}$ intersect when $\sin x = 1$, that is, when $x = \pi/2 + 2n\pi$ (where n is an integer). The graphs of $y = e^{-x} \sin x$ and $y = -e^{-x}$ intersect when $\sin x = -1$, that is, when $x = -\pi/2 + 2n\pi$.

(b) $y = e^{-x} \sin x = 0$ when $\sin x = 0$, that is, when $x = n\pi$.

(c) $f'(x) = e^{-x} \cos x - e^{-x} \sin x = e^{-x}(\cos x - \sin x) = 0$ when $\cos x = \sin x$, or $\tan x = 1$. The critical points are therefore $x = \pi/4 + n\pi$, at each of which $f'(x)$ changes sign (from plus to minus at $x = \pi/4$, from minus to plus at $x = 5\pi/4$, and so on). Hence extreme values occur at each critical point.

(d) Since $e^{-x} \to 0$ when $x \to \infty$ (while $\sin x$ varies between 1 and -1), $f(x) \to 0$.

(e) A rough sketch (Figure 16) shows why the graph is called a damped sine wave. (<u>Damping</u> a vibration means cutting it down to zero.)

32. (a) Since e^{-x} is positive, $-1 \le \cos x \le 1 \Longrightarrow -e^{-x} \le e^{-x} \cos x \le e^{-x} \cos x$, so the graph of f lies between the graphs of $y = e^{-x}$ and $y = -e^{-x}$. The graphs of $y = e^{-x} \cos x$ and $y = e^{-x}$ intersect when $\cos x = 1$, that is, when $x = 2n\pi$. The graphs of $y = e^{-x} \cos x$ and $y = -e^{-x}$ intersect when $\cos x = -1$, that is, when $x = (2n-1)\pi$.

(b) $y = e^{-x} \cos x = 0$ when $\cos x = 0$, that is, when $x = \pi/2 + n\pi$.

(c) $f'(x) = e^{-x}(-\sin x) - e^{-x} \cos x = -e^{-x}(\cos x + \sin x) = 0$ when $\cos x = -\sin x$, or $\tan x = -1$. The critical points are $x = -\pi/4 + n\pi$, at each of which $f'(x)$ changes sign. Hence an extreme value occurs at each critical point.

(d) Since $e^{-x} \to 0$ when $x \to \infty$ (while $\cos x$ varies between 1 and -1), $f(x) \to 0$.

(e) The graph is a "damped cosine wave" (like the curve shown in Figure 16, but shifted $\pi/2$ units to the left).

33. The domain is $x > 0$. We find $f'(x) = e^x - 1/x = 0$ when $e^x = 1/x$, or $e^{-x} = x$. Since $f''(x) = e^x + 1/x^2 > 0$ for all $x > 0$, we have a local (in fact global) minimum at the critical point x satisfying $e^{-x} = x$. Draw the graphs of $y = x$ and $y = e^{-x}$ on the same coordinate plane to see that they intersect at $x \approx x_0 = 0.6$. Let $g(x) = x - e^{-x}$, $g'(x) = 1 + e^{-x}$, and apply Newton's Method to find

$$x_1 = x_0 - g(x_0)/g'(x_0) = 0.6 - (0.6 - e^{-0.6})/(1 + e^{-0.6}) \approx 0.57$$

Another application yields $x_2 = 0.57 - (0.57 - e^{-0.57})/(1 + e^{-0.57}) \approx 0.5671$, so $x_1 = 0.57$ appears to be accurate to two places.

34. $f'(x) = kae^{kx} - kbe^{-kx} = k(ae^{kx} - be^{-kx}) = 0$ when $ae^{kx} = be^{-kx} \Longrightarrow ae^{2kx} = b$ $\Longrightarrow e^{2kx} = b/a \Longrightarrow e^{kx} = \sqrt{b/a}$ (and $e^{-kx} = \sqrt{a/b}$). Since

$f''(x) = k(kae^{kx} + kbe^{-kx}) = k^2(ae^{kx} + be^{-kx}) > 0$ for all x, there is a local (in fact global) minimum at the critical point satisfying $e^{kx} = \sqrt{b/a}$. This minimum value is $ae^{kx} + be^{-kx} = a\sqrt{b/a} + b\sqrt{a/b} = \sqrt{ab} + \sqrt{ab} = 2\sqrt{ab}$.

35.(a) 10! = 3,628,800, while Stirling's Formula gives $10! \approx \sqrt{20\pi}(10/e)^{10} \approx$ 3,598,696.

(b) $50! \approx 3.041 \times 10^{64}$, while Stirling's Formula gives $50! \approx \sqrt{100\pi}(50/e)^{50}$ $\approx 3.036 \times 10^{64}$.

36.(a) $\exp(u - v) = \exp[\ln(\exp u) - \ln(\exp v)] = \exp[\ln(\exp u/\exp v)]$ (because $\ln(a/b) = \ln a - \ln b$). Hence $\exp(u - v) = \exp u/\exp v$.

(b) $\exp(u - v) = \exp[u + (-v)] = \exp u \cdot \exp(-v)$ (first part of Theorem 1)

$= \exp u \cdot (\exp v)^{-1}$ (Theorem 2, with r = -1)

$= \exp u/\exp v$

37.(a) $a = e^u \iff \ln a = u$, and $b = e^v \iff \ln b = v$.

(b) $u + v = \ln a + \ln b = \ln ab \iff e^{u+v} = ab = e^u e^v$

38. $e^{r\ln a} = e^{\ln a^r}$ (Theorem 2)

$= a^r$ (because $e^{\ln x} = x$)

39. If $f(x) = e^x$, then $f'(x) = e^x$ and hence $f'(0) = e^0 = 1$. The definition of derivative says that

$$f'(0) = \lim_{h \to 0} \frac{f(h) - f(0)}{h} = \lim_{h \to 0} \frac{e^h - 1}{h}$$

so the limit is 1.

40. If $y = \ln x$, then $e^y = x$. We are assuming that the derivative of e^x is known to be e^x, so (by the Chain Rule) $\frac{d}{dx}(e^y) = e^y \frac{dy}{dx} = 1$. Then $dy/dx = 1/e^y$ $= 1/x$.

Section 8.4   GENERAL EXPONENTIAL AND LOGARITHMIC FUNCTIONS

1. $\pi^\pi = e^{\pi \ln \pi} = e^{(3.14159\cdots)(1.14472\cdots)} = e^{3.59627\cdots} = 36.462\cdots$

2. $3^{\sqrt{2}} = e^{\sqrt{2}\ln 3} = e^{(1.41421\cdots)(1.09861\cdots)} = e^{1.55367\cdots} = 4.7288\cdots$

3. $(\ln 2)^e = e^{e\ln(\ln 2)} = e^{(2.71828\cdots)(-0.366512\cdots)} = e^{-0.996285\cdots} =$ $0.36924\cdots$

4. $(-1)^x$ is meaningless if $x = \frac{1}{2}$ (for example). In general, a^x is meaningless for "most" values of x if $a < 0$.

5. A smooth curve may be drawn through the plotted points (Figure 1) because

$f(x) = 2^x$ is continuous and differentiable for all x.

6. See Figure 2.

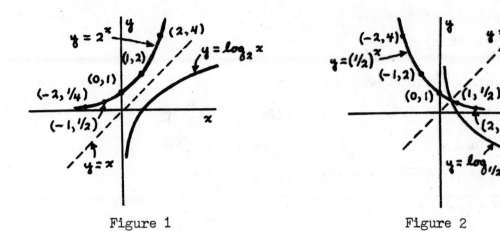

Figure 1   Figure 2

7. $f'(x) = e^x$ and $g'(x) = ex^{e-1}$, so $f'(\pi) = e^\pi$ and $g'(\pi) = e\pi^{e-1}$. A calculator gives $e^\pi \approx 23.1$ and $e\pi^{e-1} \approx 19.4$, so $f'(\pi)$ is larger. For an argument not depending on a calculator, note that $e < \pi$, so $g'(\pi) < \pi \cdot \pi^{e-1} = \pi^e < e^\pi$ (from Example 3).

8. $f'(x) = \pi^x \ln \pi$ and $g'(x) = \pi x^{\pi-1}$, so $f'(e) = \pi^e \ln \pi$ and $g'(e) = \pi e^{\pi-1}$. A calculator gives $\pi^e \ln \pi \approx 25.7$ and $\pi e^{\pi-1} \approx 26.7$, so $g'(e)$ is larger. For an argument not depending on a calculator, note that $f'(e) = \pi^e \ln \pi < \pi^e(\pi/e)$ (from Example 3). Hence (again from Example 3) $f'(e) < e^\pi(\pi/e) = \pi e^{\pi-1}$.

9. Since $\frac{d}{dx}(e^u) = e^u \frac{du}{dx}$, we have $f'(x) = e^{x \ln x} \frac{d}{dx}(x \ln x) = e^{x \ln x}(x \cdot \frac{1}{x} + \ln x) = x^x(1 + \ln x)$.

10. $f(x) = e^{\sin x \ln x} \implies f'(x) = e^{\sin x \ln x}(\sin x \cdot \frac{1}{x} + \cos x \ln x) = x^{\sin x}(\frac{1}{x} \sin x + \cos x \ln x)$. Hence $f'(1) = \sin 1$. An alternative solution is to use logarithmic differentiation.

11. $f(x) = e^{\cos x \ln(\sin x)} \implies f'(x) = e^{\cos x \ln(\sin x)}[\cos x \cot x - \sin x \ln(\sin x)] = (\sin x)^{\cos x}[\cos x \cot x - \sin x \ln(\sin x)]$. Hence $f'(\pi/2) = 0$. But f cannot be differentiated at $x = 3\pi/2$, even though the formula for f yields $f(3\pi/2) = (-1)^0 = 1$. The reason (see Problem 4) is that the negative base causes problems at nearby points. For example, $f(4.8) = (\sin 4.8)^{\cos 4.8}$ is meaningless; the base is $\sin 4.8 = -0.996\cdots$ and the exponent is $\cos 4.8 = 0.087\cdots$. Thus $f'(3\pi/2)$ is undefined; in general $f'(x)$ exists only when

$\sin x > 0$.

12. $f(x) = e^{x \ln |x|} \implies f'(x) = e^{x \ln |x|}(x \cdot \frac{1}{x} + \ln |x|) = |x|^x (1 + \ln |x|)$. The domain of both f and f' is $x \neq 0$.

13. $f(x) = e^{x \ln \sin x} \implies f'(x) = e^{x \ln \sin x}(x \cot x + \ln \sin x)$

$\qquad = (\sin x)^x (x \cot x + \ln \sin x)$

14. $f(x) = e^{(\ln x)^2} \implies f'(x) = e^{(\ln x)^2}(2 \ln x \cdot \frac{1}{x}) = x^{\ln x}(\frac{2}{x} \ln x) = 2 \ln x \cdot x^{\ln x - 1}$

15. If $x < 1$ (and $x \neq 0$), then $y > 0$ and we can write

$\qquad \ln y = \ln x^2 + \ln \sqrt{1 - x} = 2 \ln |x| + \frac{1}{2} \ln(1 - x)$

$\qquad \frac{1}{y} \frac{dy}{dx} = \frac{2}{x} - \frac{1}{2(1 - x)}$

$\qquad \frac{dy}{dx} = x^2 \sqrt{1 - x} \left[\frac{2}{x} - \frac{1}{2(1 - x)} \right]$

16. If $x \neq 0, \frac{1}{2}$, or -5, then

$\qquad \ln |y| = \ln |x|^3 + \ln |2x - 1|^4 + \ln |x + 5|^2 = 3 \ln |x| + 4 \ln |2x - 1| + 2 \ln |x + 5|$

$\qquad \frac{1}{y} \frac{dy}{dx} = \frac{3}{x} + \frac{8}{2x - 1} + \frac{2}{x + 5}$

$\qquad \frac{dy}{dx} = x^3 (2x - 1)^4 (x + 5)^2 \left(\frac{3}{x} + \frac{8}{2x - 1} + \frac{2}{x + 5} \right)$

17. If $x \neq 0, 1$, or -1, then

$\qquad \ln |y| = \ln |x| + 3 \ln |x^2 - 1| - \frac{1}{2} \ln(x^2 + 1)$

$\qquad \frac{1}{y} \frac{dy}{dx} = \frac{1}{x} + \frac{6x}{x^2 - 1} - \frac{x}{x^2 + 1}$

$\qquad \frac{dy}{dx} = \frac{x(x^2 - 1)^3}{\sqrt{x^2 + 1}} \left(\frac{1}{x} + \frac{6x}{x^2 - 1} - \frac{x}{x^2 + 1} \right)$

18. $(1 + 10^{-6})^{10^6} = (1.000001)^{1,000,000} = 2.71828046\cdots$ and $(1 - 10^{-6})^{-10^6} = (0.999999)^{-1,000,000} = 2.71828318\cdots$. The value of e is $2.71828182\cdots$.

19. Following the hint, we write

$\qquad \frac{\ln(x + h) - \ln x}{h} = \frac{1}{h} \ln\left(\frac{x + h}{x}\right) = \frac{1}{x} \cdot \frac{x}{h} \ln\left(1 + \frac{h}{x}\right) = \frac{1}{x} \ln\left(1 + \frac{h}{x}\right)^{x/h}$

$\qquad\qquad = \frac{1}{x} \ln(1 + t)^{1/t} \quad (t = h/x)$

Since $t \to 0$ when $h \to 0$, we have

$\qquad D_x \ln x = \lim_{t \to 0} \frac{1}{x} \ln(1 + t)^{1/t} = \frac{1}{x} \lim_{t \to 0} \ln(1 + t)^{1/t}$

$\qquad\qquad = \frac{1}{x} \ln[\lim_{t \to 0} (1 + t)^{1/t}] \quad \text{(Composite Function Theorem, Sec. 2.5)}$

$$= \frac{1}{x} \ln e = \frac{1}{x}$$

20. Since $a^x = e^{x \ln a}$ and $\ln e^x = x$, we have $(e^u)^v = e^{v \ln e^u} = e^{vu} = e^{uv}$.

21. Since $e^u > 0$ for all u, we have $a^x = e^{x \ln a} > 0$ for all x.

22. We know from Sec. 8.3 that $e^u e^v = e^{u+v}$. Hence

$$a^x a^{-x} = e^{x \ln a} e^{-x \ln a} = e^{x \ln a - x \ln a} = e^0 = 1$$

and therefore $a^{-x} = 1/a^x$.

23. We know from Problem 20 that $(e^u)^v = e^{uv}$. Hence $(a^u)^v = (e^{u \ln a})^v = e^{uv \ln a} = a^{uv}$.

24. We proved in the text that $a^u a^v = a^{u+v}$. Hence $a^v a^{u-v} = a^{v+u-v} = a^u$, from which $a^{u-v} = a^u/a^v$.

25. $(ab)^x = e^{x \ln ab} = e^{x(\ln a + \ln b)} = e^{x \ln a + x \ln b} = e^{x \ln a} e^{x \ln b} = a^x b^x$

26. $(a/b)^x = (ab^{-1})^x = a^x (b^{-1})^x$ (Problem 25)

$\qquad\qquad = a^x b^{-x}$ (Problem 23)

$\qquad\qquad = a^x/b^x$ (Problem 22)

27. $\log_a x = \ln x/\ln a$, which is undefined when $a = 1$ (because $\ln 1 = 0$).

28. $\log_a 1 = \ln 1/\ln a = 0$

29. $\log_a a = \ln a/\ln a = 1$

30. $\log_a uv = \ln uv/\ln a = (\ln u + \ln v)/\ln a = (\ln u/\ln a) + (\ln v/\ln a) = \log_a u + \log_a v$

31. $\log_a(u/v) = \dfrac{\ln (u/v)}{\ln a} = \dfrac{\ln u - \ln v}{\ln a} = \dfrac{\ln u}{\ln a} - \dfrac{\ln v}{\ln a} = \log_a u - \log_a v$

32. $\log_a u^v = \ln u^v/\ln a = v \ln u/\ln a = v \log_a u$

33. $\log_a a^x = \ln a^x/\ln a = x \ln a/\ln a = x$

34. Let $y = \log_a x = \ln x/\ln a$. Then $a^{\log_a x} = a^y = e^{y \ln a} = e^{\ln x} = x$.

35. $(\log_a b)(\log_b a) = \left(\dfrac{\ln b}{\ln a}\right)\left(\dfrac{\ln a}{\ln b}\right) = 1$

36. $\log_a x/\log_a b = \dfrac{\ln x/\ln a}{\ln b/\ln a} = \dfrac{\ln x}{\ln b} = \log_b x$

Section 8.5   INTEGRATION INVOLVING EXPONENTIAL AND LOGARITHMIC FUNCTIONS

1.(a) If $u = \cos x$, then $du = -\sin x\,dx$. Hence

$$\int \tan x\,dx = -\int \frac{-\sin x\,dx}{\cos x} = -\int \frac{du}{u} = -\ln |u| + C = -\ln |\cos x| + C$$

(b) If $u = \sec x$, then $du = \sec x \tan x\,dx$. Hence

$$\int \tan x\,dx = \int \frac{\sec x \tan x\,dx}{\sec x} = \int \frac{du}{u} = \ln |u| + C = \ln |\sec x| + C$$

(c) $\ln |\sec x| = \ln |\cos x|^{-1} = -\ln |\cos x|$, so the answers are the same.

2. $\int \cot x\,dx = \int \frac{\cos x\,dx}{\sin x} = \int \frac{du}{u}$ ($u = \sin x$, $du = \cos x\,dx$)

$$= \ln |u| + C = \ln |\sin x| + C = \ln | \csc x|^{-1} + C = -\ln |\csc x| + C$$

3. $\int \csc x\,dx = \int \frac{(\csc x + \cot x)\csc x\,dx}{\csc x + \cot x} = \int \frac{(\csc^2 x + \csc x \cot x)\,dx}{\csc x + \cot x}$

$$= -\int \frac{du}{u}   [u = \csc x + \cot x,\ du = -(\csc x \cot x + \csc^2 x)dx]$$

$$= -\ln |u| + C = -\ln |\csc x + \cot x| + C = \ln |\csc x + \cot x|^{-1} + C$$

But $\csc x + \cot x = \dfrac{(\csc x + \cot x)(\csc x - \cot x)}{\csc x - \cot x} = \dfrac{\csc^2 x - \cot^2 x}{\csc x - \cot x} = \dfrac{1}{\csc x - \cot x}$,

so $\int \csc x\,dx = \ln |\csc x - \cot x| + C.$

4. $\int \frac{dx}{1-x} = -\int \frac{du}{u}$ ($u = 1 - x$, $du = -dx$)

$$= -\ln |u| + C = -\ln |1 - x| + C$$

5. $\int \frac{dx}{2x+1} = \frac{1}{2}\int \frac{du}{u}$ ($u = 2x + 1$, $du = 2\,dx$)

$$= \frac{1}{2}\ln |u| + C = \frac{1}{2}\ln |2x+1| + C$$

6. $\int \frac{x\,dx}{x^2+1} = \frac{1}{2}\int \frac{du}{u}$ ($u = x^2 + 1$, $du = 2x\,dx$)

$$= \frac{1}{2}\ln |u| + C = \frac{1}{2}\ln(x^2+1) + C$$

7. $\int \frac{x\,dx}{1-x^2} = -\frac{1}{2}\int \frac{du}{u}$ ($u = 1 - x^2$, $du = -2x\,dx$)

$$= -\frac{1}{2}\ln |u| + C = -\frac{1}{2}\ln |1 - x^2| + C$$

8. $\int \frac{\cos t\,dt}{1+\sin t} = \int \frac{du}{u}$ ($u = 1 + \sin t$, $du = \cos t\,dt$)

$$= \ln |u| + C = \ln |1 + \sin t| + C$$

9. $\int \frac{\sec^2 t\,dt}{\tan t} = \int \frac{du}{u}$ ($u = \tan t$, $du = \sec^2 t\,dt$)

$$= \ln |u| + C = \ln |\tan t| + C$$

10. If $u = \ln x$, then $du = \frac{dx}{x}$, so $\int \frac{dx}{x \ln x} = \int \frac{du}{u} = \ln |u| + C = \ln |\ln x| + C.$

11. $\int \cot 2t\, dt = \frac{1}{2} \int \cot u\, du \quad (u = 2t, \; du = 2\, dt)$

$\qquad = \frac{1}{2} \ln |\sin u| + C = \frac{1}{2} \ln |\sin 2t| + C$

12. $\int \dfrac{t\, dt}{\cos t^2} = \frac{1}{2} \int \dfrac{du}{\cos u} \quad (u = t^2, \; du = 2t\, dt)$

$\qquad = \frac{1}{2} \int \sec u\, du = \frac{1}{2} \ln |\sec u + \tan u| + C = \frac{1}{2} \ln |\sec t^2 + \tan t^2| + C$

13. $\int x e^{x^2}\, dx = \frac{1}{2} \int e^u\, du \quad (u = x^2, \; du = 2x\, dx)$

$\qquad = \frac{1}{2} e^u + C = \frac{1}{2} e^{x^2} + C$

14. $\int e^{\sin 2t} \cos 2t\, dt = \frac{1}{2} \int e^u\, du \quad (u = \sin 2t, \; du = 2 \cos 2t\, dt)$

$\qquad = \frac{1}{2} e^u + C = \frac{1}{2} e^{\sin 2t} + C$

15. $\int_2^6 \dfrac{du}{u} = \ln u \Big|_2^6 = \ln 6 - \ln 2 = \ln \dfrac{6}{2} = \ln 3$

16. $\int_2^5 \dfrac{dx}{2x - 1} = \frac{1}{2} \ln (2x - 1) \Big|_2^5 = \frac{1}{2} (\ln 9 - \ln 3) = \frac{1}{2} \ln 3$

17. $\int_0^1 \dfrac{x\, dx}{x^2 + 4} = \frac{1}{2} \ln (x^2 + 4) \Big|_0^1 = \frac{1}{2} (\ln 5 - \ln 4) = \frac{1}{2} \ln \dfrac{5}{4}$

18. $\int_0^1 \dfrac{x^2\, dx}{x^3 - 8} = \frac{1}{3} \int_{-8}^{-7} \dfrac{du}{u} \quad (u = x^3 - 8, \; du = 3x^2\, dx)$

$\qquad = \frac{1}{3} \ln |u| \Big|_{-8}^{-7} = \frac{1}{3} (\ln 7 - \ln 8) = \frac{1}{3} \ln \dfrac{7}{8}$

19. $\int_2^3 \dfrac{x^3\, dx}{x^4 - 1} = \frac{1}{4} \ln (x^4 - 1) \Big|_2^3 = \frac{1}{4} (\ln 80 - \ln 15) = \frac{1}{4} \ln \dfrac{16}{3}$

20. $\int_1^2 \dfrac{x\, dx}{x^2 - 9} = \frac{1}{2} \ln |x^2 - 9| \Big|_1^2 = \frac{1}{2} (\ln 5 - \ln 8) = \frac{1}{2} \ln \dfrac{5}{8}$

21. $\int_{\pi/3}^{\pi/2} \dfrac{\sin t\, dt}{1 - \cos t} = \int_{\frac{1}{2}}^1 \dfrac{du}{u} \quad (u = 1 - \cos t, \; du = \sin t\, dt)$

$\qquad = \ln u \Big|_{\frac{1}{2}}^1 = \ln 1 - \ln \tfrac{1}{2} = 0 + \ln 2 = \ln 2$

22. $\int_0^{\pi/4} \sec x\, dx = \ln (\sec x + \tan x) \Big|_0^{\pi/4} = \ln (\sqrt{2} + 1) - \ln 1 = \ln (1 + \sqrt{2})$

23. $\int_{\pi/2}^{5\pi/6} \csc t\, dt = \ln (\csc t - \cot t) \Big|_{\pi/2}^{5\pi/6} = \ln (2 + \sqrt{3}) - \ln 1 = \ln (2 + \sqrt{3})$

24. $\int_0^{\ln 2} e^x\, dx = e^x \Big|_0^{\ln 2} = e^{\ln 2} - e^0 = 2 - 1 = 1$

25. $\int_0^2 e^{x/2} dx = 2\int_0^1 e^u du$ $(u = x/2,\ du = \frac{1}{2}dx)$

$$= 2e^u \Big|_0^1 = 2(e-1)$$

26. $\int_0^1 x^2 e^{x^3} dx = \frac{1}{3}\int_0^1 e^u du$ $(u = x^3,\ du = 3x^2 dx)$

$$= \frac{1}{3}e^u \Big|_0^1 = \frac{1}{3}(e-1)$$

27. $A = \dfrac{1}{3-1}\int_1^3 \dfrac{dx}{x} = \frac{1}{2}\ln x \Big|_1^3 = \frac{1}{2}(\ln 3 - \ln 1) = \frac{1}{2}\ln 3$

28. $A = \dfrac{3}{\pi}\int_0^{\pi/3} \tan x\, dx = \dfrac{3}{\pi}\ln \sec x \Big|_0^{\pi/3} = \dfrac{3}{\pi}(\ln 2 - \ln 1) = \dfrac{3}{\pi}\ln 2$

29. $A = \int_0^1 e^x dx = e^x \Big|_0^1 = e-1$

30. $A = \int_2^5 \dfrac{x\,dx}{x^2-1} = \frac{1}{2}\ln(x^2-1) \Big|_2^5 = \frac{1}{2}(\ln 24 - \ln 3) = \frac{1}{2}\ln 8$

31. See the solution of Problem 7, Sec. 7.1, where we found $A = \dfrac{3}{2} - 2\int_1^2 \dfrac{dx}{x}$.

At that time we were unable to do more than approximate the integral, but now we can write $A = 3/2 - 2\ln 2$. Since $\ln 2 \approx 0.693$, you can see where we got the approximation given in the earlier problem. (We said that the integral can be approximated by a Riemann sum, but that isn't really the way to do it. On the other hand, we did use a Riemann sum to approximate $\ln 2$ in Problem 1, Sec. 8.1.)

32. The curves $y = e^x$ and $y = e^{-x}$ intersect when $e^x = e^{-x} \iff e^{2x} = 1 \iff 2x = 0 \iff x = 0$. From Figure 1 we conclude that

$$A = \int_0^1 (e^x - e^{-x})dx = (e^x + e^{-x})\Big|_0^1 = (e + e^{-1}) - (1+1) = e + e^{-1} - 2$$

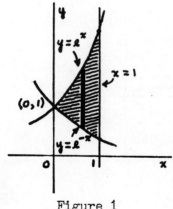

Figure 1

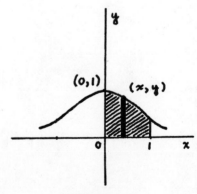

Figure 2

33. $V = \pi \int_1^4 y^2 dx = \pi \int_1^4 \dfrac{dx}{x} = \pi \ln x \Big|_1^4 = \pi(\ln 4 - \ln 1) = \pi \ln 4$

34. $V = 2\pi \int_0^1 xy\,dx = 2\pi \int_0^1 \dfrac{x\,dx}{1+x^2} = \pi \ln(1+x^2)\Big|_0^1 = \pi \ln 2$

35. From Figure 2 we conclude that

$$V = 2\pi \int_0^1 xy\,dx = 2\pi \int_0^1 xe^{-x^2} dx = -\pi e^{-x^2}\Big|_0^1 = -\pi(e^{-1}-1) = \pi(1-1/e)$$

36. If the first-quadrant vertex of the rectangle is labeled (x,y), the area of the rectangle is $A = 2xy = 2xe^{-x^2}$.   We find

$$A' = 2x(-2xe^{-x^2}) + 2e^{-x^2} = 2e^{-x^2}(1 - 2x^2) = 0 \text{ when } x = 1/\sqrt{2}$$

(because $x > 0$).   It is geometrically apparent that we have a maximum; the vertices of the critical rectangle occur at $\pm 1/\sqrt{2}$. These are inflection points of the curve (see the solution of Problem 23, Sec. 8.3).

37. $y' = \dfrac{1}{\sec x} \cdot \sec x \tan x = \tan x$ and $1 + y'^2 = 1 + \tan^2 x = \sec^2 x$.   Hence

$$s = \int_0^{\pi/3} \sec x\,dx = \ln(\sec x + \tan x)\Big|_0^{\pi/3} = \ln(2+\sqrt{3}) - \ln 1 = \ln(2+\sqrt{3})$$

38.(a) The area under the curve between $x = 0$ and $x = r > 0$ is

$$A = \int_0^r e^{-x} dx = -e^{-x}\Big|_0^r = 1 - e^{-r} \to 1 \text{ as } r \to \infty$$

Hence we need only enough paint to cover 1 square unit of area.

(b) The volume generated by rotating the region under $y = e^{-x}$, $0 \le x \le r$, about the x axis is

$$V = \pi \int_0^r y^2 dx = \pi \int_0^r e^{-2x} dx = -\dfrac{\pi}{2}e^{-2x}\Big|_0^r = \dfrac{\pi}{2}(1-e^{-2r}) \to \dfrac{\pi}{2} \text{ as } r \to \infty$$

Hence $\pi/2$ cubic units of paint are enough.

Section 8.6   APPLICATIONS OF EXPONENTIAL AND LOGARITHMIC FUNCTIONS

1. If P is the population t hours after it was 20,000, then

$$\dfrac{dP}{dt} = kP \implies \dfrac{dP}{P} = k\,dt \implies \int \dfrac{dP}{P} = \int k\,dt \implies \ln P = kt + C = kt + \ln 20{,}000$$

(because $P = 20{,}000$ when $t = 0$).   Hence $\ln(P/20{,}000) = kt$.   Since $P = 48{,}000$ when $t = 3$, we have $\ln 2.4 = 3k$, so

$$\ln(P/20{,}000) = \dfrac{t}{3}\ln 2.4 = \ln(2.4)^{t/3} \implies P/20{,}000 = (2.4)^{t/3}$$

$$\implies P = 20{,}000(2.4)^{t/3}$$

When $t = 7$, $P = 20,000(2.4)^{7/3} \approx 154,237$. When $P = 10^6$ we have

$$10^6 = (2 \times 10^4)(2.4)^{t/3} \implies (2.4)^{t/3} = 50 \implies \frac{t}{3}\ln 2.4 = \ln 50$$

$$\implies t = \frac{3\ln 50}{\ln 2.4} \approx 13.4 \text{ hr}$$

2.(a) $I = I_0$ when $t = 0$.

(b) $\frac{dI}{dt} = I_0 e^{-Rt/L}(-\frac{R}{L}) = -kI$, where $k = \frac{R}{L}$.

(c) $\frac{d^2 I}{dt^2} = -kI_0 e^{-Rt/L}(-k) = k^2 I_0 e^{-Rt/L} > 0$.

(d) $I \to 0$ when $t \to \infty$.

(e) See Figure 1.

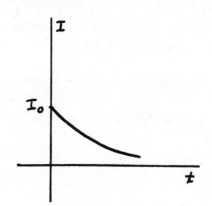

Figure 1

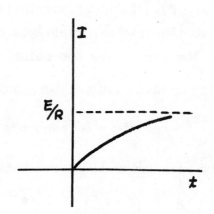

Figure 2

3. $L\frac{dI}{dt} + RI = 0 \implies L\frac{dI}{dt} = -RI \implies \frac{dI}{I} = -\frac{R}{L}dt = -k\,dt$ $(k = -R/L) \implies$

$\int \frac{dI}{I} = -k\int dt \implies \ln I = -kt + C = -kt + \ln I_0$ $(I = I_0$ when $t = 0) \implies$

$\ln (I/I_0) = -kt \implies I/I_0 = e^{-kt} \implies I = I_0 e^{-kt} = I_0 e^{-Rt/L}$

4.(a) $L\frac{dI}{dt} + RI = E \implies L\frac{dI}{dt} = E - RI \implies \frac{dI}{E - RI} = \frac{1}{L}dt \implies \int \frac{dI}{E - RI} = \frac{1}{L}\int dt \implies$

$-\frac{1}{R}\ln (E - RI) = \frac{1}{L}t + C = \frac{t}{L} - \frac{1}{R}\ln E$ $(I = 0$ when $t = 0) \implies -\frac{1}{R}\ln \frac{E - RI}{E} = \frac{t}{L} \implies$

$\ln \frac{E - RI}{E} = -\frac{Rt}{L} \implies \frac{E - RI}{E} = e^{-Rt/L} \implies E - RI = Ee^{-Rt/L} \implies RI = E - Ee^{-Rt/L} \implies$

$I = \frac{E}{R}(1 - e^{-Rt/L})$

(b) $I \to E/R$ when $t \to \infty$.

(c) See Figure 2.

5. If w is the puppy's weight t months after birth, then

$$\frac{dw}{dt} = kw \implies \frac{dw}{w} = k\,dt \implies \int \frac{dw}{w} = k\int dt \implies \ln w = kt + C = kt + \ln 3 \quad (w = 3$$

when t = 0) $\Rightarrow$ $\ln(w/3) = kt$. Since w = 5 when t = 1, we have $\ln(5/3) = k$, so

$$\ln(w/3) = t\ln(5/3) = \ln(5/3)^t \Rightarrow w/3 = (5/3)^t \Rightarrow w = 3(5/3)^t$$

When t = 6, $w = 3(5/3)^6 \approx 64.3$ lb. When w = 90, $t = \dfrac{\ln 30}{\ln(5/3)} \approx 6.7$ months.

6. If p is the pressure at altitude h, then

$$\frac{dp}{dh} = -kp \Rightarrow \frac{dp}{p} = -k\,dh \Rightarrow \int \frac{dp}{p} = -k\int dh \Rightarrow \ln p = -kh + C = -kh + \ln 30$$

(because p = 30 when h = 0). Hence $\ln(p/30) = -kh$. Since p = 29 when h = 1000, we have $\ln(29/30) = -1000k$, so $k = -0.001\ln(29/30) = 0.001\ln(30/29)$. Then $\ln(p/30) = -0.001h\ln(30/29) = \ln(30/29)^{-0.001h} \Rightarrow p/30 = (30/29)^{-0.001h}$ $\Rightarrow p = 30(30/29)^{-0.001h}$. When h = 1700, $p = 30(30/29)^{-0.001(1700)} \approx 28.3$.

7. If m is the mass of undissolved chemical t minutes after the chemical was placed in water, then

$$\frac{dm}{dt} = -km \Rightarrow \frac{dm}{m} = -k\,dt \Rightarrow \int \frac{dm}{m} = -k\int dt \Rightarrow \ln m = -kt + C = -kt + \ln 8$$

(because m = 8 when t = 0). Hence $\ln(m/8) = -kt$. Since m = 5 when t = 5, we have $\ln(5/8) = -5k$, so $k = -\frac{1}{5}\ln(5/8) = \frac{1}{5}\ln(8/5) = \frac{1}{5}\ln 1.6$. Then $\ln(m/8) = -\frac{t}{5}\ln 1.6$. The chemical will be 99% dissolved when m = 0.01(8), so

$$\ln 0.01 = -\frac{t}{5}\ln 1.6 \Rightarrow -\ln 100 = -\frac{t}{5}\ln 1.6 \Rightarrow t = \frac{5\ln 100}{\ln 1.6} \approx 49 \text{ minutes}$$

8. As in Example 3, we have

$$\frac{dT}{dt} = -k(T - 25) \Rightarrow \frac{dT}{T - 25} = -k\,dt \Rightarrow \int \frac{dT}{T - 25} = -k\int dt$$

$$\Rightarrow \ln(T - 25) = -kt + C = -kt + \ln 175 \quad (T = 200 \text{ when } t = 0)$$

$$\Rightarrow \ln\frac{T - 25}{175} = -kt$$

Since T = 150 when t = 1, we have $\ln(125/175) = -k \Rightarrow k = \ln(175/125) = \ln(7/5) = \ln 1.4$. Hence

$$\ln\frac{T - 25}{175} = -t\ln 1.4 = \ln(1.4)^{-t} \Rightarrow \frac{T - 25}{175} = (1.4)^{-t} \Rightarrow T = 25 + 175(1.4)^{-t}$$

This approaches 25 as $t \to \infty$.

9.(a) If V is the value of the machine t years after purchase, then

$$\frac{dV}{dt} = -k(V - 1000) \Rightarrow \frac{dV}{V - 1000} = -k\,dt \Rightarrow \int \frac{dV}{V - 1000} = -k\int dt$$

$$\Rightarrow \ln(V - 1000) = -kt + C = -kt + \ln 49{,}000$$

$$\Rightarrow \ln\frac{V - 1000}{49{,}000} = -kt$$

Since V = 30,000 when t = 2, we have $\ln(29/49) = -2k \Rightarrow k = \frac{1}{2}\ln(49/29)$. Thus

$$\ln \frac{V - 1000}{49,000} = -\tfrac{1}{2}t \ln(49/29) = \ln(49/29)^{-t/2} \implies \frac{V - 1000}{49,000} = (49/29)^{-t/2}$$

$$\implies V = 1000 + 49,000(49/29)^{-t/2}$$

When $t = 10$, $V = 1000 + 49,000(49/29)^{-5} \approx \$4558$

(b) $V = 1000 + 49,000(49/29)^{-t/2} \to 1000$ as $t \to \infty$.

10. If $v = kx^2 \ln(1/x) = -kx^2 \ln x$, then $\frac{dv}{dx} = -k(x^2 \cdot \frac{1}{x} + 2x \ln x) = -kx(1 + 2 \ln x)$.

Since $x > 0$, $dv/dx = 0$ when $\ln x = -\tfrac{1}{2}$, or $x = e^{-\frac{1}{2}}$. This gives a maximum

because dv/dx changes from plus to minus at $x = e^{-\frac{1}{2}}$.

11. Use the formula $S = Pe^{rt}$ from Example 5, with $P = 1$, $r = 1.00$, and $t = 1$.
Then $S = e$.

12.(a) Use the formula $S_{nt} = P(1 + r/n)^{nt}$ from the text, with $P = 10,000$, $r = $

0.08, $n = 2$, $t = 5$. This gives $S_{10} = 10,000(1 + 0.04)^{10} = \$14,802.44$.

(b) $S_{20} = 10,000(1 + 0.02)^{20} = \$14,859.47$.

(c) $S_{60} = 10,000(1 + 0.08/12)^{60} = \$14,898.46$.

(d) $S_{1800} = 10,000(1 + 0.08/360)^{1800} = \$14,917.58$.

(e) $S = Pe^{rt} = 10,000e^{0.4} = \$14,918.25$

13. $S = Pe^{rt} = 24e^{(0.05)(356)} = 24e^{17.8} \approx \$1.3$ billion.

14. If S is the value of the investment t years later, then

$$\frac{dS}{dt} = kS \implies \frac{dS}{S} = k\,dt \implies \int \frac{dS}{S} = k \int dt \implies \ln S = kt + C = kt + \ln P$$

(because $S = P$ when $t = 0$). Hence $\ln(S/P) = kt \implies S/P = e^{kt} \implies S = Pe^{kt}$.
The constant of proportionality need not be called k; label it r.

15. If we assume that the velocity $v = dx/dt$ is proportional to x, then dx/dt
$= kx$. The initial condition $x = 0$ when $t = 0$ prohibits dividing by x to
separate the variables; instead we see by inspection that the solution is the
constant function $x = 0$ (for all t). Hence the object does not fall. More
generally (ignoring the initial condition) we can write

$$\frac{dx}{dt} = kx \implies \frac{dx}{x} = k\,dt \implies \int \frac{dx}{x} = k \int dt \implies \ln x = kt + A$$

$$\implies x = e^{kt + A} = e^{kt}e^{A} = Ce^{kt} \quad (C = e^{A})$$

This general solution includes the special solution $x = 0$ if we allow $C = 0$;
Galileo's conjecture still leads to $x = 0$ for all t. (See Sec. 7.7 for a

preview of this result.)

16. $dx/dt = kt \Rightarrow x = \frac{1}{2}kt^2 + C = \frac{1}{2}kt^2$ (because $x = 0$ when $t = 0$). The constant of proportionality is usually labeled g instead of k.

17. If m is the mass at time t (the initial mass being m_0), then $m = m_0 e^{-kt}$, as shown in the text. The half-life is the value of t satisfying $\frac{1}{2}m_0 = m_0 e^{-kt}$ or $e^{kt} = 2$. This is independent of m_0.

18. $m = m_0 e^{-kt}$ (from the text). Since $m = \frac{1}{2}m_0$ when $t = 1600$, we have $\frac{1}{2}m_0 = m_0 e^{-1600k} \Rightarrow 2 = e^{1600k} \Rightarrow \ln 2 = 1600k \Rightarrow k = \frac{\ln 2}{1600}$. Hence

$$m = m_0 e^{-t \ln 2/1600}$$

This may also be put in the form $m = m_0 e^{\ln 2^{-t/1600}} = m_0(2^{-t/1600})$.

19. $m = m_0 e^{-kt}$ (from the text). The half-life is the value of t satisfying $e^{kt} = 2$ (as shown in Problem 17), that is, $t = \frac{\ln 2}{k}$. Hence we need only find k. Since $m = 0.60m_0 = \frac{3}{5}m_0$ when $t = 100$, we have $\frac{3}{5}m_0 = m_0 e^{-100k} \Rightarrow \frac{5}{3} = e^{100k} \Rightarrow k = \frac{1}{100}\ln\frac{5}{3}$. Hence the half-life is $t = \frac{100 \ln 2}{\ln(5/3)} \approx 136$ years.

20. As in Example 2, we have $t = \dfrac{-5500 \ln(m/m_0)}{\ln 2}$, where m is the amount of radioactive carbon in the fossil t years after death of the living tissue and m_0 is the initial amount. We are told that $m = 0.15m_0$ today, so the value of t today is

$$t = \frac{-5500 \ln 0.15}{\ln 2} \approx 15{,}053 \text{ years}$$

21. $y = Ce^{kx} \Rightarrow \frac{dy}{dx} = Ce^{kx} \cdot k = k(Ce^{kx}) = ky$

22.(a) $g'(x) = f(x)(-ke^{-kx}) + f'(x)e^{-kx} = e^{-kx}[f'(x) - kf(x)] = e^{-kx}(y' - ky) = 0$ (because $y' = ky$).

(b) $g(x)$ must be a constant, say $g(x) = C$. Then $f(x)e^{-kx} = C$ and hence $f(x) = Ce^{kx}$.

(c) No; the zero function $f(x) = 0$ is included in the general formula $f(x) = Ce^{kx}$ by taking the constant to be $C = 0$.

23.(a) We cannot divide by y to separate the variables if $y = 0$. However, the zero function $y = 0$ satisfies $dy/dx = ky$, so we simply note that fact and then assume that $y \neq 0$.

(b) $\int \frac{dy}{y} = \int k\,dx \Rightarrow \ln|y| = kx + A \Rightarrow |y| = e^{kx+A} = e^{kx}e^A = Be^{kx}$ (B =

$e^A > 0) \implies y = \pm Be^{kx} = Ce^{kx}$ $(C = \pm B \neq 0)$.

(c) The zero function $y = 0$ is incorporated by allowing $C = 0$.

24. If $y = e^x$, then $y' = y'' = e^x$ and the given equation reads $e^x - 2e^x + e^x = 0$ (true for all x). If $y = xe^x$, then $y' = xe^x + e^x = (x+1)e^x$ and $y'' = (x+1)e^x + e^x = (x+2)e^x$, and the equation reads $(x+2)e^x - 2(x+1)e^x + xe^x = 0$, or $e^x(x+2-2x-2+x) = 0$ (true for all x).

25. If $y = e^x \cos x$, then $y' = e^x(-\sin x) + e^x \cos x = e^x(\cos x - \sin x)$ and $y'' = e^x(-\sin x - \cos x) + e^x(\cos x - \sin x) = -2e^x \sin x$. The given equation reads $-2e^x \sin x - 2e^x(\cos x - \sin x) + 2e^x \cos x = 0$, or $2e^x(-\sin x - \cos x + \sin x + \cos x) = 0$ (true for all x). If $y = e^x \sin x$, then $y' = e^x \cos x + e^x \sin x = e^x(\cos x + \sin x)$ and $y'' = e^x(-\sin x + \cos x) + e^x(\cos x + \sin x) = 2e^x \cos x$. The equation reads $2e^x \cos x - 2e^x(\cos x + \sin x) + 2e^x \sin x = 0$, or $2e^x(\cos x - \cos x - \sin x + \sin x) = 0$ (true for all x).

26. If $y = e^{rx}$, then $y' = re^{rx}$ and $y'' = r^2 e^{rx}$. The given equation reads $ar^2 e^{rx} + bre^{rx} + ce^{rx} = 0$, or $e^{rx}(ar^2 + br + c) = 0$. Since r is a root of $ax^2 + bx + c = 0$, this is correct for all x.

27. The quadratic equation associated with $y'' - y = 0$ is $x^2 - 1 = 0$, with roots $r_1 = 1$ and $r_2 = -1$. Corresponding solutions of the differential equation (according to Problem 26) are $y = e^{r_1 x} = e^x$ and $y = e^{r_2 x} = e^{-x}$.

28. The roots of $x^2 - 3x + 2 = 0$, or $(x-1)(x-2) = 0$, are $r_1 = 1$ and $r_2 = 2$.

Corresponding solutions of $y'' - 3y' + 2y = 0$ are $y = e^x$ and $y = e^{2x}$.

29. The roots of $x^2 - x = 0$, or $x(x-1) = 0$, are $r_1 = 0$ and $r_2 = 1$.

Corresponding solutions of $y'' - y' = 0$ are $y = e^{0x} = 1$ and $y = e^x$.

30. The equation $x^2 - 2x + 1 = 0$, or $(x-1)^2 = 0$, has double root $r = 1$. This yields the solution $y = e^x$ in Problem 24, but it is not clear where the solution $y = xe^x$ comes from. See Problem 18, Sec. 19.5, for an explanation.

31. The equation $x^2 - 2x + 2 = 0$ has no real roots (because $b^2 - 4ac = 4 - 8 < 0$).

32. (a) $e^{rx} = e^{(1+i)x} = e^x e^{ix} = e^x(\cos x + i \sin x) = e^x \cos x + ie^x \sin x$

(b) If $f = g + ih$, then $f' = g' + ih'$ and $f'' = g'' + ih''$. We are told that f satisfies $ay'' + by' + cy = 0$, so $a(g'' + ih'') + b(g' + ih') + c(g + ih) = 0 \implies (ag'' + bg' + cg) + i(ah'' + bh' + ch) = 0 + 0i \implies ag'' + bg' + cg = 0$ and $ah'' + bh' + ch = 0$. Hence g and h both satisfy $ay'' + by' + cy = 0$.

(c) See the solution of Problem 26.

(d) Since $e^{rx} = e^x \cos x + i e^x \sin x$ satisfies $y'' - 2y' + 2y = 0$, so do the functions $y = e^x \cos x$ and $y = e^x \sin x$.

33. If $x = \pi$, Euler's formula reads $e^{i\pi} = \cos \pi + i \sin \pi = -1$, or $e^{\pi i} + 1 = 0$.

Chapter 8   TRUE-FALSE QUIZ

1. True. $\ln \frac{1}{2} = -\ln 2 = -\int_1^2 \frac{dt}{t}$.

2. True. $D_x \ln 2x = \frac{1}{2x} \cdot 2 = \frac{1}{x}$.

3. False. $\ln x \to \infty$ when $x \to \infty$.

4. True. $\int_2^8 \frac{dx}{x} = \ln x \Big|_2^8 = \ln 8 - \ln 2 = \ln 4 = \ln 2^2 = 2 \ln 2$.

5. True. $\ln \sin x + \ln \cos x - \ln x = \ln \left(\frac{\sin x}{x} \cdot \cos x \right)$, which approaches $\ln 1 = 0$ when $x \to 0$.

6. True. $\int \frac{x \, dx}{x^2 + 1} = \frac{1}{2} \ln(x^2 + 1) + C = \ln \sqrt{x^2 + 1} + C$.

7. True. This is the test for whether the inverse exists.

8. True. The graphs of $y = f(x)$ and $y = f^{-1}(x)$ are reflections of one another in the line $y = x$.

9. True. $x = y^3 + 2 \implies x - 2 = y^3 \implies y = \sqrt[3]{x - 2} = f^{-1}(x)$.

10. False. If $y = f^{-1}(x)$, then $D_x f^{-1}(x) = \frac{1}{f'(y)} = \frac{1}{2y}$, not $\frac{1}{2x}$. Note that since $y = \sqrt{x}$, this gives the correct derivative, $dy/dx = 1/(2y) = 1/(2\sqrt{x})$.

11. False. e^{-x} and $-e^x$ are different functions.

12. True. $\int_1^{e^x} \frac{dt}{t} = \ln t \Big|_1^{e^x} = \ln e^x - \ln 1 = x$.

13. True. $\int_0^{\ln 5} e^{2x} dx = \frac{1}{2} e^{2x} \Big|_0^{\ln 5} = \frac{1}{2}(e^{2 \ln 5} - e^0) = \frac{1}{2}(e^{\ln 25} - 1) = \frac{1}{2}(25 - 1) = 12$.

14. False. $y' = e^{-x^2}$ and $y'' = -2x e^{-x^2}$; in the first quadrant y'' is negative.

15. False. $2^\pi = e^{\pi \ln 2}$, not $e^{2 \ln \pi}$.

16. False. $D_x 2^x = D_x e^{x \ln 2} = e^{x \ln 2} \cdot \ln 2 = 2^x \ln 2$, not 2^x.

17. True. $\log e = \log_{10} e = \frac{\ln e}{\ln 10} = \frac{1}{\ln 10}$.

18. True. The functions are inverses of one another.

19. True. $\displaystyle\int_0^{\pi/2} \tan\frac{x}{2}\,dx = 2\int_0^{\pi/4} \tan u\,du$ $(u = x/2,\ du = \tfrac{1}{2}dx)$

$$= 2\ln\sec u\Big|_0^{\pi/4} = 2(\ln\sqrt{2} - \ln 1) = 2\ln 2^{1/2} = \ln 2$$

20. True. $\dfrac{dP}{dt} = kP \implies \dfrac{dP}{P} = k\,dt \implies \displaystyle\int\frac{dP}{P} = k\int dt \implies \ln P = kt + C = kt + \ln 1000$

$$\implies \ln\frac{P}{1000} = kt \implies \frac{P}{1000} = e^{kt} \implies P = 1000e^{kt}$$

Chapter 8   ADDITIONAL PROBLEMS

1. The primes less than 50 are 2, 3, 5, 7, 11, 13, 17, 19, 23, 29, 31, 37, 41, 43, 47, so p(50) = 15. We have $f(50) = 50/\ln 50 \approx 13$.

2. $D_x \ln\sqrt{1 - x^2} = D_x \tfrac{1}{2}\ln(1 - x^2) = \dfrac{1}{2}\cdot\dfrac{1}{1-x^2}(-2x) = \dfrac{-x}{1-x^2}$

3. The domain is x > 0. We have $y' = x(1/x) + \ln 2x = 1 + \ln 2x = 0$ when $\ln 2x =$ -1 $\iff 2x = e^{-1} \iff x = \tfrac{1}{2}e^{-1}$. Since $y'' = 1/x > 0$ for all x > 0, we have a local (in fact global) minimum. When $x = \tfrac{1}{2}e^{-1}$, $y = \tfrac{1}{2}e^{-1}\ln e^{-1} = -\tfrac{1}{2}e^{-1}$, so the low point is $(\tfrac{1}{2}e^{-1}, -\tfrac{1}{2}e^{-1})$. When $x\to\infty$, $y\to\infty$, but it is not clear how y behaves when $x\downarrow 0$ (because it is a product of a small positive factor x and a large negative factor $\ln 2x$). Figure 1 suggests that $y\to 0$. Note that $y'\to -\infty$ when $x\downarrow 0$, so the curve becomes vertical as it approaches the origin. But (0,0) is not on the graph. Also note that the curve hits the x axis when $y = 0 \iff \ln 2x = 0 \iff 2x = 1 \iff x = \tfrac{1}{2}$.

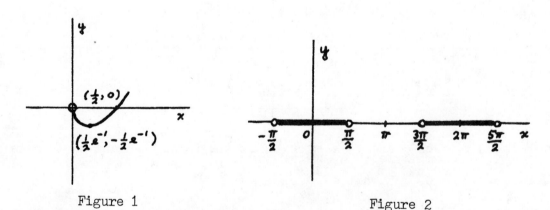

Figure 1   Figure 2

4. $y = \ln(\cos x\sec x) = \ln 1 = 0$ for all x in the domain (which consists of all x for which $\cos x > 0$). See Figure 2.

5. $\displaystyle\int_0^1 \frac{x\,dx}{x^2 - 3} = \tfrac{1}{2}\ln|x^2 - 3|\,\Big|_0^1 = \tfrac{1}{2}(\ln 2 - \ln 3) = \tfrac{1}{2}\ln(2/3) = -\tfrac{1}{2}\ln(3/2)$

6. The graph is symmetric about the origin (being above the x axis when x > 0 and below it when x < 0). Hence

$$A = 2 \int_0^1 \frac{x\,dx}{1+x^2} = \ln(1+x^2)\Big|_0^1 = \ln 2$$

7. The curves $y = x^2$ and $xy = 1$ intersect when $x^2 = 1/x \iff x^3 = 1 \iff x = 1$. From Figure 3 we conclude that

$$A = \int_1^2 (x^2 - 1/x)dx = (x^3/3 - \ln x)\Big|_1^2 = (8/3 - \ln 2) - (1/3 - \ln 1) = 7/3 - \ln 2$$

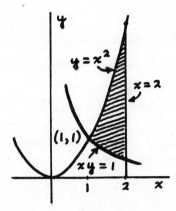

Figure 3

8. $x = \ln\sqrt{y} = \frac{1}{2}\ln y \implies 2x = \ln y \implies y = e^{2x} = f^{-1}(x)$

9. $x = \sqrt{y-1} \implies x^2 = y - 1 \implies y = x^2 + 1 = f^{-1}(x)$, $x \geq 0$. The graphs are shown in the solution of Problem 3, Sec. 8.2.

10. Since $f'(x) = 3x^2 + 1$, $\dfrac{dy}{dx} = \dfrac{1}{f'(y)} = \dfrac{1}{3y^2 + 1}$.

11. $\displaystyle\int_{\pi/6}^{\pi/2} \cot x\,dx = \ln\sin x \Big|_{\pi/6}^{\pi/2} = \ln 1 - \ln\frac{1}{2} = \ln 2$

12. $A = \dfrac{4}{\pi}\displaystyle\int_0^{\pi/4} \sec x\,dx = \dfrac{4}{\pi}\ln(\sec x + \tan x)\Big|_0^{\pi/4} = \dfrac{4}{\pi}\ln(1+\sqrt{2})$

13. $\displaystyle\lim_{x\to 0}(1+x)^{1/x} = e$, so the hole is $(0,e)$.

14. $dy/dx = 2xe^{-y} \implies e^y dy = 2x\,dx \implies \displaystyle\int e^y dy = \int 2x\,dx \implies e^y = x^2 + C = x^2 - 3$

(because $y = 0$ when $x = 2$). Hence $y = \ln(x^2 - 3)$.

15. (a) Since e^{-x} is always positive, $y > 0$ when $x > 0$ and $y < 0$ when $x < 0$.

(b) $y' = 3x(-e^{-x}) + 3e^{-x} = 3e^{-x}(1 - x)$, so the curve is rising when $x < 1$, falling when $x > 1$.

(c) $y'' = 3e^{-x}(-1) - 3e^{-x}(1 - x) = 3e^{-x}(x - 2)$, so the curve is concave up when $x > 2$, down when $x < 2$.

(d) It appears from Figure 4 that $y \to 0$ when $x \to \infty$. (Note that this is not obvious, because y is a product of a large factor $3x$ and a small factor e^{-x}. The question is settled in Problem 32, Sec. 11.2.) When $x \to -\infty$, $y \to -\infty$ (because y is a product of a large negative factor $3x$ and a large positive factor e^{-x}).

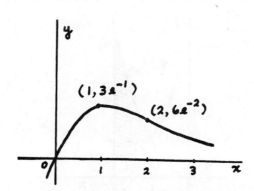

Figure 4

16. $\dfrac{d}{dx}(x \ln x - x) = x(1/x) + \ln x - 1 = \ln x$

17. $\dfrac{d}{dx} \ln |x + \sqrt{x^2 + a^2}| = \dfrac{1}{x + \sqrt{x^2 + a^2}}\left(1 + \dfrac{x}{\sqrt{x^2 + a^2}}\right) = \dfrac{1}{x + \sqrt{x^2 + a^2}}\left(\dfrac{\sqrt{x^2 + a^2} + x}{\sqrt{x^2 + a^2}}\right)$

$\qquad = \dfrac{1}{\sqrt{x^2 + a^2}}$

18. Identical in form to Problem 17.

19. Since $\dfrac{1}{2a} \ln \left|\dfrac{a + x}{a - x}\right| = \dfrac{1}{2a}(\ln |a + x| - \ln |a - x|)$, the derivative is

$\dfrac{1}{2a}\left(\dfrac{1}{a + x} + \dfrac{1}{a - x}\right) = \dfrac{1}{2a} \cdot \dfrac{a - x + a + x}{a^2 - x^2} = \dfrac{1}{a^2 - x^2}$

20. $V = \pi \displaystyle\int_0^1 y^2 dx = \pi \int_0^1 e^{-2x} dx = -\dfrac{\pi}{2} e^{-2x} \Big|_0^1 = \dfrac{\pi}{2}(1 - e^{-2})$

21. $\log_2 5 = \dfrac{\ln 5}{\ln 2}$. Or, $\log_2 5 = \dfrac{\log 5}{\log 2}$, since $\dfrac{\log 5}{\log 2} = \dfrac{\ln 5/\ln 10}{\ln 2/\ln 10} = \dfrac{\ln 5}{\ln 2}$.

22. $D_x x^{2x} = D_x e^{2x \ln x} = e^{2x \ln x}\left(2x \cdot \dfrac{1}{x} + 2 \ln x\right) = x^{2x}(2 + 2 \ln x)$

23. Since $y = e^{\sin x \ln \cos x}$, $y' = e^{\sin x \ln \cos x}[\sin x (-\tan x) + \cos x \ln \cos x] = (\cos x)^{\sin x}(-\sin x \tan x + \cos \ln \cos x) = 0$ at $x = 0$. The tangent is horizontal, with equation $y = 1$.

24. $|\Delta P/P| \approx |dP/P| = |3P_0 e^{3t} dt/(P_0 e^{3t})| = |3\,dt| = |3t|\,|dt/t|$. Since $t = 2$ and $|dt/t| = |\Delta t/t| = 0.02$, the relative error in P is about $3(2)(0.02) = 12\%$.

25. $\dfrac{dQ}{dt} = -kQ \implies \dfrac{dQ}{Q} = -k\,dt \implies \displaystyle\int \dfrac{dQ}{Q} = -k\int dt \implies \ell n\,Q = -kt + C = -kt + \ell n\,10$

(because $Q = 10$ when $t = 0$). Hence $\ell n\,(Q/10) = -kt$. Since $Q = 5$ when $t = 1$, we have $\ell n\,\tfrac{1}{2} = -k$, or $k = \ell n\,2$. Hence $\ell n\,(Q/10) = -t\,\ell n\,2 = \ell n\,(2^{-t}) \implies Q/10 = 2^{-t}$ $\implies Q = 10(2^{-t})$. When $Q = 1$,

$$t = \frac{-\ell n\,(1/10)}{\ell n\,2} = \frac{\ell n\,10}{\ell n\,2} \approx 3.3 \text{ sec}$$

26. (a) $f'(x) = 1/(1 + x^2) > 0$ for all x, so f is a continuous and increasing function. No horizontal line intersects its graph more than once, so it has an inverse.

(b) $y = g(x) \iff x = f(y) \implies 1 = f'(y)\dfrac{dy}{dx} \implies 1 = \dfrac{1}{1 + y^2}\cdot\dfrac{dy}{dx} \implies \dfrac{dy}{dx} = 1 + y^2$.

Since $f(0) = 0$, the origin is on the graph of f. Hence it is also on the graph of g, that is, $g(0) = 0$.

(c) If $y = \tan x$, then $y' = \sec^2 x = 1 + \tan^2 x = 1 + y^2$. Since $\tan 0 = 0$, the initial condition is satisfied.

(d) Since $g(x) = \tan x$ and f is the inverse of g, we have $f(x) = g^{-1}(x) = \tan^{-1} x$, that is,

$$\tan^{-1} x = \int_0^x \frac{dt}{1 + t^2}$$

27. (a) $f'(x) = 1/\sqrt{1 - x^2} > 0$ for $-1 < x < 1$. Hence f is continuous and increasing in its domain, which means it has an inverse.

(b) $g'(x) = \dfrac{1}{f'(y)} = \sqrt{1 - y^2}$ and $g''(x) = \dfrac{-y}{\sqrt{1 - y^2}}\cdot\dfrac{dy}{dx} = \dfrac{-y}{\sqrt{1 - y^2}}\cdot\sqrt{1 - y^2} = -y$.

Hence $y'' + y = 0$. Since $f(0) = 0$, the origin is on the graph of f, hence also on the graph of g, that is, $g(0) = 0$. Since $g'(x) = \sqrt{1 - y^2}$, we also have $g'(0) = 1$, because $y = g(x) = 0$ when $x = 0$.

(c) If $y = \sin x$, then $y' = \cos x$ and $y'' = -\sin x = -y$. Hence $y'' + y = 0$. Since $\sin 0 = 0$ and $\cos 0 = 1$, we have $y = 0$ and $y' = 1$ at $x = 0$.

(d) Since $g(x) = \sin x$ and f is the inverse of g, we have $f(x) = g^{-1}(x) = \sin^{-1} x$, that is,

$$\sin^{-1} x = \int_0^x \frac{dt}{\sqrt{1 - t^2}}$$

28. (a) If $u = t - 1$, then $du = dt$. Since $u = 0$ when $t = 1$ and $u = x - 1$ when $t = x$,

$$\ell n\, x = \int_1^x \frac{dt}{t} = \int_0^{x-1} \frac{du}{1+u}$$

(b) The division is shown below:

$$
\begin{array}{r}
1 - u + u^2 \\[2pt]
1 + u\,\overline{\big|\,1 } \\
\underline{1 + u} \\
-u \\
\underline{-u - u^2} \\
u^2 \\
\underline{u^2 + u^3} \\
-u^3
\end{array}
$$

Hence $\dfrac{1}{1+u} = 1 - u + u^2 - \dfrac{u^3}{1+u}$ and we find

$$\ell n\, x = \left(u - \frac{1}{2}u^2 + \frac{1}{3}u^3\right)\Big|_0^{x-1} - \int_0^{x-1} \frac{u^3 du}{1+u}$$

$$= (x-1) - \frac{1}{2}(x-1)^2 + \frac{1}{3}(x-1)^3 - \int_0^{x-1} \frac{u^3 du}{1+u}$$

(c) If $x \geq 1$, then $x - 1 \geq 0$ and the interval of integration has left-hand endpoint 0. Hence $u \geq 0$ and $0 \leq \dfrac{u^3}{1+u} \leq u^3$. Therefore

$$0 \leq \int_0^{x-1} \frac{u^3 du}{1+u} \leq \int_0^{x-1} u^3 du = \frac{1}{4}(x-1)^4$$

The error in the approximation is $\left|\int_0^{x-1} \dfrac{u^3 du}{1+u}\right| \leq \dfrac{1}{4}(x-1)^4$.

(d) $\ell n\, 1.1 \approx 0.1 - \frac{1}{2}(0.1)^2 + \frac{1}{3}(0.1)^3 = 0.095333\cdots$, with error $\leq \frac{1}{4}(0.1)^4 <$ 0.00003. Hence $\ell n\, 1.1 = 0.0953$ correct to four places.

29.(a) Carry out the division in Problem 28(b) to one more term, obtaining

$$\frac{1}{1+u} = 1 - u + u^2 - u^3 + \frac{u^4}{1+u}$$

This gives $\ell n\, x = (x-1) - \frac{1}{2}(x-1)^2 + \frac{1}{3}(x-1)^3 - \frac{1}{4}(x-1)^4 + \int_0^{x-1} \frac{u^4 du}{1+u}$, so the error in the approximation is

$$\left|\int_0^{x-1} \frac{u^4 du}{1+u}\right| \leq \int_0^{x-1} u^4 du = \frac{1}{5}(x-1)^5 \quad (x \geq 1)$$

(b) $\ell n\, 1.1 \approx 0.1 - \frac{1}{2}(0.1)^2 + \frac{1}{3}(0.1)^3 - \frac{1}{4}(0.1)^4 = 0.095308333\cdots$, with error $\leq \frac{1}{5}(0.1)^5 = 0.000002$. Hence $\ell n\, 1.1 = 0.09531$ correct to five places.

(c) $\ell n\, 0.8 = -\ell n\, 1.25 \approx -0.25 + \frac{1}{2}(0.25)^2 - \frac{1}{3}(0.25)^3 + \frac{1}{4}(0.25)^4 = -0.22298\cdots$, with error $\leq \frac{1}{5}(0.25)^5 < 0.0002$. Hence $\ell n\, 0.8 = -0.223$ correct to three places.

30.(a) Carry out the division in Problem 28(b) to obtain a quotient of degree $n - 1$. This yields a polynomial approximation of the form

$$\ln x \approx (x-1) - \frac{1}{2}(x-1)^2 + \frac{1}{3}(x-1)^3 - \cdots + \frac{(-1)^{n-1}}{n}(x-1)^n$$

with error $\leq \frac{1}{n+1}(x-1)^{n+1}$. If $1 \leq x \leq 2$, then $0 \leq x-1 \leq 1$, and hence the error approaches 0 as $n \to \infty$. The approximating polynomials approach $\ln x$, so their limit (which is what the infinite series means) is $\ln x$.

(b) Error $\leq \frac{1}{n+1}(x-1)^{n+1}$, as explained in part (a).

(c) Put $x = 2$ in the infinite series in part (a).

(d) To force the error $< \frac{1}{2} \times 10^{-5}$, we need $\frac{1}{n+1}(2-1)^{n+1} < \frac{1}{2} \times 10^{-5} \Rightarrow$ $n+1 > 2 \times 10^5 \Rightarrow n > 2 \times 10^5 - 1 = 199{,}999$. Hence n should be at least 200,000.

CHAPTER 9   INVERSE TRIGONOMETRIC, HYPERBOLIC, AND INVERSE HYPERBOLIC
            FUNCTIONS

Section 9.1   INVERSE TRIGONOMETRIC FUNCTIONS

1. $\sin^{-1}\frac{1}{2} = \frac{\pi}{6}$ because $\sin\frac{\pi}{6} = \frac{1}{2}$ and $\frac{\pi}{6} \in [-\pi/2, \pi/2]$.

2. $\cos^{-1}(-1) = \pi$ because $\cos\pi = -1$ and $\pi \in [0, \pi]$.

3. $\tan^{-1}\sqrt{3} = \pi/3$ because $\tan(\pi/3) = \sqrt{3}$ and $\pi/3 \in (-\pi/2, \pi/2)$.

4. $\cot^{-1}0 = \pi/2$ because $\cot(\pi/2) = 0$ and $\pi/2 \in (0, \pi)$.

5. $\sec^{-1}1 = 0$ because $\sec 0 = 1$ and $0 \in [0, \pi/2) \cup [-\pi, -\pi/2)$.

6. $\cos^{-1}0 = \pi/2$ because $\cos(\pi/2) = 0$ and $\pi/2 \in [0, \pi]$.

7. $\cos^{-1}2$ is undefined because $\cos t = 2$ is impossible.

8. $\sin^{-1}(-1/2) = -\pi/6$ because $\sin(-\pi/6) = -1/2$ and $-\pi/6 \in [-\pi/2, \pi/2]$.

9. $\cot^{-1}(-\sqrt{3}) = 5\pi/6$ because $\cot(5\pi/6) = -\sqrt{3}$ and $5\pi/6 \in (0, \pi)$.

10. $\sec^{-1}\sqrt{2} = \pi/4$ because $\sec(\pi/4) = \sqrt{2}$ and $\pi/4 \in [0, \pi/2) \cup [-\pi, -\pi/2)$.

11. $\tan^{-1}(-1/\sqrt{3}) = -\pi/6$ because $\tan(-\pi/6) = -1/\sqrt{3}$ and $-\pi/6 \in (-\pi/2, \pi/2)$.

12. $\sec^{-1}\frac{1}{2}$ is undefined because $\sec t = \frac{1}{2}$ is impossible.

13. $\tan(\tan^{-1}2) = 2$ because the restricted tangent and $\tan^{-1}$ are inverses.

14. $\cos^{-1}(\cos\frac{3\pi}{2}) = \cos^{-1}0 = \pi/2$ (not $3\pi/2$).

15. $\cos(\sec^{-1}3) = \cos(\cos^{-1}\frac{1}{3}) = \frac{1}{3}$.

16. If $t = \tan^{-1}3$, then $\tan t = 3$ and $0 < t < \pi/2$. Hence

$$\sin(2\tan^{-1}3) = \sin 2t = 2\sin t \cos t = 2(3/\sqrt{10})(1/\sqrt{10}) = 3/5$$

17. If $u = \sin^{-1}(3/5)$ and $v = \cos^{-1}(5/13)$, then $\sin u = 3/5$ $(0 < u < \pi/2)$, $\cos v = 5/13$ $(0 < v < \pi/2)$ and hence

$$\cos(\sin^{-1}\tfrac{3}{5} + \cos^{-1}\tfrac{5}{13}) = \cos(u + v) = \cos u \cos v - \sin u \sin v$$

$$= \frac{4}{5} \cdot \frac{5}{13} - \frac{3}{5} \cdot \frac{12}{13} = -\frac{16}{65}$$

18. If $t = \sin^{-1}(3/5)$, then $\sin t = 3/5$ $(0 < t < \pi/2)$ and

$$\tan(\tfrac{1}{2}\sin^{-1}\tfrac{3}{5}) = \tan\tfrac{1}{2}t = \frac{1 - \cos t}{\sin t} = \frac{1 - 4/5}{3/5} = \frac{1}{3}$$

19. If $x = 1/2$, the formula gives $\tan^{-1}(1/2) = \dfrac{\pi/6}{\pi/3} = \dfrac{1}{2}$. But $\tan^{-1}(1/2) \approx$ $0.46 \neq 1/2$.

20. If $x = 1$, the formula gives $\dfrac{\pi}{2} = \dfrac{1}{\sin 1}$. But $\pi/2 \approx 1.57$ and $\dfrac{1}{\sin 1} \approx 1.19$.

21.(a) If $y = \sin^{-1}x$, then $x = \sin y = \cos(\pi/2 - y)$.

(b) Since $-\pi/2 \leq y \leq \pi/2$ in part (a), it follows that $0 \leq \pi/2 - y \leq \pi$. Hence $x = \cos(\pi/2 - y) \iff \cos^{-1}x = \pi/2 - y = \pi/2 - \sin^{-1}x$.

22. Since $\dfrac{d}{dx}(\tan^{-1}x + \cot^{-1}x) = \dfrac{1}{1 + x^2} - \dfrac{1}{1 + x^2} = 0$ for all x, we have $\tan^{-1}x +$ $\cot^{-1}x = C$. Put $x = 0$ to obtain $0 + \pi/2 = C$, from which $\tan^{-1}x + \cot^{-1}x = \pi/2$.

23. $y' = \dfrac{1}{\sqrt{1 - x^2/4}} \cdot \dfrac{1}{2} = \dfrac{1}{\sqrt{4 - x^2}}$

24. $y' = \dfrac{1}{1 + 4x^2} \cdot 2 = \dfrac{2}{1 + 4x^2}$

25. $y' = \dfrac{-1}{\sqrt{1 - 1/x^4}} \cdot \dfrac{-2}{x^3} = \dfrac{2}{x\sqrt{x^4 - 1}}$

26. $y' = \dfrac{1}{x^2\sqrt{x^4 - 1}} \cdot 2x = \dfrac{2}{x\sqrt{x^4 - 1}}$

27. $y' = \dfrac{-1}{1 + (1 - x)^2}(-1) = \dfrac{1}{1 + (1 - x)^2}$

28. $y' = \dfrac{1}{1 + \left(\dfrac{x - 1}{x + 1}\right)^2} \cdot \dfrac{(x + 1) - (x - 1)}{(x + 1)^2} = \dfrac{2}{(x + 1)^2 + (x - 1)^2} = \dfrac{2}{2x^2 + 2} = \dfrac{1}{x^2 + 1}$

29. $y' = x \cdot \dfrac{1}{\sqrt{1 - x^2}} + \sin^{-1}x = \dfrac{x}{\sqrt{1 - x^2}} + \sin^{-1}x$

30. $y' = x^2 \cdot \dfrac{1}{1 + x^2} + 2x \tan^{-1}x = \dfrac{x^2}{1 + x^2} + 2x \tan^{-1}x$

31. Differentiate each side with respect to x to obtain

$$\frac{1}{1+y^2/x^2} \cdot \frac{xy'-y}{x^2} = \frac{1}{2} \cdot \frac{1}{x^2+y^2}(2x+2yy') \implies \frac{xy'-y}{x^2+y^2} = \frac{x+yy'}{x^2+y^2} \implies$$

$$xy'-y = x+yy' \implies (x-y)y' = x+y \implies y' = \frac{x+y}{x-y}$$

32. The domain of each function is $-1 \le x \le 1$ and in that domain each reduces to $y = x$.

33. $D_x \sin^{-1}(\sin x) = \frac{1}{\sqrt{1-\sin^2 x}} \cdot \cos x = \frac{\cos x}{|\cos x|} = 1$ or -1 depending on whether $\cos x > 0$ or $\cos x < 0$. Hence $y = x+C$ in each interval where $\cos x > 0$ (not necessarily the same C in each interval) and $y = -x+C$ in each interval where $\cos x < 0$. Suppose, for example, that $3\pi/2 < x < 5\pi/2$. Since $\cos x > 0$, we have $y = x+C$. Put $x = 2\pi$ to obtain $\sin^{-1}(\sin 2\pi) = 2\pi+C$, or $0 = 2\pi+C$, from which $C = -2\pi$ and $y = x-2\pi$. In this way we can check each of the formulas in Example 2, and Figure 4 follows.

34. $D_x \cos^{-1}(\cos x) = \frac{-1}{\sqrt{1-\cos^2 x}}(-\sin x) = \frac{\sin x}{|\sin x|} = 1$ or -1 depending on whether $\sin x > 0$ or $\sin x < 0$. Hence $y = x+C$ in each interval where $\sin x > 0$ and $y = -x+C$ in each interval where $\sin x < 0$. The values of C corresponding to each interval are found as in Problem 33; the result is the graph in Figure 1.

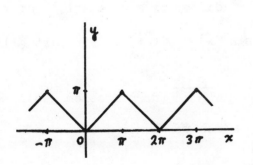

Figure 1

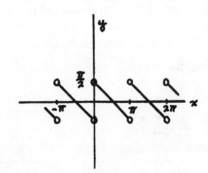

Figure 2

35. $D_x \tan^{-1}(\cot x) = \frac{1}{1+\cot^2 x}(-\csc^2 x) = \frac{-\csc^2 x}{\csc^2 x} = -1$ for all x in the domain of cot. Hence $y = -x+C$ in each interval of the domain (not necessarily the same C in each interval). In $(0,\pi)$, for example, put $x = \pi/2$ to obtain $0 = -\pi/2+C$, from which $C = \pi/2$ and hence $y = -x+\pi/2$. In $(\pi,2\pi)$ put $x = 3\pi/2$ to obtain $0 = -3\pi/2+C$, $C = 3\pi/2$, and $y = -x+3\pi/2$. The graph is shown in Figure 2.

36. See Figure 3.

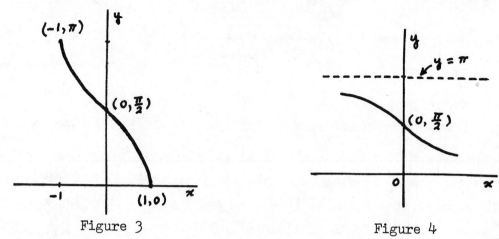

Figure 3   Figure 4

37. See Figure 8, Sec. 2.3.   The curve $y = \cot x$, $0 < x < \pi$, is in one piece, no horizontal line intersects it more than once, and it runs through the range $(-\infty, \infty)$ of cot.

38. See Figure 4.

39. (a) If $y = \sin^{-1}x$, then $x = \sin y$ and $dx/dy = \cos y$.   Hence

$$\frac{dy}{dx} = \frac{1}{dx/dy} = \frac{1}{\cos y} = \frac{1}{\cos(\sin^{-1}x)}$$

(b) Since $\frac{d}{dx}\cos(\sin^{-1}x) = -\sin(\sin^{-1}x)\cdot\frac{1}{\sqrt{1-x^2}} = \frac{-x}{\sqrt{1-x^2}}$ and $\frac{d}{dx}\sqrt{1-x^2} = $

$\frac{-x}{\sqrt{1-x^2}}$, the functions $\cos(\sin^{-1}x)$ and $\sqrt{1-x^2}$ differ by a constant.   Put $x = 0$ to show that the constant is 0.   Then $\cos(\sin^{-1}x) = \sqrt{1-x^2}$ and in part (a) we obtain $dy/dx = 1/\sqrt{1-x^2}$.

40. $\tan(\sin^{-1}x) = \sin(\sin^{-1}x)/\cos(\sin^{-1}x) = x/\sqrt{1-x^2}$ (from Problem 39b).

41. If $y = \tan^{-1}x$, then $x = \tan y$ and $dx/dy = \sec^2 y$.   Hence

$$\frac{dy}{dx} = \frac{1}{dx/dy} = \frac{1}{\sec^2 y} = \frac{1}{1 + \tan^2 y} = \frac{1}{1 + x^2}$$

42. The easiest procedure is to use the fact that $\cos^{-1}x = \pi/2 - \sin^{-1}x$ (provided that it has been established without calculus, as in Problem 21).   Then $D_x \cos^{-1}x = -D_x \sin^{-1}x = -1/\sqrt{1-x^2}$.   An alternative solution is to let $y = \cos^{-1}x$, from which $x = \cos y$ $(0 \le y \le \pi)$ and $dx/dy = -\sin y$.   Then

$$\frac{dy}{dx} = \frac{1}{dx/dy} = \frac{-1}{\sin y}$$

Since $\sin^2 y + \cos^2 y = 1$ and $\sin y \ge 0$ in $[0, \pi]$, we have $\sin y = \sqrt{1 - \cos^2 y} = \sqrt{1-x^2}$ and hence $dy/dx = -1/\sqrt{1-x^2}$.

43. Since $\cot^{-1}x = \pi/2 - \tan^{-1}x$ (Problem 22), we have $D_x\cot^{-1}x = -D_x\tan^{-1}x = -1/(1 + x^2)$. This is circular reasoning, however, if Problem 22 was done by calculus. An alternative solution is to write $y = \cot^{-1}x$, $x = \cot y$, $dx/dy = -\csc^2 y$, and hence

$$\frac{dy}{dx} = \frac{1}{dx/dy} = \frac{-1}{\csc^2 y} = \frac{-1}{1 + \cot^2 y} = \frac{-1}{1 + x^2}$$

44. (a) $D_x\cot^{-1}(1/x) = \frac{-1}{1 + 1/x^2}(-1/x^2) = \frac{1}{x^2 + 1} = D_x\tan^{-1}x$ for all $x \neq 0$.

(b) When $x = 1$ the formula $\cot^{-1}(1/x) = \tan^{-1}x + C$ reads $\pi/4 = \pi/4 + C$, so $C = 0$.

(c) When $x = -1$ the formula $\cot^{-1}(1/x) = \tan^{-1}x$ reads $3\pi/4 = -\pi/4$.

(d) Theorem 2 in Sec. 4.4 says that two functions with the same derivative in an interval differ by at most a constant in that interval. Hence $\cot^{-1}(1/x)$ and $\tan^{-1}x$ differ by a constant (namely $C = 0$) in $(0, \infty)$ and they differ by a constant (namely $C = \pi$) in $(-\infty, 0)$. The constants corresponding to different intervals need not be the same. Thus $\cot^{-1}(1/x) = \tan^{-1}x$ in $(0, \infty)$ but not in $(-\infty, 0)$.

(e) Since $\cot^{-1}(1/x) - \tan^{-1}x = C = \pi$ in $(-\infty, 0)$, $\cot^{-1}(1/x) = \pi + \tan^{-1}x$ when $x < 0$.

45. $\dfrac{d}{dx}\sec^{-1}\dfrac{1}{x} = \dfrac{1}{(1/x)\sqrt{1/x^2 - 1}}(-1/x^2)$. Since $\sqrt{1/x^2 - 1} = \sqrt{(1 - x^2)/x^2} = \sqrt{1 - x^2}/|x|$, we have

$$\frac{d}{dx}\sec^{-1}\frac{1}{x} = \frac{-|x|/x}{\sqrt{1 - x^2}}$$

Since $\dfrac{d}{dx}\cos^{-1}x = -1/\sqrt{1 - x^2}$, the derivatives are the same when $0 < x < 1$ and opposite in sign when $-1 < x < 0$. In the first case $\sec^{-1}(1/x) - \cos^{-1}x = C = 0$ (because $x = 1/2$ yields $\pi/3 - \pi/3 = C$). In the second case $\sec^{-1}(1/x) + \cos^{-1}x = C = 0$ (because $x = -1/2$ yields $-2\pi/3 + 2\pi/3 = C$). Hence $\sec^{-1}(1/x) = \pm\cos^{-1}x$, the sign depending on whether $0 < x < 1$ or $-1 < x < 0$. The endpoints $x = \pm 1$ can be checked separately; since $\sec^{-1}1 = 0 = \cos^{-1}1$ and $\sec^{-1}(-1) = -\pi = -\cos^{-1}(-1)$, they are included.

46. Since $\sin^{-1}x$ is defined for $-1 \leq x \leq 1$ and $\sec^{-1}x$ for $x \geq 1$ or $x \leq -1$, the domain consists of only two points, $x = \pm 1$. Such a function cannot be differentiated; the definition of derivative at a point requires the point to be part of an interval in the domain.

47. Since $\sin^{-1}t$ is an antiderivative of $1/\sqrt{1 - t^2}$, we have

$$\int_0^x \frac{dt}{\sqrt{1-t^2}} = \sin^{-1}t \Big|_0^x = \sin^{-1}x - \sin^{-1}0 = \sin^{-1}x$$

Similarly,

$$\int_0^x \frac{dt}{1+t^2} = \tan^{-1}t \Big|_0^x = \tan^{-1}x - \tan^{-1}0 = \tan^{-1}x$$

An alternate solution (suggested in the answer section in the text) is to observe that

$$\frac{d}{dx}\int_0^x \frac{dt}{\sqrt{1-t^2}} = \frac{1}{\sqrt{1-x^2}} = \frac{d}{dx}\sin^{-1}x$$

Hence the integral and $\sin^{-1}x$ differ by a constant (which is 0 because each function is 0 at $x = 0$).

Section 9.2   INTEGRATION INVOLVING INVERSE TRIGONOMETRIC FUNCTIONS

1. $\dfrac{d}{dx}\sin^{-1}\dfrac{x}{a} = \dfrac{1/a}{\sqrt{1-x^2/a^2}} = \dfrac{1/a}{\sqrt{a^2-x^2}/|a|} = \dfrac{1}{\sqrt{a^2-x^2}}$ (because $a > 0$)

2.(a) $\displaystyle\int \frac{dx}{a^2+x^2} = \frac{1}{a^2}\int \frac{dx}{1+x^2/a^2} = \frac{1}{a}\int \frac{du}{1+u^2}$ $(u = x/a, \; du = \frac{1}{a}dx)$

$$= \frac{1}{a}\tan^{-1}u + C = \frac{1}{a}\tan^{-1}\frac{x}{a} + C$$

(b) $\dfrac{d}{dx}\left(\dfrac{1}{a}\tan^{-1}\dfrac{x}{a}\right) = \dfrac{1}{a}\cdot\dfrac{1/a}{1+x^2/a^2} = \dfrac{1}{a^2+x^2}$

3.(a) As in Problem 2(a), let $u = x/a$. Then $x = au$, $dx = a\,du$, and

$$\int \frac{dx}{x\sqrt{x^2-a^2}} = \int \frac{a\,du}{au\sqrt{a^2u^2-a^2}} = \int \frac{du}{u\sqrt{a^2(u^2-1)}} = \frac{1}{a}\int \frac{du}{u\sqrt{u^2-1}} = \frac{1}{a}\sec^{-1}u + C$$

$$= \frac{1}{a}\sec^{-1}\frac{x}{a} + C$$

(b) $\dfrac{d}{dx}\left(\dfrac{1}{a}\sec^{-1}\dfrac{x}{a}\right) = \dfrac{1}{a}\cdot\dfrac{1/a}{(x/a)\sqrt{x^2/a^2-1}} = \dfrac{1}{x\sqrt{x^2-a^2}}$

4. $\displaystyle\int \frac{dx}{\sqrt{25-x^2}} = \sin^{-1}\frac{x}{5} + C$

5. $\displaystyle\int \frac{dx}{\sqrt{1-9x^2}} = \frac{1}{3}\int \frac{du}{\sqrt{1-u^2}}$ $(u = 3x, \; du = 3\,dx)$

$$= \frac{1}{3}\sin^{-1}u + C = \frac{1}{3}\sin^{-1}3x + C$$

6. $\displaystyle\int \frac{x\,dx}{\sqrt{9-x^4}} = \frac{1}{2}\int \frac{du}{\sqrt{9-u^2}}$ $(u = x^2, \; du = 2x\,dx)$

$$= \frac{1}{2}\sin^{-1}\frac{u}{3} + C = \frac{1}{2}\sin^{-1}\frac{x^2}{3} + C$$

7. $\displaystyle\int \frac{dx}{x^2+12} = \frac{1}{\sqrt{12}}\tan^{-1}\frac{x}{\sqrt{12}} + C = \frac{1}{2\sqrt{3}}\tan^{-1}\frac{x}{2\sqrt{3}} + C$

8. $\displaystyle\int \frac{dx}{9+16x^2} = \frac{1}{4}\int \frac{du}{9+u^2}$ $(u = 4x,\ du = 4\,dx)$

$\displaystyle\qquad = \frac{1}{4}\cdot\frac{1}{3}\tan^{-1}\frac{u}{3} + C = \frac{1}{12}\tan^{-1}\frac{4x}{3} + C$

9. $\displaystyle\int \frac{e^x dx}{1+e^{2x}} = \int \frac{du}{1+u^2}$ $(u = e^x,\ du = e^x dx)$

$\displaystyle\qquad = \tan^{-1}u + C = \tan^{-1}e^x + C$

10. $\displaystyle\int \frac{dx}{x\sqrt{9x^2-1}} = \int \frac{3\,dx}{3x\sqrt{9x^2-1}} = \int \frac{du}{u\sqrt{u^2-1}}$ $(u = 3x,\ du = 3\,dx)$

$\displaystyle\qquad = \sec^{-1}u + C = \sec^{-1}3x + C$

11. $\displaystyle\int \frac{dx}{x\sqrt{16x^2-9}} = \int \frac{4\,dx}{4x\sqrt{16x^2-9}} = \int \frac{du}{u\sqrt{u^2-9}}$ $(u = 4x,\ du = 4\,dx)$

$\displaystyle\qquad = \frac{1}{3}\sec^{-1}\frac{u}{3} + C = \frac{1}{3}\sec^{-1}\frac{4x}{3} + C$

12. $x^2 - 2x + 5 = (x^2 - 2x + 1) + 4 = (x-1)^2 + 4$.   Hence

$\displaystyle\int \frac{dx}{x^2-2x+5} = \int \frac{dx}{(x-1)^2+4} = \int \frac{du}{u^2+4}$ $(u = x-1,\ du = dx)$

$\displaystyle\qquad = \frac{1}{2}\tan^{-1}\frac{u}{2} + C = \frac{1}{2}\tan^{-1}\frac{x-1}{2} + C$

13. $6x - x^2 = -(x^2 - 6x + 9) + 9 = 9 - (x-3)^2$.   Hence

$\displaystyle\int \frac{dx}{\sqrt{6x-x^2}} = \int \frac{dx}{\sqrt{9-(x-3)^2}} = \int \frac{du}{\sqrt{9-u^2}}$ $(u = x-3,\ du = dx)$

$\displaystyle\qquad = \sin^{-1}\frac{u}{3} + C = \sin^{-1}\frac{x-3}{3} + C$

14. $\displaystyle\int_{-2}^{2} \frac{dx}{\sqrt{16-x^2}} = \sin^{-1}(x/4)\Big|_{-2}^{2} = \sin^{-1}(1/2) - \sin^{-1}(-1/2) = \pi/6 - (-\pi/6) = \pi/3$

15. $\displaystyle\int_{0}^{1} \frac{x\,dx}{\sqrt{4-x^4}} = \frac{1}{2}\int_{0}^{1} \frac{du}{\sqrt{4-u^2}}$ $(u = x^2,\ du = 2x\,dx)$

$\displaystyle\qquad = \frac{1}{2}\sin^{-1}\frac{u}{2}\Big|_{0}^{1} = \frac{1}{2}\left(\sin^{-1}\frac{1}{2} - \sin^{-1}0\right) = \frac{1}{2}\left(\frac{\pi}{6} - 0\right) = \frac{\pi}{12}$

16. $\displaystyle\int_{0}^{\pi/2} \frac{\sin x\,dx}{\sqrt{4-\cos^2 x}} = -\int_{1}^{0} \frac{du}{\sqrt{4-u^2}}$ $(u = \cos x,\ du = -\sin x\,dx)$

$\displaystyle\qquad = \int_{0}^{1} \frac{du}{\sqrt{4-u^2}} = \sin^{-1}(u/2)\Big|_{0}^{1} = \sin^{-1}(1/2) - \sin^{-1}0 = \pi/6$

17. $\displaystyle\int_{1}^{3} \frac{dx}{x^2+3} = \frac{1}{\sqrt{3}}\tan^{-1}\frac{x}{\sqrt{3}}\Big|_{1}^{3} = \frac{1}{\sqrt{3}}\left(\tan^{-1}\sqrt{3} - \tan^{-1}\frac{1}{\sqrt{3}}\right) = \frac{1}{\sqrt{3}}\left(\frac{\pi}{3} - \frac{\pi}{6}\right) = \frac{\pi}{6\sqrt{3}} = \frac{\pi\sqrt{3}}{18}$

18. $\displaystyle\int_{0}^{1} \frac{x+1}{x^2+1}\,dx = \int_{0}^{1} \frac{x\,dx}{x^2+1} + \int_{0}^{1} \frac{dx}{x^2+1} = \frac{1}{2}\ln(x^2+1)\Big|_{0}^{1} + \tan^{-1}x\Big|_{0}^{1} = \frac{1}{2}\ln 2 + \frac{\pi}{4}$

19. $\displaystyle\int_0^{\pi/2} \frac{\cos x\, dx}{9 + \sin^2 x} = \int_0^1 \frac{du}{9 + u^2}$ $(u = \sin x,\ du = \cos x\, dx)$

$$= \frac{1}{3}\tan^{-1}\frac{u}{3}\Big|_0^1 = \frac{1}{3}\tan^{-1}\frac{1}{3}$$

20. $\displaystyle\int_3^4 \frac{dx}{x\sqrt{x^2 - 4}} = \frac{1}{2}\sec^{-1}\frac{x}{2}\Big|_3^4 = \frac{1}{2}(\sec^{-1}2 - \sec^{-1}\frac{3}{2}) = \frac{1}{2}(\frac{\pi}{3} - \cos^{-1}\frac{2}{3})$

21. $\displaystyle\int_2^5 \frac{dx}{x\sqrt{9x^2 - 16}} = \int_2^5 \frac{3\, dx}{3x\sqrt{9x^2 - 16}} = \int_6^{15} \frac{du}{u\sqrt{u^2 - 16}}$ $(u = 3x,\ du = 3\, dx)$

$$= \frac{1}{4}\sec^{-1}\frac{u}{4}\Big|_6^{15} = \frac{1}{4}(\sec^{-1}\frac{15}{4} - \sec^{-1}\frac{3}{2}) = \frac{1}{4}(\cos^{-1}\frac{4}{15} - \cos^{-1}\frac{2}{3})$$

22. $x^2 - 6x + 13 = (x^2 - 6x + 9) + 4 = (x - 3)^2 + 4$. Hence

$$\int_3^5 \frac{dx}{x^2 - 6x + 13} = \int_3^5 \frac{dx}{(x - 3)^2 + 4} = \int_0^2 \frac{du}{u^2 + 4}$$ $(u = x - 3,\ du = dx)$

$$= \frac{1}{2}\tan^{-1}\frac{u}{2}\Big|_0^2 = \frac{\pi}{8}$$

23. $3 + 2x - x^2 = -(x^2 - 2x + 1) + 4 = 4 - (x - 1)^2$. Hence

$$\int_0^1 \frac{dx}{\sqrt{3 + 2x - x^2}} = \int_0^1 \frac{dx}{\sqrt{4 - (x - 1)^2}} = \int_{-1}^0 \frac{du}{\sqrt{4 - u^2}}$$ $(u = x - 1,\ du = dx)$

$$= \sin^{-1}(u/2)\Big|_{-1}^0 = 0 - \sin^{-1}(-1/2) = -(-\pi/6) = \pi/6$$

24. $\displaystyle\frac{d}{dx}(x\sin^{-1}x + \sqrt{1 - x^2}) = x\cdot\frac{1}{\sqrt{1 - x^2}} + \sin^{-1}x - \frac{x}{\sqrt{1 - x^2}} = \sin^{-1}x$

25. $\displaystyle\frac{d}{dx}(x\tan^{-1}x - \ell n\sqrt{1 + x^2}) = x\cdot\frac{1}{1 + x^2} + \tan^{-1}x - \frac{1}{2}\cdot\frac{2x}{1 + x^2} = \tan^{-1}x$

26. $\displaystyle\frac{d}{dx}(x\sec^{-1}x - \ell n|x + \sqrt{x^2 - 1}|) = x\cdot\frac{1}{x\sqrt{x^2 - 1}} + \sec^{-1}x - \frac{1}{x + \sqrt{x^2 - 1}}\Big(1 + \frac{x}{\sqrt{x^2 - 1}}\Big)$

$$= \frac{x}{x\sqrt{x^2 - 1}} + \sec^{-1}x - \frac{1}{x + \sqrt{x^2 - 1}}\cdot\frac{\sqrt{x^2 - 1} + x}{\sqrt{x^2 - 1}}$$

$$= \sec^{-1}x$$

27. $\displaystyle\frac{d}{dx}\Big(\frac{x}{2}\sqrt{a^2 - x^2} + \frac{a^2}{2}\sin^{-1}\frac{x}{a}\Big) = \frac{x}{2}\cdot\frac{-x}{\sqrt{a^2 - x^2}} + \frac{1}{2}\sqrt{a^2 - x^2} + \frac{a^2}{2}\cdot\frac{1/a}{\sqrt{1 - x^2/a^2}}$

$$= \frac{-x^2}{2\sqrt{a^2 - x^2}} + \frac{\sqrt{a^2 - x^2}}{2} + \frac{a^2}{2\sqrt{a^2 - x^2}} = \frac{-x^2 + (a^2 - x^2) + a^2}{2\sqrt{a^2 - x^2}}$$

$$= \frac{a^2 - x^2}{\sqrt{a^2 - x^2}} = \sqrt{a^2 - x^2}$$

28. Since the integrand is even, we have

$$\int_{-a}^a \sqrt{a^2 - x^2}\, dx = 2\int_0^a \sqrt{a^2 - x^2}\, dx = 2\Big(\frac{x}{2}\sqrt{a^2 - x^2} + \frac{a^2}{2}\sin^{-1}\frac{x}{a}\Big)\Big|_0^a$$

$$= 2(0 + \frac{a^2}{2}\sin^{-1}1) - 2(0 + \frac{a^2}{2}\sin^{-1}0) = a^2 \cdot \frac{\pi}{2} = \frac{\pi a^2}{2}$$

29. $\int_0^t \frac{dx}{\sqrt{4-x^2}} = \sin^{-1}\frac{x}{2}\Big|_0^t = \sin^{-1}\frac{t}{2} \to \sin^{-1}1 = \frac{\pi}{2}$ as $t \to 2$.

30. $A = \int_0^b \frac{dx}{1+x^2} = \tan^{-1}x\Big|_0^b = \tan^{-1}b \to \frac{\pi}{2}$ as $b \to \infty$.

31. The graphs intersect when $1/\sqrt{1-x^2} = 2 \iff \sqrt{1-x^2} = 1/2 \iff 1-x^2 = 1/4$ $\iff x^2 = 3/4 \iff x = \pm\sqrt{3}/2$. From Figure 1 we conclude that

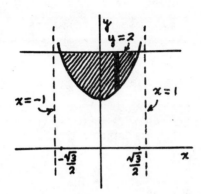

Figure 1

$$A = 2\int_0^{\sqrt{3}/2}\left(2 - \frac{1}{\sqrt{1-x^2}}\right)dx = 4\int_0^{\sqrt{3}/2}dx - 2\int_0^{\sqrt{3}/2}\frac{dx}{\sqrt{1-x^2}} = 2\sqrt{3} - 2\sin^{-1}x\Big|_0^{\sqrt{3}/2}$$

$$= 2\sqrt{3} - 2\cdot\frac{\pi}{3} = \frac{2}{3}(3\sqrt{3} - \pi)$$

32. $V = \pi\int_0^3 y^2 dx = \pi\int_0^3 \frac{dx}{9+x^2} = \frac{\pi}{3}\tan^{-1}\frac{x}{3}\Big|_0^3 = \frac{\pi}{3}\cdot\frac{\pi}{4} = \frac{\pi^2}{12}$

33. The curve is the upper half of the circle $x^2 + y^2 = r^2$, with length πr. To find its length by calculus, we use parametric equations $x = r\cos t$, $y = r\sin t$, $0 \le t \le \pi$. Since $dx = -r\sin t\, dt$ and $dy = r\cos t\, dt$, we have $(ds)^2 = (dx)^2 + (dy)^2 = r^2(dt)^2$ and hence $s = \int_0^\pi r\, dt = \pi r$.

Why is this problem placed in this section, when the above solution has nothing to do with inverse trigonometric functions? The reason is that some students may find the following "solution" more natural. Since $y = \sqrt{r^2 - x^2}$,

$$y' = \frac{-x}{\sqrt{r^2-x^2}} \text{ and } 1 + y'^2 = 1 + \frac{x^2}{r^2-x^2} = \frac{r^2}{r^2-x^2}$$

Hence $s = \int_{-r}^r \frac{r\,dx}{\sqrt{r^2-x^2}} = 2r\int_0^r \frac{dx}{\sqrt{r^2-x^2}} = 2r\sin^{-1}\frac{x}{r}\Big|_0^r = 2r\sin^{-1}1 = 2r\cdot\frac{\pi}{2} = \pi r$.

The trouble with this is that $\int_0^r \frac{dx}{\sqrt{r^2-x^2}}$ does not exist, because the integrand is unbounded in the domain of integration. To make the solution respectable, we must treat the integral as "improper" (see Problem 29), assigning it the value approached by $\int_0^t \frac{dx}{\sqrt{r^2 - x^2}}$ as $t \uparrow r$. Not every improper integral can be assigned a value, however; you must be on your guard.

34. $\frac{dy}{dx} = 16 + y^2 \implies \frac{dy}{16 + y^2} = dx \implies \int \frac{dy}{16 + y^2} = \int dx \implies \frac{1}{4} \tan^{-1} \frac{y}{4} = x + C = x$

(because $y = 0$ when $x = 0$). Then $\tan^{-1}(y/4) = 4x \implies y/4 = \tan 4x \implies$ $y = 4 \tan 4x$.

35. Let $v = dx/dt$ to put the equation in the form $dv/dt = -a^2 x$. Then use Newton's device (described in Example 4) to write

$$\frac{dv}{dt} = \frac{dv}{dx}\frac{dx}{dt} = v\frac{dv}{dx} = -a^2 x \implies v\, dv = -a^2 x\, dx \implies \int v\, dv = -a^2 \int x\, dx$$

$$\implies \tfrac{1}{2}v^2 = -\tfrac{1}{2}a^2 x^2 + C_1$$

Since $v = 0$ when $x = 1$, we find $C_1 = \tfrac{1}{2}a^2$ and hence $\tfrac{1}{2}v^2 = \tfrac{1}{2}a^2 - \tfrac{1}{2}a^2 x^2$, that is, $v^2 = a^2(1 - x^2)$. Since $v < 0$ for an interval after the motion starts, we choose the negative square root:

$$v = -a\sqrt{1 - x^2} \implies \frac{dx}{dt} = -a\sqrt{1 - x^2} \implies \frac{dx}{\sqrt{1 - x^2}} = -a\, dt \implies \int \frac{dx}{\sqrt{1 - x^2}} = -a \int dt$$

$$\implies \sin^{-1} x = -at + C_2 = \pi/2 - at \quad \text{(because } x = 1 \text{ when } t = 0\text{)}$$

$$\implies x = \sin(\pi/2 - at) = \cos at$$

36.(a) First observe that since the beacon revolves five times per minute, $d\theta/dt = 10\pi$ rad/min $= 600\pi$ rad/hr. Then from $x = \tan\theta$ we have

$$\frac{dx}{dt} = \sec^2\theta \frac{d\theta}{dt} = 600\pi \sec^2\theta \text{ km/hr}$$

(b) From $\theta = \tan^{-1} x$ we have $\frac{d\theta}{dt} = \frac{1}{1 + x^2}\frac{dx}{dt}$, or $\frac{dx}{dt} = 600\pi(1 + x^2)$.

(c) $\sec^2\theta = 1 + \tan^2\theta = 1 + x^2$

37. If x is the distance from the runners to the finish line (at time t), then $\theta = \tan^{-1}(x/10)$ and

$$\frac{d\theta}{dt} = \frac{1}{1 + x^2/100}\cdot\frac{1}{10}\frac{dx}{dt} = \frac{10}{100 + x^2}\frac{dx}{dt}$$

When $x = 10$, $dx/dt = -9$, so $d\theta/dt = -9/20$ rad/sec. The answer to the question "how fast" does not involve the direction of turning, so it is simply $9/20$ rad/sec.

38. From Figure 2 we have $\cot\alpha = x$ and $\cot\beta = x/6$, so $\theta = \beta - \alpha = \cot^{-1}(x/6) - \cot^{-1}x$. To find maximum θ, we compute

$$\frac{d\theta}{dx} = \frac{-1/6}{1 + x^2/36} + \frac{1}{1 + x^2} = \frac{-6}{36 + x^2} + \frac{1}{1 + x^2} = \frac{-6 - 6x^2 + 36 + x^2}{(36 + x^2)(1 + x^2)} = \frac{5(6 - x^2)}{(36 + x^2)(1 + x^2)}$$

This changes sign from plus to minus at $x = \sqrt{6}$, so we have maximum θ if we stand $\sqrt{6}$ ft from the wall.

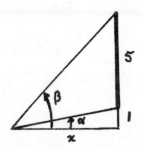

Figure 2   Figure 3

39. From Figure 3 we see that the angles of the isosceles triangle (with equal sides r) are α, α, and $\pi - 2\alpha$. Since $(\pi - 2\alpha) + \theta = \pi$, we have $\alpha = \frac{1}{2}\theta$. Moreover, $\tan\alpha = h/r$, so $\alpha = \tan^{-1}(h/r)$ and $\theta = 2\tan^{-1}(h/r)$. Since $s = r\theta = 2r\tan^{-1}(h/r)$, we find

$$\frac{ds}{dt} = 2r\cdot\frac{1}{1 + h^2/r^2}\cdot\frac{1}{r}\frac{dh}{dt} = \frac{2r^2}{r^2 + h^2}(2) \quad \text{(because } dh/dt = 2)$$

$$= \frac{4r^2}{r^2 + h^2}$$

The diver is halfway down when $h = \frac{1}{2}r$, at which point

$$\frac{ds}{dt} = \frac{4r^2}{r^2 + r^2/4} = \frac{16}{5} \text{ ft/sec}$$

Section 9.3   HYPERBOLIC FUNCTIONS

1. Since $\cosh^2 t - \sinh^2 t = 1$ and $x = \cosh t \geq 1$ for all t, the curve is the right-hand branch of the hyperbola $x^2 - y^2 = 1$. Since $y = \sinh t$ increases with t, the curve is traversed in the upward direction.

2. $\sinh(-t) = \frac{1}{2}(e^{-t} - e^t) = -\frac{1}{2}(e^t - e^{-t}) = -\sinh t$, so sinh is odd. But $\cosh(-t) = \frac{1}{2}(e^{-t} + e^t) = \cosh t$, so cosh is even.

3. $\tanh(-t) = \frac{\sinh(-t)}{\cosh(-t)} = \frac{-\sinh t}{\cosh t} = -\tanh t$, so tanh is odd. The other functions are treated similarly.

4. Divide each side of $\cosh^2 t - \sinh^2 t = 1$ by $\cosh^2 t$ to obtain

$$1 - \frac{\sinh^2 t}{\cosh^2 t} = \frac{1}{\cosh^2 t} \quad \text{or} \quad \tanh^2 t + \text{sech}^2 t = 1$$

Divide by $\sinh^2 t$ to obtain $\coth^2 t - \text{csch}^2 t = 1$.

5. If $\tanh t = -3/4$, then $\coth t = -4/3$. From Problem 4 we have $\operatorname{sech}^2 t = 1 - \tanh^2 t = 1 - 9/16 = 7/16$. Since $\operatorname{sech} t > 0$ for all t, the positive square root is required, $\operatorname{sech} t = \sqrt{7}/4$. From this it follows that $\cosh t = 4/\sqrt{7}$. Then from $\cosh^2 t - \sinh^2 t = 1$ we have $\sinh^2 t = \cosh^2 t - 1 = 16/7 - 1 = 9/7$. Since $\sinh t$ is negative (because $\tanh t = \sinh t/\cosh t < 0$ and $\cosh t > 0$), the negative square root is required, $\sinh t = -3/\sqrt{7}$. Then $\operatorname{csch} t = -\sqrt{7}/3$.

6. $\sinh u \cosh v + \cosh u \sinh v = \frac{1}{2}(e^u - e^{-u}) \cdot \frac{1}{2}(e^v + e^{-v}) + \frac{1}{2}(e^u + e^{-u}) \cdot \frac{1}{2}(e^v - e^{-v})$

$= \frac{1}{4}(e^{u+v} + e^{u-v} - e^{v-u} - e^{-(u+v)} + e^{u+v} - e^{u-v} + e^{v-u} - e^{-(u+v)}) = \frac{1}{4}(2e^{u+v} - 2e^{-(u+v)})$

$= \frac{1}{2}(e^{u+v} - e^{-(u+v)}) = \sinh(u + v)$

7. $\cosh u \cosh v + \sinh u \sinh v = \frac{1}{2}(e^u + e^{-u}) \cdot \frac{1}{2}(e^v + e^{-v}) + \frac{1}{2}(e^u - e^{-u}) \cdot \frac{1}{2}(e^v - e^{-v})$

$= \frac{1}{4}(e^{u+v} + e^{u-v} + e^{v-u} + e^{-(u+v)} + e^{u+v} - e^{u-v} - e^{v-u} + e^{-(u+v)}) = \frac{1}{4}(2e^{u+v} + 2e^{-(u+v)})$

$= \frac{1}{2}(e^{u+v} + e^{-(u+v)}) = \cosh(u + v)$

8. $\sinh(u - v) = \sinh[u + (-v)] = \sinh u \cosh(-v) + \cosh u \sinh(-v)$ (Problem 6)

$\qquad = \sinh u \cosh v - \cosh u \sinh v$ (Problem 2)

9. $\cosh(u - v) = \cosh[u + (-v)] = \cosh u \cosh(-v) + \sinh u \sinh(-v)$ (Problem 7)

$\qquad = \cosh u \cosh v - \sinh u \sinh v$ (Problem 2)

10. $\sinh 2t = \sinh(t + t) = \sinh t \cosh t + \cosh t \sinh t$ (Problem 6)

$\qquad = 2 \sinh t \cosh t$

11. $\cosh 2t = \cosh(t + t) = \cosh t \cosh t + \sinh t \sinh t$ (Problem 6)

$\qquad = \cosh^2 t + \sinh^2 t$

12. From Problem 11 (and $\cosh^2 t - \sinh^2 t = 1$) we have $\cosh 2t = \cosh^2 t + \sinh^2 t = (1 + \sinh^2 t) + \sinh^2 t = 1 + 2 \sinh^2 t$. Hence $\sinh^2 t = \frac{1}{2}(\cosh 2t - 1)$.

13. From Problem 11 (and $\cosh^2 t - \sinh^2 t = 1$) we have $\cosh 2t = \cosh^2 t + \sinh^2 t = \cosh^2 t + (\cosh^2 t - 1) = 2\cosh^2 t - 1$. Hence $\cosh^2 t = \frac{1}{2}(\cosh 2t + 1)$.

14. $D_x \cosh x = D_x \frac{1}{2}(e^x + e^{-x}) = \frac{1}{2}(e^x - e^{-x}) = \sinh x$

15. $D_x \tanh x = D_x \dfrac{\sinh x}{\cosh x} = \dfrac{\cosh x (\cosh x) - \sinh x (\sinh x)}{\cosh^2 x} = \dfrac{\cosh^2 x - \sinh^2 x}{\cosh^2 x}$

$\qquad = \dfrac{1}{\cosh^2 x} = \operatorname{sech}^2 x$

16. $D_x \coth x = D_x \dfrac{\cosh x}{\sinh x} = \dfrac{\sinh x (\sinh x) - \cosh x (\cosh x)}{\sinh^2 x} = \dfrac{\sinh^2 x - \cosh^2 x}{\sinh^2 x}$

$\qquad = \dfrac{-1}{\sinh^2 x} = -\operatorname{csch}^2 x$

17. $D_x \operatorname{sech} x = D_x (\cosh x)^{-1} = -(\cosh x)^{-2}(\sinh x) = -\dfrac{\sinh x}{\cosh^2 x} = -\dfrac{1}{\cosh x} \cdot \dfrac{\sinh x}{\cosh x}$

$$= -\text{sech}\,x\,\tanh x$$

18. $D_x\,\text{csch}\,x = D_x(\sinh x)^{-1} = -(\sinh x)^{-2}(\cosh x) = -\dfrac{\cosh x}{\sinh^2 x} = -\dfrac{1}{\sinh x}\cdot\dfrac{\cosh x}{\sinh x}$

$$= -\text{csch}\,x\,\coth x$$

19. The domain of $y = \frac{1}{2}(e^x + e^{-x})$ is R. Since cosh is even (Problem 2), the graph is symmetric about the y axis. There are no asymptotes, but $y \approx \frac{1}{2}e^x$ when x is large. Since $y' = \sinh x = 0$ when $x = 0$ and $y'' = \cosh x > 0$ for all x, the graph is always concave up, with low turning point $(0,1)$. This confirms the curve $y = \cosh x$ in Figure 3 of the text.

20. The domain of $y = \cosh x/\sinh x$ is $x \neq 0$. Since coth is odd (Problem 3), the graph is symmetric about the origin. When $x \downarrow 0$, $\cosh x$ is close to 1 and $\sinh x$ is small and positive, so $y \to \infty$. By symmetry, $y \to -\infty$ when $x \uparrow 0$. Hence the y axis is a vertical asymptote. When $x \to \infty$, $y = (e^x + e^{-x})/(e^x - e^{-x}) \approx 1$, so $y = 1$ is a horizontal asymptote. By symmetry, $y = -1$ is also a horizontal asymptote. Since $y' = -\text{csch}^2 x < 0$ for all $x \neq 0$, the curve is always falling. Since $y'' = -2\,\text{csch}\,x\,(-\text{csch}\,x\,\coth x) = 2\,\text{csch}^2 x\,\coth x$, y'' has the same sign as $\coth x$, namely positive when $x > 0$ and negative when $x < 0$. Hence the curve is concave up in the first quadrant and down in the third. See Figure 4 of the text.

21. The domain of $y = 2/(e^x + e^{-x})$ is R. Since sech is even (Problem 3), the graph is symmetric about the y axis. When $x \to \pm\infty$, $y \to 0$, so the x axis is a horizontal asymptote. We find $y' = -\text{sech}\,x\,\tanh x = 0 \iff \tanh x = 0 \iff x = 0$. (Note that sech x is always positive.) Since y' changes from plus to minus at $x = 0$, we have a high turning point at $(0,1)$. Since

$$y'' = -\text{sech}\,x\,(\text{sech}^2 x) + (\text{sech}\,x\,\tanh x)\tanh x = \text{sech}\,x\,(\tanh^2 x - \text{sech}^2 x)$$

$$= \text{sech}\,x\,(1 - 2\,\text{sech}^2 x) \quad \text{(Problem 4)}$$

there are inflection points where $\text{sech}\,x = \pm 1/\sqrt{2}$, or $x \approx \pm 0.88$ (from a calculator). See Figure 5 of the text.

22. The domain of $y = 1/\sinh x$ is $x \neq 0$. Since csch is odd (Problem 3), the graph is symmetric about the origin. Since $y \to \pm\infty$ when $x \downarrow 0$ or $x \uparrow 0$, and $y \to 0$ when $x \to \pm\infty$, the coordinate axes are asymptotes. We find

$$y' = -\text{csch}\,x\,\coth x = -\frac{\cosh x}{\sinh^2 x} < 0 \text{ for all } x \neq 0$$

so the graph is always falling. Also,

$$y'' = -\text{csch}\,x\,(-\text{csch}^2 x) + (\text{csch}\,x\,\coth x)\coth x = \text{csch}\,x\,(\text{csch}^2 x + \coth^2 x)$$

Since this has the same sign as $\text{csch}\,x$, the graph is concave up when $x > 0$

and down when $x < 0$. See Figure 6 of the text.

23. $y' = A \sinh x + B \cosh x$ and $y'' = A \cosh x + B \sinh x = y$, so $y'' - y = 0$.

24. $y' = \cosh 2x \cdot 2 = 2 \cosh 2x$

25. $y' = \sinh(1 - x) \cdot (-1) = -\sinh(1 - x)$

26. $y' = \operatorname{sech}^2 x^2 \cdot 2x = 2x \operatorname{sech}^2 x^2$

27. $y = 1$ for all x, so $y' = 0$.

28. $y' = x \cosh x + \sinh x$

29. $y' = \dfrac{1}{\cosh x} \cdot \sinh x = \tanh x$

30. $y' = \cosh x + 2 \sinh x = 0 \iff 2 \sinh x = -\cosh x \iff \tanh x = -\dfrac{1}{2} \iff$

$(e^x - e^{-x})/(e^x + e^{-x}) = -1/2 \iff 2e^x - 2e^{-x} = -e^x - e^{-x} \iff 3e^x = e^{-x} \iff$

$3e^{2x} = 1 \iff e^{2x} = 1/3 \iff 2x = \ln(1/3) = -\ln 3 \iff x = -\dfrac{1}{2}\ln 3$. Since

$y'' = \sinh x + 2 \cosh x = \sqrt{3}$ at the critical point (we omitted several steps!),
there is a minimum at the point. It is global because $y' = 0$ only once (the
curve falls to the minimum and rises thereafter).

An alternative (and easier) solution is to ignore hyperbolic functions,
writing $y = \frac{1}{2}(e^x - e^{-x}) + (e^x + e^{-x}) = \frac{1}{2}(3e^x + e^{-x})$. Then $y' = \frac{1}{2}(3e^x - e^{-x}) = 0$
when $x = -\frac{1}{2}\ln 3$ (as above). Since $y'' = \frac{1}{2}(3e^x + e^{-x}) > 0$ for all x, we have a
global minimum.

31. $\displaystyle\int_0^{\ln 2} \sinh x \, dx = \cosh x \,\Big|_0^{\ln 2} = \cosh(\ln 2) - \cosh 0 = \frac{1}{2}(e^{\ln 2} + e^{-\ln 2}) - 1$

$$= \frac{1}{2}(2 + \frac{1}{2}) - 1 = \frac{1}{4}$$

32. $\displaystyle\int_0^{\ln 3} \cosh 2x \, dx = \frac{1}{2}\sinh 2x \,\Big|_0^{\ln 3} = \frac{1}{2}\sinh(2\ln 3) - \frac{1}{2}\sinh 0 = \frac{1}{4}(e^{\ln 9} - e^{-\ln 9}) - 0$

$$= \frac{1}{4}(9 - \frac{1}{9}) = \frac{20}{9}$$

33. $\displaystyle\int_0^1 \operatorname{sech}^2 x \, dx = \tanh x \,\Big|_0^1 = \tanh 1 - \tanh 0 = \tanh 1$

34. $\displaystyle\int_0^2 \operatorname{sech}\frac{1}{2}x \tanh\frac{1}{2}x \, dx = -2 \operatorname{sech}\frac{1}{2}x \,\Big|_0^2 = -2(\operatorname{sech} 1 - \operatorname{sech} 0) = 2(1 - \operatorname{sech} 1)$

35. $\displaystyle\int_0^1 \tanh x \, dx = \int_0^1 \frac{\sinh x \, dx}{\cosh x} = \int_1^{\cosh 1} \frac{du}{u}$ $\quad (u = \cosh x, \ du = \sinh x \, dx)$

$$= \ln u \,\Big|_1^{\cosh 1} = \ln(\cosh 1)$$

36. $\displaystyle\int_1^2 \coth x \, dx = \int_1^2 \frac{\cosh x \, dx}{\sinh x} = \ln(\sinh x) \,\Big|_1^2 = \ln(\sinh 2) - \ln(\sinh 1)$

$$= \ln\left(\frac{\sinh 2}{\sinh 1}\right) = \ln\left(\frac{e^2 - e^{-2}}{e - e^{-1}}\right) = \ln\left(\frac{e^4 - 1}{e^3 - e}\right) = \ln\frac{(e^2 - 1)(e^2 + 1)}{e(e^2 - 1)}$$

$$= \ln\frac{e^2 + 1}{e} = \ln(e^2 + 1) - \ln e = \ln(e^2 + 1) - 1$$

37. From Figure 3 of the text we conclude that

$$A = \int_0^1 (\cosh x - \sinh x)\,dx = (\sinh x - \cosh x)\Big|_0^1$$

$$= (\sinh 1 - \cosh 1) - (\sinh 0 - \cosh 0) = \sinh 1 - \cosh 1 + 1$$

$$= \tfrac{1}{2}(e - e^{-1}) - \tfrac{1}{2}(e + e^{-1}) + 1 = 1 - e^{-1}$$

38. $V = \pi\int_0^1 y^2\,dx = \pi\int_0^1 \tanh^2 x\,dx = \pi\int_0^1 (1 - \operatorname{sech}^2 x)\,dx$ (Problem 4)

$$= \pi(x - \tanh x)\Big|_0^1 = \pi(1 - \tanh 1)$$

39. $V = \pi\int_0^1 y^2\,dx = \pi\int_0^1 \cosh^2 x\,dx = \frac{\pi}{2}\int_0^1 (\cosh 2x + 1)\,dx$ (Problem 13)

$$= \frac{\pi}{2}\left(\tfrac{1}{2}\sinh 2x + x\right)\Big|_0^1 = \frac{\pi}{2}\left(\tfrac{1}{2}\sinh 2 + 1\right) = \frac{\pi}{4}(\sinh 2 + 2)$$

40. $y' = \sinh x$, $\ 1 + y'^2 = 1 + \sinh^2 x = \cosh^2 x$, $\ 2\pi y\,ds = 2\pi\cosh x\cdot\cosh x\,dx = 2\pi\cosh^2 x\,dx$, so

$$A = 2\pi\int_0^1 \cosh^2 x\,dx = 2\times(\text{answer to Prob. 39}) = \frac{\pi}{2}(\sinh 2 + 2)$$

41. $y' = \sinh(x/a)$, $\ 1 + y'^2 = 1 + \sinh^2(x/a) = \cosh^2(x/a)$, so

$$s = 2\int_0^a \cosh(x/a)\,dx = 2a\sinh(x/a)\Big|_0^a = 2a\sinh 1$$

42. Using the data from Problem 41, we find

$$s = \int_0^x \cosh(t/a)\,dt = a\sinh(t/a)\Big|_0^x = a\sinh(x/a)$$

43. Since $\cosh x \geq 1$ for all x and $\sin^{-1} u$ is defined for $-1 \leq u \leq 1$, the domain consists of the single point $x = 0$. Such a function cannot be differentiated.

44. (a) $e^{-ix} = e^{i(-x)} = \cos(-x) + i\sin(-x) = \cos x - i\sin x$

(b) $\tfrac{1}{2}(e^{ix} + e^{-ix}) = \tfrac{1}{2}(\cos x + i\sin x + \cos x - i\sin x) = \cos x$ and $\frac{1}{2i}(e^{ix} - e^{-ix})$

$= \frac{1}{2i}(\cos x + i\sin x - \cos x + i\sin x) = \sin x.$

45. (a) When $n = 1$ the formula is trivial. Assume that it is true when $n = k$, $(\cos t + i\sin t)^k = \cos kt + i\sin kt$. Then

$$(\cos t + i \sin t)^{k+1} = (\cos t + i \sin t)^k (\cos t + i \sin t)$$
$$= (\cos kt + i \sin kt)(\cos t + i \sin t)$$
$$= (\cos kt \cos t - \sin kt \sin t) + i(\sin kt \cos t + \cos kt \sin t)$$
$$= \cos(kt + t) + i \sin(kt + t) = \cos(k+1)t + i \sin(k+1)t$$

This is the case corresponding to n = k+1. By the Principle of Mathematical Induction the formula is true for every positive integer n.

(b) $(\cos t + i \sin t)^n = (e^{it})^n = e^{i(nt)} = \cos nt + i \sin nt$

(c) $\cosh x + \sinh x = \frac{1}{2}(e^x + e^{-x}) + \frac{1}{2}(e^x - e^{-x}) = e^x$, so the formula reduces to $(e^t)^n = e^{nt}$, which is clearly correct.

Section 9.4   INVERSE HYPERBOLIC FUNCTIONS

1. $\sinh^{-1} 0 = 0$ because $\sinh 0 = 0$.

2. $\cosh^{-1} 1 = 0$ because $\cosh 0 = 1$.

3. $\tanh^{-1} 0 = 0$ because $\tanh 0 = 0$.

4. We use the logarithmic formula for $\sinh^{-1} x$ on page 395 to find
$$\sinh^{-1}(-1) = \ln(-1 + \sqrt{2})$$

5. We use the logarithmic formula for $\tanh^{-1} x$ on page 397 to find
$$\tanh^{-1}\tfrac{1}{2} = \tfrac{1}{2}\ln\frac{1 + \frac{1}{2}}{1 - \frac{1}{2}} = \tfrac{1}{2}\ln 3$$

6. $\cosh^{-1} 0$ is undefined because $\cosh x \geq 1$ for all x.

7. $\tanh^{-1} 2$ is undefined because $-1 < \tanh x < 1$ for all x.

8. $\sinh x = 2 \implies x = \sinh^{-1} 2 = \ln(2 + \sqrt{5})$

9. $\cosh 2x = 3 \implies 2x = \pm\cosh^{-1} 3 \implies x = \pm\tfrac{1}{2}\ln(3 + 2\sqrt{2})$. There are two answers because the graph of cosh is symmetric about the y axis (the right-hand half being used to generate $\cosh^{-1}$).

10. $\tanh\sqrt{x} = 3/5 \implies \sqrt{x} = \tanh^{-1}(3/5) = \tfrac{1}{2}\ln\frac{1 + 3/5}{1 - 3/5} = \tfrac{1}{2}\ln 4 = \ln 2 \implies$
$x = (\ln 2)^2$

11. The curves intersect when $\tanh x = \operatorname{sech} x \iff \sinh x/\cosh x = 1/\cosh x \iff \sinh x = 1 \iff x = \sinh^{-1} 1$. The corresponding value of y is

$$y = \tanh(\sinh^{-1} 1) = \frac{\sinh(\sinh^{-1} 1)}{\cosh(\sinh^{-1} 1)} = \frac{1}{\cosh(\sinh^{-1} 1)}$$

Since $\cosh^2 t - \sinh^2 t = 1$ and $\cosh t$ is positive, we have $\cosh t = \sqrt{1 + \sinh^2 t}$, from which $\cosh(\sinh^{-1} 1) = \sqrt{1 + 1^2} = \sqrt{2}.$ Hence $y = 1/\sqrt{2}.$

12. $x = \frac{1}{2}\sinh(y - 1) \implies 2x = \sinh(y - 1) \implies \sinh^{-1} 2x = y - 1 \implies y = 1 + \sinh^{-1} 2x = f^{-1}(x)$

13. $x = 2\tanh(y/2) \implies x/2 = \tanh(y/2) \implies \tanh^{-1}(x/2) = y/2 \implies y = 2\tanh^{-1}(x/2) = f^{-1}(x).$ Since $\tanh^{-1} u$ is defined for $-1 < u < 1$, the domain of f^{-1} is $-1 < x/2 < 1$, or $-2 < x < 2.$

14. See Figure 1.

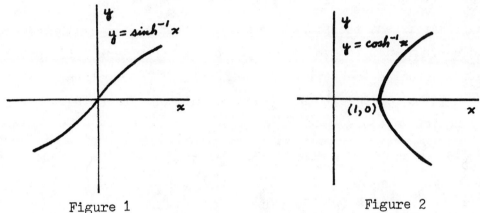

Figure 1   Figure 2

15. The inverse relation is shown in Figure 2; its upper half is the graph of $y = \cosh^{-1} x.$

16. See Figure 3.

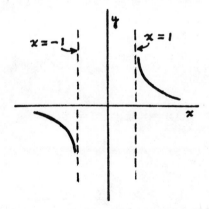

Figure 3

17. $f'(x) = \dfrac{3(2)}{\sqrt{4x^2 + 1}} = \dfrac{6}{\sqrt{4x^2 + 1}}$

18. $f'(x) = \dfrac{1/(2\sqrt{x})}{\sqrt{x - 1}} = \dfrac{1}{2\sqrt{x}(x - 1)}$

19. $f'(x) = \dfrac{1/2}{1 - x^2/4} = \dfrac{2}{4 - x^2}$

20. $\int_0^2 \frac{dx}{9-x^2} = \frac{1}{3}\tanh^{-1}\frac{x}{3}\Big|_0^2 = \frac{1}{3}\tanh^{-1}\frac{2}{3}$. Alternatively, we may use the logarithmic formula to obtain

$$\int_0^2 \frac{dx}{9-x^2} = \frac{1}{6}\ln\left|\frac{3+x}{3-x}\right|\Big|_0^2 = \frac{1}{6}(\ln 5 - \ln 1) = \frac{1}{6}\ln 5$$

21. $\int_4^6 \frac{dx}{9-x^2} = \frac{1}{3}\coth^{-1}\frac{x}{3}\Big|_4^6 = \frac{1}{3}(\coth^{-1}2 - \coth^{-1}\frac{4}{3})$. Alternatively, we may use the logarithmic formula to obtain

$$\int_4^6 \frac{dx}{9-x^2} = \frac{1}{6}\ln\left|\frac{3+x}{3-x}\right|\Big|_4^6 = \frac{1}{6}(\ln 3 - \ln 7) = \frac{1}{6}\ln\frac{3}{7} = -\frac{1}{6}\ln\frac{7}{3}$$

You can see from this and the preceding problem that the logarithmic formula is easier to use. We don't have to worry about whether $\tanh^{-1}$ or $\coth^{-1}$ is the appropriate function (depending on the domain of integration), and the answers are in terms of logarithms. (Many calculators do not have inverse hyperbolic function keys.)

22. $\int_0^3 \frac{dx}{x^2-25} = -\int_0^3 \frac{dx}{25-x^2} = -\frac{1}{10}\ln\left|\frac{5+x}{5-x}\right|\Big|_0^3 = -\frac{1}{10}(\ln 4 - \ln 1) = -\frac{1}{10}\ln 4$

23. $\int_1^2 \frac{dx}{4x^2-1} = \frac{1}{2}\int_2^4 \frac{du}{u^2-1}$ $(u = 2x, \ du = 2\,dx)$

$$= -\frac{1}{2}\int_2^4 \frac{du}{1-u^2} = -\frac{1}{4}\ln\left|\frac{1+u}{1-u}\right|\Big|_2^4 = -\frac{1}{4}(\ln\frac{5}{3} - \ln 3) = \frac{1}{4}\ln\frac{9}{5}$$

24. $\int_0^4 \frac{dx}{\sqrt{x^2+4}} = \sinh^{-1}\frac{x}{2}\Big|_0^4 = \sinh^{-1}2 = \ln(2+\sqrt{5})$. Alternatively, we may use the logarithmic formula to obtain

$$\int_0^4 \frac{dx}{\sqrt{x^2+4}} = \ln(x+\sqrt{x^2+4})\Big|_0^4 = \ln(4+2\sqrt{5}) - \ln 2 = \ln(2+\sqrt{5})$$

25. $\int_0^1 \frac{dx}{\sqrt{9x^2+25}} = \frac{1}{3}\int_0^3 \frac{du}{\sqrt{u^2+25}}$ $(u = 3x, \ du = 3\,dx)$

$$= \frac{1}{3}\sinh^{-1}\frac{u}{5}\Big|_0^3 = \frac{1}{3}\sinh^{-1}\frac{3}{5}$$

26. $\int_2^7 \frac{dx}{\sqrt{x^2-1}} = \cosh^{-1}x\Big|_2^7 = \cosh^{-1}7 - \cosh^{-1}2$. Alternatively, we may use the logarithmic formula to obtain

$$\int_2^7 \frac{dx}{\sqrt{x^2-1}} = \ln\left|x+\sqrt{x^2-1}\right|\Big|_2^7 = \ln(7+4\sqrt{3}) - \ln(2+\sqrt{3})$$

27. $\int_2^4 \frac{dx}{\sqrt{9x^2-16}} = \frac{1}{3}\int_6^{12} \frac{du}{\sqrt{u^2-16}}$ $(u = 3x, \ du = 3\,dx)$

$$= \frac{1}{3}\cosh^{-1}\frac{u}{4}\Big|_{6}^{12} = \frac{1}{3}(\cosh^{-1}3 - \cosh^{-1}\frac{3}{2})$$

28. $\displaystyle\int_{1}^{2}\frac{dx}{x\sqrt{9-x^2}} = -\frac{1}{3}\cosh^{-1}\frac{3}{x}\Big|_{1}^{2} = -\frac{1}{3}(\cosh^{-1}\frac{3}{2} - \cosh^{-1}3) = \frac{1}{3}(\cosh^{-1}3 - \cosh^{-1}\frac{3}{2})$

29. $\displaystyle\int_{2}^{3}\frac{dx}{x\sqrt{16+x^2}} = -\frac{1}{4}\sinh^{-1}\frac{4}{x}\Big|_{2}^{3} = \frac{1}{4}(\sinh^{-1}2 - \sinh^{-1}\frac{4}{3})$

30. (a) The function $y = \tanh x$ is increasing, with range $-1 < y < 1$. Hence $v = a\tanh bt$ increases with t, its least upper bound being a.

(b) The force $F = mg - kv^2$ is always positive, that is, $mg > kv^2$. Hence $v^2 < a^2$ ($a = \sqrt{mg/k}$), and $|v| < a$. Thus $v \to a$ as the air resistance decreases F to zero.

31. (a) $\dfrac{dv}{dt} = \dfrac{1600 - v^2}{50} \implies \dfrac{50\,dv}{1600 - v^2} = dt \implies 50\displaystyle\int\frac{dv}{1600-v^2} = \int dt \implies$

$\dfrac{5}{4}\tanh^{-1}\dfrac{v}{40} = t + C = t + \dfrac{5}{4}\tanh^{-1}\dfrac{1}{2}$ (because $v = 20$ when $t = 0$). Hence

$$t = \frac{5}{4}(\tanh^{-1}\frac{v}{40} - \tanh^{-1}\frac{1}{2})$$

(b) Since $dv/dt < 0$ (because v is decreasing), we have $32 - v^2/50 < 0 \implies$ $v^2 > 1600 \implies v > 40$. Hence $v \to 40$ as the force (mdv/dt) approaches zero. An alternative solution is to observe from part (a) that $\tanh^{-1}(v/40) \to \infty$ as $t \to \infty$, that is, $v/40 \to 1$. Hence $v \to 40$.

(c) When $v = 0.99(40)$ we have $t = \dfrac{5}{4}(\tanh^{-1}0.99 - \tanh^{-1}\dfrac{1}{2}) \approx 2.6$ sec.

32. $\dfrac{d}{dx}\ell n(x+\sqrt{x^2+1}) = \dfrac{1}{x+\sqrt{x^2+1}}\left(1+\dfrac{x}{\sqrt{x^2+1}}\right) = \dfrac{1}{x+\sqrt{x^2+1}}\cdot\dfrac{\sqrt{x^2+1}+x}{\sqrt{x^2+1}} = \dfrac{1}{\sqrt{x^2+1}}$

33. $\displaystyle\int\frac{dx}{\sqrt{x^2+a^2}} = \frac{1}{a}\int\frac{dx}{\sqrt{x^2/a^2+1}} = \int\frac{du}{\sqrt{u^2+1}}$ ($u = x/a$, $du = \frac{1}{a}dx$)

$$= \sinh^{-1}u + C = \sinh^{-1}\frac{x}{a} + C$$

34. (a) Since $y \geq 0$, $y = \cosh^{-1}x \iff \cosh y = x \iff \frac{1}{2}(e^y + e^{-y}) = x \iff$ $e^y + e^{-y} = 2x \iff e^{2y} - 2xe^y + 1 = 0$.

(b) $e^y = \dfrac{2x \pm \sqrt{4x^2-4}}{2} = x \pm \sqrt{x^2-1}$. Since $y \geq 0$, $e^y \geq 1$. If the minus sign were correct, we would have $x - \sqrt{x^2-1} \geq 1 \implies x - 1 \geq \sqrt{x^2-1} \implies x^2 - 2x + 1 \geq x^2 - 1 \implies 2 \geq 2x \implies x \leq 1$. But $x = \cosh y \geq 1$, so the minus sign must be rejected, that is, $e^y = x + \sqrt{x^2-1}$.

(c) $y = \ell n(x+\sqrt{x^2-1})$

35. (a) $D_x\ell n(x+\sqrt{x^2-1}) = \dfrac{1}{x+\sqrt{x^2-1}}\left(1+\dfrac{x}{\sqrt{x^2-1}}\right) = \dfrac{1}{x+\sqrt{x^2-1}}\cdot\dfrac{\sqrt{x^2-1}+x}{\sqrt{x^2-1}} = \dfrac{1}{\sqrt{x^2-1}}$

(b) Since $y \geq 0$, $y = \cosh^{-1}x \iff \cosh y = x \iff \sinh y \frac{dy}{dx} = 1 \iff$ $dy/dx = 1/\sinh y$. But $\sinh y = \sqrt{\cosh^2 y - 1} = \sqrt{x^2 - 1}$ (because $y \geq 0$ and hence $\sinh y \geq 0$). Thus $dy/dx = 1/\sqrt{x^2 - 1}$.

36. Let $u = x/a$, so $x = au$ and $dx = a\,du$. Then

$$\int \frac{dx}{\sqrt{x^2 - a^2}} = \int \frac{a\,du}{\sqrt{a^2 u^2 - a^2}} = \int \frac{du}{\sqrt{u^2 - 1}} = \cosh^{-1}u + C \ (u > 1)$$

$$= \cosh^{-1}\frac{x}{a} + C \ (x > a)$$

37. Since $\cosh^{-1}u = \ln(u + \sqrt{u^2 - 1})$ if $u \geq 1$, we have

$$\int \frac{dx}{\sqrt{x^2 - a^2}} = \cosh^{-1}(x/a) + C \ (x > a)$$

$$= \ln(x/a + \sqrt{x^2/a^2 - 1}) + C = \ln(x + \sqrt{x^2 - a^2}) - \ln a + C$$

Since $-\ln a + C$ is an arbitrary constant, relabel it C to obtain the final result.

38.(a) $y = \coth^{-1}x \iff \coth y = x \iff (e^y + e^{-y})/(e^y - e^{-y}) = x \iff$ $(e^{2y} + 1)/(e^{2y} - 1) = x \iff e^{2y} + 1 = xe^{2y} - x \iff x + 1 = (x - 1)e^{2y} \iff$ $e^{2y} = (x + 1)/(x - 1)$

(b) $2y = \ln\frac{x+1}{x-1}$ and $y = \frac{1}{2}\ln\frac{x+1}{x-1}$.

39. Since $\frac{1}{2}\ln\frac{x+1}{x-1} = \frac{1}{2}\ln(x+1) - \frac{1}{2}\ln(x-1)$, we have

$$D_x \coth^{-1}x = \frac{1}{2}\cdot\frac{1}{x+1} - \frac{1}{2}\cdot\frac{1}{x-1} = \frac{(x-1)-(x+1)}{2(x^2-1)} = \frac{1}{1-x^2}$$

40. Let $u = x/a$, so $x = au$ and $dx = a\,du$. Then

$$\int \frac{dx}{a^2 - x^2} = \int \frac{a\,du}{a^2 - a^2 u^2} = \frac{1}{a}\int \frac{du}{1 - u^2}$$

Now apply the known formulas (with u in place of x) to obtain the new ones.

41. If $|x| < a$, then

$$\int \frac{dx}{a^2 - x^2} = \frac{1}{a}\tanh^{-1}\frac{x}{a} + C = \frac{1}{a}\cdot\frac{1}{2}\ln\frac{1 + x/a}{1 - x/a} + C = \frac{1}{2a}\ln\frac{a+x}{a-x} + C = \frac{1}{2a}\ln\left|\frac{a+x}{a-x}\right| + C$$

(because $\left|\frac{a+x}{a-x}\right| = \frac{a+x}{a-x}$ when $|x| < a$).

42. $\text{sech}^{-1}x = \cosh^{-1}(1/x) = \ln(1/x + \sqrt{1/x^2 - 1}) = \ln\left(\frac{1}{x} + \frac{\sqrt{1-x^2}}{x}\right) \ (x = \text{sech}\,y > 0)$

$$= \ln\frac{1 + \sqrt{1-x^2}}{x}$$

The restriction $0 < x \leq 1$ is due to the fact that $x = \text{sech}\,y$.

43.(a) $D_x \ln\frac{1 + \sqrt{1-x^2}}{x} = \frac{x}{1 + \sqrt{1-x^2}}\cdot\frac{x(-x/\sqrt{1-x^2}) - (1 + \sqrt{1-x^2})}{x^2}$

$$= \frac{x}{1+\sqrt{1-x^2}} \cdot \frac{-x^2 - \sqrt{1-x^2} - (1-x^2)}{x^2\sqrt{1-x^2}} = \frac{x}{1+\sqrt{1-x^2}} \cdot \frac{-(1+\sqrt{1-x^2})}{x^2\sqrt{1-x^2}}$$

$$= \frac{-1}{x\sqrt{1-x^2}}$$

(b) $D_x \cosh^{-1}\frac{1}{x} = \frac{-1/x^2}{\sqrt{1/x^2 - 1}} = \frac{-1/x^2}{\sqrt{1-x^2}/x}$ (because $x > 0$)

$$= \frac{-1}{x\sqrt{1-x^2}}$$

44. $D_x \sinh^{-1}\frac{1}{x} = \frac{-1/x^2}{\sqrt{1/x^2 + 1}} = \frac{-1/x^2}{\sqrt{1+x^2}/|x|} = \frac{-1}{|x|\sqrt{1+x^2}}$

45. If $0 < x < 1$, we know from Problem 43 that $D_x \cosh^{-1}\frac{1}{x} = \frac{-1}{x\sqrt{1-x^2}}$, so

$$\int \frac{dx}{x\sqrt{1-x^2}} = -\cosh^{-1}\frac{1}{x} + C$$

If $-1 < x < 0$, the substitution $t = -x$, $dt = -dx$ yields

$$\int \frac{dx}{x\sqrt{1-x^2}} = \int \frac{dt}{t\sqrt{1-t^2}} = -\cosh^{-1}\frac{1}{t} + C \quad (\text{because } 0 < t < 1)$$

$$= -\cosh^{-1}\frac{1}{-x} + C$$

We may combine these results in the formula

$$\int \frac{dx}{x\sqrt{1-x^2}} = -\cosh^{-1}\frac{1}{|x|} + C \quad (x \neq 0)$$

To obtain the formula stated in the problem, let $u = x/a$, $x = au$, $dx = a\,du$:

$$\int \frac{dx}{x\sqrt{a^2-x^2}} = \int \frac{a\,du}{au\sqrt{a^2 - a^2u^2}} = \frac{1}{a}\int \frac{du}{u\sqrt{1-u^2}} = -\frac{1}{a}\cosh^{-1}\frac{1}{|u|} + C$$

$$= -\frac{1}{a}\cosh^{-1}\frac{a}{|x|} + C$$

The second part of the required formula follows by writing

$$-\frac{1}{a}\cosh^{-1}\frac{a}{|x|} = -\frac{1}{a}\ell n\left(a/|x| + \sqrt{a^2/x^2 - 1}\right) = -\frac{1}{a}\ell n\frac{a+\sqrt{a^2-x^2}}{|x|} = \frac{1}{a}\ell n\frac{|x|}{a+\sqrt{a^2-x^2}}$$

$$= \frac{1}{a}\ell n\frac{|x|(a-\sqrt{a^2-x^2})}{a^2 - (a^2-x^2)} = \frac{1}{a}\ell n\frac{a-\sqrt{a^2-x^2}}{|x|} = \frac{1}{a}\ell n\left|\frac{a-\sqrt{a^2-x^2}}{x}\right|$$

46. From Problem 44 we have

$$D_x \sinh^{-1}\frac{1}{x} = \frac{-1}{x\sqrt{1+x^2}} \text{ or } \frac{1}{x\sqrt{1+x^2}}$$

depending on whether $x > 0$ or $x < 0$. Hence

$$\int \frac{dx}{x\sqrt{1+x^2}} = \mp\sinh^{-1}(1/x) + C \quad (\text{minus if } x > 0, \text{ plus if } x < 0)$$

$$= -\sinh^{-1}(1/\pm x) + C \quad (\text{because } \sinh^{-1} \text{ is odd})$$

$$= -\sinh^{-1}(1/|x|) + C$$

Now let $u = x/a$, $x = au$, $dx = a\,du$ to obtain

$$\int \frac{dx}{x\sqrt{a^2 + x^2}} = \int \frac{a\,du}{au\sqrt{a^2 + a^2 u^2}} = \frac{1}{a}\int \frac{du}{u\sqrt{1 + u^2}} = -\frac{1}{a}\sinh^{-1}(1/|u|) + C$$

$$= -\frac{1}{a}\sinh^{-1}(a/|x|) + C$$

The second part of the required formula follows from

$$-\frac{1}{a}\sinh^{-1}(a/|x|) = -\frac{1}{a}\ell n\,(a/|x| + \sqrt{a^2/x^2 + 1}) = -\frac{1}{a}\ell n\,\frac{a + \sqrt{a^2 + x^2}}{|x|}$$

$$= \frac{1}{a}\ell n\,\frac{|x|}{a + \sqrt{a^2 + x^2}} = \frac{1}{a}\ell n\,\frac{|x|(a - \sqrt{a^2 + x^2})}{a^2 - (a^2 + x^2)}$$

$$= \frac{1}{a}\ell n\,\frac{a - \sqrt{a^2 + x^2}}{-|x|} = \frac{1}{a}\ell n\,\left|\frac{a - \sqrt{a^2 + x^2}}{x}\right|$$

Section 9.5 THE CATENARY

1.(a) $\tan\theta = $ slope at $(x,y) = \dfrac{d}{dx}\left(a\cosh\dfrac{x}{a}\right) = \sinh\dfrac{x}{a}$

(b) $\cosh^2(x/a) - \sinh^2(x/a) = 1$, so $\cosh^2(x/a) = 1 + \sinh^2(x/a) = 1 + \tan^2\theta$ $= \sec^2\theta$. Since $\cosh(x/a)$ and $\sec\theta$ are both positive, it follows that $\sec\theta = \cosh(x/a)$.

(c) Since $H = \delta/k = \delta a = T\cos\theta$, we have $T = \delta a\sec\theta = \delta a\cosh(x/a) = \delta y$.

2.(a) Since the crevasse is 40 ft wide, the right-hand point of support in Figure 1 has x coordinate 20. The corresponding y coordinate is $y = a\cosh(20/a)$. Hence the sag at the center is $a\cosh(20/a) - a = a\left(\cosh\dfrac{20}{a} - 1\right)$.

(b) Since the rope is 50 ft long, the length from $(0,a)$ to the right-hand point of support is 25. According to Problem 42, Sec. 9.3, this length is also $a\sinh(20/a)$. Hence $\sinh(20/a) = 25/a$.

(c) $\sinh t = \dfrac{25}{20/t} = 1.25t$. The graphs of $y = \sinh t$ and $y = 1.25t$ intersect at (t,y), where t is about $t_0 = 1.2$. Letting $f(t) = \sinh t - 1.25t$, we have $f'(t) = \cosh t - 1.25$ and hence

$$t_1 = t_0 - f(t_0)/f'(t_0) = 1.2 - \frac{\sinh 1.2 - 1.25(1.2)}{\cosh 1.2 - 1.25} \approx 1.18$$

(d) $a\left(\cosh\dfrac{20}{a} - 1\right) = \dfrac{20}{t}(\cosh t - 1) \approx \dfrac{20}{1.18}(\cosh 1.18 - 1) \approx 13.23$

(e) According to Problem 1, the tension at (x,y) is $T = \delta y$. Hence the tension at the center $(0,a)$ is $T = 0.2a = 0.2(20/t) \approx 0.2(20/1.18) \approx 3.4$ and the tension at $\left(\pm 20, a\cosh\dfrac{20}{a}\right)$ is

$$T = 0.2\left(a\cosh\dfrac{20}{a}\right) = 0.2\left(\dfrac{20}{t}\cosh t\right) \approx 0.2\left(\dfrac{20}{1.18}\cosh 1.18\right) \approx 6.0$$

3.(a) If (x,y) is the right-hand point of support in Figure 1, the sag at the center is $y - a = a\cosh(x/a) - a$. According to Problem 42, Sec. 9.3, the length of the rope from $(0,a)$ to (x,y) is $s = a\sinh(x/a)$. Since $\cosh(x/a) = \sqrt{1 + \sinh^2(x/a)}$, we have $y - a = a\sqrt{1 + s^2/a^2} - a = \sqrt{a^2 + s^2} - a$.

  (b) The sag is about $\sqrt{17^2 + 25^2} - 17 \approx 13.23$.

Chapter 9   TRUE-FALSE QUIZ

1. False. Although $\tan(3\pi/4) = -1$, $3\pi/4$ is not in $(-\pi/2, \pi/2)$. The correct answer is $-\pi/4$.

2. True. Since $-\pi/2 \le \sin^{-1}x \le \pi/2$, $\cos(\sin^{-1}x) \ge 0$.

3. False. See Problem 19, Sec. 9.1.

4. True. $\cos(\pi/2 - \sin^{-1}x) = \sin(\sin^{-1}x) = x$.

5. False. The identity is correct in the domain of the <u>restricted</u> tangent, namely $(-\pi/2, \pi/2)$. But if $x = \pi$ (for example), we have $\tan^{-1}(\tan x) = \tan^{-1}0 = 0 \ne x$.

6. True. See Problem 45, Sec. 9.1.

7. False. Since $f'(x) = \dfrac{1/2}{\sqrt{1 - x^2/4}} = \dfrac{1}{\sqrt{4 - x^2}}$, $f'(1) = 1/\sqrt{3}$.

8. False. Since $f'(x) = \dfrac{1/(2\sqrt{x})}{1 + x} = \dfrac{1}{2\sqrt{x}(1 + x)}$, $f'(1) = 1/4$.

9. False. Since $f'(x) = \dfrac{-\sin x}{\sqrt{1 - \cos^2 x}} = \dfrac{-\sin x}{|\sin x|}$, $f'(4) = 1$ (because $\sin 4 < 0$).

10. False. $\displaystyle\int_{-2}^{2} \frac{dx}{4 + x^2} = 2\int_{0}^{2} \frac{dx}{4 + x^2} = 2\cdot\frac{1}{2}\tan^{-1}\frac{x}{2}\Big|_{0}^{2} = \tan^{-1}1 = \pi/4$.

11. True. $f(x) = \sin^{-1}t\,\Big|_{0}^{x} = \sin^{-1}x$, so $f(1) = \sin^{-1}1 = \pi/2$. It follows that $f^{-1}(\pi/2) = 1$. It should be noted, however, that we have ignored an improper integral, namely $f(1) = \displaystyle\int_{0}^{1} \frac{dt}{\sqrt{1 - t^2}}$. (The integrand is unbounded in the domain of integration.) The formula $f(x) = \sin^{-1}x$ is valid in $-1 < x < 1$, but should not be considered at the endpoints $x = \pm 1$ until improper integrals are discussed. If you marked the statement "false" for that reason, you are within your rights.

12. $\displaystyle\int_{\sqrt{2}}^{2} \frac{dx}{x\sqrt{x^2 - 1}} = \sec^{-1}x\,\Big|_{\sqrt{2}}^{2} = \frac{\pi}{3} - \frac{\pi}{4} = \frac{\pi}{12}$.

13. True. $\sinh(\ln 3) = \frac{1}{2}(e^{\ln 3} - e^{-\ln 3}) = \frac{1}{2}(3 - \frac{1}{3}) = \frac{4}{3}$.

14. False. The range is $[1, \infty)$.

15. False. The domain consists of the single point $x = 0$, because if $x \neq 0$, $\cosh x > 1$ and $\sin^{-1}(\cosh x)$ is undefined.

16. False. tanh is odd.

17. True. $\cosh x \geq 1$ for all x, so $0 < \operatorname{sech} x \leq 1$.

18. False. Since $y' = \cosh x$ and $y'' = \sinh x = y$, we have $y'' - y = 0$, not $y'' + y = 0$.

19. True. $D_x \ln(\sinh x) = \dfrac{1}{\sinh x} \cdot \cosh x = \coth x$.

20. True. Since $\operatorname{sech} x = 2/(e^x + e^{-x})$, the integral is $\frac{1}{4} \int \operatorname{sech}^2 x \, dx = \frac{1}{4} \tanh x + C$.

21. False. The <u>restricted</u> hyperbolic cosine, namely $f(x) = \cosh x$, $x \geq 0$, has an inverse. Without the restriction the graph is intersected more than once by some horizontal lines.

22. False. Since $\cosh 0 = 1$, the correct statement is $\cosh^{-1} 1 = 0$.

23. True. $D_x \tanh^{-1}(\cos x) = \dfrac{-\sin x}{1 - \cos^2 x} = \dfrac{-\sin x}{\sin^2 x} = -\csc x$.

24. False. Since $|x| > 1$ in the domain of integration, the correct value of the integral is $\coth^{-1} 3 - \coth^{-1} 2$.

25. True. $\displaystyle\int_0^3 \dfrac{dx}{\sqrt{x^2 + 16}} = \ln\left(x + \sqrt{x^2 + 16}\right)\Big|_0^3 = \ln 8 - \ln 4 = \ln 2$.

Chapter 9   ADDITIONAL PROBLEMS

1. $\sin^{-1} x$ is defined only for $-1 \leq x \leq 1$.

2. $\cot^{-1} 2 = \tan^{-1} \frac{1}{2}$

3. $D_x \sin^{-1}(1 - x) = \dfrac{-1}{\sqrt{1 - (1 - x)^2}} = \dfrac{-1}{\sqrt{2x - x^2}}$

4. $D_x \tan^{-1}|x| = \dfrac{1}{1 + |x|^2} \cdot \dfrac{|x|}{x} = \dfrac{|x|}{x(1 + x^2)}$

5. $D_x \sec^{-1} 2x = \dfrac{2}{2x\sqrt{4x^2 - 1}} = \dfrac{1}{x\sqrt{4x^2 - 1}}$

6. The formula follows from
$$D_x \cos^{-1} \frac{x}{a} = \dfrac{-1/a}{\sqrt{1 - x^2/a^2}} = \dfrac{-1}{\sqrt{a^2 - x^2}}$$
Using it to evaluate the integral, we find
$$\int_0^1 \dfrac{dx}{\sqrt{4 - x^2}} = -\cos^{-1} \frac{x}{2}\Big|_0^1 = -\left(\cos^{-1} \frac{1}{2} - \cos^{-1} 0\right) = \frac{\pi}{2} - \frac{\pi}{3} = \frac{\pi}{6}$$

The standard formula yields

$$\int_0^1 \frac{dx}{\sqrt{4-x^2}} = \sin^{-1}\frac{x}{2}\Big|_0^1 = \sin^{-1}\frac{1}{2} - \sin^{-1}0 = \frac{\pi}{6} - 0 = \frac{\pi}{6}$$

7. $\int_0^2 \frac{dx}{\sqrt{16-x^2}} = \sin^{-1}\frac{x}{4}\Big|_0^2 = \frac{\pi}{6}$

8. $\int_0^{\sqrt{3}} \frac{dx}{1+x^2} = \tan^{-1}x\Big|_0^{\sqrt{3}} = \frac{\pi}{3}$

9. $\frac{dy}{dx} = 1+y^2 \implies \frac{dy}{1+y^2} = dx \implies \tan^{-1}y = x+C = x+\pi/4$ $(y = 1$ when $x = 0)$

$$\implies y = \tan(x+\pi/4)$$

10. $F'(x) = x(-x/\sqrt{1-x^2}) + \sqrt{1-x^2} - 2\sqrt{1-x^2} = -x^2/\sqrt{1-x^2} - \sqrt{1-x^2}$

$$= \frac{-x^2 - (1-x^2)}{\sqrt{1-x^2}} = \frac{-1}{\sqrt{1-x^2}}$$

Since $D_x \cos^{-1}x = -1/\sqrt{1-x^2}$, $F(x) = \cos^{-1}x + C$. Put $x = 1$ to find $F(1) = \cos^{-1}1 + C$, that is, $0 = 0+C$. Hence $C = 0$ and $F(x) = \cos^{-1}x$.

11. $D_x \cos^{-1}\frac{1}{x} = \frac{1/x^2}{\sqrt{1-1/x^2}} = \frac{1/x^2}{\sqrt{x^2-1}/|x|} = \frac{1}{|x|\sqrt{x^2-1}}$. Since $D_x \sec^{-1}x = \frac{1}{x\sqrt{x^2-1}}$,

$\sec^{-1}x = \cos^{-1}(1/x) + C_1$ when $x > 1$, $\sec^{-1}x = -\cos^{-1}(1/x) + C_2$ when $x < -1$

Put $x = 2$ in the first case to find $\pi/3 = \pi/3 + C_1$, or $C_1 = 0$. Put $x = -2$ in the second case to find $-2\pi/3 = -2\pi/3 + C_2$, or $C_2 = 0$. Hence $\sec^{-1}x = \pm\cos^{-1}(1/x)$, the sign depending on whether $x > 1$ or $x < -1$. The endpoints $x = \pm 1$ may be checked directly: $\sec^{-1}1 = \cos^{-1}1 = 0$ and $\sec^{-1}(-1) = -\cos^{-1}(-1) = -\pi$.

12. $f'(x) = 3\cosh x - 2\sinh x = \frac{3}{2}(e^x + e^{-x}) - (e^x - e^{-x}) = \frac{1}{2}e^x + \frac{5}{2}e^{-x} > 0$ for all x.

13. $\tanh(\frac{1}{2}\ell n\, x) = \tanh\ell n\sqrt{x} = (e^{\ell n\sqrt{x}} - e^{-\ell n\sqrt{x}})/(e^{\ell n\sqrt{x}} + e^{-\ell n\sqrt{x}}) = \frac{\sqrt{x} - 1/\sqrt{x}}{\sqrt{x} + 1/\sqrt{x}}$

$$= \frac{x-1}{x+1}$$

14. The slopes of the graphs at a point of intersection (x,y) are $D_x \sinh x = \cosh x$ and $D_x \operatorname{csch} x = -\operatorname{csch} x \coth x$. If the graphs intersect at right angles, then $(\cosh x)(-\operatorname{csch} x \coth x) = -1 \implies \cosh^2 x/\sinh^2 x = 1 \implies \coth^2 x = 1$. Since $|\coth x| > 1$ for all x in the domain of coth, this is impossible. Hence the graphs do not intersect at right angles.

15. $D_x \tan^{-1}(\sinh x) = \frac{\cosh x}{1+\sinh^2 x} = \frac{\cosh x}{\cosh^2 x} = \operatorname{sech} x$

16. $y' = \sinh x$, $1+y'^2 = 1+\sinh^2 x = \cosh^2 x$, so

$$s = \int_0^2 \cosh x\, dx = \sinh x\Big|_0^2 = \sinh 2$$

17. As usual, we take the density to be 1, so the mass is $m = s = 2\sinh 1$. By symmetry, $\bar{x} = 0$. Since $ds = \cosh x\, dx$,

$$M_x = \int_{x=-1}^{x=1} y\, dm = \int_{-1}^{1} \cosh^2 x\, dx = \int_0^1 (\cosh 2x + 1)\, dx = \left(\tfrac{1}{2}\sinh 2x + x\right)\Big|_0^1$$

$$= \tfrac{1}{2}\sinh 2 + 1 = \tfrac{1}{2}(\sinh 2 + 2)$$

Hence $\bar{y} = M_x / m = \dfrac{\sinh 2 + 2}{4\sinh 1}$.

18. $y' = \sinh(x/a)$, $1 + y'^2 = 1 + \sinh^2(x/a) = \cosh^2(x/a)$, and

$$2\pi y\, ds = 2\pi a \cosh(x/a)\cdot\cosh(x/a)\, dx = 2\pi a \cosh^2(x/a)\, dx$$

Hence $A = 2\pi a \displaystyle\int_{-a}^{a} \cosh^2(x/a)\, dx = 2\pi a \int_0^a \left(\cosh\dfrac{2x}{a} + 1\right)dx = 2\pi a\left(\dfrac{a}{2}\sinh\dfrac{2x}{a} + x\right)\Big|_0^a$

$$= 2\pi a\left(\dfrac{a}{2}\sinh 2 + a\right) = \pi a^2(\sinh 2 + 2)$$

19. (a) From Figure 1 we conclude that

$$V = \pi \int_0^c (\operatorname{sech}^2 x - \tanh^2 x)\, dx = \pi \int_0^c [\operatorname{sech}^2 x - (1 - \operatorname{sech}^2 x)]\, dx$$

$$= \pi \int_0^c (2\operatorname{sech}^2 x - 1)\, dx = \pi(2\tanh x - x)\Big|_0^c = \pi(2\tanh c - c)$$

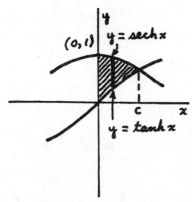

Figure 1

(b) The curves intersect when $\operatorname{sech} x = \tanh x \iff 1/\cosh x = \sinh x/\cosh x$ $\iff 1 = \sinh x \iff x = \sinh^{-1} 1 = \ln(1 + \sqrt{2})$. Hence $c = \ln(1 + \sqrt{2})$.

(c) $\tanh c = \operatorname{sech} c = \dfrac{2}{e^c + e^{-c}} = \dfrac{2}{(1 + \sqrt{2}) + (1 + \sqrt{2})^{-1}} = \dfrac{2(1 + \sqrt{2})}{(1 + \sqrt{2})^2 + 1}$

$$= \dfrac{2(1 + \sqrt{2})}{4 + 2\sqrt{2}} = \dfrac{1 + \sqrt{2}}{2 + \sqrt{2}}\cdot\dfrac{2 - \sqrt{2}}{2 - \sqrt{2}} = \dfrac{\sqrt{2}}{2}$$

Hence $V = \pi(2\tanh c - c) = \pi[\sqrt{2} - \ln(1 + \sqrt{2})]$.

20. $y'^2 = y^2 - 1 \implies \dfrac{dy}{dx} = \pm\sqrt{y^2 - 1}$. Since $y = 1$ when $x = 0$, we cannot divide by

$\sqrt{y^2 - 1}$ to separate the variables. This suggests the special solution $y = 1$, which (as you can check by inspection) satisfies the given conditions.

This solution is not very interesting. Suppose that we separate the variables anyway, to see what happens:

$$\frac{dy}{\sqrt{y^2 - 1}} = \pm dx \implies \int \frac{dy}{\sqrt{y^2 - 1}} = \pm \int dx$$

The original differential equation requires $y \geq 1$ or $y \leq -1$ and the initial condition excludes $y \leq -1$. The restriction $y \geq 1$ enables us to use $\cosh^{-1} y$ for the integral on the left, so we have $\cosh^{-1} y = \pm x + C = \pm x$ (because $y = 1$ when $x = 0$). Hence $y = \cosh(\pm x) = \cosh x$ (because $\cosh$ is even). The function $y = \cosh x$ is an answer to the original question, as you can check. Thus there are two answers, $y = 1$ and $y = \cosh x$.

The student who is trying to be careful about details should disapprove our second solution (in which division by zero was overlooked and an improper integral was fudged). Nevertheless the function $y = \cosh x$ is a correct answer. Differential equations are often solved by methods that are technically deficient; the excuse is that such methods sometimes turn up answers. Of course any solution of this kind should be checked.

21. Since $\tan x$ takes on all real values in $(-\pi/2, \pi/2)$, there must be a number x in this interval such that $\tan x = \sinh t$. Then

$\cosh t = \sqrt{1 + \sinh^2 t} = \sqrt{1 + \tan^2 x} = |\sec x| = \sec x$ (because $-\pi/2 < x < \pi/2$)

$\tanh t = \sinh t / \cosh t = \tan x / \sec x = \sin x$

$\coth t = 1/\tanh t = 1/\sin x = \csc x$ (if $t \neq 0$)

$\operatorname{sech} t = 1/\cosh t = 1/\sec x = \cos x$

$\operatorname{csch} t = 1/\sinh t = 1/\tan x = \cot x$ (if $t \neq 0$)

22.(a) Since $-\pi/2 < x < \pi/2$, $x = \tan^{-1}(\sinh t)$.

(b) $\dfrac{dx}{dt} = \dfrac{\cosh t}{1 + \sinh^2 t} = \dfrac{\cosh t}{\cosh^2 t} = \dfrac{1}{\cosh t} = \dfrac{1}{\sec x}$ (from Problem 21).

(c) $\dfrac{dx}{dt} = \dfrac{1}{\sec x} \implies \sec x \, dx = dt \implies \int \sec x \, dx = \int dt = t + C$

$= \sinh^{-1}(\tan x) + C$

(d) $\displaystyle\int \sec x \, dx = \sinh^{-1}(\tan x) + C = \ln(\tan x + \sqrt{\tan^2 x + 1}) + C$

$\qquad\qquad = \ln(\tan x + \sec x) + C$ ($\sec x > 0$ because $-\pi/2 < x < \pi/2$)

$\qquad\qquad = \ln(\sec x + \tan x) + C$, $-\pi/2 < x < \pi/2$

Example 3 in Sec. 8.5 is more general, giving $\displaystyle\int \sec x \, dx = \ln |\sec x + \tan x| + C$

without the restriction $-\pi/2 < x < \pi/2$.

23.(a) In Problem 21 we showed that for every t there is an x between $-\pi/2$ and $\pi/2$ such that $\sinh t = \tan x$. It follows that $x = \tan^{-1}(\sinh t)$. We also found $\tanh t = \sin x$, from which $x = \sin^{-1}(\tanh t)$. Hence $\tan^{-1}(\sinh t) = \sin^{-1}(\tanh t)$ for all t.

(b) $D_t \tan^{-1}(\sinh t) = \dfrac{\cosh t}{1 + \sinh^2 t} = \dfrac{\cosh t}{\cosh^2 t} = \operatorname{sech} t$ and $D_t \sin^{-1}(\tanh t) =$

$\dfrac{\operatorname{sech}^2 t}{\sqrt{1 - \tanh^2 t}} = \dfrac{\operatorname{sech}^2 t}{\sqrt{\operatorname{sech}^2 t}} = \dfrac{\operatorname{sech}^2 t}{\operatorname{sech} t} = \operatorname{sech} t$. Hence $\tan^{-1}(\sinh t) = \sin^{-1}(\tanh t) + C$.
Put $t = 0$ to find $0 = 0 + C$, or $C = 0$.

24.(a) If x is any number in $(-\pi/2, \pi/2)$, there is a t such that $\sinh t = \tan x$ (because $\sinh$ takes on all real values). Then $t = \sinh^{-1}(\tan x)$. From Problem 21 we also have $\tanh t = \sin x$, from which $t = \tanh^{-1}(\sin x)$. Hence $\sinh^{-1}(\tan x) = \tanh^{-1}(\sin x)$.

(b) $D_x \sinh^{-1}(\tan x) = \dfrac{\sec^2 x}{\sqrt{\tan^2 x + 1}} = \dfrac{\sec^2 x}{\sec x} = \sec x$. Moreover, $D_x \tanh^{-1}(\sin x)$

$= \dfrac{\cos x}{1 - \sin^2 x} = \dfrac{\cos x}{\cos^2 x} = \sec x$. Hence $\sinh^{-1}(\tan x) = \tanh^{-1}(\sin x) + C$. Put $x = 0$ to obtain $0 = 0 + C$, or $C = 0$.

CHAPTER 10   TECHNIQUES OF INTEGRATION

Section 10.1   INTEGRATION BY PARTS

1. Let $u = x$, $dv = e^{2x}dx$. Then $du = dx$ and $v = \frac{1}{2}e^{2x}$, so
$$\int xe^{2x}dx = uv - \int v\,du = \tfrac{1}{2}xe^{2x} - \tfrac{1}{2}\int e^{2x}dx = \tfrac{1}{2}xe^{2x} - \tfrac{1}{4}e^{2x} + C$$

2. Let $u = x^2$, $dv = e^x dx$. Then $du = 2x\,dx$ and $v = e^x$, so
$$\int x^2 e^x dx = x^2 e^x - 2\int xe^x dx$$

In the new integral let $u = x$, $dv = e^x dx$. Then $du = dx$ and $v = e^x$, so
$$\int xe^x dx = xe^x - \int e^x dx = xe^x - e^x \quad \text{(arbitrary constant omitted)}$$

Hence $\int x^2 e^x dx = x^2 e^x - 2xe^x + 2e^x + C$. An easier solution (by the formula for repeated integration by parts) is
$$\int x^2 e^x dx = (x^2)(e^x) - (2x)(e^x) + (2)(e^x) + C = x^2 e^x - 2xe^x + 2e^x + C$$

3. Let $u = x$, $dv = \sin x\,dx$. Then $du = dx$ and $v = -\cos x$, so
$$\int x \sin x\,dx = -x \cos x + \int \cos x\,dx = -x \cos x + \sin x + C$$

4. Let $u = x$, $dv = (x+1)^4 dx$. Then $du = dx$ and $v = \frac{1}{5}(x+1)^5$, so

$$\int x(x+1)^4 dx = \frac{1}{5}x(x+1)^5 - \frac{1}{5}\int (x+1)^5 dx = \frac{1}{5}x(x+1)^5 - \frac{1}{30}(x+1)^6 + C$$

5. Let $u = x$, $dv = \sec^2 x\, dx$. Then $du = dx$ and $v = \tan x$, so

$$\int x \sec^2 x\, dx = x \tan x - \int \tan x\, dx = x \tan x - \ell n \,|\sec x| + C$$

6. Let $u = \ell n\, x$, $dv = x\, dx$. Then $du = dx/x$ and $v = \frac{1}{2}x^2$, so

$$\int x \ell n\, x\, dx = \frac{1}{2}x^2 \ell n\, x - \frac{1}{2}\int x\, dx = \frac{1}{2}x^2 \ell n\, x - \frac{1}{4}x^2 + C$$

7. Let $u = \ell n\,(x^2+1)$, $dv = dx$. Then $du = 2x\, dx/(x^2+1)$ and $v = x$, so

$$\int \ell n\,(x^2+1)\, dx = x \ell n\,(x^2+1) - 2\int \frac{x^2 dx}{x^2+1}$$

Division of x^2 by x^2+1 yields $x^2/(x^2+1) = 1 - 1/(x^2+1)$, so

$$\int \frac{x^2 dx}{x^2+1} = \int \left(1 - \frac{1}{x^2+1}\right) dx = x - \tan^{-1} x \quad \text{(arbitrary constant omitted)}$$

Hence $\int \ell n\,(x^2+1)\, dx = x \ell n\,(x^2+1) - 2x + 2\tan^{-1} x + C$.

8. Let $u = e^x$, $dv = \sin x\, dx$. Then $du = e^x dx$ and $v = -\cos x$, so

$$\int e^x \sin x\, dx = -e^x \cos x + \int e^x \cos x\, dx$$

In the new integral let $u = e^x$, $dv = \cos x\, dx$. Then $du = e^x dx$ and $v = \sin x$,

so $\int e^x \sin x\, dx = -e^x \cos x + e^x \sin x - \int e^x \sin x\, dx$. Solve for the integral to

obtain $\int e^x \sin x\, dx = \frac{1}{2}e^x(\sin x - \cos x) + C$.

9. Let $u = \sin(\ell n\, x)$, $dv = dx$. Then $du = \dfrac{\cos(\ell n\, x) dx}{x}$ and $v = x$, so

$$\int \sin(\ell n\, x)\, dx = x \sin(\ell n\, x) - \int \cos(\ell n\, x)\, dx$$

In the new integral let $u = \cos(\ell n\, x)$, $dv = dx$. Then $du = \dfrac{-\sin(\ell n\, x) dx}{x}$ and

$v = x$, so

$$\int \sin(\ell n\, x)\, dx = x \sin(\ell n\, x) - x \cos(\ell n\, x) - \int \sin(\ell n\, x)\, dx$$

Solve for the integral to obtain

$$\int \sin(\ell n\, x)\, dx = \frac{1}{2}x \sin(\ell n\, x) - \frac{1}{2}x \cos(\ell n\, x) + C$$

10. Let $u = \sec x$, $dv = \sec^2 x\, dx$. Then $du = \sec x \tan x\, dx$ and $v = \tan x$, so

$$\int \sec^3 x\, dx = \sec x \tan x - \int \sec x \tan^2 x\, dx = \sec x \tan x - \int \sec x\,(\sec^2 x - 1)\, dx$$

$$= \sec x \tan x - \int \sec^3 x\, dx + \int \sec x\, dx$$

$$= \sec x \tan x - \int \sec^3 x\, dx + \ell n\,|\sec x + \tan x|$$

Solve for the integral to obtain

$$\int \sec^3 x \, dx = \tfrac{1}{2} \sec x \tan x + \tfrac{1}{2} \ell n \, |\sec x + \tan x| + C$$

11. Let $u = \tan^{-1} x$, $dv = dx$. Then $du = dx/(1 + x^2)$ and $v = x$, so

$$\int \tan^{-1} x \, dx = x \tan^{-1} x - \int \frac{x \, dx}{1 + x^2} = x \tan^{-1} x - \tfrac{1}{2} \ell n \, (1 + x^2) + C$$

12. Let $u = \sinh^{-1} x$, $dv = dx$. Then $du = dx/\sqrt{x^2 + 1}$ and $v = x$, so

$$\int \sinh^{-1} x \, dx = x \sinh^{-1} x - \int \frac{x \, dx}{\sqrt{x^2 + 1}}$$

$$= x \sinh^{-1} x - \tfrac{1}{2} \int t^{-1/2} dt \quad (t = x^2 + 1, \; dt = 2x \, dx)$$

$$= x \sinh^{-1} x - t^{1/2} + C = x \sinh^{-1} x - \sqrt{x^2 + 1} + C$$

13. Let $u = \tan^{-1} x$, $dv = x \, dx$. Then $du = dx/(1 + x^2)$ and $v = \tfrac{1}{2} x^2$, so

$$\int x \tan^{-1} x \, dx = \tfrac{1}{2} x^2 \tan^{-1} x - \tfrac{1}{2} \int \frac{x^2 dx}{1 + x^2}$$

$$= \tfrac{1}{2} x^2 \tan^{-1} x - \tfrac{1}{2} \int \left(1 - \frac{1}{x^2 + 1} \right) dx \quad \text{(see the solution of Prob. 7)}$$

$$= \tfrac{1}{2} x^2 \tan^{-1} x - \tfrac{1}{2} x + \tfrac{1}{2} \tan^{-1} x + C$$

14. Let $u = \sin x$, $dv = \sin 3x \, dx$. Then $du = \cos x \, dx$ and $v = -\dfrac{1}{3} \cos 3x$, so

$$\int \sin x \sin 3x \, dx = -\frac{1}{3} \sin x \cos 3x + \frac{1}{3} \int \cos x \cos 3x \, dx$$

In the new integral let $u = \cos x$, $dv = \cos 3x \, dx$. Then $du = -\sin x \, dx$ and $v = \dfrac{1}{3} \sin 3x$, so

$$\int \sin x \sin 3x \, dx = -\frac{1}{3} \sin x \cos 3x + \frac{1}{9} \cos x \sin 3x + \frac{1}{9} \int \sin x \sin 3x \, dx$$

Solve for the integral to obtain

$$\int \sin x \sin 3x \, dx = -\frac{3}{8} \sin x \cos 3x + \frac{1}{8} \cos x \sin 3x + C$$

15. Let $u = \cos 2x$, $dv = \cos 3x \, dx$. Then $du = -2 \sin 2x \, dx$ and $v = \dfrac{1}{3} \sin 3x$, so

$$\int \cos 2x \cos 3x \, dx = \frac{1}{3} \cos 2x \sin 3x + \frac{2}{3} \int \sin 2x \sin 3x \, dx$$

In the new integral let $u = \sin 2x$, $dv = \sin 3x \, dx$. Then $du = 2 \cos 2x \, dx$ and $v = -\dfrac{1}{3} \cos 3x$, so

$$\int \cos 2x \cos 3x \, dx = \frac{1}{3} \cos 2x \sin 3x - \frac{2}{9} \sin 2x \cos 3x + \frac{4}{9} \int \cos 2x \cos 3x \, dx$$

Solve for the integral to find

$$\int \cos 2x \cos 3x \, dx = \frac{3}{5} \cos 2x \sin 3x - \frac{2}{5} \sin 2x \cos 3x + C$$

Note: In Problems 16-27 we omit the arbitrary constant when finding antiderivatives.

16. Let $u = x$, $dv = e^{-x}dx$. Then $du = dx$ and $v = -e^{-x}$, so

$$\int xe^{-x}dx = -xe^{-x} + \int e^{-x}dx = -xe^{-x} - e^{-x} = -(x+1)e^{-x}$$

$$\int_0^1 xe^{-x}dx = 1 - 2e^{-1}$$

17. Let $u = x$, $dv = \sinh x\,dx$. Then $du = dx$ and $v = \cosh x$, so

$$\int x\sinh x\,dx = x\cosh x - \int \cosh x\,dx = x\cosh x - \sinh x$$

$$\int_0^1 x\sinh x\,dx = \cosh 1 - \sinh 1 = \tfrac{1}{2}(e + e^{-1}) - \tfrac{1}{2}(e - e^{-1}) = 1/e$$

18. Let $u = x$, $dv = (2x-1)^3 dx$. Then $du = dx$ and $v = \tfrac{1}{8}(2x-1)^4$, so

$$\int x(2x-1)^3 dx = \tfrac{1}{8}x(2x-1)^4 - \tfrac{1}{8}\int (2x-1)^4 dx = \tfrac{1}{8}x(2x-1)^4 - \tfrac{1}{80}(2x-1)^5$$

$$\int_0^1 x(2x-1)^3 dx = \left(\tfrac{1}{8} - \tfrac{1}{80}\right) - \tfrac{1}{80} = \tfrac{1}{10}$$

19. Let $u = x$, $dv = \csc^2 x\,dx$. Then $du = dx$ and $v = -\cot x$, so

$$\int x\csc^2 x\,dx = -x\cot x + \int \cot x\,dx = -x\cot x + \ln|\sin x|$$

$$\int_{\pi/6}^{\pi/2} x\csc^2 x\,dx = 0 - \left(-\tfrac{\pi}{6}\sqrt{3} + \ln\tfrac{1}{2}\right) = \tfrac{\pi}{6}\sqrt{3} + \ln 2$$

20. Let $u = \ln x$, $dv = x^2 dx$. Then $du = dx/x$ and $v = \tfrac{1}{3}x^3$, so

$$\int x^2 \ln x\,dx = \tfrac{1}{3}x^3 \ln x - \tfrac{1}{3}\int x^2 dx = \tfrac{1}{3}x^3 \ln x - \tfrac{1}{9}x^3$$

$$\int_1^2 x^2 \ln x\,dx = \left(\tfrac{8}{3}\ln 2 - \tfrac{8}{9}\right) - \left(-\tfrac{1}{9}\right) = \tfrac{8}{3}\ln 2 - \tfrac{7}{9}$$

21. Let $u = \ln(x^2+4)$, $dv = dx$. Then $du = 2x\,dx/(x^2+4)$ and $v = x$, so

$$\int \ln(x^2+4)dx = x\ln(x^2+4) - 2\int \frac{x^2 dx}{x^2+4} = x\ln(x^2+4) - 2\int\left(1 - \frac{4}{x^2+4}\right)dx$$

$$= x\ln(x^2+4) - 2x + 4\tan^{-1}\frac{x}{2}$$

$$\int_1^2 \ln(x^2+4)dx = (2\ln 8 - 4 + \pi) - (\ln 5 - 2 + 4\tan^{-1}\tfrac{1}{2}) = \ln\frac{64}{5} - 2 + \pi - 4\tan^{-1}\tfrac{1}{2}$$

22. Let $u = e^{-x}$, $dv = \sin x\,dx$. Then $du = -e^{-x}dx$ and $v = -\cos x$, so

$$\int e^{-x}\sin x\,dx = -e^{-x}\cos x - \int e^{-x}\cos x\,dx$$

In the new integral let $u = e^{-x}$, $dv = \cos x\, dx$. Then $du = -e^{-x}dx$ and $v = \sin x$, so $\int e^{-x}\sin x\, dx = -e^{-x}\cos x - e^{-x}\sin x - \int e^{-x}\sin x\, dx$. Solve for the integral to obtain $\int e^{-x}\sin x\, dx = -\frac{1}{2}e^{-x}(\cos x + \sin x)$ and hence

$$\int_0^\pi e^{-x}\sin x\, dx = -\frac{1}{2}e^{-\pi}(-1) + \frac{1}{2}(1) = \frac{1}{2}(e^{-\pi} + 1)$$

23. Let $u = \cos(\ell n\, x)$, $dv = dx$. Then $du = \dfrac{-\sin(\ell n\, x)dx}{x}$ and $v = x$, so

$$\int \cos(\ell n\, x)\, dx = x\cos(\ell n\, x) + \int \sin(\ell n\, x)\, dx$$

In the new integral let $u = \sin(\ell n\, x)$, $dv = dx$. Then $du = \dfrac{\cos(\ell n\, x)dx}{x}$ and $v = x$, so

$$\int \cos(\ell n\, x)\, dx = x\cos(\ell n\, x) + x\sin(\ell n\, x) - \int \cos(\ell n\, x)\, dx$$

Solve for the integral to obtain

$$\int \cos(\ell n\, x)\, dx = \tfrac{1}{2}x\cos(\ell n\, x) + \tfrac{1}{2}x\sin(\ell n\, x)$$

$$\int_{e^{-\pi}}^{e^{\pi}} \cos(\ell n\, x)\, dx = (\tfrac{1}{2}e^{\pi}\cos\pi + \tfrac{1}{2}e^{\pi}\sin\pi) - [\tfrac{1}{2}e^{-\pi}\cos(-\pi) + \tfrac{1}{2}e^{-\pi}\sin(-\pi)]$$
$$= -\tfrac{1}{2}e^{\pi} + \tfrac{1}{2}e^{-\pi} = -\tfrac{1}{2}(e^{\pi} - e^{-\pi}) = -\sinh\pi$$

24. Let $u = \csc x$, $dv = \csc^2 x$. Then $du = -\csc x\cot x\, dx$ and $v = -\cot x$, so

$$\int \csc^3 x\, dx = -\csc x\cot x - \int \csc x\cot^2 x\, dx = -\csc x\cot x - \int \csc x(\csc^2 x - 1)dx$$

$$= -\csc x\cot x - \int \csc^3 x\, dx + \int \csc x\, dx$$

$$= -\csc x\cot x - \int \csc^3 x\, dx + \ell n\,|\csc x - \cot x|$$

Solve for the integral to obtain

$$\int \csc^3 x\, dx = -\tfrac{1}{2}\csc x\cot x + \tfrac{1}{2}\ell n\,|\csc x - \cot x|$$

$$\int_{\pi/4}^{\pi/2} \csc^3 x\, dx = 0 - [-\tfrac{1}{2}\sqrt{2} + \tfrac{1}{2}\ell n(\sqrt{2} - 1)] = \tfrac{1}{2}\sqrt{2} - \tfrac{1}{2}\ell n(\sqrt{2} - 1)$$

25. Let $u = \sec^{-1}x$, $dv = dx$. Then $du = \dfrac{dx}{x\sqrt{x^2 - 1}}$ and $v = x$, so

$$\int \sec^{-1}x\, dx = x\sec^{-1}x - \int \frac{dx}{\sqrt{x^2 - 1}} = x\sec^{-1}x - \ell n\,|x + \sqrt{x^2 - 1}|$$

$$\int_1^2 \sec^{-1}x\, dx = [2\sec^{-1}2 - \ell n(2 + \sqrt{3})] - \sec^{-1}1 = \frac{2\pi}{3} - \ell n(2 + \sqrt{3})$$

Note that although the original integral is an ordinary (proper) integral, we sailed by an improper integral in the solution, namely $\int_1^2 \dfrac{dx}{\sqrt{x^2 - 1}}$. (The integrand is unbounded in the domain of integration.) Justification awaits our discussion of improper integrals in Chapter 11.

26. Let $u = \tanh^{-1} x$, $dv = dx$. Then $du = dx/(1 - x^2)$ and $v = x$, so

$$\int \tanh^{-1} x\, dx = x \tanh^{-1} x - \int \frac{x\, dx}{1 - x^2} = x \tanh^{-1} x + \tfrac{1}{2} \ell n\, |1 - x^2|$$

$$\int_0^{1/2} \tanh^{-1} x\, dx = \left(\tfrac{1}{2} \tanh^{-1} \tfrac{1}{2} + \tfrac{1}{2} \ell n\, \tfrac{3}{4}\right) - 0 = \tfrac{1}{2} \tanh^{-1} \tfrac{1}{2} + \tfrac{1}{2} \ell n\, \tfrac{3}{4}$$

By using the logarithmic formula for $\tanh^{-1} x$, we can put this in the form

$$\tfrac{1}{2} \cdot \tfrac{1}{2} \ell n\, \frac{1 + 1/2}{1 - 1/2} + \tfrac{1}{2} \ell n\, \tfrac{3}{4} = \tfrac{1}{4} \ell n\, 3 + \tfrac{1}{2} \ell n\, \tfrac{3}{4} = \tfrac{1}{4} \ell n\, 3 + \tfrac{1}{2} \ell n\, 3 - \tfrac{1}{2} \ell n\, 4 = \tfrac{3}{4} \ell n\, 3 - \ell n\, 2$$

(It is not really worthwhile to do this, except for the practice gained in manipulating logarithms.)

27. Let $u = \sin 2x$, $dv = \cos 3x\, dx$. Then $du = 2 \cos 2x\, dx$ and $v = \tfrac{1}{3} \sin 3x$, so

$$\int \sin 2x \cos 3x\, dx = \tfrac{1}{3} \sin 2x \sin 3x - \tfrac{2}{3} \int \cos 2x \sin 3x\, dx$$

In the new integral let $u = \cos 2x$, $dv = \sin 3x\, dx$. Then $du = -2 \sin 2x\, dx$ and $v = -\tfrac{1}{3} \cos 3x$, so

$$\int \sin 2x \cos 3x\, dx = \tfrac{1}{3} \sin 2x \sin 3x + \tfrac{2}{9} \cos 2x \cos 3x + \tfrac{4}{9} \int \sin 2x \cos 3x\, dx$$

Solve for the integral to obtain

$$\int \sin 2x \cos 3x\, dx = \tfrac{2}{5} \sin 2x \sin 3x + \tfrac{2}{5} \cos 2x \cos 3x$$

$$\int_0^{\pi/6} \sin 2x \cos 3x\, dx = \left(\tfrac{2}{5} \cdot \tfrac{\sqrt{3}}{2} + 0\right) - \left(0 + \tfrac{2}{5}\right) = \tfrac{3}{10}\sqrt{3} - \tfrac{2}{5} = \tfrac{1}{10}(3\sqrt{3} - 4)$$

28. $\displaystyle \int e^x \sinh x\, dx = \int e^x \cdot \tfrac{1}{2}(e^x - e^{-x})dx = \tfrac{1}{2} \int (e^{2x} - 1)dx = \tfrac{1}{2}(\tfrac{1}{2} e^{2x} - x) + C$

$$= \tfrac{1}{4} e^{2x} - \tfrac{1}{2}x + C$$

29. $\displaystyle A = \int_1^e \ell n\, x\, dx = (x \ell n\, x - x)\Big|_1^e$ (Example 2)

$$= (e \ell n\, e - e) - (0 - 1) = 1$$

30. $\displaystyle V = 2\pi \int_0^{\pi/2} xy\, dx = 2\pi \int_0^{\pi/2} x \sin x\, dx = 2\pi(-x \cos x + \sin x)\Big|_0^{\pi/2}$ (Problem 3)

$$= 2\pi(1 - 0) = 2\pi$$

31. Assuming constant density 1, we have $m = A = \displaystyle\int_0^{\pi/2} \cos x\, dx = 1$. Also,

$$M_y = \int_{x=0}^{x=\pi/2} x\, dm = \int_0^{\pi/2} xy\, dx = \int_0^{\pi/2} x \cos x\, dx$$

$$= (x \sin x + \cos x)\Big|_0^{\pi/2} \text{(Example 4)}$$

$$= \pi/2 - 1$$

$$M_x = \int_0^{\pi/2} \frac{y}{2} \cdot y \, dx = \frac{1}{2} \int_0^{\pi/2} \cos^2 x \, dx = \frac{1}{2} \cdot \frac{1}{2} \int_0^{\pi/2} dx \quad \text{(reduction formula, page 412)}$$

$$= \frac{1}{4} \cdot \frac{\pi}{2} = \frac{\pi}{8}$$

Hence $\bar{x} = M_y/m = \pi/2 - 1$ and $\bar{y} = M_x/m = \pi/8$.

32. $\int x^2 e^{-x} dx = (x^2)(-e^{-x}) - (2x)(e^{-x}) + (2)(-e^{-x}) + C = -e^{-x}(x^2 + 2x + 2) + C$

33. $\int x^3 e^{2x} dx = (x^3)(\frac{1}{2}e^{2x}) - (3x^2)(\frac{1}{4}e^{2x}) + (6x)(\frac{1}{8}e^{2x}) - (6)(\frac{1}{16}e^{2x}) + C$

$$= \frac{1}{8}e^{2x}(4x^3 - 6x^2 + 6x - 3) + C$$

34. $\int (x^2 - x + 1)\cos x \, dx = (x^2 - x + 1)(\sin x) - (2x - 1)(-\cos x) + (2)(-\sin x) + C$

$$= (2x - 1)\cos x + (x^2 - x - 1)\sin x + C$$

35. $\int x^4 \sin 2x \, dx = (x^4)(-\frac{1}{2}\cos 2x) - (4x^3)(-\frac{1}{4}\sin 2x) + (12x^2)(\frac{1}{8}\cos 2x)$

$$- (24x)(\frac{1}{16}\sin 2x) + (24)(-\frac{1}{32}\cos 2x) + C$$

$$= -\frac{1}{4}(2x^4 - 6x^2 + 3)\cos 2x + \frac{1}{2}x(2x^2 - 3)\sin 2x + C$$

Hence $\int_0^{\pi/4} x^4 \sin 2x \, dx = [0 + \frac{\pi}{8}(\frac{\pi^2}{8} - 3)] - (-\frac{3}{4}) = \frac{1}{64}\pi^3 - \frac{3}{8}\pi + \frac{3}{4}$.

36. Let $u = e^{ax}$, $dv = \sin bx \, dx$. Then $du = ae^{ax}dx$ and $v = -\frac{1}{b}\cos bx$, so

$$\int e^{ax}\sin bx \, dx = -\frac{1}{b}e^{ax}\cos bx + \frac{a}{b}\int e^{ax}\cos bx \, dx$$

In the new integral let $u = e^{ax}$, $dv = \cos bx \, dx$. Then $du = ae^{ax}dx$ and $v = \frac{1}{b}\sin bx$, so

$$\int e^{ax}\sin bx \, dx = -\frac{1}{b}e^{ax}\cos bx + \frac{a}{b^2}e^{ax}\sin bx - \frac{a^2}{b^2}\int e^{ax}\sin bx \, dx$$

Solve for the integral to obtain

$$\int e^{ax}\sin bx \, dx = \frac{b^2}{a^2 + b^2}(-\frac{1}{b}e^{ax}\cos bx + \frac{a}{b^2}e^{ax}\sin bx) + C$$

$$= \frac{e^{ax}(a\sin bx - b\cos bx)}{a^2 + b^2} + C$$

If $b = 0$, the original integral is zero (plus a constant). The above formula covers that case (if $a \neq 0$) because it reduces to zero, too.

37. Let $u = e^{ax}$, $dv = \cos bx \, dx$. Then $du = ae^{ax}dx$ and $v = \frac{1}{b}\sin bx$, so

$$\int e^{ax}\cos bx \, dx = \frac{1}{b}e^{ax}\sin bx - \frac{a}{b}\int e^{ax}\sin bx \, dx$$

In the new integral let $u = e^{ax}$, $dv = \sin bx \, dx$. Then $du = ae^{ax}dx$ and $v = -\frac{1}{b}\cos bx$, so

$$\int e^{ax}\cos bx \, dx = \frac{1}{b}e^{ax}\sin bx + \frac{a}{b^2}e^{ax}\cos bx - \frac{a^2}{b^2}\int e^{ax}\cos bx \, dx$$

Solve for the integral to obtain

$$\int e^{ax}\cos bx \, dx = \frac{b^2}{a^2+b^2}\left(\frac{1}{b}e^{ax}\sin bx + \frac{a}{b^2}e^{ax}\cos bx\right) + C$$

$$= \frac{e^{ax}(b\sin bx + a\cos bx)}{a^2+b^2} + C$$

If $b = 0$ (and $a \neq 0$), the original integral is $\int e^{ax}dx = \frac{1}{a}e^{ax} + C$. The above

formula covers that case because it reduces to the same thing.

38. Let $u = \cos^{n-1}x$, $dv = \cos x \, dx$. Then $du = -(n-1)\cos^{n-2}x \sin x \, dx$ and

$v = \sin x$, so

$$\int \cos^n x \, dx = \cos^{n-1}x \sin x + (n-1)\int \cos^{n-2}x \sin^2 x \, dx$$

$$= \cos^{n-1}x \sin x + (n-1)\int \cos^{n-2}x (1-\cos^2 x)dx$$

$$= \cos^{n-1}x \sin x + (n-1)\int \cos^{n-2}x \, dx - (n-1)\int \cos^n x \, dx$$

Solve for the integral to obtain

$$\int \cos^n x \, dx = \frac{\cos^{n-1}x \sin x}{n} + \frac{n-1}{n}\int \cos^{n-2}x \, dx$$

39. When the limits 0 and $\pi/2$ are inserted in the formula in Problem 38, the

first term on the right side drops out. Hence

$$\int_0^{\pi/2}\cos^n x \, dx = \frac{n-1}{n}\int_0^{\pi/2}\cos^{n-2}x \, dx$$

40. $\displaystyle\int_0^{\pi/2}\cos^6 x \, dx = \frac{5}{6}\cdot\frac{3}{4}\cdot\frac{1}{2}\int_0^{\pi/2}dx = \frac{5}{16}\cdot\frac{\pi}{2} = \frac{5\pi}{32}$

41. $\displaystyle\int_0^{\pi/2}\sin^8 x \, dx = \frac{7}{8}\cdot\frac{5}{6}\cdot\frac{3}{4}\cdot\frac{1}{2}\cdot\frac{\pi}{2} = \frac{35\pi}{256}$

42. $\displaystyle\int_0^{\pi}\sin^5\frac{x}{2}dx = 2\int_0^{\pi/2}\sin^5 u \, du \quad (u = \frac{x}{2}, \quad du = \frac{1}{2}dx)$

$$= 2\cdot\frac{4}{5}\cdot\frac{2}{3}\int_0^{\pi/2}\sin u \, du = \frac{16}{15}$$

43. $\displaystyle\int_0^{\pi/2}\sin^{2k}x \, dx = \frac{2k-1}{2k}\int_0^{\pi/2}\sin^{2k-2}x \, dx = \frac{2k-1}{2k}\cdot\frac{2k-3}{2k-2}\int_0^{\pi/2}\sin^{2k-4}x \, dx$, and so

on, until the exponent is reduced to 0. Hence (writing the product in reverse

order) we have

$$\int_0^{\pi/2}\sin^{2k}x \, dx = \frac{1\cdot 3\cdot 5\cdots(2k-1)}{2\cdot 4\cdot 6\cdots(2k)}\cdot\frac{\pi}{2}$$

The second formula is

$$\int_0^{\pi/2} \sin^{2k+1} x \, dx = \frac{2k}{2k+1} \int_0^{\pi/2} \sin^{2k-1} x \, dx = \frac{2k}{2k+1} \cdot \frac{2k-2}{2k-1} \int_0^{\pi/2} \sin^{2k-3} x \, dx$$

and so on, until the exponent is reduced to 1. Since

$$\int_0^{\pi/2} \sin x \, dx = 1, \text{ we have } \int_0^{\pi/2} \sin^{2k+1} x \, dx = \frac{2 \cdot 4 \cdot 6 \cdots (2k)}{1 \cdot 3 \cdot 5 \cdots (2k+1)}$$

44. (a) For each $k = 1, 2, 3, \ldots$ the ratio of the integrals is

$$r_k = \frac{1 \cdot 3 \cdot 5 \cdots (2k-1)}{2 \cdot 4 \cdot 6 \cdots (2k)} \cdot \frac{\pi}{2} \cdot \frac{1 \cdot 3 \cdot 5 \cdots (2k+1)}{2 \cdot 4 \cdot 6 \cdots (2k)}$$

$$= \frac{\pi}{2} \cdot \frac{1 \cdot 1 \cdot 3 \cdot 3 \cdot 5 \cdot 5 \cdots (2k-1)(2k-1)(2k+1)}{2 \cdot 2 \cdot 4 \cdot 4 \cdot 6 \cdot 6 \cdots (2k)(2k)}$$

Hence $\dfrac{\pi}{2} = \dfrac{2}{1} \cdot \dfrac{2}{3} \cdot \dfrac{4}{3} \cdot \dfrac{4}{5} \cdot \dfrac{6}{5} \cdot \dfrac{6}{7} \cdots \dfrac{2k}{2k-1} \cdot \dfrac{2k}{2k+1} \cdot r_k,$ $k = 1, 2, 3, \cdots$. As k increases, $r_k \to 1$ and we obtain the given infinite product.

(b) Multiply each side of the formula in part (a) by 2 and combine two fractions at a time.

(c) As an example, the product of the first 26 factors gives

$$\pi \approx 2 \cdot \frac{4}{3} \cdot \frac{16}{15} \cdot \frac{36}{35} \cdot \frac{64}{63} \cdots \frac{2304}{2303} \cdot \frac{2500}{2499} \approx 3.11$$

As you can see, the convergence is slow.

Section 10.2   TRIGONOMETRIC SUBSTITUTIONS

1. Let $x = a \sin t$ $(-\pi/2 \le t \le \pi/2)$. Then $dx = a \cos t \, dt$ and $\sqrt{a^2 - x^2} = a \cos t$ and $\int \dfrac{dx}{\sqrt{a^2 - x^2}} = \int \dfrac{a \cos t \, dt}{a \cos t} = \int dt = t + C = \sin^{-1} \dfrac{x}{a} + C.$

2. Let $x = a \tan t$ $(-\pi/2 < t < \pi/2)$. Then $dx = a \sec^2 t \, dt$, $a^2 + x^2 = a^2 \sec^2 t$, and $\int \dfrac{dx}{a^2 + x^2} = \int \dfrac{a \sec^2 t \, dt}{a^2 \sec^2 t} = \dfrac{1}{a} \int dt = \dfrac{1}{a} t + C = \dfrac{1}{a} \tan^{-1} \dfrac{x}{a} + C.$

3. Let $x = a \sec t$ $(0 \le t < \pi/2$ or $-\pi \le t < -\pi/2)$. Then $dx = a \sec t \tan t \, dt$, $\sqrt{x^2 - a^2} = a \tan t$, and

$$\int \frac{dx}{x \sqrt{x^2 - a^2}} = \int \frac{a \sec t \tan t \, dt}{a \sec t \cdot a \tan t} = \frac{1}{a} \int dt = \frac{1}{a} t + C = \frac{1}{a} \sec^{-1} \frac{x}{a} + C$$

4. Let $x = a \tan t$ $(-\pi/2 < t < \pi/2)$. Then $dx = a \sec^2 t \, dt$, $\sqrt{x^2 + a^2} = a \sec t$, and $\int \dfrac{dx}{\sqrt{x^2 + a^2}} = \int \dfrac{a \sec^2 t \, dt}{a \sec t} = \int \sec t \, dt = \ell n \, |\sec t + \tan t| + C$

$$= \ell n \left| \frac{\sqrt{x^2 + a^2}}{a} + \frac{x}{a} \right| + C = \ell n \, (x + \sqrt{x^2 + a^2}) + C \text{ (because } x + \sqrt{x^2 + a^2} > 0)$$

(We absorbed $-\ell n \, a$ into the constant and called the new constant C.)

5. Using the substitution in Problem 3, we have

$$\int \frac{dx}{\sqrt{x^2 - a^2}} = \int \frac{a \sec t \tan t\, dt}{a \tan t} = \int \sec t\, dt = \ell n\, |\sec t + \tan t| + C$$

$$= \ell n\, \left| \frac{x}{a} + \frac{\sqrt{x^2 - a^2}}{a} \right| + C = \ell n\, |x + \sqrt{x^2 - a^2}| + C \quad \text{(new constant,}$$
$$\text{absorbing } -\ell n\, a\text{)}$$

6. Using the substitution in Problem 1, we have

$$\int \frac{dx}{x\sqrt{a^2 - x^2}} = \int \frac{a \cos t\, dt}{a \sin t \cdot a \cos t} = \frac{1}{a} \int \csc t\, dt = \frac{1}{a} \ell n\, |\csc t - \cot t| + C$$

$$= \frac{1}{a} \ell n\, \left| \frac{a}{x} - \frac{\sqrt{a^2 - x^2}}{x} \right| + C \quad \text{(see Figure 4 in the text)}$$

$$= \frac{1}{a} \ell n\, \left| \frac{a - \sqrt{a^2 - x^2}}{x} \right| + C$$

7. Using the substitution in Problem 4, we have

$$\int \frac{dx}{x\sqrt{a^2 + x^2}} = \int \frac{a \sec^2 t\, dt}{a \tan t \cdot a \sec t} = \frac{1}{a} \int \csc t\, dt = \frac{1}{a} \ell n\, |\csc t - \cot t| + C$$

$$= \frac{1}{a} \ell n\, \left| \frac{\sqrt{a^2 + x^2}}{x} - \frac{a}{x} \right| + C \quad \text{(see Figure 4 in the text)}$$

$$= \frac{1}{a} \ell n\, \left| \frac{a - \sqrt{a^2 + x^2}}{x} \right| + C$$

8. Using the substitution in Problem 1, we have

$$\int \frac{dx}{a^2 - x^2} = \int \frac{a \cos t\, dt}{a^2 \cos^2 t} = \frac{1}{a} \int \sec t\, dt = \frac{1}{a} \ell n\, |\sec t + \tan t| + C$$

$$= \frac{1}{a} \ell n\, \left| \frac{a}{\sqrt{a^2 - x^2}} + \frac{x}{\sqrt{a^2 - x^2}} \right| + C \quad \text{(see Figure 4 in the text)}$$

$$= \frac{1}{a} \ell n\, \left| \frac{a + x}{\sqrt{a^2 - x^2}} \right| + C = \frac{1}{a}(\ell n\, |a + x| - \tfrac{1}{2} \ell n\, |a^2 - x^2|) + C$$

$$= \frac{1}{a}(\ell n\, |a + x| - \tfrac{1}{2} \ell n\, |a - x| - \tfrac{1}{2} \ell n\, |a + x|) + C$$

$$= \frac{1}{2a}(\ell n\, |a + x| - \ell n\, |a - x|) + C = \frac{1}{2a} \ell n\, \left| \frac{a + x}{a - x} \right| + C$$

9. Using the substitution in Problem 4, we have

$$\int \sqrt{x^2 + a^2}\, dx = \int a \sec t \cdot a \sec^2 t\, dt = a^2 \int \sec^3 t\, dt$$

$$= a^2(\tfrac{1}{2} \sec t \tan t + \tfrac{1}{2} \ell n\, |\sec t + \tan t|) + C$$

$$= \frac{a^2}{2}\left(\frac{\sqrt{x^2 + a^2}}{a} \cdot \frac{x}{a} + \ell n\, \left| \frac{\sqrt{x^2 + a^2}}{a} + \frac{x}{a} \right| \right) + C$$

$$= \frac{x}{2} \sqrt{x^2 + a^2} + \frac{a^2}{2} \ell n\, |x + \sqrt{x^2 + a^2}| + C \quad \text{(new constant, absorbing}$$
$$-\frac{a^2}{2} \ell n\, a\text{)}$$

10. Let $x = 2 \sin t$, $dx = 2 \cos t\, dt$, $\sqrt{4 - x^2} = 2 \cos t$ $(-\pi/2 \le t \le \pi/2)$. Then

$$\int \frac{dx}{x^2\sqrt{4-x^2}} = \int \frac{2\cos t\,dt}{4\sin^2 t \cdot 2\cos t} = \frac{1}{4}\int \csc^2 t\,dt = -\frac{1}{4}\cot t + C$$

$$= -\frac{1}{4}\cdot\frac{\sqrt{4-x^2}}{x} + C = -\frac{\sqrt{4-x^2}}{4x} + C$$

11. Let $x = 5\sin t$, $dx = 5\cos t\,dt$, $\sqrt{25-x^2} = 5\cos t$ $(-\pi/2 \le t \le \pi/2)$.   Then

$$\int \frac{x^2\,dx}{\sqrt{25-x^2}} = \int \frac{25\sin^2 t \cdot 5\cos t\,dt}{5\cos t} = \frac{25}{2}\int (1-\cos 2t)\,dt = \frac{25}{2}\left(t - \frac{1}{2}\sin 2t\right) + C$$

$$= \frac{25}{2}(t - \sin t\cos t) + C = \frac{25}{2}\left(\sin^{-1}\frac{x}{5} - \frac{x}{5}\cdot\frac{\sqrt{25-x^2}}{5}\right) + C$$

$$= \frac{25}{2}\sin^{-1}\frac{x}{5} - \frac{1}{2}x\sqrt{25-x^2} + C$$

12. Let $x = \tan t$, $dx = \sec^2 t\,dt$, $\sqrt{1+x^2} = \sec t$ $(-\pi/2 < t < \pi/2)$.   Then

$$\int \frac{\sqrt{1+x^2}}{x^2}\,dx = \int \frac{\sec t\cdot\sec^2 t\,dt}{\tan^2 t} = \int \frac{\sec t\,(\tan^2 t+1)\,dt}{\tan^2 t} = \int \sec t\,dt + \int \frac{\sec t\,dt}{\tan^2 t}$$

$$= \ln|\sec t + \tan t| + \int (\sin t)^{-2}\cos t\,dt$$

$$= \ln|\sec t + \tan t| - (\sin t)^{-1} + C = \ln|\sec t + \tan t| - \csc t + C$$

$$= \ln|\sqrt{1+x^2} + x| - \frac{\sqrt{1+x^2}}{x} + C$$

13. Let $x = 3\tan t$, $dx = 3\sec^2 t\,dt$, $9+x^2 = 9\sec^2 t$.   Then

$$\int \frac{dx}{(9+x^2)^2} = \int \frac{3\sec^2 t\,dt}{81\sec^4 t} = \frac{1}{27}\int \cos^2 t\,dt = \frac{1}{54}\int (1+\cos 2t)\,dt$$

$$= \frac{1}{54}\left(t + \frac{1}{2}\sin 2t\right) + C = \frac{1}{54}(t + \sin t\cos t) + C$$

$$= \frac{1}{54}\left(\tan^{-1}\frac{x}{3} + \frac{x}{\sqrt{9+x^2}}\cdot\frac{3}{\sqrt{9+x^2}}\right) + C = \frac{1}{54}\left(\tan^{-1}\frac{x}{3} + \frac{3x}{9+x^2}\right) + C$$

14. Let $x = \sec t$, $dx = \sec t\tan t\,dt$, $\sqrt{x^2-1} = \tan t$ $(0 \le t < \pi/2$ or $-\pi \le t < -\pi/2)$.   Then

$$\int \frac{x^2\,dx}{\sqrt{x^2-1}} = \int \frac{\sec^2 t\,\sec t\tan t\,dt}{\tan t} = \int \sec^3 t\,dt$$

$$= \frac{1}{2}\sec t\tan t + \frac{1}{2}\ln|\sec t + \tan t| + C$$

$$= \frac{1}{2}x\sqrt{x^2-1} + \frac{1}{2}\ln|x + \sqrt{x^2-1}| + C$$

15. Using the substitution in Problem 14, we have

$$\int \frac{dx}{x^4\sqrt{x^2-1}} = \int \frac{\sec t\tan t\,dt}{\sec^4 t\tan t} = \int \cos^3 t\,dt = \int (1-\sin^2 t)\cos t\,dt$$

$$= \int \cos t\,dt - \int \sin^2 t\cos t\,dt = \sin t - \frac{1}{3}\sin^3 t + C$$

$$= \frac{1}{3}\sin t\,(3 - \sin^2 t) + C = \frac{\sqrt{x^2-1}}{3x}\left(3 - \frac{x^2-1}{x^2}\right) + C$$

$$= \frac{2x^2 + 1}{3x^3} \sqrt{x^2 - 1} + C$$

16. Let $x = \sin t$, $dx = \cos t \, dt$, $(1 - x^2)^{3/2} = \cos^3 t$ $(-\pi/2 \leq t \leq \pi/2)$. Then

$$\int \frac{dx}{(1 - x^2)^{3/2}} = \int \frac{\cos t \, dt}{\cos^3 t} = \int \sec^2 t \, dt = \tan t + C = \frac{x}{\sqrt{1 - x^2}} + C$$

17. Let $3x = 2 \tan t$, $dx = \frac{2}{3} \sec^2 t \, dt$, $(4 + 9x^2)^{3/2} = 8 \sec^3 t$ $(-\pi/2 < t < \pi/2)$.

Then $\int \frac{dx}{(4 + 9x^2)^{3/2}} = \int \frac{(2/3) \sec^2 t \, dt}{8 \sec^3 t} = \frac{1}{12} \int \cos t \, dt = \frac{1}{12} \sin t + C$

$$= \frac{1}{12} \cdot \frac{3x}{\sqrt{4 + 9x^2}} + C = \frac{x}{4\sqrt{4 + 9x^2}} + C$$

18. Let $2x = \sin t$, $x = \frac{1}{2} \sin t$, $dx = \frac{1}{2} \cos t \, dt$, $\sqrt{1 - 4x^2} = \cos t$ $(-\pi/2 \leq t \leq \pi/2)$. Then

$$\int \frac{\sqrt{1 - 4x^2}}{x^2} dx = \int \frac{\cos t \cdot \frac{1}{2} \cos t \, dt}{\frac{1}{4} \sin^2 t} = 2 \int \cot^2 t \, dt = 2 \int (\csc^2 t - 1) dt$$

$$= 2(-\cot t - t) + C = -\frac{\sqrt{1 - 4x^2}}{x} - 2 \sin^{-1} 2x + C$$

19. Use integration by parts, with $u = \sin^{-1} x$, $dv = x \, dx$. Then $du = dx/\sqrt{1 - x^2}$ and $v = \frac{1}{2} x^2$, so

$$\int x \sin^{-1} x \, dx = \frac{1}{2} x^2 \sin^{-1} x - \frac{1}{2} \int \frac{x^2 dx}{\sqrt{1 - x^2}}$$

In the new integral let $x = \sin t$, $dx = \cos t \, dt$, $\sqrt{1 - x^2} = \cos t$ $(-\pi/2 \leq t \leq \pi/2)$. Then

$$\int \frac{x^2 dx}{\sqrt{1 - x^2}} = \int \frac{\sin^2 t \cos t \, dt}{\cos t} = \int \sin^2 t \, dt = \frac{1}{2} \int (1 - \cos 2t) dt$$

$$= \frac{1}{2}(t - \frac{1}{2} \sin 2t) \quad \text{(arbitrary constant omitted)}$$

$$= \frac{1}{2}(t - \sin t \cos t) = \frac{1}{2}(\sin^{-1} x - x\sqrt{1 - x^2})$$

Hence $\int x \sin^{-1} x \, dx = \frac{1}{2} x^2 \sin^{-1} x - \frac{1}{4} \sin^{-1} x + \frac{1}{4} x\sqrt{1 - x^2} + C$.

20. Let $x = 4 \sin t$, $dx = 4 \cos t \, dt$, $\sqrt{16 - x^2} = 4 \cos t$ $(-\pi/2 \leq t \leq \pi/2)$. Then

$$\int_2^4 \frac{\sqrt{16 - x^2}}{x^2} dx = \int_{\pi/6}^{\pi/2} \frac{4 \cos t \cdot 4 \cos t \, dt}{16 \sin^2 t} = \int_{\pi/6}^{\pi/2} \cot^2 t \, dt = \int_{\pi/6}^{\pi/2} (\csc^2 t - 1) dt$$

$$= (-\cot t - t) \Big|_{\pi/6}^{\pi/2} = (0 - \pi/2) + (1/\sqrt{3} + \pi/6) = 1/\sqrt{3} - \pi/3$$

21. Let $x = 3 \sin t$, $dx = 3 \cos t \, dt$, $\sqrt{9 - x^2} = 3 \cos t$ $(-\pi/2 \leq t \leq \pi/2)$. Then

$$\int_0^3 x^2 \sqrt{9 - x^2} \, dx = \int_0^{\pi/2} 9 \sin^2 t \cdot 3 \cos t \cdot 3 \cos t \, dt = 81 \int_0^{\pi/2} \sin^2 t \cos^2 t \, dt$$

$$= \frac{81}{4} \int_0^{\pi/2} \sin^2 2t \, dt \quad \text{(because } \sin t \cos t = \tfrac{1}{2} \sin 2t\text{)}$$

$$= \frac{81}{8} \int_0^{\pi/2} (1 - \cos 4t) dt = \frac{81}{8}\left(t - \frac{1}{4}\sin 4t\right)\Big|_0^{\pi/2} = \frac{81}{8} \cdot \frac{\pi}{2} = \frac{81\pi}{16}$$

22. Let $x = 2\tan t$, $dx = 2\sec^2 t \, dt$, $x^2 + 4 = 4\sec^2 t$. Then

$$\int_2^{2\sqrt{3}} \frac{dx}{x(x^2+4)} = \int_{\pi/4}^{\pi/3} \frac{2\sec^2 t \, dt}{2\tan t \cdot 4\sec^2 t} = \frac{1}{4}\int_{\pi/4}^{\pi/3} \cot t \, dt$$

$$= \frac{1}{4}\ell n \,|\csc t - \cot t| \Big|_{\pi/4}^{\pi/3} = \frac{1}{4}[\ell n \,(2/\sqrt{3} - 1/\sqrt{3}) - \ell n \,(\sqrt{2} - 1)]$$

$$= \frac{1}{4}\ell n \left(\frac{1/\sqrt{3}}{\sqrt{2}-1}\right) = \frac{1}{4}\ell n \left(\frac{1}{\sqrt{6}-\sqrt{3}}\right) = -\frac{1}{4}\ell n \,(\sqrt{6} - \sqrt{3})$$

23. Using the substitution in Problem 22, we have

$$\int_0^2 \frac{x^2 dx}{\sqrt{4+x^2}} = \int_0^{\pi/4} \frac{4\tan^2 t \cdot 2\sec^2 t \, dt}{2\sec t} = 4\int_0^{\pi/4} \tan^2 t \sec t \, dt$$

$$= 4\int_0^{\pi/4} (\sec^2 t - 1)\sec t \, dt = 4\int_0^{\pi/4} (\sec^3 t - \sec t) dt$$

$$= 4\left(\frac{1}{2}\sec t \tan t + \frac{1}{2}\ell n \,|\sec t + \tan t| - \ell n \,|\sec t + \tan t|\right)\Big|_0^{\pi/4}$$

$$= 2(\sec t \tan t - \ell n \,|\sec t + \tan t|)\Big|_0^{\pi/4} = 2[\sqrt{2} - \ell n \,(\sqrt{2}+1)]$$

$$= 2\sqrt{2} - 2\ell n \,(1 + \sqrt{2})$$

24. Let $x = 2\sin t$, $dx = 2\cos t \, dt$, $(4-x^2)^{3/2} = 8\cos^3 t$ $(-\pi/2 \leq t \leq \pi/2)$.

Then $\displaystyle\int_0^1 \frac{x^2 dx}{(4-x^2)^{3/2}} = \int_0^{\pi/6} \frac{4\sin^2 t \cdot 2\cos t \, dt}{8\cos^3 t} = \int_0^{\pi/6} \tan^2 t \, dt = \int_0^{\pi/6} (\sec^2 t - 1) dt$

$$= (\tan t - t)\Big|_0^{\pi/6} = \sqrt{3}/3 - \pi/6$$

25. Using the substitution in Problem 20, we have

$$\int_2^3 \frac{dx}{x^4\sqrt{16-x^2}} = \int_{\pi/6}^{\alpha} \frac{4\cos t \, dt}{256\sin^4 t \cdot 4\cos t} \quad \left(\text{where } \alpha = \sin^{-1}\frac{3}{4}\right)$$

$$= \frac{1}{256}\int_{\pi/6}^{\alpha} \csc^4 t \, dt = \frac{1}{256}\int_{\pi/6}^{\alpha} (\cot^2 t + 1)\csc^2 t \, dt$$

$$= \frac{1}{256}\left(-\frac{1}{3}\cot^3 t - \cot t\right)\Big|_{\pi/6}^{\alpha} = \frac{1}{768}\cot t \,(\cot^2 t + 3)\Big|_{\alpha}^{\pi/6}$$

Since $\sin \alpha = 3/4$, we find $\cot \alpha = \sqrt{7}/3$ and hence the integral becomes

$$\frac{\sqrt{3}}{768}(3+3) - \frac{\sqrt{7}}{2304}\left(\frac{7}{9}+3\right) = \frac{\sqrt{3}}{128} - \frac{17\sqrt{7}}{10,368} = \frac{81\sqrt{3} - 17\sqrt{7}}{10,368}$$

26. Let $2x = \tan t$, $x = \frac{1}{2}\tan t$, $dx = \frac{1}{2}\sec^2 t \, dt$, $\sqrt{1+4x^2} = \sec t$ $(-\pi/2 < t <$

$\pi/2$).   Then

$$\int_1^2 \frac{\sqrt{1+4x^2}}{x^4}dx = \int_\alpha^\beta \frac{\sec t \cdot \frac{1}{2}\sec^2 t\, dt}{(1/16)\tan^4 t} \quad (\text{where } \alpha = \tan^{-1}2, \ \beta = \tan^{-1}4)$$

$$= 8\int_\alpha^\beta (\sin t)^{-4}\cos t\, dt = -\frac{8}{3}(\sin t)^{-3}\Big|_\alpha^\beta = \frac{8}{3}\csc^3 t\Big|_\beta^\alpha$$

Since $\tan\alpha = 2$ and $\tan\beta = 4$, we find $\csc\alpha = \sqrt{5}/2$ and $\csc\beta = \sqrt{17}/4$, so the integral becomes

$$\frac{8}{3}(5\sqrt{5}/8 - 17\sqrt{17}/64) = \frac{1}{24}(40\sqrt{5} - 17\sqrt{17})$$

27.(a) $\int \frac{x\,dx}{x^2+9} = \frac{1}{2}\int \frac{du}{u} \quad (u = x^2+9, \ du = 2x\,dx)$

$\qquad = \frac{1}{2}\ln|u| + C = \frac{1}{2}\ln(x^2+9) + C$

(b) Let $x = 3\tan t$, $dx = 3\sec^2 t\, dt$, $x^2+9 = 9\sec^2 t$. Then

$$\int \frac{x\,dx}{x^2+9} = \int \frac{3\tan t \cdot 3\sec^2 t\, dt}{9\sec^2 t} = \int \tan t\, dt = \ln|\sec t| + C = \ln\frac{\sqrt{x^2+9}}{3} + C$$

(c) $\ln\frac{\sqrt{x^2+9}}{3} = \frac{1}{2}\ln(x^2+9) - \ln 3$, which differs from the result in part (a) by only a constant.

28.(a) $\int \frac{x\,dx}{\sqrt{x^2-1}} = \frac{1}{2}\int u^{-1/2}du \quad (u = x^2-1, \ du = 2x\,dx)$

$\qquad = \sqrt{u} + C = \sqrt{x^2-1} + C$

(b) Using the substitution in Problem 14, we have

$$\int \frac{x\,dx}{\sqrt{x^2-1}} = \int \frac{\sec t \cdot \sec t \tan t\, dt}{\tan t} = \int \sec^2 t\, dt = \tan t + C = \sqrt{x^2-1} + C$$

(c) The results are identical.

29. $\int_0^3 \frac{x^3 dx}{\sqrt{9+x^2}} = \int_3^{3\sqrt{2}} \frac{(u^2-9)u\,du}{u} = \int_3^{3\sqrt{2}}(u^2-9)du = \left(\frac{u^3}{3} - 9u\right)\Big|_3^{3\sqrt{2}}$

$\qquad = \frac{u}{3}(u^2-27)\Big|_3^{3\sqrt{2}} = \sqrt{2}(18-27) - (9-27) = 9(2-\sqrt{2})$

30.(a) If $u = \sqrt{4-x^2}$, then $u^2 = 4 - x^2$, $2u\,du = -2x\,dx$, and $u\,du = -x\,dx$. Hence

$$\int_1^2 \frac{\sqrt{4-x^2}}{x}dx = \int_{\sqrt{3}}^0 \frac{u(-u\,du)}{4-u^2} = \int_0^{\sqrt{3}} \frac{u^2 du}{4-u^2} = \int_0^{\sqrt{3}}\left(\frac{4}{4-u^2} - 1\right) \text{ (by division)}$$

$$= \ln\left(\frac{2+u}{2-u}\right)\Big|_0^{\sqrt{3}} - \sqrt{3} = \ln\left(\frac{2+\sqrt{3}}{2-\sqrt{3}}\right) - \sqrt{3}$$

(b) Using the substitution in Problem 10, we have

$$\int_1^2 \frac{\sqrt{4-x^2}}{x}dx = \int_{\pi/6}^{\pi/2} \frac{2\cos t \cdot 2\cos t\, dt}{2\sin t} = 2\int_{\pi/6}^{\pi/2} \frac{(1-\sin^2 t)dt}{\sin t}$$

$$= 2 \int_{\pi/6}^{\pi/2} (\csc t - \sin t)dt = 2(\ell n \, |\csc t - \cot t| + \cos t) \Big|_{\pi/6}^{\pi/2}$$

$$= 2[0 - \ell n \, (2 - \sqrt{3}) - \sqrt{3}/2] = -2\ell n(2 - \sqrt{3}) - \sqrt{3}$$

This is the same as the result in part (a) because

$$\ell n \left(\frac{2 + \sqrt{3}}{2 - \sqrt{3}}\right) = \ell n \, \frac{(2 + \sqrt{3})^2}{4 - 3} = 2\ell n \, (2 + \sqrt{3})$$

and $-2\ell n \, (2 - \sqrt{3}) = 2\ell n \left(\frac{1}{2 - \sqrt{3}}\right) = 2\ell n \left(\frac{2 + \sqrt{3}}{4 - 3}\right) = 2\ell n \, (2 + \sqrt{3})$.

31. $y' = x$, $1 + y'^2 = 1 + x^2$, so

$$s = \int_0^2 \sqrt{1 + x^2} \, dx = [\tfrac{1}{2}x\sqrt{1 + x^2} + \tfrac{1}{2}\ell n(x + \sqrt{1 + x^2})] \Big|_0^2 \quad \text{(see the standard form}$$
$$\text{preceding Example 4)}$$

$$= \sqrt{5} + \tfrac{1}{2}\ell n(2 + \sqrt{5})$$

32. $y' = 1/x$, $1 + y'^2 = 1 + 1/x^2 = (x^2 + 1)/x^2$, so

$$s = \int_1^2 \frac{\sqrt{x^2 + 1}}{x} dx = \int_{\pi/4}^{\alpha} \frac{\sec t \cdot \sec^2 t \, dt}{\tan t} \quad (x = \tan t, \ dx = \sec^2 t \, dt, \ \alpha = \tan^{-1} 2)$$

$$= \int_{\pi/4}^{\alpha} \frac{\sec t \, (\tan^2 t + 1) \, dt}{\tan t} = \int_{\pi/4}^{\alpha} (\sec t \tan t + \csc t) dt$$

$$= (\sec t + \ell n \, |\csc t - \cot t|) \Big|_{\pi/4}^{\alpha}$$

Since $\tan \alpha = 2$, we find $\sec \alpha = \sqrt{5}$, $\csc \alpha = \sqrt{5}/2$, and $\cot \alpha = 1/2$, so

$$s = \sqrt{5} + \ell n \left(\frac{\sqrt{5}}{2} - \frac{1}{2}\right) - \sqrt{2} - \ell n \, (\sqrt{2} - 1) = \sqrt{5} - \sqrt{2} + \ell n \left(\frac{\sqrt{5} - 1}{2}\right) - \ell n \, (\sqrt{2} - 1)$$

33. Using the substitution in Problem 14, we have

$$\int \frac{\sqrt{x^2 - 1}}{x^2} dx = \int \frac{\tan t \cdot \sec t \tan t \, dt}{\sec^2 t} = \int \frac{\tan^2 t \, dt}{\sec t} = \int \frac{(\sec^2 t - 1) dt}{\sec t}$$

$$= \int (\sec t - \cos t) dt = \ell n \, |\sec t + \tan t| - \sin t + C$$

$$= \ell n \, |x + \sqrt{x^2 - 1}| - \frac{\sqrt{x^2 - 1}}{x} + C$$

Since $y = 0$ when $x = 1$, $C = 0$. Moreover, the original problem requires $x \geq 1$, so we may drop the absolute value to obtain $y = \ell n \, (x + \sqrt{x^2 - 1}) - \sqrt{x^2 - 1}/x$.

34. The first figure in the text (referring to the substitution $x = a \sin t$) should be drawn as in Figure 1 when $-\pi/2 < t < 0$ (which implies $x < 0$). Then (as in the case $0 < t < \pi/2$) we have $\cos t = \sqrt{a^2 - x^2}/a$, $\tan t = x/\sqrt{a^2 - x^2}$, and so on. The second figure in the text (referring to $x = a \tan t$) should be drawn as in Figure 2 when $-\pi/2 < t < 0$ (which implies $x < 0$). Then (as in the case $0 < t < \pi/2$) we have $\sin t = x/\sqrt{a^2 + x^2}$, $\cos t = a/\sqrt{a^2 + x^2}$, and so on.

35. If $x = a \sinh t$, then $dx = a \cosh t \, dt$ and $\sqrt{a^2 + x^2} = a\sqrt{1 + \sinh^2 t} = a\sqrt{\cosh^2 t}$

= $a \cosh t$ (because $\cosh t > 0$).   Hence

$$\int \frac{dx}{\sqrt{a^2 + x^2}} = \int \frac{a \cosh t \, dt}{a \cosh t} = \int dt = t + C = \sinh^{-1} \frac{x}{a} + C$$

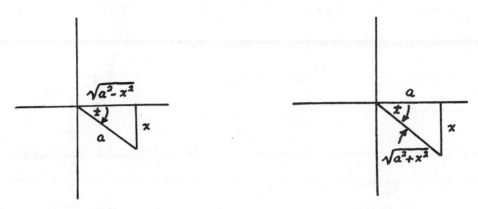

Figure 1   Figure 2

36. Using the data in Problem 35, we have

$$\int \frac{dx}{a^2 + x^2} = \int \frac{a \cosh t \, dt}{a^2 \cosh^2 t} = \frac{1}{a} \int \operatorname{sech} t \, dt = \frac{1}{a} \tan^{-1}(\sinh t) + C = \frac{1}{a} \tan^{-1} \frac{x}{a} + C$$

37.(a) If $x = a \tanh t$, then $dx = a \operatorname{sech}^2 t \, dt$ and $\sqrt{a^2 - x^2} = a\sqrt{1 - \tanh^2 t} = a\sqrt{\operatorname{sech}^2 t} = a \operatorname{sech} t$ (because $\operatorname{sech} t > 0$). Hence

$$\int \frac{dx}{\sqrt{a^2 - x^2}} = \int \frac{a \operatorname{sech}^2 t \, dt}{a \operatorname{sech} t} = \int \operatorname{sech} t \, dt = \tan^{-1}(\sinh t) + C$$

(b) $\tan^{-1}(\sinh t) = \sin^{-1}(\tanh t) = \sin^{-1} \frac{x}{a}$

38. If $x = 2 \sinh t$, then $dx = 2 \cosh t \, dt$ and $\sqrt{4 + x^2} = 2 \cosh t$, so

$$\int_2^6 \frac{dx}{x^2 \sqrt{4 + x^2}} = \int_\alpha^\beta \frac{2 \cosh t \, dt}{4 \sinh^2 t \cdot 2 \cosh t} \quad \text{(where } \alpha = \sinh^{-1} 1, \ \beta = \sinh^{-1} 3)$$

$$= \frac{1}{4} \int_\alpha^\beta \operatorname{csch}^2 t \, dt = -\frac{1}{4} \coth t \Big|_\alpha^\beta$$

Since $\sinh \alpha = 1$, $\coth^2 \alpha = \operatorname{csch}^2 \alpha + 1 = 2$ and $\coth \alpha = \sqrt{2}$; similarly, $\sinh \beta = 3$, $\coth^2 \beta = 1/9 + 1 = 10/9$, and $\coth \beta = \sqrt{10}/3$. Hence the integral is

$$\frac{1}{4}(\sqrt{2} - \sqrt{10}/3) = \frac{1}{12}(3\sqrt{2} - \sqrt{10})$$

as in Example 5. Note that the hyperbolic substitution is easier.

39. If $x = 2 \tan^{-1} u$, then $dx = 2 \, du/(1 + u^2)$. Since $\tan(x/2) = u$, the usual triangle yields $\sin(x/2) = u/\sqrt{1 + u^2}$ and $\cos(x/2) = 1/\sqrt{1 + u^2}$. Hence

$$\sin x = 2 \sin(x/2)\cos(x/2) = \frac{2u}{1 + u^2}$$

$$\cos x = \cos^2(x/2) - \sin^2(x/2) = \frac{1}{1 + u^2} - \frac{u^2}{1 + u^2} = \frac{1 - u^2}{1 + u^2}$$

40. Using the data in Problem 39, we have

$$\frac{dx}{1 + \cos x} = \frac{1}{1 + (1 - u^2)/(1 + u^2)} \cdot \frac{2\,du}{1 + u^2} = \frac{2\,du}{(1 + u^2) + (1 - u^2)} = du$$

Hence $\int \frac{dx}{1 + \cos x} = \int du = u + C = \tan(x/2) + C.$

41. Using the data in Problem 39, we have

$$\frac{dx}{1 - \sin x} = \frac{1}{1 - 2u/(1 + u^2)} \cdot \frac{2\,du}{1 + u^2} = \frac{2\,du}{(1 + u^2) - 2u} = \frac{2\,du}{(u - 1)^2}$$

Hence $\int_0^{\pi/3} \frac{dx}{1 - \sin x} = 2\int_0^{1/\sqrt{3}} \frac{du}{(u - 1)^2} = -2(u - 1)^{-1} \Big|_0^{1/\sqrt{3}} = \frac{2}{1 - u}\Big|_0^{1/\sqrt{3}}$

$$= \frac{2}{1 - 1/\sqrt{3}} - 2 = \frac{2\sqrt{3}}{\sqrt{3} - 1} - 2 = \frac{2\sqrt{3} - 2(\sqrt{3} - 1)}{\sqrt{3} - 1} = \frac{2}{\sqrt{3} - 1} = 1 + \sqrt{3}$$

42. Using the data in Problem 39, we have

$$\frac{dx}{\sin x + \tan x} = \frac{1}{2u/(1 + u^2) + 2u/(1 - u^2)} \cdot \frac{2\,du}{1 + u^2} = \frac{2(1 - u^2)\,du}{2u(1 - u^2) + 2u(1 + u^2)}$$

$$= \frac{2(1 - u^2)\,du}{4u} = \frac{1}{2}\left(\frac{1}{u} - u\right)du$$

Hence $\int \frac{dx}{\sin x + \tan x} = \frac{1}{2}\int \left(\frac{1}{u} - u\right)du = \frac{1}{2}\left(\ell n\,|u| - \frac{1}{2}u^2\right) + C$

$$= \frac{1}{2}\ell n\,|\tan(x/2)| - \frac{1}{4}\tan^2(x/2) + C$$

Section 10.3   DECOMPOSITION OF RATIONAL FUNCTIONS

1. Since $P(10 - P) = -(P^2 - 10P + 25) + 25 = 25 - (P - 5)^2$,

$$\int \frac{dP}{P(10 - P)} = \int \frac{dP}{25 - (P - 5)^2} = \int \frac{dx}{25 - x^2} \quad (x = P - 5,\ dx = dP)$$

$$= \frac{1}{10}\ell n\left|\frac{5 + x}{5 - x}\right| + C = \frac{1}{10}\ell n\,\frac{P}{10 - P} + C \quad (\text{because } 0 < P < 10)$$

2. Since $x^2 + 2x - 3 = (x^2 + 2x + 1) - 4 = (x + 1)^2 - 4$, we have

$$\int \frac{dx}{x^2 + 2x - 3} = \int \frac{dx}{(x + 1)^2 - 4} = -\int \frac{du}{4 - u^2} \quad (u = x + 1,\ du = dx)$$

$$= -\frac{1}{4}\ell n\left|\frac{2 + u}{2 - u}\right| + C = -\frac{1}{4}\ell n\left|\frac{3 + x}{1 - x}\right| + C$$

3. $\frac{1}{x^2 + 2x - 3} = \frac{1}{(x - 1)(x + 3)} = \frac{A}{x - 1} + \frac{B}{x + 3} \implies 1 = A(x + 3) + B(x - 1).$ Put $x = 1$
to find $A = 1/4$ and $x = -3$ to find $B = -1/4$. Then

$$\int \frac{dx}{x^2 + 2x - 3} = \frac{1}{4}\int \frac{dx}{x - 1} - \frac{1}{4}\int \frac{dx}{x + 3} = \frac{1}{4}\ell n\,|x - 1| - \frac{1}{4}\ell n\,|x + 3| + C = \frac{1}{4}\ell n\left|\frac{x - 1}{x + 3}\right| + C$$

This is the same as $-\frac{1}{4}\ell n\left|\frac{3 + x}{1 - x}\right| + C = \frac{1}{4}\ell n\left|\frac{1 - x}{3 + x}\right| + C$ in Problem 2.

4. $\frac{x^2 + 1}{x(x^2 - 1)} = \frac{x^2 + 1}{x(x - 1)(x + 1)} = \frac{A}{x} + \frac{B}{x - 1} + \frac{C}{x + 1} \implies x^2 + 1 = A(x - 1)(x + 1) +$

$Bx(x+1) + Cx(x-1)$. Put $x = 0$ to find $A = -1$, $x = 1$ to find $B = 1$, and $x = -1$ to find $C = 1$. Then

$$\int \frac{x^2+1}{x(x^2-1)} dx = -\int \frac{dx}{x} + \int \frac{dx}{x-1} + \int \frac{dx}{x+1} = -\ell n\,|x| + \ell n\,|x-1| + \ell n\,|x+1| + C$$

$$= \ell n\left|\frac{x^2-1}{x}\right| + C$$

5. $\dfrac{1}{x^3-x^2} = \dfrac{1}{x^2(x-1)} = \dfrac{A}{x} + \dfrac{B}{x^2} + \dfrac{C}{x-1} \Longrightarrow 1 = Ax(x-1) + B(x-1) + Cx^2$. Put $x = 0$ to find $B = -1$ and $x = 1$ to find $C = 1$. Equate the coefficients of x^2 to find $0 = A + C$, from which $A = -1$. Hence

$$\int \frac{dx}{x^3-x^2} = -\int\frac{dx}{x} - \int\frac{dx}{x^2} + \int\frac{dx}{x-1} = -\ell n\,|x| + \frac{1}{x} + \ell n\,|x-1| + C = \frac{1}{x} + \ell n\left|\frac{x-1}{x}\right| + C$$

6. $\dfrac{1}{x(x-1)^2} = \dfrac{A}{x} + \dfrac{B}{x-1} + \dfrac{C}{(x-1)^2} \Longrightarrow 1 = A(x-1)^2 + Bx(x-1) + Cx$. Put $x = 0$ to find $A = 1$ and $x = 1$ to find $C = 1$. Equate the coefficients of x^2 to find $0 = A + B$, from which $B = -1$. Hence

$$\int \frac{dx}{x(x-1)^2} = \int\frac{dx}{x} - \int\frac{dx}{x-1} + \int\frac{dx}{(x-1)^2} = \ell n\,|x| - \ell n\,|x-1| - \frac{1}{x-1} + C$$

$$= \ell n\left|\frac{x}{x-1}\right| - \frac{1}{x-1} + C$$

7. $\dfrac{1}{x(x^2+4)} = \dfrac{A}{x} + \dfrac{Bx+C}{x^2+4} \Longrightarrow 1 = A(x^2+4) + x(Bx+C)$. Put $x = 0$ to find $A = 1/4$. Equate the coefficients of x^2, and of x, to find $0 = A + B$ (so $B = -1/4$) and $0 = C$. Hence

$$\int \frac{dx}{x(x^2+4)} = \frac{1}{4}\int\frac{dx}{x} - \frac{1}{4}\int \frac{x\,dx}{x^2+4} = \frac{1}{4}\ell n\,|x| - \frac{1}{8}\ell n(x^2+4) + C = \frac{1}{8}\ell n\left(\frac{x^2}{x^2+4}\right) + C$$

8. $\dfrac{1}{x^2(x^2+9)} = \dfrac{A}{x} + \dfrac{B}{x^2} + \dfrac{Cx+D}{x^2+9} \Longrightarrow 1 = Ax(x^2+9) + B(x^2+9) + x^2(Cx+D)$. Put $x = 0$ to find $B = 1/9$. Equate the coefficients of x, of x^2, and of x^3, to find $0 = 9A$ (so $A = 0$), $0 = B + D$ (so $D = -1/9$), $0 = A + C$ (so $C = 0$). Hence

$$\int \frac{dx}{x^2(x^2+9)} = \frac{1}{9}\int\frac{dx}{x^2} - \frac{1}{9}\int\frac{dx}{x^2+9} = \frac{-1}{9x} - \frac{1}{27}\tan^{-1}\frac{x}{3} + C$$

9. $\dfrac{1}{x^4-1} = \dfrac{1}{(x-1)(x+1)(x^2+1)} = \dfrac{A}{x-1} + \dfrac{B}{x+1} + \dfrac{Cx+D}{x^2+1} \Longrightarrow 1 = A(x+1)(x^2+1) +$ $B(x-1)(x^2+1) + (x^2-1)(Cx+D)$. Put $x = 1$ to find $A = 1/4$ and $x = -1$ to find $B = -1/4$. Equate the coefficients of x^0, and of x^3, to find $1 = A - B - D$ (so $D = -1/2$) and $0 = A + B + C$ (so $C = 0$). Hence

$$\int \frac{dx}{x^4-1} = \frac{1}{4}\int\frac{dx}{x-1} - \frac{1}{4}\int\frac{dx}{x+1} - \frac{1}{2}\int\frac{dx}{x^2+1} = \frac{1}{4}\ell n\,|x-1| - \frac{1}{4}\ell n\,|x+1| - \frac{1}{2}\tan^{-1}x + C$$

$$= \frac{1}{4}\ell n\left|\frac{x-1}{x+1}\right| - \frac{1}{2}\tan^{-1}x + C$$

10. $\dfrac{x^3}{(x^2+1)^2} = \dfrac{Ax+B}{x^2+1} + \dfrac{Cx+D}{(x^2+1)^2} \implies x^3 = (x^2+1)(Ax+B) + (Cx+D)$.   Equating

coefficients of each power of x, we have

$$x^3: 1 = A; \quad x^2: 0 = B; \quad x^1: 0 = A+C \text{ (so } C = -1\text{)}; \quad x^0: 0 = B+D \text{ (so } D = 0\text{)}$$

Hence $\displaystyle\int \dfrac{x^3\,dx}{(x^2+1)^2} = \int \dfrac{x\,dx}{x^2+1} - \int \dfrac{x\,dx}{(x^2+1)^2} = \tfrac{1}{2}\int\dfrac{du}{u} - \tfrac{1}{2}\int\dfrac{du}{u^2}$ $(u = x^2+1, \; du = 2x\,dx)$

$$= \tfrac{1}{2}\ell n\,|u| + \dfrac{1}{2u} + C = \tfrac{1}{2}\ell n\,(x^2+1) + \dfrac{1}{2(x^2+1)} + C$$

11. $\dfrac{1}{x^3-8} = \dfrac{1}{(x-2)(x^2+2x+4)} = \dfrac{A}{x-2} + \dfrac{Bx+C}{x^2+2x+4} \implies 1 = A(x^2+2x+4) +$

$(x-2)(Bx+C)$.   Put $x = 2$ to find $A = 1/12$.   Equate the coefficients of x^2,

and of x^0, to find $0 = A+B$ (so $B = -1/12$) and $1 = 4A - 2C$ (so $C = -1/3$). Hence

$$\int \dfrac{dx}{x^3-8} = \dfrac{1}{12}\int\dfrac{dx}{x-2} - \dfrac{1}{12}\int\dfrac{(x+4)dx}{x^2+2x+4}$$

The first integral is $\ell n\,|x-2|$.   To find the second, let $u = x^2+2x+4$, $du = (2x+2)dx$.   Since $x+4 = \tfrac{1}{2}(2x+2) + 3$, we have

$$\int\dfrac{(x+4)dx}{x^2+2x+4} = \tfrac{1}{2}\int\dfrac{(2x+2)dx}{x^2+2x+4} + 3\int\dfrac{dx}{x^2+2x+4} = \tfrac{1}{2}\int\dfrac{du}{u} + 3\int\dfrac{dx}{(x+1)^2+3}$$

$$= \tfrac{1}{2}\ell n\,|u| + \dfrac{3}{\sqrt{3}}\tan^{-1}\!\left(\dfrac{x+1}{\sqrt{3}}\right) \quad \text{(arbitrary constant omitted)}$$

$$= \tfrac{1}{2}\ell n\,(x^2+2x+4) + \sqrt{3}\tan^{-1}\!\left(\dfrac{x+1}{\sqrt{3}}\right)$$

Thus $\displaystyle\int\dfrac{dx}{x^3-8} = \dfrac{1}{12}\ell n\,|x-2| - \dfrac{1}{24}\ell n\,(x^2+2x+4) - \dfrac{\sqrt{3}}{12}\tan^{-1}\!\left(\dfrac{x+1}{\sqrt{3}}\right) + C$

$$= \dfrac{1}{24}\ell n\dfrac{(x-2)^2}{x^2+2x+4} - \dfrac{\sqrt{3}}{12}\tan^{-1}\!\left(\dfrac{x+1}{\sqrt{3}}\right) + C$$

12. $\dfrac{x}{x^2-x-2} = \dfrac{x}{(x-2)(x+1)} = \dfrac{A}{x-2} + \dfrac{B}{x+1} \implies x = A(x+1) + B(x-2)$.   Put $x = 2$

to find $A = 2/3$ and $x = -1$ to find $B = 1/3$.   Then

$$\int\dfrac{x\,dx}{x^2-x-2} = \dfrac{2}{3}\int\dfrac{dx}{x-2} + \dfrac{1}{3}\int\dfrac{dx}{x+1} = \dfrac{2}{3}\ell n\,|x-2| + \dfrac{1}{3}\ell n\,|x+1| \quad \text{(constant omitted)}$$

$$= \dfrac{1}{3}\ell n\,|(x-2)^2(x+1)|$$

Hence $\displaystyle\int_0^1 \dfrac{x\,dx}{x^2-x-2} = \dfrac{1}{3}(\ell n\,2 - \ell n\,4) = -\dfrac{1}{3}\ell n\,2$

13. $\dfrac{1}{x^3+x} = \dfrac{1}{x(x^2+1)} = \dfrac{A}{x} + \dfrac{Bx+C}{x^2+1} \implies 1 = A(x^2+1) + x(Bx+C)$.   Put $x = 0$ to find

$A = 1$.   Equate the coefficients of x^2, and of x, to find $0 = A+B$ (so $B = -1$)

and $0 = C$.   Then

$$\int\dfrac{dx}{x^3+x} = \int\dfrac{dx}{x} - \int\dfrac{x\,dx}{x^2+1} = \ell n\,|x| - \tfrac{1}{2}\ell n\,(x^2+1) = \tfrac{1}{2}\ell n\!\left(\dfrac{x^2}{x^2+1}\right) + C$$

$$\int_1^2 \frac{dx}{x^3 + x} = \frac{1}{2}(\ln\frac{4}{5} - \ln\frac{1}{2}) = \frac{1}{2}\ln\frac{8}{5}$$

14. $\dfrac{x}{(x-1)^2} = \dfrac{A}{x-1} + \dfrac{B}{(x-1)^2} \implies x = A(x-1) + B.$ Put $x = 1$ to find $B = 1.$

Equate the coefficients of x to find $1 = A.$ Then

$$\int \frac{x\,dx}{(x-1)^2} = \int \frac{dx}{x-1} + \int \frac{dx}{(x-1)^2} = \ln|x-1| - \frac{1}{x-1} + C$$

$$\int_2^3 \frac{x\,dx}{(x-1)^2} = \ln 2 - \ln 1 - \frac{1}{2} + 1 = \frac{1}{2} + \ln 2$$

15. $\dfrac{1}{x^3(x+2)} = \dfrac{A}{x} + \dfrac{B}{x^2} + \dfrac{C}{x^3} + \dfrac{D}{x+2} \implies 1 = Ax^2(x+2) + Bx(x+2) + C(x+2) + Dx^3.$ Put

$x = 0$ to find $C = 1/2$ and $x = -2$ to find $D = -1/8.$ Equate the coefficients of

x^3, and of x^2, to find $0 = A + D$ (so $A = 1/8$) and $0 = 2A + B$ (so $B = -1/4$). Then

$$\int \frac{dx}{x^3(x+2)} = \frac{1}{8}\int\frac{dx}{x} - \frac{1}{4}\int\frac{dx}{x^2} + \frac{1}{2}\int\frac{dx}{x^3} - \frac{1}{8}\int\frac{dx}{x+2} = \frac{1}{8}\ln|x| + \frac{1}{4x} - \frac{1}{4x^2} - \frac{1}{8}\ln|x+2| + C$$

$$= \frac{1}{8}\ln\left|\frac{x}{x+2}\right| + \frac{1}{4x} - \frac{1}{4x^2} + C$$

$$\int_1^2 \frac{dx}{x^3(x+2)} = (\frac{1}{8}\ln\frac{1}{2} + \frac{1}{8} - \frac{1}{16}) - (\frac{1}{8}\ln\frac{1}{3} + \frac{1}{4} - \frac{1}{4}) = \frac{1}{16} + \frac{1}{8}\ln\frac{3}{2}$$

16. $\dfrac{x^2}{16 - x^4} = \dfrac{x^2}{(2-x)(2+x)(4+x^2)} = \dfrac{A}{2-x} + \dfrac{B}{2+x} + \dfrac{Cx+D}{4+x^2} \implies x^2 = A(2+x)(4+x^2) +$

$B(2-x)(4+x^2) + (4-x^2)(Cx+D).$ Put $x = 2$ to find $A = 1/8$ and $x = -2$ to find

$B = 1/8.$ Equate the coefficients of x^3, and of x^0, to find $0 = A - B - C$ (so

$C = 0$) and $0 = 8A + 8B + 4D$ (so $D = -1/2$). Then

$$\int \frac{x^2\,dx}{16 - x^4} = \frac{1}{8}\int\frac{dx}{2-x} + \frac{1}{8}\int\frac{dx}{2+x} - \frac{1}{2}\int\frac{dx}{4+x^2} = -\frac{1}{8}\ln|2-x| + \frac{1}{8}\ln|2+x| - \frac{1}{4}\tan^{-1}\frac{x}{2}$$

$$= \frac{1}{8}\ln\left|\frac{2+x}{2-x}\right| - \frac{1}{4}\tan^{-1}\frac{x}{2} \quad \text{(arbitrary constant omitted)}$$

$$\int_0^1 \frac{x^2\,dx}{16 - x^4} = \frac{1}{8}\ln 3 - \frac{1}{4}\tan^{-1}\frac{1}{2}$$

17. $\dfrac{1}{x^3+1} = \dfrac{1}{(x+1)(x^2-x+1)} = \dfrac{A}{x+1} + \dfrac{Bx+C}{x^2-x+1} \implies 1 = A(x^2-x+1) +$

$(x+1)(Bx+C).$ Put $x = -1$ to find $A = 1/3.$ Equate the coefficients of x^2,

and of x^0, to find $0 = A + B$ (so $B = -1/3$) and $1 = A + C$ (so $C = 2/3$). Then

$$\int \frac{dx}{x^3+1} = \frac{1}{3}\int\frac{dx}{x+1} - \frac{1}{3}\int\frac{(x-2)dx}{x^2-x+1}$$

The first integral is $\ln|x+1|.$ To find the second, let $u = x^2 - x + 1,$ $du =$

$(2x-1)dx.$ Since $x - 2 = \frac{1}{2}(2x-1) - \frac{3}{2},$ we have

85

$$\int \frac{(x-2)dx}{x^2-x+1} = \frac{1}{2}\int\frac{(2x-1)dx}{x^2-x+1} - \frac{3}{2}\int\frac{dx}{x^2-x+1} = \frac{1}{2}\int\frac{du}{u} - \frac{3}{2}\int\frac{dx}{(x-1/2)^2+3/4}$$

$$= \frac{1}{2}\ell n\,|u| - \frac{3}{2}\cdot\frac{2}{\sqrt{3}}\tan^{-1}\!\left(\frac{x-1/2}{\sqrt{3}/2}\right) = \frac{1}{2}\ell n\,(x^2-x+1) - \sqrt{3}\tan^{-1}\!\left(\frac{2x-1}{\sqrt{3}}\right)$$

(arbitrary constant omitted). Hence

$$\int_0^1 \frac{dx}{x^3+1} = \left[\frac{1}{3}\ell n\,|x+1| - \frac{1}{6}\ell n\,(x^2-x+1) + \frac{\sqrt{3}}{3}\tan^{-1}\!\left(\frac{2x-1}{\sqrt{3}}\right)\right]\Big|_0^1$$

$$= \left(\frac{1}{3}\ell n\,2 + \frac{\sqrt{3}}{3}\tan^{-1}(1/\sqrt{3})\right) - \frac{\sqrt{3}}{3}\tan^{-1}(-1/\sqrt{3}) = \frac{1}{3}\ell n\,2 + \frac{2\sqrt{3}}{3}\tan^{-1}(1/\sqrt{3})$$

$$= \frac{1}{3}\ell n\,2 + \frac{2\sqrt{3}}{3}\cdot\frac{\pi}{6} = \frac{1}{3}\ell n\,2 + \frac{\pi\sqrt{3}}{9}$$

18.(a) $x^3+1 = A(x^2+1) + x(Bx+C)$. Put $x=0$ to find $A=1$. Equate the coefficients of x^2, and of x, to find $0 = A+B$ (so $B=-1$) and $0=C$. Thus the original supposition implies $A=1$, $B=-1$, $C=0$. (It also implies $1=0$, by equating the coefficients of x^3, so something is already wrong!)

(b) What went wrong is that the original integrand is not a proper fraction; division of x^3+1 by $x(x^2+1)$ is called for before any decomposition is attempted.

(c) Division of x^3+1 by x^3+x yields

$$\int \frac{x^3+1}{x(x^2+1)}\,dx = \int\left[1 - \frac{x-1}{x(x^2+1)}\right]dx = x - \int\frac{(x-1)dx}{x(x^2+1)}$$

To find the integral, write

$$\frac{x-1}{x(x^2+1)} = \frac{A}{x} + \frac{Bx+C}{x^2+1} \implies x-1 = A(x^2+1) + x(Bx+C)$$

Put $x=0$ to find $A=-1$. Equate the coefficients of x^2, and of x, to find $0 = A+B$ (so $B=1$) and $1=C$. Then

$$\int\frac{(x-1)dx}{x(x^2+1)} = -\int\frac{dx}{x} + \int\frac{(x+1)dx}{x^2+1} = -\ell n\,|x| + \int\frac{x\,dx}{x^2+1} + \int\frac{dx}{x^2+1}$$

$$= -\ell n\,|x| + \frac{1}{2}\ell n\,(x^2+1) + \tan^{-1}x + C = \frac{1}{2}\ell n\left(\frac{x^2+1}{x^2}\right) + \tan^{-1}x + C$$

Hence the original integral is

$$\int\frac{x^3+1}{x(x^2+1)}\,dx = x - \frac{1}{2}\ell n\left(\frac{x^2+1}{x^2}\right) - \tan^{-1}x + C \quad \text{(not the same C as above)}$$

19.(a) $1 = (x^2+1)(Ax+B) + (Cx+D)$. Equate coefficients:

x^3: $0=A$; x^2: $0=B$; x^1: $0 = A+C$ (so $C=0$); x^0: $1 = B+D$ (so $D=1$)

Thus $\dfrac{1}{(x^2+1)^2} = \dfrac{1}{(x^2+1)^2}$. (!) The integrand is already decomposed.

(b) Let $x = \tan t$, $dx = \sec^2t\,dt$, $x^2+1 = \sec^2t$. Then

$$\int\frac{dx}{(x^2+1)^2} = \int\frac{\sec^2t\,dt}{\sec^4t} = \int\cos^2t\,dt = \frac{1}{2}\int(1+\cos 2t)dt = \frac{1}{2}(t + \frac{1}{2}\sin 2t) + C$$

$$= \tfrac{1}{2}(t + \sin t \cos t) + C = \tfrac{1}{2}\left(\tan^{-1}x + \frac{x}{\sqrt{x^2+1}} \cdot \frac{1}{\sqrt{x^2+1}}\right) + C$$

$$= \tfrac{1}{2}\tan^{-1}x + \frac{x}{2(x^2+1)} + C$$

20. $\dfrac{1}{a^2 - x^2} = \dfrac{1}{(a-x)(a+x)} = \dfrac{A}{a-x} + \dfrac{B}{a+x} \Longrightarrow 1 = A(a+x) + B(a-x).$ Put $x = a$ to

find $A = 1/(2a)$ and $x = -a$ to find $B = 1/(2a)$. Then

$$\int \frac{dx}{a^2 - x^2} = \frac{1}{2a}\int \frac{dx}{a-x} + \frac{1}{2a}\int \frac{dx}{a+x} = -\frac{1}{2a}\ell n\,|a-x| + \frac{1}{2a}\ell n\,|a+x| + C$$

$$= \frac{1}{2a}\ell n\left|\frac{a+x}{a-x}\right| + C$$

21. $\dfrac{1}{x(ax+b)} = \dfrac{A}{x} + \dfrac{B}{ax+b} \Longrightarrow 1 = A(ax+b) + Bx.$ Put $x = 0$ to find $A = 1/b$ and

$x = -b/a$ to find $B = -a/b$. Then

$$\int \frac{dx}{x(ax+b)} = \frac{1}{b}\int \frac{dx}{x} - \frac{a}{b}\int \frac{dx}{ax+b} = \frac{1}{b}\ell n\,|x| - \frac{1}{b}\ell n\,|ax+b| + C = \frac{1}{b}\ell n\left|\frac{x}{ax+b}\right| + C$$

22. $\dfrac{1}{x^2(ax+b)} = \dfrac{A}{x} + \dfrac{B}{x^2} + \dfrac{C}{ax+b} \Longrightarrow 1 = Ax(ax+b) + B(ax+b) + Cx^2.$ Put $x = 0$ to

find $B = 1/b$ and $x = -b/a$ to find $C = a^2/b^2$. Equate the coefficients of x^2 to

find $0 = aA + C$ (so $A = -a/b^2$). Then

$$\int \frac{dx}{x^2(ax+b)} = -\frac{a}{b^2}\int \frac{dx}{x} + \frac{1}{b}\int \frac{dx}{x^2} + \frac{a^2}{b^2}\int \frac{dx}{ax+b} = -\frac{a}{b^2}\ell n\,|x| - \frac{1}{bx} + \frac{a}{b^2}\ell n\,|ax+b| + C$$

$$= -\frac{1}{bx} + \frac{a}{b^2}\ell n\left|\frac{ax+b}{x}\right| + C$$

23. (a) $\dfrac{dx}{dt} = k(a-x)(b-x) \Longrightarrow \dfrac{dx}{(a-x)(b-x)} = k\,dt.$ To integrate the left side,

write $\dfrac{1}{(a-x)(b-x)} = \dfrac{A}{a-x} + \dfrac{B}{b-x} \Longrightarrow 1 = A(b-x) + B(a-x).$ Put $x = a$ to find

$A = 1/(b-a)$ and $x = b$ to find $B = 1/(a-b)$. Then

$$\int \frac{dx}{(a-x)(b-x)} = \frac{1}{b-a}\int \frac{dx}{a-x} + \frac{1}{a-b}\int \frac{dx}{b-x} = \frac{1}{a-b}\ell n\,|a-x| - \frac{1}{a-b}\ell n\,|b-x|$$

$$= \frac{1}{a-b}\ell n\left|\frac{a-x}{b-x}\right| \quad \text{(arbitrary constant omitted)}$$

The original differential equation therefore leads to

$$\frac{1}{a-b}\ell n\left|\frac{a-x}{b-x}\right| = kt + C, \text{ or } \ell n\left|\frac{a-x}{b-x}\right| = (a-b)kt + C \quad \text{(new } C)$$

Since $x = 0$ when $t = 0$, we find $C = \ell n\,(a/b)$, and we note that the original

differential equation requires $x < a$ and $x < b$ (so the absolute value may be

dropped). Hence

$$\ell n\,\frac{b(a-x)}{a(b-x)} = (a-b)kt \Longrightarrow \frac{b(a-x)}{a(b-x)} = e^{(a-b)kt} \Longrightarrow \frac{a-x}{b-x} = \frac{a}{b}e^{(a-b)kt}$$

(b) If $a < b$, the exponential on the right side approaches 0 as $t \to \infty$, so the fraction on the left side also approaches 0, that is, $x \to a$. If $a > b$, take reciprocals of each side to conclude in the same way that $x \to b$. In any case x approaches the smaller of a and b.

(c) The equation becomes $\dfrac{3-x}{6-x} = \dfrac{1}{2}e^{-3kt}$. Since $x = 1$ when $t = 10$, we have $\dfrac{2}{5} = \dfrac{1}{2}e^{-30k} \Rightarrow \dfrac{5}{4} = e^{30k} \Rightarrow \ell n\,\dfrac{5}{4} = 30k \Rightarrow k = \dfrac{1}{30}\ell n\,1.25$. Hence

$$\frac{3-x}{6-x} = \frac{1}{2}e^{-0.1t\,\ell n\,1.25} \Longrightarrow \frac{6-x}{3-x} = 2e^{0.1t\,\ell n\,1.25} = 2(1.25)^{0.1t}$$

When $t = 20$ we have

$$\frac{6-x}{3-x} = 2(1.25)^2 = \frac{25}{8} \Longrightarrow 48 - 8x = 75 - 25x \Longrightarrow x = \frac{27}{17}\ \text{gm}$$

(d) If $a = b$, the original differential equation is

$$\frac{dx}{dt} = k(a-x)^2 \Longrightarrow \frac{dx}{(a-x)^2} = k\,dt \Longrightarrow \frac{1}{a-x} = kt + C = kt + \frac{1}{a}\ (x=0\ \text{at}\ t=0)$$

$$\Longrightarrow \frac{1}{a-x} = \frac{akt+1}{a} \Longrightarrow a - x = \frac{a}{akt+1}$$

$$\Longrightarrow x = a - \frac{a}{akt+1} = \frac{a^2kt}{akt+1}$$

24.(a) At the beginning of this section we used the Law of Inhibited Growth to find $\displaystyle\int \frac{dP}{P(10-P)} = kt + C$, or $\dfrac{1}{10}\ell n\,\dfrac{P}{10-P} = kt + C$. Since $P = 2$ when $t = 0$, we find $C = \dfrac{1}{10}\ell n\,\dfrac{1}{4}$, so $\dfrac{1}{10}\ell n\,\dfrac{4P}{10-P} = kt$. Since $P = 4$ when $t = 60$, we have $\dfrac{1}{10}\ell n\,\dfrac{8}{3} = 60k$, or $k = \dfrac{1}{600}\ell n\,\dfrac{8}{3}$. Solve for P:

$$\ell n\,\frac{4P}{10-P} = 10kt \Longrightarrow \frac{4P}{10-P} = e^{10kt} \Longrightarrow 4P = 10e^{10kt} - Pe^{10kt}$$

$$\Longrightarrow P(4 + e^{10kt}) = 10e^{10kt} \Longrightarrow P = \frac{10e^{10kt}}{4 + e^{10kt}} = \frac{10}{1 + 4e^{-10kt}}$$

This approaches 10 as $t \to \infty$.

(b) Put $P = 8$ in the equation $\dfrac{1}{10}\ell n\,\dfrac{4P}{10-P} = kt$ (where $k = \dfrac{1}{600}\ell n\,\dfrac{8}{3}$) to find $\dfrac{1}{10}\ell n\,16 = \dfrac{t}{600}\ell n\,\dfrac{8}{3} \Longrightarrow t = \dfrac{60\,\ell n\,16}{\ell n\,(8/3)} \approx 170$ years. Hence $P = 8$ in about the year 2090.

(c) Since the population doubled in 60 years, it will double again in 60 more years, so $P = 8$ in the year 2040.

25.(a) $\dfrac{dP}{dt} = kP(8-P) \Longrightarrow \dfrac{dP}{P(8-P)} = k\,dt$. To integrate the left side, write

$\dfrac{1}{P(8-P)} = \dfrac{A}{P} + \dfrac{B}{8-P} \implies 1 = A(8-P) + BP$.   Put $P = 0$ to find $A = 1/8$ and $P = 8$ to find $B = 1/8$.   Then

$$\int \frac{dP}{P(8-P)} = \frac{1}{8}\int \frac{dP}{P} + \frac{1}{8}\int \frac{dP}{8-P} = \frac{1}{8}\ln P - \frac{1}{8}\ln(8-P) = \frac{1}{8}\ln \frac{P}{8-P}$$

$$= kt + C = kt + \frac{1}{8}\ln \frac{1}{3} \quad \text{(because } P = 2 \text{ when } t = 0\text{)}$$

Hence $\dfrac{1}{8}\ln \dfrac{3P}{8-P} = kt$.   Since $P = 4$ when $t = 60$, we have $\dfrac{1}{8}\ln 3 = 60k$, or

$k = \dfrac{1}{480}\ln 3$.   Then $\ln \dfrac{3P}{8-P} = 8kt \implies \dfrac{3P}{8-P} = e^{8kt} \implies 3P = 8e^{8kt} - Pe^{8kt} \implies$

$P(3 + e^{8kt}) = 8e^{8kt} \implies P = \dfrac{8e^{8kt}}{3 + e^{8kt}} = \dfrac{8}{1 + 3e^{-8kt}}$.   This approaches 8 when $t \to \infty$.

(b) Since $k = \dfrac{1}{480}\ln 3$, we have $e^{-8kt} = e^{-(t/60)\ln 3} = 3^{-t/60}$.   Hence

$P = \dfrac{8}{1 + 3(3^{-t/60})} = \dfrac{8}{1 + 3^{1-(t/60)}}$.   When $P = 6$ we find $6 + 6 \cdot 3^{1-(t/60)} = 8 \implies$

$3^{1-(t/60)} = 3^{-1} \implies 1 - t/60 = -1 \implies t = 120$.   Hence $P = 6$ in the year 2040.

(c) $P = P_0 e^{ct} = 2e^{ct}$ (because $P = 2$ when $t = 0$).   Since $P = 4$ when $t = 60$,

we have $2 = e^{60c}$, or $e^c = 2^{1/60}$.   Hence $P = 2(2^{t/60})$.   When $P = 6$ we have

$3 = 2^{t/60} \implies \ln 3 = \dfrac{t}{60}\ln 2 \implies t = \dfrac{60\ln 3}{\ln 2} \approx 95$.   Hence $P = 6$ in about the

year 2015.

26.(a) $\dfrac{dP}{dt} = kP + aP^2 = P(k + aP) \implies \dfrac{dP}{P(k + aP)} = dt$.   Use Problem 21 to integrate

the left side: $\displaystyle\int \frac{dP}{P(k + aP)} = \frac{1}{k}\ln\left(\frac{P}{k + aP}\right) = t + C = t + \frac{1}{k}\ln\left(\frac{P_0}{k + aP_0}\right)$ (because $P = P_0$

when $t = 0$).   Hence

$$\frac{1}{k}\ln \frac{P(k + aP_0)}{P_0(k + aP)} = t \implies \frac{P(k + aP_0)}{P_0(k + aP)} = e^{kt} \implies kP + aP_0 P = kP_0 e^{kt} + aP_0 P e^{kt}$$

$$\implies P(k + aP_0 - aP_0 e^{kt}) = kP_0 e^{kt}$$

$$\implies P = \frac{kP_0 e^{kt}}{k + aP_0 - aP_0 e^{kt}} = \frac{k}{(a + k/P_0)e^{-kt} - a}$$

When $a = 0$ this becomes

$$P = \frac{k}{(k/P_0)e^{-kt}} = P_0 e^{kt}$$

which is correct because the original differential equation is $dP/dt = kP$.

(b) Since $e^{-kt} \to 0$ when $t \to \infty$, there is a time when the denominator in the formula for P is 0. We cannot allow t to reach that value.

(c) The denominator is 0 when $(a + k/P_0)e^{-kt} = a \implies 1 + k/(aP_0) = e^{kt} \implies$ $\ln(1 + k/(aP_0)) = kt \implies t = \frac{1}{k}\ln(1 + k/(aP_0))$. When t approaches this value, $P \to \infty$.

27. Using the data in Problem 39, Sec. 10.2, we have

$$\frac{dx}{1 + \sin x - \cos x} = \frac{1}{1 + 2u/(1+u^2) - (1-u^2)/(1+u^2)} \cdot \frac{2\,du}{1+u^2}$$

$$= \frac{2\,du}{(1+u^2) + 2u - (1-u^2)} = \frac{du}{u(u+1)}$$

Hence $\displaystyle\int \frac{dx}{1 + \sin x - \cos x} = \int \frac{du}{u(u+1)} = \ln\left|\frac{u}{u+1}\right| + C$ (by Problem 21)

$$= \ln\left|\frac{\tan\frac{1}{2}x}{1 + \tan\frac{1}{2}x}\right| + C \quad \text{(because } u = \tan\frac{1}{2}x\text{)}$$

Section 10.4   MISCELLANEOUS INTEGRATION PROBLEMS

1. Let $u = \sqrt{4 - x}$. Then $u^2 = 4 - x$ and $2u\,du = -dx$, so

$$\int_1^3 \frac{dx}{x\sqrt{4-x}} = \int_{\sqrt{3}}^1 \frac{-2u\,du}{(4-u^2)(u)} = 2\int_1^{\sqrt{3}} \frac{du}{4-u^2} = \frac{1}{2}\ln\left(\frac{2+u}{2-u}\right)\Big|_1^{\sqrt{3}}$$

$$= \frac{1}{2}\ln\left(\frac{2+\sqrt{3}}{2-\sqrt{3}}\right) - \frac{1}{2}\ln 3 = \frac{1}{2}\ln\frac{(2+\sqrt{3})^2}{4-3} - \frac{1}{2}\ln 3$$

$$= \frac{1}{2}\ln(7 + 4\sqrt{3}) - \frac{1}{2}\ln 3 = \frac{1}{2}\ln\left(\frac{7+4\sqrt{3}}{3}\right)$$

2. $\displaystyle\int \frac{dx}{x^2 + 8x + 20} = \int \frac{dx}{(x+4)^2 + 4} = \frac{1}{2}\tan^{-1}\left(\frac{x+4}{2}\right) + C$

3. Let $t = \sqrt{x}$. Then $t^2 = x$ and $2t\,dt = dx$, so

$$\int \sin\sqrt{x}\,dx = \int \sin t\,(2t\,dt) = \int 2t \sin t\,dt$$

Now use integration by parts, with $u = 2t$, $dv = \sin t\,dt$. Then $du = 2\,dt$ and $v = -\cos t$, so

$$\int \sin\sqrt{x}\,dx = -2t\cos t + 2\int \cos t\,dt = -2t\cos t + 2\sin t + C$$

$$= 2\sin\sqrt{x} - 2\sqrt{x}\cos\sqrt{x} + C$$

4. $\displaystyle\int_0^1 \frac{e^x dx}{e^{2x} + 1} = \int_1^e \frac{du}{u^2 + 1} \quad (u = e^x,\ du = e^x dx)$

$$= \tan^{-1}u\Big|_1^e = \tan^{-1}e - \pi/4$$

5. $\displaystyle\int_0^{\pi/6} \frac{\sin x \cos x\, dx}{1 - \sin x} = \int_0^{\frac{1}{2}} \frac{u\, du}{1 - u}$ ($u = \sin x$, $du = \cos x\, dx$)

$$= \int_0^{\frac{1}{2}}\left(\frac{1}{1-u} - 1\right)du \quad \text{(division of } u \text{ by } 1 - u)$$

$$= \left[-\ell n\,(1 - u) - u\right]\Big|_0^{\frac{1}{2}} = -\ell n\,\tfrac{1}{2} - \tfrac{1}{2} = \ell n\,2 - \tfrac{1}{2}$$

6. Use integration by parts, with $u = \tan^{-1}x$, $dv = x^2 dx$. Then $du = dx/(1+x^2)$ and $v = x^3/3$, so

$$\int x^2 \tan^{-1}x\, dx = \tfrac{1}{3}x^3 \tan^{-1}x - \tfrac{1}{x}\int \frac{x^3 dx}{1 + x^2} = \tfrac{1}{3}x^3 \tan^{-1}x - \tfrac{1}{3}\int\left(x - \frac{x}{x^2 + 1}\right)dx$$

$$= \tfrac{1}{3}x^3 \tan^{-1}x - \tfrac{1}{6}x^2 + \tfrac{1}{6}\ell n\,(x^2 + 1) + C$$

7. $\dfrac{1}{x^2 - 2x} = \dfrac{1}{x(x - 2)} = \dfrac{A}{x} + \dfrac{B}{x - 2} \implies 1 = A(x - 2) + Bx$. Put $x = 0$ to find $A = -1/2$ and $x = 2$ to find $B = 1/2$. Then

$$\int \frac{dx}{x^2 - 2x} = -\tfrac{1}{2}\int\frac{dx}{x} + \tfrac{1}{2}\int\frac{dx}{x - 2} = -\tfrac{1}{2}\ell n\,|x| + \tfrac{1}{2}\ell n\,|x - 2| + C = \tfrac{1}{2}\ell n\left|\frac{x - 2}{x}\right| + C$$

An alternative solution is to use Problem 21, Sec. 10.3, to write

$$\int \frac{dx}{x(x - 2)} = -\tfrac{1}{2}\ell n\left|\frac{x}{x - 2}\right| + C = \tfrac{1}{2}\ell n\left|\frac{x - 2}{x}\right| + C$$

8. Let $x = a\sin t$, $dx = a\cos t\, dt$, $(a^2 - x^2)^{3/2} = a^3\cos^3 t$ $(-\pi/2 \le t \le \pi/2)$.

Then $\displaystyle\int \frac{dx}{(a^2 - x^2)^{3/2}} = \int \frac{a\cos t\, dt}{a^3\cos^3 t} = \frac{1}{a^2}\int\sec^2 t\, dt = \frac{1}{a^2}\tan t + C = \frac{x}{a^2\sqrt{a^2 - x^2}} + C$

9. Let $x = \tan t$, $dx = \sec^2 t\, dt$, $(x^2 + 1)^3 = \sec^6 t$. Then

$$\int_0^1 \frac{x^2 dx}{(x^2 + 1)^3} = \int_0^{\pi/4}\frac{\tan^2 t \sec^2 t\, dt}{\sec^6 t} = \int_0^{\pi/4}\sin^2 t \cos^2 t\, dt = \tfrac{1}{4}\int_0^{\pi/4}\sin^2 2t\, dt$$

$$= \tfrac{1}{8}\int_0^{\pi/4}(1 - \cos 4t)dt = \tfrac{1}{8}\left(t - \tfrac{1}{4}\sin 4t\right)\Big|_0^{\pi/4} = \frac{\pi}{32}$$

10. $\displaystyle\int_0^{\pi/4}\frac{\tan^2 x + 1}{\tan x + 1}dx = \int_0^{\pi/4}\frac{\sec^2 x\, dx}{\tan x + 1} = \int_1^2 \frac{du}{u}$ ($u = \tan x + 1$, $du = \sec^2 x\, dx$)

$$= \ell n\,2$$

11. Use the substitution $x = 2\tan^{-1}u$ in Example 4 to write

$$\frac{dx}{1 + \sin x} = \frac{1}{1 + 2u/(1 + u^2)}\cdot\frac{2\, du}{1 + u^2} = \frac{2\, du}{(1 + u^2) + 2u} = \frac{2\, du}{(u + 1)^2}$$

Then $\displaystyle\int_0^{\pi/2}\frac{dx}{1 + \sin x} = 2\int_0^1\frac{du}{(u + 1)^2} = \frac{-2}{u + 1}\Big|_0^1 = 1$

12. $\dfrac{x^2}{(x - 1)^3} = \dfrac{A}{x - 1} + \dfrac{B}{(x - 1)^2} + \dfrac{C}{(x - 1)^3} \implies x^2 = A(x - 1)^2 + B(x - 1) + C$. Put $x = 1$

to find C = 1. Equate the coefficients of x^2, and of x^0, to find 1 = A and

0 = A - B + C (so B = 2). Then

$$\int \frac{x^2 dx}{(x-1)^3} = \int \frac{dx}{x-1} + 2\int \frac{dx}{(x-1)^2} + \int \frac{dx}{(x-1)^3} = \ell n \,|x-1| - \frac{2}{x-1} - \frac{1}{2(x-1)^2} + C$$

13. Divide $x^4 + 1$ by $x^4 - 1$ to find

$$\int \frac{x^4+1}{x^4-1}dx = \int \left(1 + \frac{2}{x^4-1}\right)dx = x + 2\int \frac{dx}{x^4-1}$$

Then write

$$\frac{1}{x^4-1} = \frac{1}{(x-1)(x+1)(x^2+1)} = \frac{A}{x-1} + \frac{B}{x+1} + \frac{Cx+D}{x^2+1} \implies 1 = A(x+1)(x^2+1) +$$

$B(x-1)(x^2+1) + (x^2-1)(Cx+D)$. Put x = 1 to find A = 1/4 and x = -1 to find

B = -1/4. Equate the coefficients of x^3, and of x^0, to find 0 = A + B + C (so

C = 0) and 1 = A - B - D (so D = -1/2). Then

$$\int \frac{x^4+1}{x^4-1}dx = x + \tfrac{1}{2}\int \frac{dx}{x-1} - \tfrac{1}{2}\int \frac{dx}{x+1} - \int \frac{dx}{x^2+1}$$

$$= x + \tfrac{1}{2}\ell n\,|x-1| - \tfrac{1}{2}\ell n\,|x+1| - \tan^{-1}x + C = x + \tfrac{1}{2}\ell n\left|\frac{x-1}{x+1}\right| - \tan^{-1}x + C$$

14. Use the substitution $x = 2\tan^{-1}u$ in Example 4 to write

$$\frac{dx}{1+\sec x} = \frac{1}{1+(1+u^2)/(1-u^2)} \cdot \frac{2\,du}{1+u^2} = \frac{2(1-u^2)du}{(1-u^2+1+u^2)(1+u^2)}$$

$$= \frac{(1-u^2)du}{1+u^2} = \left(\frac{2}{u^2+1} - 1\right)du \quad \text{(by division)}$$

Hence $\int \dfrac{dx}{1+\sec x} = \int\left(\dfrac{2}{u^2+1} - 1\right)du = 2\tan^{-1}u - u + C = x - \tan\dfrac{x}{2} + C$

15. Since $4x - x^2 = -(x^2 - 4x + 4) + 4 = 4 - (x-2)^2$, we have

$$\int_0^1 \sqrt{4x-x^2}\,dx = \int_0^1 \sqrt{4-(x-2)^2}\,dx = \int_{-2}^{-1} \sqrt{4-u^2}\,du \quad (u = x-2,\ du = dx)$$

$$= \int_1^2 \sqrt{4-v^2}\,dv \quad (v = -u,\ dv = -du)$$

$$= \left(\tfrac{1}{2}v\sqrt{4-v^2} + 2\sin^{-1}\tfrac{v}{2}\right)\Big|_1^2 \quad \text{(Example 1, Sec. 10.2)}$$

$$= \left(0 + 2\cdot\tfrac{\pi}{2}\right) - \left(\tfrac{1}{2}\sqrt{3} + 2\cdot\tfrac{\pi}{6}\right) = \frac{2\pi}{3} - \frac{\sqrt{3}}{2}$$

16. $\displaystyle\int_0^{\pi/4} \sec^4 x\,dx = \int_0^{\pi/4}\sec^2 x\sec^2 x\,dx = \int_0^{\pi/4}(\tan^2 x + 1)\sec^2 x\,dx$

$$= \left(\tfrac{1}{3}\tan^3 x + \tan x\right)\Big|_0^{\pi/4} = \frac{1}{3} + 1 = \frac{4}{3}$$

17. Use the formula for repeated integration by parts (Sec. 10.1) to obtain

$$\int (x^3+1)e^x dx = (x^3+1)(e^x) - (3x^2)(e^x) + (6x)(e^x) - (6)(e^x) + C$$

$$= e^x(x^3 - 3x^2 + 6x - 5) + C$$

18. Use integration by parts, with $u = x$, $dv = \sec x \tan x \, dx$. Then $du = dx$ and $v = \sec x$, so

$$\int x \sec x \tan x \, dx = x \sec x - \int \sec x \, dx = x \sec x - \ln |\sec x + \tan x| + C$$

19. Let $u = \sqrt{x^2 + 1}$, $u^2 = x^2 + 1$, $2u\,du = 2x\,dx$, and $u\,du = x\,dx$. Then

$$\int_0^1 x^3 \sqrt{x^2 + 1} \, dx = \int_1^{\sqrt{2}} (u^2 - 1)(u)(u\,du) = \int_1^{\sqrt{2}} (u^4 - u^2)du = \left(\frac{u^5}{5} - \frac{u^3}{3}\right)\Big|_1^{\sqrt{2}}$$

$$= \frac{u^3}{15}(3u^2 - 5)\Big|_1^{\sqrt{2}} = \frac{2\sqrt{2}}{15}(1) - \frac{1}{15}(-2) = \frac{2}{15}(1 + \sqrt{2})$$

20. Let $u = \sqrt[3]{x}$, $u^3 = x$, $3u^2 du = dx$. Then

$$\int_0^1 \frac{dx}{2 - \sqrt[3]{x}} = \int_0^1 \frac{3u^2 du}{2 - u} = 3\int_0^1 \left[\frac{4}{2 - u} - (u + 2)\right] du \quad \text{(by division)}$$

$$= 3\left[-4\ln(2 - u) - \frac{1}{2}(u + 2)^2\right]\Big|_0^1 = 12\ln 2 - 15/2$$

Section 10.5   NUMERICAL INTEGRATION

1.(a) The partition is $\{1, 5/4, 3/2, 7/4, 2\}$, with $\Delta x = 1/4$. Hence

$$\int_1^2 \frac{dx}{x} \approx \frac{1}{4}\left(\frac{1}{2} + \frac{4}{5} + \frac{2}{3} + \frac{4}{7} + \frac{1}{4}\right) \approx 0.697024$$

(b) $\int_1^2 \frac{dx}{x} \approx \frac{1}{12}\left(1 + \frac{16}{5} + \frac{4}{3} + \frac{16}{7} + \frac{1}{2}\right) \approx 0.693254$

The true value is $\ln 2 \approx 0.693147$.

2.(a) The partition is $\{0, 1/6, 1/3, 1/2, 2/3, 5/6, 1\}$, with $\Delta x = 1/6$. Hence

$$\int_0^1 e^x dx \approx \frac{1}{6}\left(\frac{1}{2} + e^{1/6} + e^{1/3} + e^{1/2} + e^{2/3} + e^{5/6} + \frac{1}{2}e\right) \approx 1.722257$$

(b) $\int_0^1 e^x dx \approx \frac{1}{18}\left(1 + 4e^{1/6} + 2e^{1/3} + 4e^{1/2} + 2e^{2/3} + 4e^{5/6} + e\right) \approx 1.718289$

The true value is $e - 1 \approx 1.718282$.

3.(a) The partition is $\{0, \pi/6, \pi/3, \pi/2, 2\pi/3, 5\pi/6, \pi\}$, with $\Delta x = \pi/6$. Hence

$$\int_0^\pi \sin x \, dx \approx \frac{\pi}{6}\left(0 + \frac{1}{2} + \frac{\sqrt{3}}{2} + 1 + \frac{\sqrt{3}}{2} + \frac{1}{2} + 0\right) \approx 1.954097$$

(b) $\int_0^\pi \sin x \, dx \approx \frac{\pi}{18}\left(0 + 2 + \sqrt{3} + 4 + \sqrt{3} + 2 + 0\right) \approx 2.000863$

The true value is $-\cos x \Big|_0^\pi = 2$.

4.(a) The partition is $\{0, 0.25, 0.5, 0.75, 1\}$, with $\Delta x = 0.25$. Hence

$$\int_0^1 \frac{dx}{1+x^2} \approx 0.25\left(0.5 + \frac{1}{1+0.25^2} + \frac{1}{1+0.5^2} + \frac{1}{1+0.75^2} + 0.25\right) \approx 0.782794$$

(b) $\displaystyle\int_0^1 \frac{dx}{1+x^2} \approx \frac{0.25}{3}\left(1 + \frac{4}{1+0.25^2} + \frac{2}{1+0.5^2} + \frac{4}{1+0.75^2} + 0.5\right) \approx 0.785392$

The true value is $\tan^{-1} 1 = \pi/4 \approx 0.785398$.

5.(a) The partition is the same as in Problem 4.   Hence

$$\int_0^1 \sqrt{1-x^2}\, dx \approx 0.25\left(0.5 + \sqrt{1-0.25^2} + \sqrt{1-0.5^2} + \sqrt{1-0.75^2} + 0\right) \approx 0.748927$$

(b) $\displaystyle\int_0^1 \sqrt{1-x^2}\, dx \approx \frac{0.25}{3}\left(1 + 4\sqrt{1-0.25^2} + 2\sqrt{1-0.5^2} + 4\sqrt{1-0.75^2} + 0\right) \approx 0.770899$

The true value is the first-quadrant area of the unit circle, $\pi/4 \approx 0.785398$.

6.(a) The partition is $\{0, \pi/4, \pi/2, 3\pi/4, \pi\}$, with $\Delta x = \pi/4$. Since $(\sin x)/x \to 1$ when $x \to 0$, we take the value of the integrand to be 1 at $x = 0$. (This choice is arbitrary, making no difference in the value of the integral itself. But it affects our approximations, so of course we choose to make the integrand continuous.)   Thus

$$\int_0^1 \frac{\sin x}{x}\, dx \approx \frac{\pi}{4}\left(\frac{1}{2} + \frac{1}{\sqrt{2}}\cdot\frac{4}{\pi} + \frac{2}{\pi} + \frac{1}{\sqrt{2}}\cdot\frac{4}{3\pi} + 0\right) \approx 1.835508$$

(b) $\displaystyle\int_0^1 \frac{\sin x}{x}\, dx \approx \frac{\pi}{12}\left(1 + \frac{16}{\pi\sqrt{2}} + \frac{4}{\pi} + \frac{16}{3\pi\sqrt{2}} + 0\right) \approx 1.852211$

7.(a) The partition is the same as in Problem 4.   Hence

$$\int_0^1 \sqrt{1+x^4}\, dx \approx 0.25\left(0.5 + \sqrt{1+0.25^4} + \sqrt{1+0.5^4} + \sqrt{1+0.75^4} + 0.5\sqrt{2}\right) \approx 1.096795$$

(b) $\displaystyle\int_0^1 \sqrt{1+x^4}\, dx \approx \frac{0.25}{3}\left(1 + 4\sqrt{1+0.25^4} + 2\sqrt{1+0.5^4} + 4\sqrt{1+0.75^4} + \sqrt{2}\right) \approx 1.089413$

8.(a) The partition is $\{0, 0.5, 1, 1.5, 2\}$, with $\Delta x = 0.5$.   Hence

$$\int_0^2 e^{-x^2}\, dx \approx 0.5\left(0.5 + e^{-0.5^2} + e^{-1} + e^{-1.5^2} + 0.5e^{-4}\right) \approx 0.880619$$

(b) $\displaystyle\int_0^2 e^{-x^2}\, dx \approx \frac{0.5}{3}\left(1 + 4e^{-0.5^2} + 2e^{-1} + 4e^{-1.5^2} + e^{-4}\right) \approx 0.881812$

9.(a) If $f(x) = 1/x$, then $f'(x) = -x^{-2}$ and $f''(x) = 2x^{-3} = 2/x^3$. The maximum value of $|f''(x)|$ in $[1,2]$ is $M = 2$, so $E_n \leq \frac{1}{12}(2-1)(2)(\frac{1}{4})^2 < 0.02$. Thus the answer in Problem 1(a) should be rounded to 0.7.

(b) $f'''(x) = -6x^{-4}$ and $f^{(4)}(x) = 24x^{-5} = 24/x^5$. The maximum value of $|f^{(4)}(x)|$ in $[1,2]$ is $N = 24$, so $E_n \leq \frac{1}{180}(2-1)(24)(\frac{1}{4})^4 < 0.0006$. The answer in Problem 1(b) should be rounded to 0.69.

10.(a) If $f(x) = e^x$, then $f''(x) = e^x$, with upper bound $M = e$ in $[0,1]$. Hence $E_n \leq \frac{1}{12}(1 - 0)(e)(\frac{1}{6})^2 < 0.007$. The answer in Problem 2(a) should be rounded to 1.7.

  (b) $f^{(4)}(x) = e^x$, with upper bound $N = e$ in $[0,1]$. Hence $E_n \leq \frac{1}{180}(1 - 0)(e)(\frac{1}{6})^4 < 0.00002$. The answer in Problem 2(b) should be rounded to 1.7183.

11.(a) If $f(x) = \sin x$, then $f'(x) = \cos x$ and $f''(x) = -\sin x$. The maximum value of $|f''(x)|$ in $[0,\pi]$ is $M = 1$, so $E_n \leq \frac{1}{12}(\pi - 0)(1)(\frac{\pi}{6})^2 < 0.08$. This does not guarantee even one-place accuracy, so the best we can do with the answer in Problem 3(a) is to report it as somewhere between 1.87 and 2.04.

  (b) $f'''(x) = -\cos x$ and $f^{(4)}(x) = \sin x$, so we may take $N = 1$. Then $E_n \leq \frac{1}{180}(\pi - 0)(1)(\frac{\pi}{6})^4 < 0.002$. The answer in Problem 3(b) should be rounded to 2.00.

12. From Problem 4(b) we have $\int_0^1 \frac{dx}{1 + x^2} = \tan^{-1} x \Big|_0^1 = \frac{\pi}{4} \approx 0.785392$. Hence $\pi \approx 3.141568$. The actual value is $\pi = 3.141592\cdots$, so we have four-place accuracy.

13.(a) The area is $A = \int_0^{12} f(x)dx$, where $f(x)$ is the width at x. The partition is $\{0, 2, 4, \ldots, 12\}$, with $\Delta x = 2$. Hence $A \approx 2(0 + 3 + 4 + 7 + 6 + 5 + 0) = 50$ in^2.

  (b) $A \approx \frac{2}{3}(0 + 12 + 8 + 28 + 12 + 20 + 0) = 53\frac{1}{3}$ in^2.

14.(a) The distance traveled is $D = \int_0^4 v(t)dt$, where $v(t)$ is the velocity at time t. The partition is $\{0, 1, 2, 3, 4\}$, with $\Delta t = 1$. Hence $D \approx 1.3 + 3.0 + 3.2 + 4.0 + 2.2 = 13.7$ m/sec.

  (b) $D \approx \frac{1}{3}(2.6 + 12 + 6.4 + 16 + 4.4) = 13.8$ m/sec.

15.(a) The work is $W = \int_0^2 F(x)dx$, where $F(x)$ is the force at x. The partition is $\{0, 0.5, 1, 1.5, 2\}$, with $\Delta x = 0.5$. Hence $W \approx 0.5(7.5 + 18 + 20 + 16 + 9) = 35.25$.

  (b) $W \approx \frac{0.5}{3}(15 + 72 + 40 + 64 + 18) \approx 34.833$.

16. $y' = \cos x$, $1 + y'^2 = 1 + \cos^2 x$, so $s = \int_0^\pi \sqrt{1 + \cos^2 x}\, dx \approx \frac{\pi}{12}(\sqrt{2} + 4\sqrt{1.5} + 2 + 4\sqrt{1.5} + \sqrt{2}) \approx 3.83$.

17.(a) If $f(x) = 1/x$, then $f''(x) = 2/x^3$, with upper bound $M = 2$ in $[1,2]$. If a partition with n subintervals is used, then $\Delta x = 1/n$ and

$$E_n \leq \frac{1}{12}(2-1)(2)(\frac{1}{n})^2 = \frac{1}{6n^2}$$

To guarantee five-place accuracy, we choose n satisfying

$$\frac{1}{6n^2} < \frac{1}{2} \times 10^{-5} \implies 6n^2 > 2 \times 10^5 \implies n^2 > \frac{1}{3} \times 10^5 = \frac{1}{30} \times 10^6$$

$$\implies n > \frac{10^3}{\sqrt{30}} \approx 182.6$$

Hence n should be at least 183.

(b) $f^{(4)}(x) = 24/x^5$, with upper bound $N = 24$ in $[1,2]$. Hence

$$E_n \leq \frac{1}{180}(2-1)(24)(\frac{1}{n})^4 = \frac{2}{15n^4} < \frac{1}{2} \times 10^{-5} \implies \frac{15n^4}{2} > 2 \times 10^5$$

$$\implies n^4 > \frac{4}{15} \times 10^5 = \frac{8}{3} \times 10^4 \implies n > \sqrt[4]{8/3} \times 10 \approx 12.8$$

Hence n should be at least 14 (because it must be even).

18. The area under $y = f(x)$, $a \leq x \leq b$, is estimated by trapezoids as shown in Figure 1 of the text, except that the curve is concave up because $f''(x) > 0$. Hence each trapezoid overestimates the area corresponding to the typical subinterval. If $f''(x) < 0$, then each trapezoid underestimates the area (as indicated in Figure 1).

19. $E_n = 0$ because $f^{(4)}(x) = 0$ for all x.

20. (a) $\displaystyle\int_r^s p(x)dx = \int_r^s (Ax^2 + Bx + C)dx = (\frac{1}{3}Ax^3 + \frac{1}{2}Bx^2 + Cx)\Big|_r^s = \frac{x}{6}(2Ax^2 + 3Bx + 6C)\Big|_r^s$

$$= \frac{s}{6}(2As^2 + 3Bs + 6C) - \frac{r}{6}(2Ar^2 + 3Br + 6C)$$

$$= \frac{1}{6}[2A(s^3 - r^3) + 3B(s^2 - r^2) + 6C(s-r)]$$

$$= \frac{1}{6}(s-r)[2A(s^2 + sr + r^2) + 3B(s+r) + 6C]$$

(b) $y_0 + 4y_1 + y_2 = p(x_0) + 4p(x_1) + p(x_2) = (Ar^2 + Br + C) + 4[A \cdot \frac{1}{4}(r+s)^2 +$

$B \cdot \frac{1}{2}(r+s) + C] + (As^2 + Bs + C) = A(r^2 + r^2 + 2rs + s^2 + s^2) + B(r + 2r + 2s + s) + 6C =$

$2A(s^2 + rs + r^2) + 3B(s+r) + 6C$

(c) $\displaystyle\int_r^s p(x)dx = \frac{1}{6}(s-r)(y_0 + 4y_1 + y_2) = \frac{1}{6}(2\Delta x)(y_0 + 4y_1 + y_2)$

$$= \frac{1}{3}\Delta x(y_0 + 4y_1 + y_2)$$

Chapter 10   ADDITIONAL PROBLEMS

1. $\displaystyle\int_0^{\pi/4} \sec^2 x \tan^2 x \, dx = \frac{1}{3}\tan^3 x \Big|_0^{\pi/4} = \frac{1}{3}$

2. $\int_3^5 \frac{dx}{x^2 - 6x + 13} = \int_3^5 \frac{dx}{(x-3)^2 + 4} = \frac{1}{2} \tan^{-1}\left(\frac{x-3}{2}\right)\Big|_3^5 = \frac{1}{2}\left(\frac{\pi}{4} - 0\right) = \frac{\pi}{8}$

3. Since $15 + 2x - x^2 = -(x^2 - 2x + 1) + 16 = 16 - (x-1)^2$,

$$\int \frac{dx}{\sqrt{15 + 2x - x^2}} = \int \frac{dx}{\sqrt{16 - (x-1)^2}} = \sin^{-1}\left(\frac{x-1}{4}\right) + C$$

4. $\int_0^1 \frac{x^2 dx}{x+1} = \int_0^1 \left(x - 1 + \frac{1}{x+1}\right) dx$ (by division)

$$= \left[\frac{1}{2}(x-1)^2 + \ln(x+1)\right]\Big|_0^1 = \ln 2 - \frac{1}{2}$$

5. Let $u = \sqrt{x}$, $u^2 = x$, $2u\,du = dx$. Then

$$\int_1^4 \frac{dx}{x + 2\sqrt{x}} = \int_1^2 \frac{2u\,du}{u^2 + 2u} = 2\int_1^2 \frac{du}{u+2} = 2\ln(u+2)\Big|_1^2 = 2(\ln 4 - \ln 3) = 2\ln \frac{4}{3}$$

6. Use integration by parts, with $u = \ln x$, $dv = x\,dx$. Then $du = dx/x$ and $v = \frac{1}{2}x^2$, so

$$\int x \ln x\,dx = \frac{1}{2}x^2 \ln x - \frac{1}{2}\int x\,dx = \frac{1}{2}x^2 \ln x - \frac{1}{4}x^2 = \frac{1}{4}x^2(2\ln x - 1) + C$$

$$\int_1^2 x \ln x\,dx = (2\ln 2 - 1) - \frac{1}{4}(-1) = 2\ln 2 - \frac{3}{4}$$

7. Use the formula for repeated integration by parts in Sec. 10.1 to obtain

$$\int x^3 \cosh x\,dx = (x^3)(\sinh x) - (3x^2)(\cosh x) + (6x)(\sinh x) - (6)(\cosh x) + C$$
$$= x(x^2 + 6)\sinh x - 3(x^2 + 2)\cosh x + C$$

$$\int_0^1 x^3 \cosh x\,dx = (7\sinh 1 - 9\cosh 1) - (-6\cosh 0) = 7\sinh 1 - 9\cosh 1 + 6$$

8. Let $x = 4\sin t$, $dx = 4\cos t\,dt$, $\sqrt{16 - x^2} = 4\cos t$ $(-\pi/2 \le t \le \pi/2)$. Then

$$\int_0^2 \frac{x^2 dx}{\sqrt{16 - x^2}} = \int_0^{\pi/6} \frac{16\sin^2 t \cdot 4\cos t\,dt}{4\cos t} = 16\int_0^{\pi/6} \sin^2 t\,dt = 8\int_0^{\pi/6}(1 - \cos 2t)dt$$

$$= 8\left(t - \frac{1}{2}\sin 2t\right)\Big|_0^{\pi/6} = 8\left(\frac{\pi}{6} - \frac{\sqrt{3}}{4}\right) = \frac{2}{3}(2\pi - 3\sqrt{3})$$

9. Use the data in Example 4, Sec. 10.4, to write

$$\frac{dx}{2 + \sin x} = \frac{1}{2 + 2u/(1 + u^2)} \cdot \frac{2\,du}{1 + u^2} = \frac{2\,du}{2(1 + u^2) + 2u} = \frac{du}{u^2 + u + 1} = \frac{du}{(u + 1/2)^2 + 3/4}$$

$$\int_0^{\pi/2} \frac{dx}{2 + \sin x} = \int_0^1 \frac{du}{(u + 1/2)^2 + 3/4} = \frac{2}{\sqrt{3}} \tan^{-1}\left(\frac{u + 1/2}{\sqrt{3}/2}\right)\Big|_0^1 = \frac{2}{\sqrt{3}} \tan^{-1}\left(\frac{2u + 1}{\sqrt{3}}\right)\Big|_0^1$$

$$= \frac{2}{\sqrt{3}}\left(\frac{\pi}{3} - \frac{\pi}{6}\right) = \frac{\pi}{3\sqrt{3}} = \frac{\pi\sqrt{3}}{9}$$

10. $\frac{x^2 - 2}{x^3 - x^2} = \frac{x^2 - 2}{x^2(x-1)} = \frac{A}{x} + \frac{B}{x^2} + \frac{C}{x-1} \Rightarrow x^2 - 2 = Ax(x-1) + B(x-1) + Cx^2$. Put $x = 0$ to find $B = 2$ and $x = 1$ to find $C = -1$. Equate the coefficients of x^2 to find $1 = A + C$ (so $A = 2$). Then

$$\int \frac{x^2 - 2}{x^3 - x^2}\,dx = 2\int \frac{dx}{x} + 2\int \frac{dx}{x^2} - \int \frac{dx}{x-1} = 2\ell n\,|x| - \frac{2}{x} - \ell n\,|x-1| + C$$

$$= \ell n\left|\frac{x^2}{x-1}\right| - \frac{2}{x} + C$$

11. $\dfrac{2x^2 + 1}{x^3 + x} = \dfrac{2x^2 + 1}{x(x^2 + 1)} = \dfrac{A}{x} + \dfrac{Bx + C}{x^2 + 1} \implies 2x^2 + 1 = A(x^2 + 1) + x(Bx + C)$. Put $x = 0$ to find $A = 1$. Equate the coefficients of x^2, and of x, to find $2 = A + B$ (so $B = 1$) and $0 = C$. Then

$$\int \frac{2x^2 + 1}{x^3 + x}\,dx = \int \frac{dx}{x} + \int \frac{x\,dx}{x^2 + 1} = \ell n\,|x| + \tfrac{1}{2}\ell n\,(x^2 + 1) + C = \tfrac{1}{2}\ell n\,x^2(x^2 + 1) + C$$

12.(a) Let $u = \sqrt{x^2 + 9}$, $u^2 = x^2 + 9$, $u\,du = x\,dx$. Then

$$\int_0^4 \frac{x^3\,dx}{\sqrt{x^2 + 9}} = \int_3^5 \frac{(u^2 - 9)u\,du}{u} = \int_3^5 (u^2 - 9)\,du = \left.\left(\frac{u^3}{3} - 9u\right)\right|_3^5 = \left.\frac{u}{3}(u^2 - 27)\right|_3^5$$

$$= \frac{5}{3}(-2) - (-18) = \frac{44}{3}$$

(b) Let $x = 3\tan t$, $dx = 3\sec^2 t\,dt$, $\sqrt{x^2 + 9} = 3\sec t$ $(-\pi/2 < t < \pi/2)$. Then

$$\int_0^4 \frac{x^3\,dx}{\sqrt{x^2 + 9}} = \int_0^\alpha \frac{27\tan^3 t \cdot 3\sec^2 t\,dt}{3\sec t} \qquad \left(\text{where } \alpha = \tan^{-1}\frac{4}{3}\right)$$

$$= 27\int_0^\alpha \tan^3 t \sec t\,dt = 27\int_0^\alpha (\sec^2 t - 1)\sec t \tan t\,dt$$

$$= \left.(9\sec^3 t - 27\sec t)\right|_0^\alpha = \left.9\sec t\,(\sec^2 t - 3)\right|_0^\alpha$$

Since $\tan \alpha = 4/3$, we have $\sec \alpha = 5/3$ and hence the integral is

$$9 \cdot \frac{5}{3}\left(\frac{25}{9} - 3\right) - 9(1 - 3) = \frac{44}{3}$$

13. Use integration by parts, with $u = \sinh^{-1}x$, $dv = dx$. Then $du = dx/\sqrt{x^2 + 1}$ and $v = x$, so

$$\int \sinh^{-1}x\,dx = x\sinh^{-1}x - \int \frac{x\,dx}{\sqrt{x^2 + 1}} = x\sinh^{-1}x - \sqrt{x^2 + 1} + C$$

$$\int_0^1 \sinh^{-1}x\,dx = \sinh^{-1}1 - \sqrt{2} + 1 = 1 - \sqrt{2} + \ell n\,(1 + \sqrt{2})$$

14. The graph of $y = \tan^{-1}x$ is shown in Figure 6, Sec. 9.1. The area is $A = \displaystyle\int_0^1 \tan^{-1}x\,dx$. Use integration by parts, with $u = \tan^{-1}x$, $dv = dx$. Then $du = dx/(1 + x^2)$ and $v = x$, so

$$A = \left.x\tan^{-1}x\right|_0^1 - \int_0^1 \frac{x\,dx}{1 + x^2} = \frac{\pi}{4} - \left.\frac{1}{2}\ell n\,(1 + x^2)\right|_0^1 = \frac{\pi}{4} - \frac{1}{2}\ell n\,2$$

An alternative solution is to use horizontal strips to generate the area:

$$A = \int_0^{\pi/4}(1 - x)\,dy = \int_0^{\pi/4}(1 - \tan y)\,dy = \left.(y - \ell n\,\sec y)\right|_0^{\pi/4} = \frac{\pi}{4} - \frac{1}{2}\ell n\,2$$

15. (a) The curve is an ellipse, $x^2/a^2 + y^2/b^2 = 1$. The part in the first quadrant corresponds to the interval $0 \leq x \leq a$ (the parameter running from $\pi/2$ to 0). Hence

$$V = 2\pi \int_0^a y^2 dx = 2\pi \int_{\pi/2}^0 b^2 \sin^2 t(-a\sin t\, dt) = 2\pi a b^2 \int_0^{\pi/2} \sin^3 t\, dt$$

$$= 2\pi a b^2 \cdot \frac{2}{3} \quad \text{(see the reduction formulas at the end of Sec. 10.1)}$$

$$= \frac{4}{3}\pi a b^2$$

(b) Since $x^2/a^2 + y^2/b^2 = 1$, $V = 2\pi b^2 \int_0^a (1 - x^2/a^2) dx = 2\pi b^2 (x - \frac{x^3}{3a^2})\Big|_0^a = \frac{4}{3}\pi a b^2$.

(c) $V = \frac{4}{3}\pi a^3$, the volume of a sphere of radius a.

16. (a) The power is $P = IV = I_0 V_0 \cos^2(\omega t)$. One cycle corresponds to the interval $-\pi/\omega \leq t \leq \pi/\omega$; the average power during this cycle is

$$A = \frac{\omega}{2\pi}\int_{-\pi/\omega}^{\pi/\omega} I_0 V_0 \cos^2(\omega t) dt = I_0 V_0/(2\pi)\int_{-\pi}^{\pi} \cos^2 u\, du \quad (u = \omega t, \; du = \omega dt)$$

$$= I_0 V_0/(2\pi)\int_0^{\pi}(1 + \cos 2u)du = I_0 V_0/(2\pi)\cdot(u + \frac{1}{2}\sin 2u)\Big|_0^{\pi} = \frac{1}{2}I_0 V_0$$

(b) $A = \frac{\omega}{2\pi}\int_{-\pi/\omega}^{\pi/\omega} I_0 V_0 \cos(\omega t)\cos(\omega t + \alpha)dt$

$$= I_0 V_0/(2\pi)\int_{-\pi}^{\pi}\cos u\cos(u + \alpha)du \quad (u = \omega t, \; du = \omega dt)$$

Since $\cos(u + \alpha) = \cos u \cos\alpha - \sin u \sin\alpha$, the integral is

$$\cos\alpha\int_{-\pi}^{\pi}\cos^2 u\, du - \sin\alpha\int_{-\pi}^{\pi}\sin u \cos u\, du$$

As in part (a), the first integral is π; the second is 0 because the integrand is odd. Hence $A = I_0 V_0/(2\pi)\cdot\pi\cos\alpha = \frac{1}{2}I_0 V_0 \cos\alpha$. Note that this is less than the answer in part (a) because $\cos\alpha < 1$.

17. (a) The partition is $\{0, \pi/4, \pi/2, 3\pi/4, \pi\}$, with $\Delta x = \pi/4$. Hence

$$\int_0^{\pi} e^{\sin x} dx \approx \frac{\pi}{4}(\frac{1}{2} + e^{\sqrt{2}/2} + e + e^{\sqrt{2}/2} + \frac{1}{2}) \approx 6.106087$$

(b) $\int_0^{\pi} e^{\sin x} dx \approx \frac{\pi}{12}(1 + 4e^{\sqrt{2}/2} + 2e + 4e^{\sqrt{2}/2} + 1) \approx 6.194562$

18. (a) The partition is $\{0, 1/3, 2/3, 1, 4/3, 5/3, 2\}$, with $\Delta x = 1/3$. Hence

$$\int_0^2 \frac{dx}{x^3 + 2} \approx \frac{1}{3}(\frac{1}{4} + \frac{1}{(1/3)^3 + 2} + \frac{1}{(2/3)^3 + 2} + \frac{1}{3} + \frac{1}{(4/3)^3 + 2} + \frac{1}{(5/3)^3 + 2} + \frac{1}{20})$$

$$\approx 0.646459$$

(b) $\int_0^2 \frac{dx}{x^3+2} \approx \frac{1}{9}(\frac{1}{2} + \frac{4}{(1/3)^3+2} + \frac{2}{(2/3)^3+2} + \frac{4}{3} + \frac{2}{(4/3)^3+2} + \frac{4}{(5/3)^3+2} + \frac{1}{10})$

≈ 0.647657

19.(a) The partition is $\{0, 0.25, 0.5, 0.75, 1\}$, with $\Delta x = 0.25$. Since $(\tan x)/x \to 1$ when $x \to 0$, we take the value of the integrand to be 1 at $x = 0$.

Then $\int_0^1 \frac{\tan x}{x} dx \approx 0.25(0.5 + \frac{\tan 0.25}{0.25} + \frac{\tan 0.5}{0.5} + \frac{\tan 0.75}{0.75} + \frac{1}{2}\tan 1) \approx 1.158701.$

(b) $\int_0^1 \frac{\tan x}{x} dx \approx \frac{0.25}{3}(1 + \frac{4\tan 0.25}{0.25} + \frac{2\tan 0.5}{0.5} + \frac{4\tan 0.75}{0.75} + \tan 1) \approx 1.149717$

CHAPTER 11   MORE ABOUT LIMITS

Section 11.1   LIMITS INVOLVING INFINITY

1. $\frac{x^2-x+1}{x^2+x+1} = \frac{1-(1/x)+(1/x^2)}{1+(1/x)+(1/x^2)} \to 1$ when $x \to \infty$.

2. $\frac{x^3}{x^2+1} \approx \frac{x^3}{x^2} = x \to -\infty$ when $x \to -\infty$.

3. When x is negatively large, $x\sqrt{3-x}$ is a product of a large negative number and a large positive number. Hence the limit is $-\infty$.

4. $\frac{1}{x} - \frac{1}{x^2} = \frac{x-1}{x^2} \approx \frac{x}{x^2} = \frac{1}{x} \to 0$ when $x \to \infty$.

5. $x^2 - \frac{1}{x^2} \approx -\frac{1}{x^2} \to -\infty$ when $x \to 0$.

6. $x - \sqrt{x^2+1} \approx x - \sqrt{x^2} = x - x = 0$ when x is large. Hence the limit is 0.

7. When x is negatively large, $x - \sqrt{x^2+1}$ is a large negative number minus a large positive number. Hence the limit is $-\infty$.

8. $\frac{\cos x}{x} \approx \frac{1}{x} \to \infty$ when $x \downarrow 0$.

9. When x is small and positive, $\ell n\, x$ is negatively large. Division by x makes it even larger negatively. Hence the limit is $-\infty$.

10. When x is small and positive, $\ell n\, x$ is negatively large. Subtraction of the large positive number $1/x$ makes it even larger negatively. Hence the limit is $-\infty$.

11. $\lim_{x\to\infty} (\sin \frac{1}{x}) = \sin(\lim_{x\to\infty} \frac{1}{x}) = \sin 0 = 0.$

12. $\lim_{x\to\infty} x\sin \frac{1}{x} = \lim_{t\to 0} \frac{\sin t}{t} = 1$ (where $t = 1/x$).

13. $x\cos\frac{1}{x} \approx x\cdot 1 \to \infty$ when $x \to \infty$.

14. $\sinh x \to \infty$ when $x \to \infty$, so the limit is ∞.

15. $(2/5)^x \to 0$ when $x \to \infty$.

16. $(5/2)^x \to \infty$ when $x \to \infty$.

17. $1/x \to \infty$ when $x \downarrow 0$, so the limit is ∞.

18. $1/x \to -\infty$ when $x \uparrow 0$, so the limit is 0.

19. $\dfrac{1+x}{1-x} \approx \dfrac{2}{1-x} \to \infty$ when $x \uparrow 1$, so the limit is ∞.

20. $1/x \to \infty$ or $-\infty$ depending on whether $x \downarrow 0$ or $x \uparrow 0$.

21. $\tan x \to \infty$ or $-\infty$ depending on whether $x \uparrow \pi/2$ or $x \downarrow \pi/2$.

22. $\sin x$ oscillates between 1 and -1 as $x \to \infty$.

23. The oscillation in Problem 22 is now magnified by a factor x which increases without bound.

24. The domain of $1 - \sqrt{x}$ is $x \geq 0$.

25. $\lim\limits_{x \to \infty} (1+1/x)^x = \lim\limits_{h \to 0} (1+h)^{1/h} = e$.   (See Sec. 8.4.)

26. $\lim\limits_{x \to \infty} (1+1/x)^{2x} = [\lim\limits_{x \to \infty} (1+1/x)^x]^2 = e^2$ (by Problem 25).

27. When $0 \leq x < 1$, $x^n \to 0$ as $n \to \infty$. When $x = 1$, $x^n = 1$ for all n, so the limit is 1. When $x > 1$, $x^n \to \infty$ as $n \to \infty$. When $x < 0$, the exponential function x^n (n being the variable) is undefined except for special values of n.

28. When $0 \leq x < 1$, $x^n \to 0$ as $n \to \infty$, so $f(x) = 0$. When $x = 1$, $2x^n/(x^n+1) = 1$ for all n, so $f(1) = 1$. When $x > 1$, $x^n \to \infty$ as $n \to \infty$. Hence

$$\frac{2x^n}{x^n+1} \approx \frac{2x^n}{x^n} = 2$$

and $f(x) = 2$.   See Figure 1.

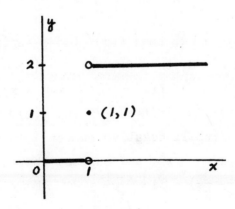

Figure 1

29. If $f(x) \to L$ and $g(x) \to \infty$, then $f(x) + g(x) \approx L + (\text{large number}) \to \infty$. If $f(x) \to \infty$ and $g(x) \to \infty$, then $f(x) + g(x) = (\text{large number}) + (\text{large number}) \to \infty$.

If $f(x) \to L$ and $g(x) \to -\infty$, then $f(x) + g(x) \approx L +$ (negatively large number) $\to -\infty$.

If $f(x) \to -\infty$ and $g(x) \to -\infty$, then $f(x) + g(x) =$ (negatively large number) + (negatively large number) $\to -\infty$.

30. If $f(x) \to L > 0$ and $g(x) \to \infty$, then $f(x)g(x) \approx L$(large number) $\to \infty$. If $f(x) \to \infty$ and $g(x) \to \infty$, then $f(x)g(x) =$ (large number)(large number) $\to \infty$. If $f(x) \to L > 0$ and $g(x) \to -\infty$, then $f(x)g(x) \approx L$(negatively large number) $\to -\infty$. If $f(x) \to \infty$ and $g(x) \to -\infty$, then $f(x)g(x) =$ (large number)(negatively large number) $\to -\infty$.

31. If $f(x) \to -L < 0$ and $g(x) \to \infty$, then $f(x)g(x) \approx -L$(large number) $\to -\infty$. If $f(x) \to -\infty$ and $g(x) \to \infty$, then $f(x)g(x) =$ (negatively large number)(large number) $\to -\infty$. If $f(x) \to -L < 0$ and $g(x) \to -\infty$, then $f(x)g(x) \approx -L$(negatively large number) $\to \infty$. If $f(x) \to -\infty$ and $g(x) \to -\infty$, then $f(x)g(x) =$ (negatively large number)(negatively large number) $\to \infty$.

32. If $f(x) \to L$ and $g(x) \to \infty$, then $f(x)/g(x) \approx L/$(large number) $\to 0$. If $f(x) \to L$ and $g(x) \to -\infty$, then $f(x)/g(x) \approx L/$(negatively large number) $\to 0$.

33. If $f(x) \to \infty$ and $g(x) \to L > 0$, then $f(x)/g(x) \approx$ (large number)$/L \to \infty$. If $f(x) \to -\infty$ and $g(x) \to L > 0$, then $f(x)/g(x) \approx$ (negatively large number)$/L \to -\infty$.

34. If $f(x) \to \infty$ and $g(x) \to -L < 0$, then $f(x)/g(x) \approx$ (large number)$/(-L) \to -\infty$. If $f(x) \to -\infty$ and $g(x) \to -L < 0$, then $f(x)/g(x) \approx$ (negatively large number)$/(-L) \to \infty$.

35. If $f(x) \to L > 0$ and $g(x) \downarrow 0$, then $f(x)/g(x) \approx L/$(small positive number) $\to \infty$. If $f(x) \to \infty$ and $g(x) \downarrow 0$, then $f(x)/g(x) =$ (large number)$/$(small positive number) $\to \infty$. If $f(x) \to L > 0$ and $g(x) \uparrow 0$, then $f(x)/g(x) \approx L/$(small negative number) $\to -\infty$. If $f(x) \to \infty$ and $g(x) \uparrow 0$, then $f(x)/g(x) =$ (large number)$/$(small negative number) $\to -\infty$.

36. If $f(x) \to -L < 0$ and $g(x) \downarrow 0$, then $f(x)/g(x) \approx -L/$(small positive number) $\to -\infty$. If $f(x) \to -\infty$ and $g(x) \downarrow 0$, then $f(x)/g(x) =$ (negatively large number)$/$(small positive number) $\to -\infty$. If $f(x) \to -L < 0$ and $g(x) \uparrow 0$, then $f(x)/g(x) \approx -L/$(small negative number) $\to \infty$. If $f(x) \to -\infty$ and $g(x) \uparrow 0$, then $f(x)/g(x) =$ (negatively large number)$/$(small negative number) $\to \infty$.

37. Let $f(x) = 1/x$ and $g(x) = 1/x^2$, and suppose that $x \downarrow 0$. Then $\lim f(x) = \lim g(x) = \infty$, but $\lim \left(\frac{1}{x} - \frac{1}{x^2}\right) = \lim \frac{x-1}{x^2} = -\infty$. Many other counterexamples can be given.

38. Let $f(x) = x^2$ and $g(x) = x$, and suppose that $x \to 0$. Then $\lim f(x) = \lim g(x) = 0$, but $\lim (x^2/x) = \lim x = 0$, not 1.

39. Use the same data as in Problem 37. Then $\lim f(x) = \lim g(x) = \infty$, but

102

$\lim \dfrac{1/x}{1/x^2} = \lim x = 0$, not 1.

40. If $a^2 > b^2$ (and a and b are positive), then $a > b$. Hence $x > B^2 \implies \sqrt{x} > B$. A critic who doubts that $\sqrt{x} \to \infty$ as $x \to \infty$ would name a number B that he doesn't think $\sqrt{x}$ ever exceeds. We prove him wrong by naming A such that $x > A \implies \sqrt{x} > B$. Our choice is $A = B^2$.

41. If $a > b$ (and a and b are positive), then $a^2 > b^2$. Hence $x < -\sqrt{B} \implies -x > \sqrt{B} \implies x^2 > B$. A critic who doubts that $x^2 \to \infty$ as $x \to -\infty$ would name a number B that he doesn't think x^2 ever exceeds. We prove him wrong by naming -A such that $x < -A \implies x^2 > B$. Our choice is $-A = -\sqrt{B}$.

42. $0 < x < 1/(B+1) \implies 1/x > B+1 \implies -1/x < -(B+1) \implies 1 - 1/x < 1 - (B+1) = -B$. A critic who doubts that $1 - 1/x \to -\infty$ as $x \downarrow 0$ would name a number -B that he doesn't think $1 - 1/x$ ever goes below. We prove him wrong by naming δ such that $0 < x < \delta \implies 1 - 1/x < -B$. Our choice is $\delta = 1/(B+1)$.

43. $x > 2/\epsilon \implies 0 < 1/x < \epsilon/2 \implies 0 < 2/x < \epsilon \implies |2/x| < \epsilon$ (because $x > 0$). A critic who doubts that $2/x \to 0$ as $x \to \infty$ would name a number ϵ that he doesn't think $|2/x - 0| = |2/x|$ can be made less than. We prove him wrong by naming A such that $x > A \implies |2/x| < \epsilon$. Our choice is $A = 2/\epsilon$.

44. $x > 1/\epsilon + 1 \implies x - 1 > 1/\epsilon \implies 0 < 1/(x-1) < \epsilon \implies 0 < \dfrac{x}{x-1} - 1 < \epsilon \implies \left| \dfrac{x}{x-1} - 1 \right| < \epsilon$ (because $\dfrac{x}{x-1} - 1 > 0$). The student has a right to complain that the above steps are not obvious! What we do to construct them is to work backwards from the conclusion desired by the critic. For if he doubts that $\dfrac{x}{x-1} \to 1$ as $x \to \infty$, he will name a number ϵ that he doesn't think $\left| \dfrac{x}{x-1} - 1 \right|$ can be made less than, challenging us to respond with a number A such that $x > A \implies \left| \dfrac{x}{x-1} - 1 \right| < \epsilon$. We name A by working on scratch paper (which the critic need not be shown). It is safe to assume $x > 1$ (since we are thinking of $x \to \infty$). Then $\dfrac{x}{x-1} > 1$, so the critic's inequality yields the following equivalences:

$$\left| \dfrac{x}{x-1} - 1 \right| < \epsilon \iff 0 < \dfrac{x}{x-1} - 1 < \epsilon \ \left(\text{because } \dfrac{x}{x-1} - 1 > 0\right)$$

$$\iff 0 < \dfrac{x - (x-1)}{x-1} < \epsilon \iff 0 < \dfrac{1}{x-1} < \epsilon \iff x - 1 > \dfrac{1}{\epsilon}$$

$$\iff x > \dfrac{1}{\epsilon} + 1$$

This scratchwork suggests the choice $A = 1/\epsilon + 1$ and enables us to write the implications given at the beginning.

45. The limit is $-\infty$. To prove it, suppose that we are given -B (where $B > 0$)

and challenged to name A such that $x > A \implies 1 - \sqrt{x} < -B$. Since

$$1 - \sqrt{x} < -B \iff \sqrt{x} > B + 1 \iff x > (B+1)^2$$

our choice is $A = (B+1)^2$.

46. The limit is ∞. To prove it, suppose that we are given $B > 0$ and challenged to name δ such that $0 < x < \delta \implies 1/x > B$. Since $1/x > B \iff 0 < x < 1/B$, our choice is $\delta = 1/B$.

47. The limit is 0. To prove it, suppose that we are given $\epsilon > 0$ and challenged to name A such that $x > A \implies |e^{-x} - 0| < \epsilon$. Since $|e^{-x} - 0| < \epsilon \iff e^x > 1/\epsilon \iff x > \ln(1/\epsilon)$, our choice is $A = \ln(1/\epsilon)$.

48. The limit is ∞. To prove it, suppose that we are given $B > 0$ and challenged to name δ such that $0 < 1 - x < \delta \implies 1/\sqrt{1 - x^2} > B$. Restricting x to the domain $-1 < x < 1$, we have

$$\frac{1}{\sqrt{1 - x^2}} > B \iff \frac{1}{1 - x^2} > B^2 \iff 0 < 1 - x^2 < \frac{1}{B^2} \iff 1 - \frac{1}{B^2} < x^2 < 1$$

The critic cannot object if we assume his B to be at least 1, in which case $1 - 1/B^2 \geq 0$ and we may take square roots:

$$\sqrt{1 - 1/B^2} < x < 1 \iff -1 < -x < -\sqrt{1 - 1/B^2} \iff 0 < 1 - x < 1 - \sqrt{1 - 1/B^2}$$

Our choice is $\delta = 1 - \sqrt{1 - 1/B^2}$.

49. The limit is 1. To prove it, suppose that we are given $\epsilon > 0$ and challenged to name A such that $x > A \implies \left| \frac{x^2}{x^2 + 1} - 1 \right| < \epsilon$. Since $\frac{x^2}{x^2 + 1} < 1$ for all x, we have

$$\left| \frac{x^2}{x^2 + 1} - 1 \right| < \epsilon \iff 1 - \frac{x^2}{x^2 + 1} < \epsilon \iff \frac{1}{x^2 + 1} < \epsilon \iff x^2 + 1 > \frac{1}{\epsilon}$$
$$\iff x^2 > \frac{1}{\epsilon} - 1$$

Our critic cannot object if we assume his ϵ to be no larger than 1, in which case $\frac{1}{\epsilon} - 1 \geq 0$ and we may take square roots: $|x| > \sqrt{1/\epsilon - 1}$. Our choice is $A = \sqrt{1/\epsilon - 1}$. Then $x > A \implies |x| > \sqrt{1/\epsilon - 1} \implies \cdots \implies \left| \frac{x^2}{x^2 + 1} - 1 \right| < \epsilon$.

Section 11.2   L'HÔPITAL'S RULE AND INDETERMINATE FORMS

1. $\frac{\sin^2 x}{1 - \cos x} = \frac{1 - \cos^2 x}{1 - \cos x} = \frac{(1 - \cos x)(1 + \cos x)}{1 - \cos x} = 1 + \cos x \to 2$ as $x \to 0$.

L'Hôpital's Rule gives

$$\lim_{x \to 0} \frac{\sin^2 x}{1 - \cos x} = \lim_{x \to 0} \frac{2 \sin x \cos x}{\sin x} = \lim_{x \to 0} 2 \cos x = 2$$

2. $\frac{x + \tan x}{\sin x} = \frac{x}{\sin x} + \frac{1}{\cos x} \to 1 + 1 = 2$ as $x \to 0$. L'Hôpital's Rule gives

$$\lim_{x\to 0} \frac{x+\tan x}{\sin x} = \lim_{x\to 0} \frac{1+\sec^2 x}{\cos x} = 2$$

3. $\frac{x-2}{x^2-4} = \frac{1}{x+2} \to 0$ as $x\to\infty$. L'Hôpital's Rule gives $\lim_{x\to\infty} \frac{x-2}{x^2-4} = \lim_{x\to\infty} \frac{1}{2x} = 0$.

4. $\frac{2x^3 - 5x^2 + 1}{x^3 - 1} = \frac{2-(5/x)+(1/x^3)}{1-(1/x^3)} \to 2$ as $x\to\infty$. L'Hôpital's Rule gives

$$\lim_{x\to\infty} \frac{2x^3 - 5x^2 + 1}{x^3 - 1} = \lim_{x\to\infty} \frac{6x^2 - 10x}{3x^2} = \lim_{x\to\infty} \frac{6x-10}{3x} \quad \text{(cancellation of x)}$$

$$= \lim_{x\to\infty} \frac{6}{3} = 2$$

5. $\lim_{x\to 0} \frac{x-\sin x}{\tan x} = \lim_{x\to 0} \frac{1-\cos x}{\sec^2 x} = \frac{0}{1} = 0$

6. $\lim_{x\to\infty} \frac{\sqrt{x}}{x^2-1} = \lim_{x\to\infty} \frac{1/(2\sqrt{x})}{2x} = \lim_{x\to\infty} \frac{1}{4x^{3/2}} = 0$

7. $\lim_{x\to 0} \frac{e^x - 1}{xe^x} = \lim_{x\to 0} \frac{e^x}{xe^x + e^x} = \lim_{x\to 0} \frac{1}{x+1} = 1$

8. $\lim_{x\to 0} \frac{\sinh x}{\sin x} = \lim_{x\to 0} \frac{\cosh x}{\cos x} = 1$

9. $\lim_{x\to 0} \frac{\ln \cos x}{x} = \lim_{x\to 0} \frac{-\tan x}{1} = 0$

10. $x \csc x = \frac{x}{\sin x} \to 1$ as $x\to 0$.

11. $\lim_{x\to 0} \frac{\ln(1+x)}{x} = \lim_{x\to 0} \frac{1/(1+x)}{1} = 1$

12. $\lim_{x\to 1} \frac{x^2-1}{\ln x} = \lim_{x\to 1} \frac{2x}{1/x} = 2$

13. $\lim_{x\to\pi/2} \frac{\sec x + 1}{\tan x - 1} = \lim_{x\to\pi/2} \frac{\sec x \tan x}{\sec^2 x} = \lim_{x\to\pi/2} \sin x = 1$

14. $\lim_{x\downarrow 0} \frac{x^2}{\sin x - x} = \lim_{x\downarrow 0} \frac{2x}{\cos x - 1} = \lim_{x\downarrow 0} \frac{2}{-\sin x} = -\infty$ (because $\sin x \downarrow 0$ as $x\downarrow 0$).

15. $\lim_{x\to 0} \frac{\tan x}{\tan 2x} = \lim_{x\to 0} \frac{\sec^2 x}{2\sec^2 2x} = \frac{1}{2}$

16. $\lim_{x\to 0} \frac{1-\cos x}{x^2} = \lim_{x\to 0} \frac{\sin x}{2x} = \frac{1}{2}$ (because $\frac{\sin x}{x} \to 1$ as $x\to 0$).

17. $\lim_{x\to 1} \frac{x^2-1}{\sqrt[3]{x}-1} = \lim_{x\to 1} \frac{2x}{\frac{1}{3}x^{-2/3}} = \lim_{x\to 1} 6x^{5/3} = 6$

18. $\displaystyle\lim_{x\to\pi/2}(\sec x - \tan x) = \lim_{x\to\pi/2}\frac{1-\sin x}{\cos x} = \lim_{x\to\pi/2}\frac{-\cos x}{-\sin x} = 0$

19. $\displaystyle\lim_{x\to 0}(\csc x - \cot x) = \lim_{x\to 0}\frac{1-\cos x}{\sin x} = \lim_{x\to 0}\frac{\sin x}{\cos x} = 0$

20. $\csc x - \dfrac{1}{x} = \dfrac{1}{\sin x} - \dfrac{1}{x} = \dfrac{x-\sin x}{x\sin x}$, so the limit is

$$\lim_{x\to 0}\frac{1-\cos x}{x\cos x + \sin x} = \lim_{x\to 0}\frac{\sin x}{-x\sin x + \cos x + \cos x} = \frac{0}{2} = 0$$

21. $x - \cosh x = x\left(1 - \dfrac{\cosh x}{x}\right)$. Since $\displaystyle\lim_{x\to\infty}\frac{\cosh x}{x} = \lim_{x\to\infty}\frac{\sinh x}{1} = \infty$, the

function $x\left(1 - \dfrac{\cosh x}{x}\right)$ is a product of a large factor x and a negatively large

factor $1 - \dfrac{\cosh x}{x}$. Hence the limit is $-\infty$.

22. $x^2 - \sinh x$ is of the form $f(x) - g(x)$, where $f(x) \to \infty$ and $g(x) \to -\infty$ as $x \to -\infty$.
Hence the limit is ∞.

23. $\displaystyle\lim_{x\to\infty}\frac{x^3}{e^x} = \lim_{x\to\infty}\frac{3x^2}{e^x} = \lim_{x\to\infty}\frac{6x}{e^x} = \lim_{x\to\infty}\frac{6}{e^x} = 0$

24. $\displaystyle\lim_{x\to\infty}\frac{e^x + 1}{x^2} = \lim_{x\to\infty}\frac{e^x}{2x} = \lim_{x\to\infty}\frac{e^x}{2} = \infty$

25. $\displaystyle\lim_{x\to 0}x^2\ln x = \lim_{x\to 0}\frac{\ln x}{1/x^2} = \lim_{x\to 0}\frac{1/x}{-2/x^3} = \lim_{x\to 0}\left(-\tfrac{1}{2}x^2\right) = 0$

26. $\displaystyle\lim_{x\downarrow 0}xe^{1/x} = \lim_{x\downarrow 0}\frac{e^{1/x}}{1/x} = \lim_{x\downarrow 0}\frac{e^{1/x}(-1/x^2)}{-1/x^2} = \lim_{x\downarrow 0}e^{1/x} = \infty$

27. Let $h = -x$. Then $\displaystyle\lim_{x\to 0}(1-x)^{1/x} = \lim_{h\to 0}(1+h)^{-1/h} = \left[\lim_{h\to 0}(1+h)^{1/h}\right]^{-1}$

$$= e^{-1} = 1/e$$

28. Let $y = (x^2+1)^{1/x}$. Then $\ln y = \dfrac{1}{x}\ln(x^2+1) = \dfrac{\ln(x^2+1)}{x}$ and

$$\lim_{x\to\infty}\ln y = \lim_{x\to\infty}\frac{2x/(x^2+1)}{1} = \lim_{x\to\infty}\frac{2}{2x} = 0$$

Hence $\ln\left(\displaystyle\lim_{x\to\infty}y\right) = 0$ and $\displaystyle\lim_{x\to\infty}y = 1$.

29. Let $y = x^{\sin x}$. Then $\ln y = \sin x \cdot \ln x = \dfrac{\ln x}{\csc x}$ and

$$\lim_{x\downarrow 0}\ln y = \lim_{x\downarrow 0}\frac{1/x}{-\csc x\cot x} = -\lim_{x\downarrow 0}\frac{\sin x\tan x}{x} = -\lim_{x\downarrow 0}\left(\frac{\sin x}{x}\right)(\tan x) = 0$$

Hence $\ln\left(\displaystyle\lim_{x\downarrow 0}y\right) = 0$ and $\displaystyle\lim_{x\downarrow 0}y = 1$.

30. Let $y = (\tan x)^{\cos x}$. Then $\ln y = \cos x \cdot \ln \tan x = \dfrac{\ln \tan x}{\sec x}$ and

$$\lim_{x \uparrow \pi/2} \ln y = \lim_{x \uparrow \pi/2} \frac{\sec^2 x / \tan x}{\sec x \tan x} = \lim_{x \uparrow \pi/2} \frac{\sec x}{\tan^2 x} = \lim_{x \uparrow \pi/2} \frac{\cos x}{\sin^2 x} = 0.$$

Hence $\ln \left(\lim_{x \uparrow \pi/2} y \right) = 0$ and $\lim_{x \uparrow \pi/2} y = 1$.

31. $\lim_{x \to \infty} x e^x = \infty$ by inspection, while $\lim_{x \to -\infty} x e^x = \lim_{x \to -\infty} \dfrac{x}{e^{-x}} = \lim_{x \to -\infty} \dfrac{1}{-e^{-x}} = 0.$

(See the solution of Problem 24, Sec. 8.3.)

32. $\lim_{x \to \infty} x e^{-x} = \lim_{x \to \infty} \dfrac{x}{e^x} = \lim_{x \to \infty} \dfrac{1}{e^x} = 0$, while $\lim_{x \to -\infty} x e^{-x} = -\infty$ by inspection. (See

the solution of Problem 25, Sec. 8.3.)

33. $\lim_{x \downarrow 0} \dfrac{e^x}{x} = \infty$, $\lim_{x \uparrow 0} \dfrac{e^x}{x} = -\infty$, and $\lim_{x \to -\infty} \dfrac{e^x}{x} = 0$ by inspection, while

$\lim_{x \to \infty} \dfrac{e^x}{x} = \lim_{x \to \infty} \dfrac{e^x}{1} = \infty$. (See the solution of Problem 26, Sec. 8.3.)

34. $e^x - x = x\left(\dfrac{e^x}{x} - 1\right)$. Since $e^x/x \to \infty$ as $x \to \infty$ (Problem 33), $\lim_{x \to \infty} (e^x - x) = \infty$.

When $x \to -\infty$, $e^x - x \to \infty$ by inspection. (See the solution of Problem 27,

Sec. 8.3.)

35. $\lim_{x \downarrow 0} x \ln x = \lim_{x \downarrow 0} \dfrac{\ln x}{1/x} = \lim_{x \downarrow 0} \dfrac{1/x}{-1/x^2} = \lim_{x \downarrow 0} (-x) = 0$, while $\lim_{x \to \infty} x \ln x = \infty$ by

inspection. (See the solution of Problem 28, Sec. 8.3.)

36. $\lim_{x \downarrow 0} (x \ln x - x) = \lim_{x \downarrow 0} \dfrac{\ln x - 1}{1/x} = \lim_{x \downarrow 0} \dfrac{1/x}{-1/x^2} = \lim_{x \downarrow 0} (-x) = 0$, while

$\lim_{x \to \infty} (x \ln x - x) = \lim_{x \to \infty} x(\ln x - 1) = \infty$ by inspection. (See the solution of

Problem 29, Sec. 8.3.)

37. $\lim_{x \downarrow 0} \dfrac{\ln x}{x} = -\infty$ by inspection, while $\lim_{x \to \infty} \dfrac{\ln x}{x} = \lim_{x \to \infty} \dfrac{1/x}{1} = 0$. (See the

solution of Problem 30, Sec. 8.3.)

38. The first student is right because $\dfrac{x^3 - x^2}{x^3 - 1} = \dfrac{x^2(x-1)}{(x-1)(x^2+x+1)} = \dfrac{x^2}{x^2+x+1}$

$\to 1/3$ as $x \to 1$. The second student is right in the first step,

$$\lim_{x \to 1} \frac{x^3 - x^2}{x^3 - 1} = \lim_{x \to 1} \frac{3x^2 - 2x}{3x^2}$$

But the new limit is not indeterminate; L'Hôpital's Rule should not be used

again. Instead the limit is $1/3$ by inspection.

39. Two applications of the rule yield

$$\lim_{x\to\infty}\frac{\sqrt{1+x^2}}{x} = \lim_{x\to\infty}\frac{x}{\sqrt{1+x^2}} = \lim_{x\to\infty}\frac{\sqrt{1+x^2}}{x}$$

back where we started. There is nothing incorrect about this, but it is not going anywhere. Instead, use ordinary algebra to write (for $x > 0$)

$$\frac{\sqrt{1+x^2}}{x} = \sqrt{(1+x^2)/x^2} = \sqrt{1+1/x^2} \to 1 \text{ as } x\to\infty$$

40. $\lim\limits_{x\to\infty}\dfrac{x-\sin x}{x} = \lim\limits_{x\to\infty}\left(1-\dfrac{\sin x}{x}\right) = 1 - 0 = 1$. If L'Hôpital's Rule is used

(the original limit is of the form ∞/∞), we obtain $\lim\limits_{x\to\infty}(1-\cos x)$, which does not exist. This illustrates Remark 3 at the end of the section.

41. (a) $\lim\limits_{x\to0}\dfrac{\sin x}{x} = \lim\limits_{x\to0}\dfrac{\cos x}{1} = 1$

(b) No. In using the rule in part (a) we differentiated $\sin x$. The formula $D_x \sin x = \cos x$, however, was derived in Sec. 2.3 by using the limit of $(\sin x)/x$ as $x\to0$.

42. Since $e^{-x}\to0$ and $1/x\to0$ as $x\to\infty$, the first limit is of the type 0^0. But its value is e^{-1}, because $(e^{-x})^{1/x} = e^{-1}$ for all $x\neq0$. Since $e^x\to\infty$ and $1/x \to 0$ as $x\to\infty$, the second limit is of the type ∞^0. But its value is e, because $(e^x)^{1/x} = e$ for all $x\neq0$.

43. Let $u = xh$. Since $u\to0$ when $h\to0$, we have

$$\lim_{h\to0}(1+xh)^{1/h} = \lim_{u\to0}(1+u)^{x/u} = [\lim_{u\to0}(1+u)^{1/u}]^x = e^x$$

44. $0/\infty$ refers to a function $f(x) \approx$ (small number)/(large number) $\to 0$. Similarly, $\infty/0$ refers to $f(x) \approx$ (large number)/(small number). This is definite if the small number is positive (the answer is ∞) or if the small number is negative (the answer is $-\infty$). If the small number is unrestricted, we can still be definite; the limit is neither a real number, nor ∞, nor $-\infty$, but is simply meaningless. Hence in any case we can come to a decision.

$\infty + \infty$ refers to $f(x) \approx$ (large number) + (large number) $\to \infty$

$\infty \cdot \infty$ refers to $f(x) \approx$ (large number)·(large number) $\to \infty$

∞^1 refers to $f(x) \approx$ (large number)$^{\text{(number close to 1)}} \to \infty$

0^∞ refers to $f(x) \approx$ (small positive number)$^{\text{(large number)}} \to 0$

∞^∞ refers to $f(x) \approx$ (large number)$^{\text{(large number)}} \to \infty$

45. When $x = 100$, $x - \sinh x \approx -1.3 \times 10^{43}$. When $x = 228$, $\sinh x$ is already too large for the author's calculator to compute it. When $x = 227$ it yields $x - \sinh x \approx -1.9 \times 10^{98}$, which is an enormous negative number.

46.(a) $f'(0) = \lim\limits_{x \to 0} \dfrac{f(x) - f(0)}{x - 0} = \lim\limits_{x \to 0} \dfrac{1}{x} e^{-1/x^2}$

(b) Using the hint, we have

$$\lim\limits_{x \downarrow 0} \frac{1}{x} e^{-1/x^2} = \lim\limits_{t \to \infty} te^{-t^2} = \lim\limits_{t \to \infty} \frac{t}{e^{t^2}} = \lim\limits_{t \to \infty} \frac{1}{2te^{t^2}} = 0$$

and $\lim\limits_{x \uparrow 0} \dfrac{1}{x} e^{-1/x^2} = \lim\limits_{t \to -\infty} te^{-t^2} = \lim\limits_{t \to -\infty} \dfrac{t}{e^{t^2}} = \lim\limits_{t \to -\infty} \dfrac{1}{2te^{t^2}} = 0$

Hence $f'(0) = 0$.

47. If $n \neq -1$, then $\displaystyle\int_1^x t^n dt = \dfrac{t^{n+1}}{n+1}\Big|_1^x = \dfrac{x^{n+1} - 1}{n+1}$. For a fixed $x > 0$, this takes the $0/0$ form as $n \to -1$, so we may use L'Hôpital's Rule (differentiating with respect to n). Since

$$\frac{d}{dn} x^{n+1} = \frac{d}{dn} e^{(n+1)\ell n\, x} = e^{(n+1)\ell n\, x} \cdot \ell n\, x = x^{n+1} \ell n\, x$$

we have $\lim\limits_{n \to -1} \dfrac{x^{n+1} - 1}{n+1} = \lim\limits_{n \to -1} (x^{n+1} \ell n\, x) = \ell n\, x$.

48.(a) The variable is L. Since R and t are positive, $e^{-Rt/L} \to 0$ as $L \downarrow 0$. Hence $I \to E/R$.

(b) The variable is R. Since $e^{-Rt/L} \to 1$ as $R \downarrow 0$, the limit of I is a $0/0$ form. Hence we may use L'Hôpital's Rule (differentiating with respect to R) to find $\lim\limits_{R \downarrow 0} \dfrac{E(1 - e^{-Rt/L})}{R} = \lim\limits_{R \downarrow 0} E(\dfrac{t}{L} e^{-Rt/L}) = \dfrac{E}{L} t$.

(c) In a circuit with no inductance the current $I = E/R$ is a constant function (obeying Ohm's Law). In a circuit with no resistance the current is the linear function $I = \dfrac{E}{L} t$ (which increases without bound as time goes on). Neither of these formulas is realistic! But they tell us something about circuits with small inductance or small resistance.

49.(a) P and Q both approach $(1,0)$. It is not obvious what B approaches; part (b) settles the question.

(b) For fixed t, the slope of PQ is $\dfrac{\sin t - 0}{\cos t - (1 - t)} = \dfrac{\sin t}{\cos t - 1 + t}$. If b is the y coordinate of B, the slope of BQ is $\dfrac{b - 0}{0 - (1 - t)} = \dfrac{b}{t - 1}$. Hence $\dfrac{b}{t - 1} = \dfrac{\sin t}{\cos t - 1 + t}$, from which $b = \dfrac{(t - 1)\sin t}{(t - 1) + \cos t}$. Use L'Hôpital's Rule to find $\lim_{t\to 0} b = \lim_{t\to 0} \frac{(t-1)\cos t + \sin t}{1 - \sin t} = -1$. Hence B approaches $(0,-1)$. If you guessed right, your intuition is in good shape!

50.(a) F and G are continuous and differentiable in N because f and g are. Since $\lim_{x\to a} F(x) = \lim_{x\to a} f(x) = 0 = F(a)$ and (similarly) $\lim_{x\to a} G(x) = G(a)$, F and G are also continuous at $x = a$. Hence they satisfy the hypotheses of Cauchy's Theorem in the interval with endpoints a and x.

(b) Cauchy's Theorem yields a point c between a and x such that $G'(c)[F(x) - F(a)] = F'(c)[G(x) - G(a)]$. Since $G'(x) = g'(x)$ is never zero, we can write this equation in the form

$$\frac{F(x) - F(a)}{G(x) - G(a)} = \frac{F'(c)}{G'(c)}$$ (see part (d) of Problem 27, Sec. 4.3)

This reduces to $f(x)/g(x) = f'(c)/g'(c)$ because of the way F and G are defined.

(c) When $x \to a$, $c \to a$, so $\lim_{x\to a} \frac{f(x)}{g(x)} = \lim_{c\to a} \frac{f'(c)}{g'(c)} = \lim_{x\to a} \frac{f'(x)}{g'(x)}$ (the last step being merely a change of letter from c to x).

Section 11.3   IMPROPER INTEGRALS

1. $\int_0^t \frac{dx}{\sqrt{2-x}} = -2\sqrt{2-x}\Big|_0^t = 2(\sqrt{2} - \sqrt{2-t}) \to 2\sqrt{2}$ as $t \uparrow 2$.

2. $\int_t^1 \frac{dx}{x^2} = -\frac{1}{x}\Big|_t^1 = \frac{1}{t} - 1 \to \infty$ as $t \downarrow 0$. (The integral diverges.)

3. The integral is improper because of the unbounded behavior of $\sec x \tan x$ near $x = \pi/2$. (If we overlooked this, we might think that the integral is $\sec x \Big|_0^\pi = -1 - 1 = -2$, which is nonsense in view of the positive integrand.) To investigate $\int_0^{\pi/2} \sec x \tan x\, dx$, we write

$$\int_0^t \sec x \tan x\, dx = \sec t \Big|_0^t = \sec t - 1 \to \infty \text{ when } x \uparrow \pi/2$$

Hence this integral (and therefore also the original integral) diverges.

4. The integral is improper because of the unbounded behavior of $1/(4 - x^2)$ near $x = 2$. To investigate $\int_0^2 \frac{dx}{4 - x^2}$, we write

$$\int_0^t \frac{dx}{4 - x^2} = \frac{1}{4} \ln\frac{2+x}{2-x}\Big|_0^t = \frac{1}{4} \ln\frac{2+t}{2-t} \to \infty \text{ as } t \uparrow 2$$

Hence the original integral diverges.

5. $\int_0^t \frac{dx}{\sqrt{4 - x^2}} = \sin^{-1}\frac{x}{2}\Big|_0^t = \sin^{-1}\frac{t}{2} \to \pi/2$ as $t \uparrow 2$.

6. $\int_0^t \frac{dx}{\sqrt{1-x}} = -2\sqrt{1-x}\,\Big|_0^t = 2(1 - \sqrt{1-t}) \to 2$ as $t \uparrow 1$.

7. $\int_t^1 \frac{dx}{x^3} = \frac{-1}{2x^2}\,\Big|_t^1 = \frac{1}{2}(\frac{1}{t^2} - 1) \to \infty$ as $t \downarrow 0$.   (The integral diverges.)

8. $\int_0^t \frac{dx}{x-3} = \ell n\,|x-3|\,\Big|_0^t = \ell n\,|t-3| - \ell n\,3 \to -\infty$ as $t \uparrow 3$.   (The integral

diverges.)

9. The integral is improper because of the unbounded behavior of $1/(x-1)^2$

near $x = 1$. To investigate $\int_0^1 \frac{dx}{(x-1)^2}$, we write

$$\int_0^t \frac{dx}{(x-1)^2} = \frac{-1}{x-1}\,\Big|_0^t = \frac{1}{1-t} - 1 \to \infty \text{ as } t \uparrow 1.$$

The integral diverges.

10. $\int_0^t \tan x\,dx = \ell n\,\sec t \to \infty$ as $t \uparrow \pi/2$. The integral from 0 to $\pi/2$ (and hence

also the original integral) diverges.

11. $\int_t^1 \frac{dx}{\sqrt[3]{x}} = \frac{3}{2}x^{2/3}\,\Big|_t^1 = \frac{3}{2}(1 - t^{2/3}) \to 3/2$ as $t \downarrow 0$. Hence $\int_0^1 \frac{dx}{\sqrt[3]{x}} = 3/2$. Since the

integrand is odd, $\int_{-1}^0 \frac{dx}{\sqrt[3]{x}} = -3/2$, so the original integral is 0.

12. Integration by parts (Example 2, Sec. 10.1) yields

$$\int_t^1 \ell n\,x\,dx = (x\,\ell n\,x - x)\,\Big|_t^1 = t - t\,\ell n\,t - 1$$

Since $\lim_{t \downarrow 0} t\,\ell n\,t = \lim_{t \downarrow 0} \frac{\ell n\,t}{1/t} = \lim_{t \downarrow 0} \frac{1/t}{-1/t^2} = \lim_{t \downarrow 0} (-t) = 0$, we have $t - t\,\ell n\,t - 1 \to -1$

as $t \downarrow 0$.

13. Using the data from Example 4, Sec. 10.4, we find

$$\frac{dx}{1-\sin x} = \frac{1}{1 - 2u/(1+u^2)} \cdot \frac{2\,du}{1+u^2} = \frac{2\,du}{(1+u^2) - 2u} = \frac{2\,du}{(u-1)^2}$$

Hence $\int_0^t \frac{dx}{1-\sin x} = 2\int_0^{\tan(t/2)} \frac{du}{(u-1)^2} = \frac{-2}{u-1}\,\Big|_0^{\tan(t/2)} = \frac{2}{1-\tan(t/2)} - 2 \to \infty$

as $t \uparrow \pi/2$. The integral diverges. An alternative solution is to write

$$\int_0^{\pi/2} \frac{dx}{1-\sin x} = 2\int_0^1 \frac{du}{(u-1)^2}$$

(changing from one improper integral to another by substitution). Since

$$\int_0^t \frac{du}{(u-1)^2} = \frac{-1}{u-1}\,\Big|_0^t = \frac{1}{1-t} - 1 \to \infty \text{ as } t \uparrow 1$$

the new integral (and therefore the original one) diverges. However, we have

not proved that our substitution theorems apply directly to improper

integrals. The first solution is safer.

111

14. $2x - x^2 = -(x^2 - 2x + 1) + 1 = 1 - (x - 1)^2$. Hence

$$\int \frac{dx}{\sqrt{2x - x^2}} = \int \frac{dx}{\sqrt{1 - (x-1)^2}} = \sin^{-1}(x - 1) + C$$

The original integral is improper at both endpoints, so we break it up:

$$\int_0^2 \frac{dx}{\sqrt{2x - x^2}} = \int_0^1 \frac{dx}{\sqrt{2x - x^2}} + \int_1^2 \frac{dx}{\sqrt{2x - x^2}} \quad \text{(assuming that both integrals converge)}$$

The first integral is

$$\lim_{t \downarrow 0} \sin^{-1}(x - 1) \Big|_t^1 = -\lim_{t \downarrow 0} \sin^{-1}(t - 1) = -\sin^{-1}(-1) = \pi/2$$

while the second is

$$\lim_{t \uparrow 2} \sin^{-1}(x - 1) \Big|_1^t = \lim_{t \uparrow 2} \sin^{-1}(t - 1) = \sin^{-1} 1 = \pi/2$$

Hence the original integral is π. Note that we might have overlooked the whole thing by writing

$$\int_0^2 \frac{dx}{\sqrt{2x - x^2}} = \sin^{-1}(x - 1) \Big|_0^2 = \sin^{-1} 1 - \sin^{-1}(-1) = \pi$$

This is more luck than skill, however.

15. $\int_0^1 \frac{dx}{e^x - e^{-x}} = \frac{1}{2} \int_0^1 \operatorname{csch} x \, dx$, which is improper at the lower endpoint. Since

$$\int_t^1 \operatorname{csch} x \, dx = \ln\left(\tanh \frac{x}{2}\right) \Big|_t^1 = \ln\left(\tanh \frac{1}{2}\right) - \ln\left(\tanh \frac{t}{2}\right) \to \infty \text{ as } t \downarrow 0$$

(because $\tanh \frac{t}{2} \downarrow 0$), the integral diverges.

16. If $p < 1$, $\int_t^1 \frac{dx}{x^p} = \int_t^1 x^{-p} dx = \frac{x^{1-p}}{1 - p} \Big|_t^1 = \frac{1}{1-p}(1 - t^{1-p}) \to \frac{1}{1-p}$ as $t \downarrow 0$ (because the exponent $1 - p$ is positive). Note that the integral is **proper** if $p \le 0$. It does not hurt to treat it as improper, however. (See Problem 26.)

If $p = 1$, $\int_t^1 \frac{dx}{x^p} = \int_t^1 \frac{dx}{x} = -\ln t \to \infty$ as $t \downarrow 0$, so the integral diverges.

If $p > 1$, $\int_t^1 \frac{dx}{x^p} = \frac{1}{1-p}(1 - t^{1-p}) = \frac{1}{1-p}\left(1 - \frac{1}{t^{p-1}}\right) = \frac{1}{p-1}\left(\frac{1}{t^{p-1}} - 1\right) \to \infty$ as $t \downarrow 0$ (because $p - 1$ is positive). Again the integral diverges.

17. $\int_0^t (\sec^2 x - \sec x \tan x) dx = (\tan x - \sec x) \Big|_0^t = (\tan t - \sec t) + 1$

$$= \frac{\sin t - 1 + \cos t}{\cos t}$$

Since $\lim_{x \uparrow \pi/2} \frac{\sin t - 1 + \cos t}{\cos t} = \lim_{x \uparrow \pi/2} \frac{\cos t - \sin t}{-\sin t} = 1$, the integral converges. We have already seen (Example 4 and Problem 3) that $\int_0^{\pi/2} \sec^2 x \, dx$ and

$\int_0^{\pi/2} \sec x \tan x \, dx$ diverge. Note that if we attempt to use the formula

$$\int_0^{\pi/2}(\sec^2 x - \sec x \tan x)dx = \int_0^{\pi/2}\sec^2 x \, dx - \int_0^{\pi/2}\sec x \tan x \, dx$$

we get $1 = \infty - \infty$. (!)

18. See the graph in the solution of Problem 28, Sec. 8.3. The area is

$$A = \int_0^1 (0 - x \ln x)dx = -\int_0^1 x \ln x \, dx$$

Despite appearances ($\ln x$ is unbounded near $x = 0$), this integral is proper.
For the integrand $x \ln x$ is not unbounded, but approaches 0 as $x \downarrow 0$. (Use
L'Hôpital's Rule to see why.) The region whose area we seek is normal except
that the origin is missing from its boundary. We could fill in the
discontinuity by defining the integrand to be $x \ln x$ when $x > 0$ and 0 when
$x = 0$, but it is simpler to treat the integral as though it were improper
after all. Integration by parts (Problem 6, Sec. 10.1) yields

$$\int_t^1 x \ln x \, dx = (\tfrac{1}{2}x^2 \ln x - \tfrac{1}{4}x^2)\Big|_t^1 = -\tfrac{1}{4} - \tfrac{1}{2}t^2 \ln t + \tfrac{1}{4}t^2$$

Since $t^2 \ln t \to 0$ as $t \downarrow 0$, we find $A = \lim_{t \downarrow 0}(\tfrac{1}{4} + \tfrac{1}{2}t^2 \ln t - \tfrac{1}{4}t^2) = \tfrac{1}{4}$.

19. $A = \int_0^1 \dfrac{dx}{\sqrt{x}} = \lim_{t \downarrow 0} 2\sqrt{x}\Big|_t^1 = \lim_{t \downarrow 0}(2 - 2\sqrt{t}) = 2$

20. If a volume exists, it is

$$V = \pi \int_0^1 y^2 dx = \pi \int_0^1 \frac{dx}{x}$$

This integral diverges, however (Problem 16), so the answer is no.

21. The asymptotes are $x = \pm 1$. If the area exists, it is

$$A = 2\int_0^1 \frac{x \, dx}{\sqrt{1 - x^2}} = \lim_{t \uparrow 1}(-2\sqrt{1 - x^2})\Big|_0^t = \lim_{t \uparrow 1}(2 - 2\sqrt{1 - t^2}) = 2$$

22. Differentiate implicitly in $15y^2 = x^3 - 10x^2 + 25x$ to obtain

$$30yy' = 3x^2 - 20x + 25 \implies y' = \frac{(3x - 5)(x - 5)}{30y}$$

Then $1 + y'^2 = 1 + \dfrac{(3x - 5)^2(x - 5)^2}{900y^2} = 1 + \dfrac{(3x - 5)^2(x - 5)^2}{60x(x - 5)^2} = 1 + \dfrac{(3x - 5)^2}{60x}$

$$= \frac{9x^2 + 30x + 25}{60x} = \frac{(3x + 5)^2}{60x}$$

The loop is like the one in Figure 1 of the text, except that its intercepts
are $x = 0$ and $x = 5$. Hence

$$s = 2 \int_0^5 \sqrt{1 + y'^2}\, dx = \frac{1}{\sqrt{15}} \int_0^5 \frac{3x + 5}{\sqrt{x}}\, dx = \frac{1}{\sqrt{15}} \int_0^5 (3x^{1/2} + 5x^{-1/2})\, dx$$

$$= \frac{1}{\sqrt{15}} \lim_{t \downarrow 0} (2x^{3/2} + 10x^{1/2}) \Big|_t^5 = \frac{1}{\sqrt{15}} \lim_{t \downarrow 0} (20\sqrt{5} - 2t^{3/2} - 10t^{1/2}) = \frac{20}{\sqrt{3}}$$

23.(a) $\sqrt{\dfrac{1 + x}{1 - x}} = \sqrt{\dfrac{(1 + x)^2}{1 - x^2}} = \dfrac{1 + x}{\sqrt{1 - x^2}}$ $(-1 < x < 1)$

 (b) $\int \sqrt{\dfrac{1 + x}{1 - x}}\, dx = \int \dfrac{dx}{\sqrt{1 - x^2}} + \int \dfrac{x\,dx}{\sqrt{1 - x^2}} = \sin^{-1} x - \sqrt{1 - x^2} + C.$ Hence the

original integral is $\lim_{t \uparrow 1} (\sin^{-1} t - \sqrt{1 - t^2} + \pi/2) = \pi/2 + \pi/2 = \pi.$

24. $\int \ln t\, dt = t \ln t - t + C$ (Example 2, Sec. 10.1), so

$$\int_0^x \ln t\, dt = \lim_{u \downarrow 0} (x \ln x - x - u \ln u + u)$$

Since $u \ln u \to 0$ as $u \downarrow 0$ (by L'Hôpital's Rule), we find $\int_0^x \ln t\, dt = x \ln x - x.$ The

integral is 0 when $x \ln x = x \iff \ln x = 1$ (because $x > 0$) $\iff x = e.$

25. The integrand has only one discontinuity (at $x = 0$) and is bounded.

26. Let F be an antiderivative of f. Then

$$\lim_{t \uparrow b} \int_a^t f(x)dx = \lim_{t \uparrow b} [F(t) - F(a)] = F(b) - F(a) \quad \text{(because F is continuous)}$$

$$= \int_a^b f(x)dx$$

27. The integral is defined as $\int_{-1}^0 \dfrac{dx}{x} + \int_0^1 \dfrac{dx}{x}$ (if each of these exists), but

neither one does.

28. The first error is the notation for the limits. The sum is actually

$\lim_{t \uparrow 0} \ln |t| + \lim_{t \downarrow 0} (-\ln |t|).$ Even if this were overlooked, it is still incorrect

to write $\lim_{t \to 0} \ln |t| + \lim_{t \to 0} (-\ln |t|) = \lim_{t \to 0} (\ln |t| - \ln |t|).$ The algebra of limits

requires that each individual limit should exist. But $\lim_{t \to 0} \ln |t| = -\infty$ and

$\lim_{t \to 0} (-\ln |t|) = \infty.$ It is no good to argue that $-\infty + \infty = 0.$ (See Problem 17,

for example, where the attempt to give meaning to $\infty - \infty$ leads to the nonsense

$1 = \infty - \infty.$)

Section 11.4   OTHER TYPES OF IMPROPER INTEGRALS

1. $\int_0^b \frac{dx}{4+x^2} = \frac{1}{2}\tan^{-1}\frac{x}{2}\Big|_0^b = \frac{1}{2}\tan^{-1}\frac{b}{2} \to \frac{1}{2}\cdot\frac{\pi}{2} = \frac{\pi}{4}$ as $b \to \infty$.

2. $\int_0^b e^{-x}dx = -e^{-x}\Big|_0^b = 1 - e^{-b} \to 1$ as $b \to \infty$.

3. Integration by parts gives

$\int_0^b xe^{-x}dx = -(x+1)e^{-x}\Big|_0^b = 1 - (b+1)e^{-b} \to 1$ as $b \to \infty$ (by L'Hôpital's Rule)

4. $\int_0^b xe^{-x^2}dx = -\frac{1}{2}e^{-x^2}\Big|_0^b = \frac{1}{2} - \frac{1}{2}e^{-b^2} \to \frac{1}{2}$ as $b \to \infty$. Hence $\int_0^\infty xe^{-x^2}dx = \frac{1}{2}$. Since

the integrand is odd, $\int_{-\infty}^0 xe^{-x^2}dx = -\frac{1}{2}$, so the original integral is 0.

5. $\int_0^b \sin x\,dx = -\cos x\Big|_0^b = 1 - \cos b$, which does not have a limit as $b \to \infty$.

Hence the integral diverges.

6. $\int_0^b \operatorname{sech} x\,dx = \tan^{-1}(\sinh x)\Big|_0^b = \tan^{-1}(\sinh b) \to \pi/2$ as $b \to \infty$. Since the

integrand is even, the original integral is $2\int_0^\infty \operatorname{sech} x\,dx = \pi$.

7. Integration by parts (Problem 36, Sec. 10.1) gives

$\int_0^b e^{-x}\sin x\,dx = -\frac{1}{2}e^{-x}(\sin x + \cos x)\Big|_0^b = \frac{1}{2} - \frac{1}{2}e^{-b}(\sin b + \cos b) \to \frac{1}{2}$ as $b \to \infty$.

8. If $u = \sqrt{x}$, then $u^2 = x$, $2u\,du = dx$, and

$\int \frac{dx}{\sqrt{x}(1+x)} = \int \frac{2u\,du}{u(1+u^2)} = 2\int \frac{du}{1+u^2} = 2\tan^{-1}u + C = 2\tan^{-1}\sqrt{x} + C$

The original integral is improper in two ways, so we break it up:

$\int_0^\infty \frac{dx}{\sqrt{x}(1+x)} = \int_0^1 \frac{dx}{\sqrt{x}(1+x)} + \int_1^\infty \frac{dx}{\sqrt{x}(1+x)}$

$= \lim_{t\downarrow 0} 2(\frac{\pi}{4} - \tan^{-1}\sqrt{t}) + \lim_{b\to\infty} 2(\tan^{-1}\sqrt{b} - \frac{\pi}{4}) = \frac{\pi}{2} + 2(\frac{\pi}{2} - \frac{\pi}{4}) = \pi$

9. The integral is improper in two ways, so we write

$\int_1^\infty \frac{dx}{x\sqrt{x^2-1}} = \int_1^2 \frac{dx}{x\sqrt{x^2-1}} + \int_2^\infty \frac{dx}{x\sqrt{x^2-1}} = \lim_{t\downarrow 1}(\frac{\pi}{3} - \sec^{-1}t) + \lim_{b\to\infty}(\sec^{-1}b - \frac{\pi}{3})$

$= \frac{\pi}{3} - 0 + \frac{\pi}{2} - \frac{\pi}{3} = \frac{\pi}{2}$

10. $\int_0^\infty \frac{dx}{2-x} = \int_0^2 \frac{dx}{2-x} + \int_2^3 \frac{dx}{2-x} + \int_3^\infty \frac{dx}{2-x}$ (provided that each of these improper

integrals converges). To investigate the first one, we write

$$\int_0^t \frac{dx}{2-x} = -\ln(2-x)\Big|_0^t = \ln 2 - \ln(2-t) \to \infty \text{ as } t \uparrow 2$$

Hence this integral (and therefore the original integral) diverges.

11. If $p > 1$, $\int_1^b \frac{dx}{x^p} = \frac{x^{1-p}}{1-p}\Big|_1^b = \frac{1}{1-p}(b^{1-p}-1) = \frac{1}{p-1}\left(1-\frac{1}{b^{p-1}}\right) \to \frac{1}{p-1}$ as $b \to \infty$

(because $p-1 > 0$). If $p = 1$, $\int_1^b \frac{dx}{x^p} = \ln x\Big|_1^b = \ln b \to \infty$ as $b \to \infty$, so the

integral diverges. If $p < 1$, $\int_1^b \frac{dx}{x^p} = \frac{1}{1-p}(b^{1-p}-1) \to \infty$ as $b \to \infty$ (because

$1-p > 0$). Again the integral diverges.

12. $\int_0^\infty \frac{dx}{x^p} = \int_0^1 \frac{dx}{x^p} + \int_1^\infty \frac{dx}{x^p}$, provided that each of these integrals converges.
The first one, however, converges only if $p < 1$ and the second only if $p > 1$.
Hence the original integral diverges no matter what p is.

13.(a) $\frac{1}{x(x+1)} = \frac{A}{x} + \frac{B}{x+1} \implies 1 = A(x+1) + Bx$. Put $x = 0$ to find $A = 1$ and

$x = -1$ to find $B = -1$. Then if $x > 0$,

$$\int \frac{dx}{x(x+1)} = \int \frac{dx}{x} - \int \frac{dx}{x+1} = \ln x - \ln(x+1) + C = \ln \frac{x}{x+1} + C$$

(b) $\int_1^b \frac{dx}{x(x+1)} = \ln \frac{b}{b+1} - \ln \frac{1}{2} = \ln \frac{2b}{b+1} \to \ln 2$ as $b \to \infty$.

14. The left side is $\ln 2$, but the right side is meaningless. (The first
integral, for example, diverges by Problem 11.)

15. The curve and its asymptotes are shown in Figure 1. The area of the

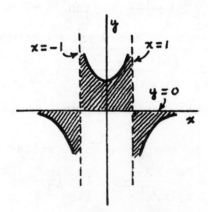

Figure 1

central region (if it exists) is $2\int_0^1 \frac{dx}{1-x^2} = \lim_{t \uparrow 1} \ln \frac{1+t}{1-t}$. The limit, however,

is ∞. The area of the right-hand region (and also the left-hand region) is

$\int_1^\infty (0 - \frac{1}{1 - x^2})dx = -\int_1^2 \frac{dx}{1 - x^2} - \int_2^\infty \frac{dx}{1 - x^2}$, provided that each integral converges.

The first one, however, is $\lim_{t \downarrow 1} \left(\ln 3 - \ln \left| \frac{1 + t}{1 - t} \right| \right) = -\infty$. Hence none of the regions can be assigned a finite area.

16. The work done in sending an object to a distance R from the center of the earth is

$$\int_{4000}^R F(x)dx = \int_{4000}^R \frac{k}{x}dx = k(\ln R - \ln 4000)$$

Since this increases without bound as $R \to \infty$, no object can be sent out of the planet's gravitational field.

17. $P(r) = \int_0^\infty e^{-rt}f(t)dt = k\int_0^\infty e^{-rt}dt = k\lim_{b \to \infty} \left(-\frac{1}{r}e^{-rt} \right) \Big|_0^b = \frac{k}{r}\lim_{b \to \infty}(1 - e^{-br}) = \frac{k}{r}$

18. The present value is $P(r) = \int_0^\infty e^{-rt}f(t)dt$, where $f(t)$ is the annual profit t years from now. Observe that (for all $t > 0$) $r_1 < r_2 \Rightarrow r_1 t < r_2 t \Rightarrow$

$e^{r_1 t} < e^{r_2 t} \Rightarrow e^{-r_1 t} > e^{-r_2 t} \Rightarrow e^{-r_1 t}f(t) > e^{-r_2 t}f(t)$ (assuming positive annual profit!). In other words, the graph of $y = e^{-r_1 t}f(t)$ is above the graph of $y = e^{-r_2 t}f(t)$ in the ty plane. Hence $\int_0^\infty e^{-r_1 t}f(t)dt > \int_0^\infty e^{-r_2 t}f(t)dt$, that is, $P(r_1) > P(r_2)$. Thus when the interest rate increases from r_1 to r_2, the present value decreases from $P(r_1)$ to $P(r_2)$.

19. $\int_{-\infty}^c f(x)dx + \int_c^\infty f(x)dx = \int_{-\infty}^0 f(x)dx + \int_0^c f(x)dx + \int_c^0 f(x)dx + \int_0^\infty f(x)dx$

$$= \int_{-\infty}^0 f(x)dx + \int_0^\infty f(x)dx = \int_{-\infty}^\infty f(x)dx$$

20. According to the definition in the text, $\int_{-\infty}^\infty \frac{x\,dx}{1 + x^2}$ diverges because

$\int_0^\infty \frac{x\,dx}{1 + x^2} = \lim_{b \to \infty} \frac{1}{2}\ln(1 + b^2) = \infty$

The suggested alternate definition gives $\int_{-\infty}^\infty \frac{x\,dx}{1 + x^2} = \lim_{b \to \infty} \frac{1}{2}\ln(1 + x^2) \Big|_{-b}^b = \lim_{b \to \infty} 0$

$= 0$, so the definitions are not equivalent.

21.(a) $x \geq 1 \Rightarrow x^2 \geq x \Rightarrow e^{x^2} \geq e^x \Rightarrow 0 < e^{-x^2} \leq e^{-x}$

$$\Rightarrow 0 \leq \int_1^b e^{-x^2}dx \leq \int_1^b e^{-x}dx \quad \text{(for } b \geq 1)$$

117

(b) The area under the graph of $y = e^{-x^2}$, $1 \leq x \leq b$, increases as b increases. Alternatively, we may observe that

$$\frac{d}{db} \int_1^b e^{-x^2} dx = e^{-b^2} > 0$$

so the integral is an increasing function of b. It does not increase without bound, however, because of the inequality in part (a):

$$\int_1^b e^{-x^2} dx \leq \int_1^b e^{-x} dx = e^{-1} - e^{-b} < e^{-1} \quad \text{for all b}$$

(c) Since $\int_1^b e^{-x^2} dx$ is an increasing function which is less than e^{-1} for all b, it has a limit as $b \to \infty$, that is, $\int_1^\infty e^{-x^2} dx$ exists. (This is geometrically apparent; a formal argument involves the concept of <u>least</u> <u>upper</u> <u>bound</u>.) Moreover, this limit cannot be larger than e^{-1}.

22.(a) $\Gamma(1) = \int_0^\infty e^{-t} dt = \lim_{b \to \infty} (1 - e^{-b}) = 1$. Using integration by parts, we have $\int te^{-t} dt = -(t+1)e^{-t} + C$. Hence

$$\Gamma(2) = \int_0^\infty te^{-t} dt = \lim_{b \to \infty} [1 - (b+1)e^{-b}] = 1$$

because $(b+1)e^{-b} \to 0$ as $b \to \infty$ (by L'Hôpital's Rule).

(b) $\Gamma(x+1) = \int_0^\infty t^x e^{-t} dt$. Letting $u = t^x$, $dv = e^{-t} dt$, we have $du = xt^{x-1} dt$ and $v = -e^{-t}$. Hence

$$\int_0^b t^x e^{-t} dt = -t^x e^{-t} \Big|_0^b + x \int_0^b t^{x-1} e^{-t} dt = -b^x e^{-b} + x \int_0^b t^{x-1} e^{-t} dt$$

If x is a positive integer, we know by L'Hôpital's Rule that $b^x e^{-b} \to 0$ as $b \to \infty$. If x is not a positive integer, let n be the smallest positive integer greater than x. Then $0 < b^x e^{-b} < b^n e^{-b} \to 0$ as $b \to \infty$. Hence $b^x e^{-b} \to 0$ in any case. Therefore

$$\Gamma(x+1) = \lim_{b \to \infty} (-b^x e^{-b} + x \int_0^b t^{x-1} e^{-t} dt) = x \int_0^\infty t^{x-1} e^{-t} dt = x\Gamma(x)$$

(c) The formula $\Gamma(n) = (n-1)!$ is correct when $n = 1$ because $\Gamma(1) = 1$ from part (a) and $(1-1)! = 0! = 1$ by the agreed convention. Assume that the formula is correct when $n = k$, that is, $\Gamma(k) = (k-1)!$ (where k is an arbitrary positive integer). Then by part (b) we have $\Gamma(k+1) = k\Gamma(k) = k(k-1)! = k!$, so the formula is correct when $n = k+1$. By the Principle of Mathematical Induction it is correct for every positive integer n.

23. If $f(t) = 1$, then (for all $x > 0$) $L(x) = \int_0^\infty e^{-xt}dt = \lim\limits_{b \to \infty} \frac{1}{x}(1 - e^{-xb}) = \frac{1}{x}$.

24. If $f(t) = t$, then (for all $x > 0$)

$$L(x) = \int_0^\infty te^{-xt}dt = \lim\limits_{b \to \infty} \frac{1}{x^2}[1 - (xb+1)e^{-xb}] = \frac{1}{x^2}$$

(We used integration by parts, with $u = t$, $dv = e^{-xt}dt$.)

25. If $f(t) = \sin t$, then $L(x) = \int_0^\infty e^{-xt}\sin t\, dt$. Using integration by parts
(Problem 36, Sec. 10.1), we have

$$\int e^{-xt}\sin t\, dt = \frac{e^{-xt}(-x\sin t - \cos t)}{x^2 + 1} + C$$

Hence $L(x) = \lim\limits_{b \to \infty} \frac{1}{1 + x^2}[1 - e^{-xb}(x\sin b + \cos b)] = \frac{1}{1+x^2}$ (provided that $x > 0$).

Section 11.5   TAYLOR POLYNOMIALS

1. The values of f and its successive derivatives at $x = 0$ are

$$f(x) = 5 - 2x + x^2 + 6x^3 + 2x^4 = 5$$
$$f'(x) = -2 + 2x + 18x^2 + 8x^3 = -2$$
$$f''(x) = 2 + 36x + 24x^2 = 2$$
$$f'''(x) = 36 + 48x = 36$$
$$f^{(4)}(x) = 48$$

All higher-order derivatives are zero. Hence $R_4(x) = 0$ and

$$P_4(x) = 5 - 2x + x^2 + 6x^3 + 2x^4 = f(x)$$

In other words, $f(x)$ is its own fourth-order Taylor polynomial. More
generally, any polynomial of degree n is its own nth-order Taylor polynomial.

2. The base point is $a = 1$. The values of f and its successive derivatives
at $x = 1$ are

$$f(x) = 2 + x^2 - 5x^3 = -2$$
$$f'(x) = 2x - 15x^2 = -13$$
$$f''(x) = 2 - 30x = -28$$
$$f'''(x) = -30$$

All higher-order derivatives are zero. Hence $R_3(x) = 0$ and

$$f(x) = P_3(x) = -2 - 13(x - 1) - 14(x - 1)^2 - 5(x - 1)^3$$

By expanding and collecting terms on the right side, you can check that it is
the same as the original polynomial $f(x)$.

3. Every derivative is $e^x = 1$ at $x = 0$. Hence the nth-order Taylor

polynomial associated with e^x at a = 0 is

$$P_n(x) = 1 + x + \frac{x^2}{2!} + \frac{x^3}{3!} + \cdots + \frac{x^n}{n!}$$

Moreover, $e^x \approx P_n(x)$.

4. $R_n(x) = \frac{e^c}{(n+1)!} x^{n+1}$ for some c between 0 and x. Since $0 < |c| < |x|$,

$e^c \le e^{|c|} \le e^{|x|}$, so $|R_n(x)| \le \frac{e^{|x|}}{(n+1)!} |x|^{n+1}$.

5. $e^{0.2} \approx 1 + 0.2 + \frac{(0.2)^2}{2!} + \frac{(0.2)^3}{3!} + \frac{(0.2)^4}{4!} = 1.2214$, with error

$$|R_4(0.2)| \le \frac{e^{0.2}}{5!}(0.2)^5$$

Since $e^{0.2} < e < 3$, $|R_4(0.2)| < \frac{3(0.2)^5}{5!} = 0.8 \times 10^{-5} < 0.00001$. Hence

$e^{0.2} = 1.2214$ correct to four places.

6.(a) By Problem 4, $|R_n(1)| \le \frac{e^{|1|}}{(n+1)!} |1|^{n+1} < \frac{3}{(n+1)!}$.

(b) Choose n satisfying

$$\frac{3}{(n+1)!} < \frac{1}{2} \times 10^{-3} \implies \frac{(n+1)!}{3} > 2 \times 10^3 \implies (n+1)! > 6000$$

Since 7! = 5040 and 8! = 40,320, n + 1 should be 8, that is, n should be 7. Hence we compute

$$e \approx 1 + 1 + \frac{1}{2!} + \frac{1}{3!} + \cdots + \frac{1}{7!} = 2.71825\cdots$$

or e = 2.718 correct to three places.

7. The values of f and its successive derivatives at x = 0 are $f(x) = e^{-x}$ = 1, $f'(x) = -e^{-x} = -1$, $f''(x) = e^{-x} = 1$, and so on, the general formula being $f^{(n)}(0) = (-1)^n$. Hence $e^{-x} = 1 - x + \frac{x^2}{2!} - \frac{x^3}{3!} + \cdots + (-1)^n \frac{x^n}{n!}$.

8. $e^{-x} = 1 + (-x) + \frac{(-x)^2}{2!} + \frac{(-x)^3}{3!} + \cdots + \frac{(-x)^n}{n!} = 1 - x + \frac{x^2}{2!} - \frac{x^3}{3!} + \cdots + (-1)^n \frac{x^n}{n!}$

9. The values of f and its successive derivatives at x = 0 are $f(x) = \cosh x$ = 1, $f'(x) = \sinh x = 0$, $f''(x) = \cosh x = 1$, and so on. Hence (taking n = 4) we have $\cosh x \approx 1 + 0x + \frac{x^2}{2!} + 0x^3 + \frac{x^4}{4!} = 1 + \frac{x^2}{2!} + \frac{x^4}{4!}$.

10. $\cosh x \approx \frac{1}{2}(1 + x + \frac{x^2}{2!} + \frac{x^3}{3!} + \frac{x^4}{4!}) + \frac{1}{2}(1 - x + \frac{x^2}{2!} - \frac{x^3}{3!} + \frac{x^4}{4!}) = 1 + \frac{x^2}{2!} + \frac{x^4}{4!}$

11. The values of f and its successive derivatives at x = 0 are $f(x) = \sinh x$ = 0, $f'(x) = \cosh x = 1$, $f''(x) = \sinh x = 0$, and so on. Hence (taking n = 5)

we have $\sinh x \approx 0 + x + 0x^2 + \frac{x^3}{3!} + 0x^4 + \frac{x^5}{5!} = x + \frac{x^3}{3!} + \frac{x^5}{5!}$.

12. $\sinh x = \frac{1}{2}e^x - \frac{1}{2}e^{-x} \approx \frac{1}{2}(1 + x + \frac{x^2}{2!} + \frac{x^3}{3!} + \frac{x^4}{4!} + \frac{x^5}{5!}) - \frac{1}{2}(1 - x + \frac{x^2}{2!} - \frac{x^3}{3!} + \frac{x^4}{4!} - \frac{x^5}{5!})$

$= x + \frac{x^3}{3!} + \frac{x^5}{5!}$

13. Using the hint, we have $f^{(k)}(0) = \sin\frac{k\pi}{2}$, $k = 0, 1, 2, \cdots$. Hence

$\sin x \approx \sin 0 + (\sin\frac{\pi}{2})x + (\sin\pi)\frac{x^2}{2!} + (\sin\frac{3\pi}{2})\frac{x^3}{3!} + \cdots + (\sin\frac{n\pi}{2})\frac{x^n}{n!}$

$= 0 + x + 0x^2 - \frac{x^3}{3!} + 0x^4 + \frac{x^5}{5!} + \cdots + (\frac{1}{n!}\sin\frac{n\pi}{2})x^n$

14. $R_n(x) = \frac{f^{(n+1)}(c)}{(n+1)!}x^{n+1}$, where c is between 0 and x. Since

$|f^{(n+1)}(c)| = |\sin[c + \frac{1}{2}(n+1)\pi]| \leq 1$, we have $|R_n(x)| \leq \frac{|x|^{n+1}}{(n+1)!}$.

15. When $n = 2m$ is even, the formula in Problem 13 ends with the term $0x^{2m}$, rather than with the preceding nonzero term. The remainder is smaller when we include this extra term (at least for values of x close to 0). The coefficient of the last nonzero term is $\frac{1}{(2m-1)!}\sin\frac{1}{2}(2m-1)\pi = \frac{(-1)^{m-1}}{(2m-1)!}$, so

$\sin x \approx x - \frac{x^3}{3!} + \frac{x^5}{5!} - \cdots + \frac{(-1)^{m-1}}{(2m-1)!}x^{2m-1}$

16. When $n = 4$ the formula in Problem 13 is

$\sin x \approx 0 + x + 0x^2 - \frac{x^3}{3!} + 0x^4 = x - \frac{1}{6}x^3$

and the error in Problem 14 is

$|R_4(x)| \leq \frac{|x|^5}{5!} = \frac{1}{5!}$ when $x = 1$

Hence $\sin 1 \approx 1 - \frac{1}{6} = 0.8\overline{3}$, with error $\leq 0.008\overline{3}$. Since $0.8\overline{3} + 0.008\overline{3} = 0.841\overline{6}$ and $0.8\overline{3} - 0.008\overline{3} = 0.825\overline{0}$, we have $0.825\overline{0} \leq \sin 1 \leq 0.841\overline{6}$. The best value we can report is $\sin 1 = 0.8$ (correct to one place).

17. $\sin 0.2 \approx 0.2 - \frac{1}{6}(0.2)^3 = 0.198\overline{6}$, with error $\leq \frac{(0.2)^5}{5!} = 0.000002\overline{6}$. Since $0.198\overline{6} + 0.000002\overline{6} = 0.198669\overline{3}$ and $0.198\overline{6} - 0.000002\overline{6} = 0.198664\overline{0}$, we have $0.198664\overline{0} \leq \sin 0.2 \leq 0.198669\overline{3}$. The best value we can report is $\sin 0.2 = 0.1987$ (correct to four places).

18. The given formula may be considered to end with $0x^{10}$, that is, we are taking $n = 10$ (not 9). Since $0 < x < \pi/2$, the error (from Problem 14) is

$|R_{10}(x)| < \frac{(\pi/2)^{11}}{11!} < 0.000004$

This yields five-place accuracy.

19. We know from Problems 13 and 14 that (for all x) $\sin x = 0 + x + 0x^2 + R_2(x)$,

where $|R_2(x)| \le \dfrac{|x|^3}{3!}$. Hence $|\sin x - x| = |R_2(x)| \le \dfrac{1}{6}|x|^3$. If $x \ne 0$, we may

divide by $|x|$ to obtain $\left|\dfrac{\sin x}{x} - 1\right| \le \dfrac{1}{6}|x|^2$. Since $\dfrac{1}{6}|x|^2 \to 0$ when $x \to 0$, the

left side can be made arbitrarily small by taking x close to 0. Hence

$\lim\limits_{x \to 0} \dfrac{\sin x}{x} = 1$. (Actually this is circular reasoning! The Taylor formula for

$\sin x$ requires the derivative of $\sin x$, which depends on this limit.)

20. As the hint suggests, we may regard the given formula as ending with $0x^3$,

that is, we are taking n = 3 (not 2). The error (from Example 3) is $|R_3(x)|$

$\le |x|^4/4!$. If $|x| \le 0.3$, the error is $\le (0.3)^4/4! < 0.0004$, which guarantees

three-place accuracy.

21. We know that $\cos x = 1 + 0x + R_1(x)$, where $|R_1(x)| \le |x|^2/2!$. Hence

$|1 - \cos x| = |R_1(x)| \le \dfrac{1}{2}|x|^2$. If $x \ne 0$, we may divide by $|x|$ to obtain

$\left|\dfrac{1 - \cos x}{x}\right| \le \dfrac{1}{2}|x|$. Since $\dfrac{1}{2}|x| \to 0$ when $x \to 0$, $\lim\limits_{x \to 0} \dfrac{1 - \cos x}{x} = 0$.

22. $\cos 0.1 \approx 1 - \dfrac{(0.1)^2}{2!} + \dfrac{(0.1)^4}{4!} = 0.995004166\cdots$ (plus a zero term), with

error $|R_5(0.1)| \le (0.1)^6/6! < 0.000000002$. Hence $\cos 0.1 = 0.99500417$ correct

to eight places.

23. $\cos 0.2 \approx 1 - \dfrac{(0.2)^2}{2!} + \dfrac{(0.2)^4}{4!} - \dfrac{(0.2)^6}{6!} = 0.9800665777\cdots$ (plus a zero term),

with error $|R_7(0.2)| \le (0.2)^8/8! < 0.0000000002$. Hence $\cos 0.2 = 0.980066578$

correct to nine places.

24.(a) $f(x) = \tan x = 0$ at $x = 0$ and $f'(x) = \sec^2 x = 1$ at $x = 0$. Hence

$\tan x \approx P_1(x) = 0 + 1x = x$.

 (b) $f''(x) = 2 \sec x \cdot \sec x \tan x = 2 \sec^2 x \tan x = 0$ at $x = 0$ and $f'''(x) =$

$2 \sec^2 x \cdot \sec^2 x + 4 \sec x \cdot \sec x \tan x \cdot \tan x = 2 \sec^2 x (\sec^2 x + 2 \tan^2 x) = 2$ at $x = 0$.

Hence $\tan x \approx P_3(x) = 0 + 1x + 0x^2 + 2x^3/3! = x + \dfrac{1}{3}x^3$.

 (c) $f^{(4)}(x) = 2 \sec^2 x (2 \sec x \cdot \sec x \tan x + 4 \tan x \cdot \sec^2 x) +$

$4 \sec x \cdot \sec x \tan x (\sec^2 x + 2 \tan^2 x) = 8 \sec^2 x \tan x (2 \sec^2 x + \tan^2 x) = 0$ at $x = 0$

and $f^{(5)}(x) = 8 \sec^2 x \tan x (4 \sec x \cdot \sec x \tan x + 2 \tan x \cdot \sec^2 x) +$

$(8 \sec^2 x \cdot \sec^2 x + 16 \sec x \cdot \sec x \tan x \cdot \tan x)(2 \sec^2 x + \tan^2 x) = 16$ at $x = 0$. Hence

$$\tan x \approx P_5(x) = 0 + 1x + 0x^2 + \frac{2x^3}{3!} + 0x^4 + \frac{16x^5}{5!} = x + \frac{1}{3}x^3 + \frac{2}{15}x^5$$

25.

$$1 - \frac{x^2}{2} + \frac{x^4}{24} \;\Big|\; \begin{array}{l} x + \frac{1}{3}x^3 + \frac{2}{15}x^5 \\[4pt] \hline x - \frac{x^3}{6} + \frac{x^5}{120} \\[6pt] \underline{x - \frac{x^3}{2} + \frac{x^5}{24}} \\[6pt] \frac{x^3}{3} - \frac{x^5}{30} \\[6pt] \underline{\frac{x^3}{3} - \frac{x^5}{6} + \frac{x^7}{72}} \\[6pt] \frac{2x^5}{15} - \frac{x^7}{72} \end{array}$$

Ignoring all further terms, we have $\tan x \approx x + \frac{1}{3}x^3 + \frac{2}{15}x^5$. (This is not as arbitrary as it may look. In the next chapter we will express $\sin x$ and $\cos x$ as _infinite_ _series_; then the above division continues in a coherent way to produce a series for $\tan x$.)

26. Referring to Problem 24, we have $\tan x = 0 + x + 0x^2 + R_2(x)$, where $R_2(x) = \frac{f'''(c)}{3!}x^3$ (c is between 0 and x). Hence $|\tan x - x| = |R_2(x)| = \frac{|f'''(c)|}{3!}|x|^3$.

Since $f'''(c) = 2\sec^2 c\,(\sec^2 c + 2\tan^2 c)$ (Problem 24) and since $|c| < |x| \leq \pi/6$, we have $|f'''(c)| \leq 2\sec^2\frac{\pi}{6}(\sec^2\frac{\pi}{6} + 2\tan^2\frac{\pi}{6}) = 2 \cdot \frac{4}{3}(\frac{4}{3} + 2 \cdot \frac{1}{3}) = \frac{16}{3}$. Hence $|\tan x - x| \leq \frac{16/3}{3!}|x|^3 = \frac{8}{9}|x|^3$. If $x \neq 0$, we may divide by $|x|$ to obtain $\left|\frac{\tan x}{x} - 1\right| \leq \frac{8}{9}|x|^2$. Since $\frac{8}{9}|x|^2 \to 0$ when $x \to 0$, $\lim\limits_{x \to 0} \frac{\tan x}{x} = 1$.

27. The base point is $a = \pi/4$. Using the derivatives computed in Problem 24, we find $f(\pi/4) = 1$, $f'(\pi/4) = 2$, and $f''(\pi/4) = 4$. Hence

$$\tan x = P_2(x) + R_2(x) = 1 + 2(x - \pi/4) + 2(x - \pi/4)^2 + R_2(x)$$

Since $R_2(x) = \frac{f'''(c)}{3!}(x - \pi/4)^3$, where $\pi/4 < c < x < \pi/3$, and since $f'''(c) = 2\sec^2 c\,(\sec^2 c + 2\tan^2 c)$, we have $0 \leq R_2(x) \leq \frac{1}{3!} \cdot 2 \cdot 4(4 + 2 \cdot 3)(x - \pi/4)^3 = \frac{40}{3}(x - \pi/4)^3$.

28. $\tan 0.8 \approx 1 + 2(0.8 - \pi/4) + 2(0.8 - \pi/4)^2 = 1.0296301\cdots$, with error $R_2(0.8) \leq \frac{40}{3}(0.8 - \pi/4)^3 < 0.00005$. Hence $\tan 0.8 = 1.0296$ correct to four places.

29. At $x = 1$ we have $f(x) = \sqrt{x} = 1$, $f'(x) = \frac{1}{2}x^{-1/2} = \frac{1}{2}$, and $f''(x) = -\frac{1}{4}x^{-3/2} = -\frac{1}{4}$. Hence $\sqrt{x} \approx 1 + \frac{1}{2}(x - 1) - \frac{1}{8}(x - 1)^2$ and $\sqrt{0.98} \approx 1 + \frac{1}{2}(-0.02) - \frac{1}{8}(-0.02)^2 = 0.98995$.

30. At $x = 0$ we have $f(x) = \sec x = 1$, $f'(x) = \sec x \tan x = 0$, $f''(x) = \sec x \cdot \sec^2 x + \sec x \tan x \cdot \tan x = 1$. Hence $\sec x \approx 1 + 0x + x^2/2! = 1 + \frac{1}{2}x^2$ and $\sec 0.2 \approx 1 + \frac{1}{2}(0.2)^2 = 1.02$.

31. The values of f and its successive derivatives at $x = 1$ are $f(x) = \ln x = 0$, $f'(x) = x^{-1} = 1$, $f''(x) = -x^{-2} = -1$, $f'''(x) = 2x^{-3} = 2$, $f^{(4)}(x) = -3!\,x^{-4} = -3!$, and (in general) $f^{(n)}(x) = (-1)^{n-1}(n-1)!\,x^{-n} = (-1)^{n-1}(n-1)!$. Hence

$$P_n(x) = 0 + 1(x-1) - \frac{1}{2!}(x-1)^2 + \frac{2}{3!}(x-1)^3 - \frac{3!}{4!}(x-1)^4 + \cdots$$

$$+ \frac{(-1)^{n-1}(n-1)!}{n!}(x-1)^n$$

$$= (x-1) - \frac{(x-1)^2}{2} + \frac{(x-1)^3}{3} - \frac{(x-1)^4}{4} + \cdots + (-1)^{n-1}\frac{(x-1)^n}{n}$$

32. Since $f^{(n+1)}(x) = (-1)^n n!\,x^{-(n+1)}$, we have

$$R_n(x) = \frac{(-1)^n n!\,c^{-(n+1)}}{(n+1)!}(x-1)^{n+1} = \frac{(-1)^n}{n+1}\left(\frac{x-1}{c}\right)^{n+1}$$

where c is between 1 and x.

33. $\ln 1.1 \approx 0.1 - \frac{(0.1)^2}{2} + \frac{(0.1)^3}{3} - \frac{(0.1)^4}{4} = 0.0953083\overline{3}$, with error

$$|R_4(1.1)| = \frac{1}{5}\left(\frac{0.1}{c}\right)^5 \quad \text{(where } c \text{ is between 1 and 1.1)}$$

Hence the error is $\leq \frac{1}{5}(0.1)^5 = 0.000002$ and we have $0.0953063\overline{3} \leq \ln 1.1 \leq$ $0.0953103\overline{3}$. The best value we can report is $\ln 1.1 = 0.09531$ (correct to five places).

34. The values of f and its successive derivatives at $x = 0$ are $f(x) = (1-x)^{-1} = 1$, $f'(x) = (1-x)^{-2} = 1$, $f''(x) = 2(1-x)^{-3} = 2$, $f'''(x) = 3!(1-x)^{-4}$, and (in general) $f^{(n)}(x) = n!(1-x)^{-(n+1)} = n!$. Hence

$$P_n(x) = 1 + 1x + \frac{2}{2!}x^2 + \frac{3!}{3!}x^3 + \cdots + \frac{n!}{n!}x^n = 1 + x + x^2 + x^3 + \cdots + x^n$$

35. $P_n(x) - xP_n(x) = (1 + x + x^2 + \cdots + x^n) - (x + x^2 + x^3 + \cdots + x^{n+1})$, which telescopes to $1 - x^{n+1}$. Hence $(1-x)P_n(x) = 1 - x^{n+1}$ and $P_n(x) = \frac{1 - x^{n+1}}{1 - x}$ (if $x \neq 1$).

36. $R_n(x) = \frac{1}{1-x} - P_n(x) = \frac{1}{1-x} - \frac{1 - x^{n+1}}{1-x} = \frac{x^{n+1}}{1-x}$

37. If $|x| < 1$, then $x^{n+1} \to 0$ as $n \to \infty$. Hence $\lim_{n \to \infty} R_n(x) = 0$.

38. (a) $\int_0^x \frac{dt}{1-t} \approx \left(t + \frac{t^2}{2} + \frac{t^3}{3} + \cdots + \frac{t^n}{n}\right)\Big|_0^x = x + \frac{x^2}{2} + \frac{x^3}{3} + \cdots + \frac{x^n}{n}$. The only restriction required here is $x < 1$ (to avoid an improper integral). We impose $-1 < x < 1$ to stay in the domain of the series in Problem 37.

(b) If $-1 < x < 1$, then $\int_0^x \frac{dt}{1-t} = -\ln(1-t)\Big|_0^x = -\ln(1-x)$. Hence from part (a) we have $\ln(1-x) \approx -x - \frac{x^2}{2} - \frac{x^3}{3} - \cdots - \frac{x^n}{n}$.

(c) $\ln x \approx -(1-x) - \frac{(1-x)^2}{2} - \frac{(1-x)^3}{3} - \cdots - \frac{(1-x)^n}{n}$

$\qquad = (x-1) - \frac{(x-1)^2}{2} + \frac{(x-1)^3}{3} - \cdots + (-1)^{n-1}\frac{(x-1)^n}{n}$

where $-1 < 1-x < 1$, that is, $0 < x < 2$.

39. At $x = 0$ we have $f(x) = \tan^{-1}x = 0$ and $f'(x) = 1/(1+x^2) = 1$. Hence $P_1(x) = 0 + x = x$. Since $f''(x) = -2x/(1+x^2)^2$, we have

$$R_1(x) = \frac{f''(c)}{2!}x^2 = \frac{-2cx^2}{2!(1+c^2)^2} = \frac{-cx^2}{(1+c^2)^2} \quad \text{(where } c \text{ is between 0 and } x)$$

Thus $\tan^{-1}x = P_1(x) + R_1(x) = x - \frac{cx^2}{(1+c^2)^2}$

40. Since $0 < c < 0.2$, the error is $|R_1(0.2)| = \frac{c(0.2)^2}{(1+c^2)^2} < \frac{(0.2)^3}{1^2} = 0.008 < 0.01$. This guarantees one-place accuracy.

41.(a) $\frac{1}{1-(-t^2)} \approx 1 + (-t^2) + (-t^2)^2 + \cdots + (-t^2)^{n-1}$, that is,

$\qquad \frac{1}{1+t^2} \approx 1 - t^2 + t^4 - \cdots + (-1)^{n-1}t^{2n-2}$

(b) $\int_0^x \frac{dt}{1+t^2} \approx \left(t - \frac{t^3}{3} + \frac{t^5}{5} - \cdots + (-1)^{n-1}\frac{t^{2n-1}}{2n-1} \right)\Big|_0^x$, that is,

$\qquad \tan^{-1}x \approx x - \frac{x^3}{3} + \frac{x^5}{5} - \cdots + (-1)^{n-1}\frac{x^{2n-1}}{2n-1}$

42. $\tan^{-1}0.2 \approx 0.2 - \frac{(0.2)^3}{3} = 0.197\overline{3}$. A calculator gives $\tan^{-1}0.2 = 0.19739\cdots$ so we have three-place accuracy.

43. The equation $\sin x = x^2$ becomes $x - \frac{1}{6}x^3 = x^2$ if the approximation is considered exact. Since we are looking for the nonzero root, we may divide by x: $1 - \frac{1}{6}x^2 = x \iff x^2 + 6x - 6 = 0 \iff x = \frac{1}{2}(-6 \pm \sqrt{36+24}) = -3 \pm \sqrt{15}$. The root we seek is positive, namely $\sqrt{15} - 3 \approx 0.87$.

44.(a) The line $y = 1 + 2x$ intersects the curve $y = e^x$ at $(0,1)$ and at a point with positive x coordinate r. Thus the only root besides r is 0.

(b) The equation $e^x = 1 + 2x$ becomes $1 + x + \frac{x^2}{2} + \frac{x^3}{6} = 1 + 2x \iff x^3 + 3x^2 - 6x = 0$ if the approximation is considered exact. Since we are looking for the positive root, we may divide by x: $x^2 + 3x - 6 = 0 \iff x = \frac{1}{2}(-3 \pm \sqrt{33})$. The positive root is $\frac{1}{2}(-3 + \sqrt{33}) \approx 1.37$.

(c) Let $f(x) = e^x - 1 - 2x$, $f'(x) = e^x - 2$. If $x = 1.37$, then

$$x_1 = x_0 - f(x_0)/f'(x_0) = 1.37 - (e^{1.37} - 1 - 2.74)/(e^{1.37} - 2) \approx 1.27$$

$$x_2 = 1.27 - (e^{1.27} - 1 - 2.54)/(e^{1.27} - 2) \approx 1.2566$$

$$x_3 = 1.2566 - (e^{1.2566} - 1 - 2.5132)/(e^{1.2566} - 2) \approx 1.2564$$

It seems safe to say that the root is 1.26 correct to two places.

45.(a) $e^{-x^2} \approx 1 - x^2 + \dfrac{x^4}{2} - \dfrac{x^6}{6}$, so

$$\int_0^{0.5} e^{-x^2} dx \approx 0.5 - \frac{(0.5)^3}{3} + \frac{(0.5)^5}{10} - \frac{(0.5)^7}{42} \approx 0.461272$$

(b) The partition is $\{0, 0.125, 0.25, 0.375, 0.5\}$, with $\Delta x = 0.125$. Hence

$$\int_0^{0.5} e^{-x^2} dx \approx \frac{0.125}{3}[1 + 4e^{-(0.125)^2} + 2e^{-(0.25)^2} + 4e^{-(0.375)^2} + e^{-(0.5)^2}]$$

$$\approx 0.461286$$

46.(a) $\dfrac{\sin x}{x} \approx 1 - \dfrac{x^2}{6} + \dfrac{x^4}{120}$, so $\displaystyle\int_0^1 \frac{\sin x}{x} dx \approx 1 - \frac{1}{18} + \frac{1}{600} \approx 0.946111.$

(b) The partition is $\{0, 0.25, 0.5, 0.75, 1\}$, with $\Delta x = 0.25$. Hence

$$\int_0^1 \frac{\sin x}{x} dx \approx \frac{0.25}{3}(1 + \frac{4 \sin 0.25}{0.25} + \frac{2 \sin 0.5}{0.5} + \frac{4 \sin 0.75}{0.75} + \sin 1) \approx 0.946087$$

47.(a) If $x = a$, Taylor's Formula reduces to $f(a) = f(a)$, which is trivial. If $x \neq a$, and we let $b = x$, the approximation $f(b) \approx P_n(b)$ becomes exact by writing $f(b) = P_n(b) + R_n(b)$, where $R_n(b) = f(b) - P_n(b)$. This is trivial, too, since we have done nothing more than use the label $R_n(b)$ for the difference $f(b) - P_n(b)$. The problem is to show that this expression has the form given in the statement of Taylor's Formula (with x replaced by b).

(b) When x is replaced by a in the formula for $F(x)$, the expression in brackets becomes $P_n(b)$. Hence

$$F(a) = P_n(b) + \frac{R_n(b)}{(b-a)^{n+1}}(b-a)^{n+1} - f(b) = P_n(b) + R_n(b) - f(b)$$

$$= f(b) - f(b) = 0$$

We see by inspection that $F(b) = f(b) - f(b) = 0$, since every term but the first and last is zero.

To find $F'(x)$, differentiate the expression in brackets first. The typical term (not counting the first one) is $\dfrac{1}{k!}f^{(k)}(x)(b-x)^k$, $k = 1, 2, \ldots, n$. The derivative of this term (by the Product Rule) is

$$\frac{1}{k!}f^{(k+1)}(x)(b-x)^k - \frac{1}{(k-1)!}f^{(k)}(x)(b-x)^{k-1}$$

Hence the derivative of the expression in brackets is

$$f'(x) + [f''(x)(b-x) - f'(x)] + [\frac{f'''(x)}{2!}(b-x)^2 - f''(x)(b-x)] + \cdots$$

$$+ [\frac{f^{(n+1)}(x)}{n!}(b-x)^n - \frac{f^{(n)}(x)}{(n-1)!}(b-x)^{n-1}]$$

This telescopes (the second term in each bracket cancelling the first term in the preceding bracket), that is, it collapses to $\frac{f^{(n+1)}(x)}{n!}(b-x)^n$. Differentiating the rest of $F(x)$, we find

$$F'(x) = \frac{f^{(n+1)}(x)}{n!}(b-x)^n - \frac{(n+1)R_n(b)}{(b-a)^{n+1}}(b-x)^n$$

(c) Rolle's Theorem yields a point c between a and b such that $F'(c) = 0$.

Hence $\frac{f^{(n+1)}(c)}{n!}(b-c)^n = \frac{(n+1)R_n(b)}{(b-a)^{n+1}}(b-c)^n \Rightarrow R_n(b) = \frac{f^{(n+1)}(c)}{(n+1)!}(b-a)^{n+1}$.

Chapter 11   TRUE-FALSE QUIZ

1. True. A critic who doubts that $e^{-x} \to 0$ as $x \to \infty$ would name $\epsilon > 0$ and challenge us to name A such that $x > A \Rightarrow |e^{-x} - 0| < \epsilon$. Since $|e^{-x} - 0| < \epsilon$ $\Leftrightarrow e^{-x} < \epsilon \Leftrightarrow -x < \ln \epsilon \Leftrightarrow x > -\ln \epsilon = \ln(1/\epsilon)$, our choice is $A = \ln(1/\epsilon)$.

2. True. $e^{1/x} \to 1$ as $x \to \infty$, so $xe^{1/x} \to \infty$.

3. False. $\frac{1984x^3}{x^4+1} = \frac{1984}{x+(1/x^3)} \to 0$ as $x \to \infty$.

4. False. If $f(x) = 1/x^2$ and $g(x) = 2/x^2$, for example, then $\lim\limits_{x \to 0} f(x) = \lim\limits_{x \to 0} g(x) = \infty$, but $\lim\limits_{x \to 0} \frac{f(x)}{g(x)} = \frac{1}{2}$.

5. True. $f(x)g(x) \approx (-1)(\text{large number}) \to -\infty$ as $x \to a$.

6. False. By L'Hôpital's Rule, $\lim\limits_{x \to \infty} \frac{x}{\ln x} = \lim\limits_{x \to \infty} \frac{1}{1/x} = \lim\limits_{x \to \infty} x = \infty$.

7. False. This is a misapplication of L'Hôpital's Rule. The first limit is not indeterminate, but is equal to 0 by inspection. The second limit is $\frac{1}{2}$.

8. False. $\int_0^t \frac{x\,dx}{1-x} = \int_0^t (\frac{1}{1-x} - 1)dx = [-\ln(1-x) - x]\Big|_0^t = -\ln(1-t) - t \to \infty$ as $t \uparrow 1$.

9. True. $\int_{-\infty}^{\infty} f(x)dx = \int_{-\infty}^{0} f(x)dx + \int_{0}^{\infty} f(x)dx$. If the second integral converges, the first is its negative, so the sum is 0. To see why, let $u = -x$, $du = -dx$ in the first integral. Its value is

$$\int_{-\infty}^0 f(x)dx = \int_{\infty}^0 f(-u)(-du) = \int_{\infty}^0 f(u)du \quad \text{(because f is odd)}$$

$$= -\int_0^{\infty} f(u)du$$

10. True. The formula for repeated integration by parts (Sec. 10.1) yields

$$\int x^2 e^{-x}dx = (x^2)(-e^{-x}) - (2x)(e^{-x}) + (2)(-e^{-x}) + C = -(x^2 + 2x + 2)e^{-x} + C$$

Hence $\int_0^{\infty} x^2 e^{-x}dx = \lim_{b\to\infty}\left(2 - \dfrac{b^2 + 2b + 2}{e^b}\right) = 2.$

11. True. At $x = 1$ we have $f(x) = x^2 = 1$, $f'(x) = 2x = 2$, $f''(x) = 2$. Hence $P_2(x) = 1 + 2(x - 1) + (x - 1)^2.$

12. True. At $x = 0$ we have $f(x) = e^{-x^2} = 1$, $f'(x) = -2xe^{-x^2} = 0$, $f''(x) = -2x(-2xe^{-x^2}) - 2e^{-x^2} = -2.$ Hence $P_2(x) = 1 + 0x - \dfrac{2}{2!}x^2 = 1 - x^2.$

Chapter 11   ADDITIONAL PROBLEMS

1. $\dfrac{x + 1}{x^2 + 1} = \dfrac{1 + 1/x}{x + 1/x} \approx \dfrac{1}{x} \to 0$ when $x \to \infty$.

2. $\dfrac{2x - 1}{x + 1} = \dfrac{2 - 1/x}{1 + 1/x} \to 2$ when $x \to \infty$.

3. $1 - 1/x \to 1$ when $x \to \infty$, so $(1 - 1/x)^3 \to 1^3 = 1.$

4. $x^2 - 2x = x^2(1 - 2/x) \approx x^2 \to \infty$ when $x \to \infty$.

5. $\cot x \approx \dfrac{\cos x}{\sin x} \approx \dfrac{1}{\text{small positive number}} \to \infty$ when $x \downarrow 0$.

6. $\cot x \approx \dfrac{\cos x}{\sin x} \approx \dfrac{1}{\text{small negative number}} \to -\infty$ when $x \uparrow 0$.

7. $\sqrt{1 + \tan^2 x} = |\sec x| \to \infty$ when $x \to \pi/2$.

8. $\tan x \cot x = 1$ for all x near 0, so the limit is 1.

9. $1/x \to 0$ when $x \to \infty$, so $\tan(1/x) \to \tan 0 = 0.$

10. $\sin(1/x)$ is bounded between 1 and -1 while $x \to 0$, so the limit is 0.

11. Let $t = 1/x$. Then $\lim_{x\to\infty} x^2 \sin(1/x) = \lim_{t\downarrow 0} \dfrac{\sin t}{t^2} = \lim_{t\downarrow 0}\left(\dfrac{\sin t}{t}\right)\left(\dfrac{1}{t}\right).$ Since $(\sin t)/t \to 1$ when $t \downarrow 0$, and $1/t \to \infty$, the limit is ∞.

12. $\tanh x = \dfrac{e^x - e^{-x}}{e^x + e^{-x}} \approx \dfrac{e^x}{e^x} = 1$ when $x \to \infty$, so the limit is 1.

13. Since $e^x > 1$ when $x > 0$, $(e^x + 1)/(e^x - 1) \approx 2/(\text{small positive number}) \to \infty$ when $x \downarrow 0$.

14. $2 - x \to -\infty$ when $x \to \infty$, so $\tan^{-1}(2 - x) \to -\pi/2.$

15. $2 - \sin x$ is bounded between 1 and 3 while $\ln x \to \infty$ when $x \to \infty$. The limit is ∞.

16. $\dfrac{e^x - \ell n\, x}{e^x} = 1 - (\ell n\, x)/e^x$. Use L'Hôpital's Rule to find

$$\lim_{x \to \infty} \frac{\ell n\, x}{e^x} = \lim_{x \to \infty} \frac{1/x}{e^x} = \lim_{x \to \infty} \frac{1}{xe^x} = 0$$

Hence the original limit is 1.

17. $x > \tfrac{1}{2}\ell n\, B \Longrightarrow 2x > \ell n\, B \Longrightarrow e^{2x} > B$, which proves that $\lim_{x \to \infty} e^{2x} = \infty$.

18. $0 < |x| < 1/\sqrt{B} \Longrightarrow 1/|x| > \sqrt{B} \Longrightarrow 1/x^2 > B$, which proves that $\lim_{x \to 0} \dfrac{1}{x^2} = \infty$.

19. $0 < 1 - x < 1/B \Longrightarrow \dfrac{1}{1-x} > B$, which proves that $\lim_{x \uparrow 1} \dfrac{1}{1-x} = \infty$.

20. $x < -2/\epsilon \Longrightarrow \epsilon x < -2 \Longrightarrow \epsilon(-x) > 2 \Longrightarrow \epsilon|x| > 2$ (because x is negative)

$\Longrightarrow |2/x| < \epsilon$, which proves that $\lim_{x \to -\infty} \dfrac{2}{x} = 0$.

21. This is not easy to do directly, so we start with the conclusion:

$$\frac{x}{x-2} < -B \iff \frac{x}{x-2} + B < 0 \iff \frac{(B+1)x - 2B}{x-2} < 0 \iff \frac{x - 2B/(B+1)}{x-2} < 0$$

(dividing by $B+1$, which is positive). Let $a = 2B/(B+1)$, which is less than

2. Then our inequality is $\dfrac{x-a}{x-2} < 0$. The sign change diagram in Figure 1

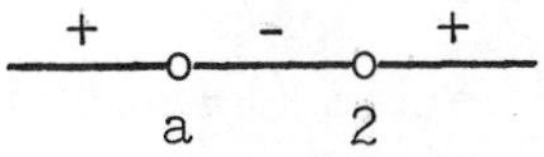

Sign of $\dfrac{x-a}{x-2}$

Figure 1

shows that $\dfrac{x-a}{x-2} < 0 \iff a < x < 2$, so the original statement,

$$\frac{2B}{B+1} < x < 2 \Longrightarrow \frac{x}{x-2} < -B$$

is correct. This proves that $\lim_{x \uparrow 2} \dfrac{x}{x-2} = -\infty$.

22. The limit is 1. To prove it, suppose that a critic chooses $\epsilon > 0$,

challenging us to name A such that $x > A \Longrightarrow \left| \dfrac{x-1}{x} - 1 \right| < \epsilon$. Since

$$\left| \frac{x-1}{x} - 1 \right| < \epsilon \iff |-1/x| < \epsilon \iff |x| > 1/\epsilon$$

we choose $A = 1/\epsilon$.

23. The limit is ∞. To prove it, suppose that a critic chooses B, challenging us to name $-A$ such that $x < -A \Longrightarrow 2 - x > B$. Since $2 - x > B \iff x < 2 - B$, we choose $-A = 2 - B$.

24. The limit is $-\infty$. To prove it, suppose that a critic chooses $-B$ (where $B > 0$), challenging us to name δ such that $-\delta < x < 0 \Longrightarrow 1/x < -B$. Since $1/x < -B \Longleftrightarrow -1/x > B \Longleftrightarrow 0 < -x < 1/B \Longleftrightarrow -1/B < x < 0$, we choose $\delta = 1/B$.

25. The limit is $-\infty$. To prove it, suppose that a critic chooses $-B$ (where $B > 0$), challenging us to name δ such that $0 < x < \delta \Longrightarrow 2 - 1/x < -B$. Since $2 - 1/x < -B \Longleftrightarrow B + 2 < 1/x \Longleftrightarrow 0 < x < 1/(B+2)$, we choose $\delta = 1/(B+2)$.

26. The limit is $-\infty$. To prove it, suppose that a critic chooses $-B$ (where $B > 0$), challenging us to name A such that $x > A \Longrightarrow 1 - \ln x < -B$. Since $1 - \ln x < -B \Longleftrightarrow B + 1 < \ln x \Longleftrightarrow x > e^{B+1}$, we choose $A = e^{B+1}$.

27. The limit is 0. To prove it, suppose that a critic chooses $\epsilon > 0$, challenging us to name A such that $x > A \Longrightarrow |(\sin x)/x - 0| < \epsilon$. Since $|\sin x| \le 1$ for all x, we have $|(\sin x)/x - 0| = |(\sin x)/x| \le 1/|x|$ for all $x \ne 0$. Moreover, $1/|x| < \epsilon \Longleftrightarrow |x| > 1/\epsilon$. Hence we name $A = 1/\epsilon$. Then $x > A \Longrightarrow |x| > 1/\epsilon \Longrightarrow 1/|x| < \epsilon \Longrightarrow |(\sin x)/x| \le 1/|x| < \epsilon$.

28. $\dfrac{1 - \cos x}{\sin^2 x} = \dfrac{1 - \cos x}{(1 - \cos x)(1 + \cos x)} = \dfrac{1}{1 + \cos x} \to \dfrac{1}{2}$ when $x \to 0$. L'Hôpital's Rule

yields $\lim\limits_{x \to 0} \dfrac{1 - \cos x}{\sin^2 x} = \lim\limits_{x \to 0} \dfrac{\sin x}{2 \sin x \cos x} = \lim\limits_{x \to 0} \dfrac{1}{2 \cos x} = \dfrac{1}{2}$.

29. If we try to apply the rule, we obtain

$$\lim\limits_{x \to \infty} \frac{x - \cos x}{x} = \lim\limits_{x \to \infty} \frac{1 + \sin x}{1} = \lim\limits_{x \to \infty} (1 + \sin x)$$

The new limit, however, is meaningless; L'Hôpital's Rule does not apply. Instead we write $(x - \cos x)/x = 1 - (\cos x)/x \to 1$ as $x \to \infty$.

30. $\lim\limits_{x \downarrow 0} \dfrac{x^2 - \tan x}{1 - \cos x} = \lim\limits_{x \downarrow 0} \dfrac{2x - \sec^2 x}{\sin x} = -\infty$.

31. Let $y = (1 - \sin x)^{1/x}$. Then $\ln y = \dfrac{1}{x} \ln(1 - \sin x)$ and

$$\lim\limits_{x \to 0} \ln y = \lim\limits_{x \to 0} \frac{\ln(1 - \sin x)}{x} = \lim\limits_{x \to 0} \frac{-\cos x}{1 - \sin x} = -1$$

Hence $\ln(\lim\limits_{x \to 0} y) = -1$ and $\lim\limits_{x \to 0} y = e^{-1}$.

32.(a) The domain is $x > 0$.

(b) $\lim\limits_{x \downarrow 0} \left(\ln x + \dfrac{1}{x}\right) = \lim\limits_{x \downarrow 0} \dfrac{x \ln x + 1}{x}$. Since $\lim\limits_{x \downarrow 0} x \ln x = \lim\limits_{x \downarrow 0} \dfrac{\ln x}{1/x} = \lim\limits_{x \downarrow 0} \dfrac{1/x}{-1/x^2} =$

$\lim\limits_{x \downarrow 0} (-x) = 0$, the original limit is ∞, that is, $y \to \infty$ as $x \downarrow 0$.

(c) $y = \ln x + \dfrac{1}{x} \approx \ln x \to \infty$ when $x \to \infty$.

(d) $y' = \dfrac{1}{x} - \dfrac{1}{x^2} = \dfrac{x - 1}{x^2}$. Since this changes from minus to plus at $x = 1$, we have a local minimum at $x = 1$, namely $y = 1$.

(e) $y' = x^{-1} - x^{-2}$, so $y'' = -x^{-2} + 2x^{-3} = \dfrac{-1}{x^2} + \dfrac{2}{x^3} = \dfrac{2 - x}{x^3}$. This changes sign at $x = 2$, so we have an inflection point $(2, \ln 2 + \frac{1}{2})$. Note that the apparent sign change at $x = 0$ is not considered because the domain is $x > 0$. The graph is shown in Figure 2.

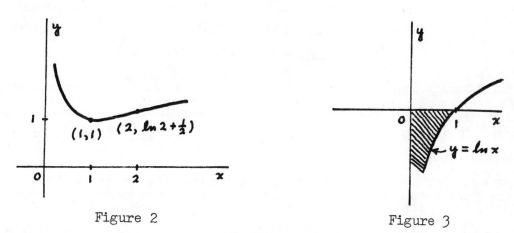

Figure 2   Figure 3

33. From Figure 3 we conclude that the area (if it exists) is

$$A = \int_0^1 (0 - \ln x)dx = \lim_{t \downarrow 0} (x - x\ln x)\Big|_t^1 = \lim_{t \downarrow 0} (1 - t + t\ln t)$$

Since $t\ln t \to 0$ when $t \downarrow 0$, we find $A = 1$.

34. Since the curve is symmetric about the y axis, the area is

$$A = 2\int_0^1 \frac{dx}{\sqrt{1 - x^2}} = 2\lim_{t \uparrow 1}(\sin^{-1}t) = 2(\pi/2) = \pi$$

35. $\int_0^\infty \dfrac{x\,dx}{x^2 + 1} = \lim_{b \to \infty} \frac{1}{2}\ln(b^2 + 1) = \infty$, so the integral diverges.

36. At $x = 1$ we have $f(x) = x^{-2} = 1$, $f'(x) = -2x^{-3} = -2$, $f''(x) = 3!x^{-4} = 3!$, $f'''(x) = -4!x^{-5} = -4!$. Hence $1/x^2 \approx 1 - 2(x - 1) + 3(x - 1)^2 - 4(x - 1)^3$ and $1/(1.1)^2 \approx 1 - 2(0.1) + 3(0.1)^2 - 4(0.1)^3 = 0.826$. Since $f^{(4)}(x) = 5!x^{-6}$, the error is $|R_3(1.1)| = \dfrac{5!c^{-6}}{4!}(0.1)^4 = \dfrac{5(0.1)^4}{c^6} < 5(0.1)^4 = 0.0005$ (because c is between 1 and 1.1). Hence $1/(1.1)^2 = 0.826$ correct to three places. The value given by a calculator is $0.826446\cdots$.

37. At $x = 0$ we have $f(x) = \sin^{-1}x = 0$, $f'(x) = 1/\sqrt{1 - x^2} = 1$,

$$f''(x) = \frac{x}{(1 - x^2)^{3/2}} = 0, \quad f'''(x) = \frac{(1 - x^2)^{3/2} - x(3/2)(1 - x^2)^{1/2}(-2x)}{(1 - x^2)^3} = 1$$

Hence $\sin^{-1} x \approx 0 + x + 0x^2 + \frac{x^3}{3!} = x + \frac{1}{6}x^3$ and $\sin^{-1} 0.2 \approx 0.2 + \frac{1}{6}(0.2)^3 = 0.201\overline{3}$. This is correct to three places.

CHAPTER 12   INFINITE SERIES

Section 12.1   PRELIMINARIES

1. $S_1 = \cos 0 = 1$, $S_2 = 1 + \cos \pi = 0$, $S_3 = 0 + \cos 2\pi = 1$, $S_4 = 1 + \cos 3\pi = 0$, and so on. The sequence $1, 0, 1, 0, \cdots$ has no limit, so the series diverges.

2. $S_1 = \sin(\pi/2) = 1$, $S_2 = 1 + \sin \pi = 1$, $S_3 = 1 + \sin(3\pi/2) = 0$, $S_4 = 0 + \sin 2\pi = 0$, $S_5 = 0 + \sin(5\pi/2) = 1$, and so on. The sequence $1, 1, 0, 0,$ $1, 1, 0, 0, \cdots$ has no limit, so the series diverges.

3. $S_n = \ell n\, 1 + \ell n\, \frac{1}{2} + \ell n\, \frac{1}{3} + \cdots + \ell n\, \frac{1}{n} = \ell n\, (1 \cdot \frac{1}{2} \cdot \frac{1}{3} \cdots \frac{1}{n}) = \ell n\, \frac{1}{n!} = -\ell n\, n! \to -\infty$ as $n \to \infty$, so the series diverges.

4. $S_n = 1 + 2 + 3 + \cdots + n = \frac{1}{2}n(n+1)$. (This formula may be proved by mathematical induction; it has appeared before in Problem 19, Sec. 6.1.) Since $S_n \to \infty$ as $n \to \infty$, the series diverges.

5. $\dfrac{1}{(k+1)(k+2)} = \dfrac{A}{k+1} + \dfrac{B}{k+2} \Longrightarrow 1 = A(k+2) + B(k+1)$. Put $k = -1$ to find $A = 1$ and $k = -2$ to find $B = -1$. Then $\dfrac{1}{(k+1)(k+2)} = \dfrac{1}{k+1} - \dfrac{1}{k+2}$, from which

$$S_n = (\tfrac{1}{2} - \tfrac{1}{3}) + (\tfrac{1}{3} - \tfrac{1}{4}) + (\tfrac{1}{4} - \tfrac{1}{5}) + \cdots + (\tfrac{1}{n+1} - \tfrac{1}{n+2})$$

This telescopes to $S_n = \frac{1}{2} - \dfrac{1}{n+2}$, which approaches $\frac{1}{2}$ as $n \to \infty$. Hence the sum of the series is $\frac{1}{2}$. An alternate solution is to use the result of Example 1, $\dfrac{1}{1 \cdot 2} + \dfrac{1}{2 \cdot 3} + \dfrac{1}{3 \cdot 4} + \cdots = 1$. The series in this problem is $\dfrac{1}{2 \cdot 3} + \dfrac{1}{3 \cdot 4} + \dfrac{1}{4 \cdot 5} + \cdots$, which is the same except for the missing first term. Hence its sum is $1 - \frac{1}{2} = \frac{1}{2}$.

6. The typical term may be decomposed by writing

$$\frac{1}{(2k-1)(2k+1)} = \frac{A}{2k-1} + \frac{B}{2k+1} \Longrightarrow 1 = A(2k+1) + B(2k-1)$$

Put $k = \frac{1}{2}$ to find $A = \frac{1}{2}$ and $k = -\frac{1}{2}$ to find $B = -\frac{1}{2}$. Then

$$\frac{1}{(2k-1)(2k+1)} = \frac{1}{2}\left(\frac{1}{2k-1} - \frac{1}{2k+1}\right)$$

from which $S_n = \frac{1}{2}[(1 - \frac{1}{3}) + (\frac{1}{3} - \frac{1}{5}) + (\frac{1}{5} - \frac{1}{7}) + \cdots + (\dfrac{1}{2n-1} - \dfrac{1}{2n+1})]$. This telescopes to $S_n = \frac{1}{2}(1 - \dfrac{1}{2n+1})$, which approaches $\frac{1}{2}$ as $n \to \infty$. The sum of the series is 1/2.

7. $S_n = \int_1^2 \frac{dx}{x^2} + \int_2^3 \frac{dx}{x^2} + \cdots + \int_n^{n+1} \frac{dx}{x^2} = \int_1^{n+1} \frac{dx}{x^2} = -\frac{1}{x}\Big|_1^{n+1} = 1 - \frac{1}{n+1}$. This

approaches 1 as $n \to \infty$, so the series converges to 1.

8. This is a geometric series $1 + x + x^2 + \cdots$ with $x = 1/3$, so its sum is

$\frac{1}{1-x} = \frac{1}{1-1/3} = \frac{3}{2}$.

9. This is a geometric series $1 + x + x^2 + \cdots$ with $x = -1/3$, so its sum is

$\frac{1}{1-x} = \frac{1}{1+1/3} = \frac{3}{4}$.

10. Geometric with $x = 1.01 > 1$, so it diverges. An alternate solution is to observe that the typical term is $(1.01)^n$, which does not approach 0 as $n \to \infty$. Hence the series diverges.

11. This is a geometric series $a + ar + ar^2 + \cdots$ with $a = 1/2$ and $r = 1/2$, so

its sum is $\frac{a}{1-r} = \frac{1/2}{1-1/2} = 1$.

12. Geometric with $x = -1/2$, so its sum is $\frac{1}{1-x} = \frac{1}{1+1/2} = \frac{2}{3}$.

13. Geometric with $a = 2$ and $r = 1/2$, so its sum is $\frac{a}{1-r} = \frac{2}{1-1/2} = 4$.

14. Geometric with $a = 0.1$ and $r = 0.1$, so its sum is $\frac{a}{1-r} = \frac{0.1}{1-0.1} = \frac{1}{9}$.

15. The series is $1 + 2/3 + (2/3)^2 + \cdots$, which is geometric with $x = 2/3$. The

sum is $\frac{1}{1-x} = \frac{1}{1-2/3} = 3$.

16. The series is $e^{-1} + e^{-2} + e^{-3} + \cdots$, which is geometric with $a = e^{-1}$ and

$r = e^{-1}$. The sum is $\frac{a}{1-r} = \frac{e^{-1}}{1-e^{-1}} = \frac{1}{e-1}$.

17. Geometric with $x = 2 > 1$, so the series diverges. Also, the typical term does not approach 0, which implies divergence.

18. Geometric with $x = \pi/3 > 1$, so the series diverges.

19. Geometric with $x = 3/\pi < 1$, so the series converges to $\frac{1}{1-3/\pi} = \frac{\pi}{\pi-3}$.

20. The series is $1 + \sin^2 x + \sin^4 x + \sin^6 x + \cdots$, which is geometric with $a = 1$ and $r = \sin^2 x < 1$ (because $-\pi/2 < x < \pi/2$). Hence the series converges to

$\frac{1}{1-\sin^2 x} = \frac{1}{\cos^2 x} = \sec^2 x$.

21. The series is $\cos^2 x + \cos^4 x + \cos^6 x + \cdots$, which is geometric with $a = \cos^2 x$ and $r = \cos^2 x < 1$ (because $0 < x < \pi$). The sum is $\frac{\cos^2 x}{1-\cos^2 x} = \frac{\cos^2 x}{\sin^2 x} = \cot^2 x$.

22. Geometric, with a = 1 and r = $1/(1+x^2) < 1$ (because x $\neq$ 0). The sum is

$$\frac{1}{1 - 1/(x^2+1)} = \frac{x^2+1}{(x^2+1)-1} = \frac{x^2+1}{x^2}$$

23. The typical term is $n/(n+1)$, which does not approach 0 as $n \to \infty$. Hence the series diverges.

24. The typical term is $n/(2n-1)$, which does not approach 0 as $n \to \infty$. Hence the series diverges.

25. L'Hôpital's Rule yields $\lim\limits_{k \to \infty} \dfrac{\sinh k}{k} = \lim\limits_{k \to \infty} \cosh k = \infty$. Thus the typical term does not approach 0 and the series diverges.

26. The typical term is the value at x = n of the function $y = x^{-1/x}$. To find its limit as $n \to \infty$, we write

$$\ell n\, y = -\frac{1}{x} \ell n\, x \implies \lim_{x \to \infty} \ell n\, y = \lim_{x \to \infty}\left(\frac{-\ell n\, x}{x}\right) = \lim_{x \to \infty}\left(-\frac{1}{x}\right) = 0 \implies \lim_{x \to \infty} y = 1$$

Thus the typical term approaches 1 (not 0) as $n \to \infty$ and the series diverges.

27.(a) $S_n = 1 + 1/\sqrt{2} + 1/\sqrt{3} + \cdots + 1/\sqrt{n}$. Each term of this sum is $\geq 1/\sqrt{n}$, so $S_n \geq n(1/\sqrt{n}) = \sqrt{n}$.

(b) Since $\sqrt{n} \to \infty$ as $n \to \infty$, $\lim\limits_{n \to \infty} S_n = \infty$.

28.(a) The inequalities given for S_1, S_2, S_4, S_8, S_{16} are self-explanatory (in the sense that you can check their correctness, not that the pattern shown is obvious). Once you have perceived the pattern, the statement $S_n > 1 + \frac{1}{2}r$ if $n = 2^r$ is merely a generalization (which can be formally established by mathematical induction). The point of the problem is not to be formal, but to obtain a useful inequality leading to the conclusion in part (b).

(b) As we run through the sequence S_1, S_2, S_3, S_4, S_5, ..., we encounter the special sums S_1, S_2, S_4, S_8, S_{16}, $\cdots$. By part (a) the typical member of this sequence (with index 2^r, r = 0, 1, 2, ...) is larger than $1 + \frac{1}{2}r$. Since $1 + \frac{1}{2}r \to \infty$ as $r \to \infty$, the sums S_1, S_2, S_4, S_8, S_{16}, ... increase without bound. Hence the original sequence S_1, S_2, S_3, S_4, S_5, ... cannot have a finite limit and the series diverges.

29. The series is geometric, with a = 1 and r = x - 2. It converges if and only if $|r| < 1 \iff |x-2| < 1 \iff -1 < x - 2 < 1 \iff 1 < x < 3$. For these values of x, the sum is $\dfrac{a}{1-r} = \dfrac{1}{1-(x-2)} = \dfrac{1}{3-x}$.

30. Replace x by x^2 in the geometric series to obtain $f(x) = 1 + x^2 + x^4 + x^6 +$

$\cdots$. The domain is $x^2 < 1$, that is, $-1 < x < 1$.

31. Replace x by $-x$ in the geometric series to obtain $f(x) = 1 - x + x^2 - x^3 + \cdots$. The domain is $|-x| < 1$, that is, $-1 < x < 1$.

32. $f(x) = \dfrac{1}{2} \cdot \dfrac{1}{1 - (x/2)} = \dfrac{1}{2}(1 + \dfrac{x}{2} + \dfrac{x^2}{4} + \dfrac{x^3}{8} + \cdots)$. The domain is $|x/2| < 1$, that is, $-2 < x < 2$.

33. $f(x) = x \cdot \dfrac{1}{1 - x} = x(1 + x + x^2 + \cdots) = x + x^2 + x^3 + \cdots$. The domain is $|x| < 1$, that is, $-1 < x < 1$.

34. $0.\overline{36} = 0.363636\cdots = 0.36 + 0.0036 + 0.000036 + \cdots$, which is geometric with $a = 0.36$ and $r = 0.01$. The sum is $\dfrac{a}{1-r} = \dfrac{0.36}{1 - 0.01} = \dfrac{4}{11}$.

35. A periodic decimal need not start repeating right away, for example, $1.6272727\cdots = 1.6\overline{27}$. When we locate the repeating part of it, however, we can represent that part by a geometric series. Thus $1.6272727\cdots = 1.6 + (0.027 + 0.00027 + \cdots)$. The sum of the series is a rational number. (In this example it is $0.027/(1 - 0.01) = 3/110$.) The first part of the decimal (in this case $1.6 = 8/5$) is also a rational number. Hence the original decimal must be rational. In this example it is $8/5 + 3/110 = 179/110$. (You can check by division that $179/110 = 1.6272727\cdots$.) It would be hard to put this argument in a form that applies to an arbitrary periodic decimal, but the idea ought to be clear.

36. The ball falls 5 ft, rebounds 60% of 5 ft (or 3 ft) and falls 3 ft, rebounds 60% of 3 ft and falls, and so on. The distance traveled is

$$5 + 2(5)(0.6) + 2(5)(0.6)^2 + \cdots = 5 + 6[1 + 0.6 + (0.6)^2 + \cdots] = 5 + 6 \cdot \dfrac{1}{1 - 0.6}$$
$$= 5 + 15 = 20 \text{ ft}$$

37. The distance traveled is $a + 2ar + 2ar^2 + \cdots = a + 2ar(1 + r + r^2 + \cdots) = a + \dfrac{2ar}{1-r} = \dfrac{a(1+r)}{1-r}$.

38. The ball falls 1 ft, rebounds $\frac{1}{2}$ ft and falls, rebounds $\frac{1}{4}$ ft and falls, and so on. The times corresponding to these distances form the sum

$$\sqrt{2/g} + 2\sqrt{1/g} + 2\sqrt{1/(2g)} + 2\sqrt{1/(4g)} + \cdots = \sqrt{2/g} + 2\sqrt{1/g}(1 + 1/\sqrt{2} + 1/\sqrt{4} + \cdots)$$
$$= \dfrac{1}{4} + \dfrac{1}{2\sqrt{2}} \cdot \dfrac{1}{1 - 1/\sqrt{2}} = \dfrac{1}{4} + \dfrac{1}{2(\sqrt{2} - 1)} = \dfrac{1}{4} + \dfrac{\sqrt{2} + 1}{2} = \dfrac{1}{4}(3 + 2\sqrt{2}) \approx 1.46 \text{ sec}$$

39. The original population P produces $0.8P$ new bacteria, which in turn produce $(0.8)^2 P$ new bacteria, and so on. The total is eventually

$$P + 0.8P + (0.8)^2 P + \cdots = \dfrac{P}{1 - 0.8} = 5P$$

40. The original \$100 generates deposits of \$100(0.4), which are lent out and spent again, generating deposits of \$100(0.4)^2, and so on. Total deposits are

$$100 + 100(0.4) + 100(0.4)^2 + \cdots = \frac{100}{1 - 0.4} = \$166.67$$

41. The original \$1 billion generates spending of \$1(0.75) billion, which generates more spending of \$1(0.75)^2 billion, and so on. Total spending is

$$1 + 0.75 + (0.75)^2 + \cdots = \frac{1}{1 - 0.75} = \$4 \text{ billion}$$

42. The first loan of $D - d$ generates deposits of $(D-d)p$, which are completely loaned out because the legal requirement d is still on deposit. This generates deposits of $(D-d)p^2$, which are completely loaned out again, and so on. Total loans are

$$(D-d) + (D-d)p + (D-d)p^2 + \cdots = \frac{D-d}{1-p}$$

43. $\frac{5}{6^2} + \frac{5^3}{6^4} + \frac{5^5}{6^6} + \cdots = \frac{5/(6^2)}{1 - 5^2/6^2} = \frac{5}{6^2 - 5^2} = \frac{5}{11}$. Thus by going first you win about 45% of the time (and lose about 55% of the time). To see how the original formula is derived, observe that the probability of your not throwing a 1 on the first trial is 5/6, while the probability of your opponent throwing a 1 is 1/6. Hence the probability that you win in the first round is $\frac{5}{6} \cdot \frac{1}{6} = \frac{5}{6^2}$. Assuming no result from the first round (which has probability $\frac{5}{6} \cdot \frac{5}{6} = \frac{5^2}{6^2}$), the probability that you win in the second round is $\frac{5}{6^2}$ again. Hence the probability that you win in the first or second round is $\frac{5}{6^2} + \frac{5^2}{6^2} \cdot \frac{5}{6^2} = \frac{5}{6^2} + \frac{5^3}{6^4}$. Continuing in this way, we conclude that the probability of your winning eventually is the given series.

44. If $S_n = a_1 + a_2 + \cdots + a_n$ is the nth partial sum of $\sum a_k$, the nth partial sum of $\sum ca_k$ is $ca_1 + ca_2 + \cdots + ca_n = cS_n$. Convergence of $\sum a_k$ to $S = \lim_{n \to \infty} S_n$ implies convergence of $\sum ca_k$ to $\lim_{n \to \infty} cS_n = c \lim_{n \to \infty} S_n = cS$, that is, $\sum ca_k = c \sum a_k$. Conversely, convergence of $\sum ca_k$ implies existence of $\lim_{n \to \infty} cS_n$, so $\lim_{n \to \infty} S_n = \frac{1}{c} \lim_{n \to \infty} cS_n$ also exists (because $c \neq 0$). Hence $\sum a_k$ converges.

45. Let S_n and T_n be the nth partial sums of $\sum a_k$ and $\sum b_k$, respectively, with finite limits S and T. Then $S_n + T_n = (a_1 + a_2 + \cdots + a_n) + (b_1 + b_2 + \cdots + b_n) = (a_1 + b_1) + (a_2 + b_2) + \cdots + (a_n + b_n)$ is the nth partial sum of $\sum (a_k + b_k)$. Since

$\lim\limits_{n\to\infty}(S_n + T_n) = \lim\limits_{n\to\infty}S_n + \lim\limits_{n\to\infty}T_n = S + T$, $\sum(a_k + b_k)$ converges and $\sum(a_k + b_k) =$

$\sum a_k + \sum b_k$.

46. Let $a_k = 1$ and $b_k = -1$ for $k = 1, 2, 3, \cdots$. Then $a_k + b_k = 0$ and hence

$\sum(a_k + b_k) = 0$. But $\sum a_k$ and $\sum b_k$ both diverge.

47. The series $(1-1)+(1-1)+(1-1)+\cdots$ has typical term 0, with nth

partial sum 0. Hence it converges, with sum 0.

48. The nth partial sum of the series is

$$S_n = (a_2 - a_1) + (a_3 - a_2) + (a_4 - a_3) + \cdots + (a_{n+1} - a_n) = a_{n+1} - a_1$$

If the sequence a_1, a_2, a_3, ... has a finite limit, say $L = \lim\limits_{n\to\infty} a_n$, then

$\lim\limits_{n\to\infty} S_n = L - a_1$, so the series converges. Conversely, if the series converges,

with sum $S = \lim\limits_{n\to\infty} S_n$, then $\lim\limits_{n\to\infty} a_n = \lim\limits_{n\to\infty} a_{n+1} = \lim\limits_{n\to\infty}(a_1 + S_n) = a_1 + S$. Hence the

sequence has a limit.

49. If $\sum a_k$ converges, then $\lim\limits_{k\to\infty} a_k = 0$ and hence $\lim\limits_{k\to\infty} \cos a_k = \cos 0 = 1 \neq 0$.

This implies divergence of $\sum \cos a_k$.

Section 12.2   THE INTEGRAL TEST

1. Let $f(x) = 1/x^{3/2}$. Then f is continuous, positive, and decreasing for
$x \geq 1$, and $f(n) = 1/n\sqrt{n}$ is the typical term of the series. Since $\int_1^\infty f(x)dx$

converges (Problem 11, Sec. 11.4), so does the series. More directly, we can
use Example 2 to conclude the same thing, since the series is a p-series with
$p = 3/2 > 1$.

2. This is a p-series with $p = 1/3 < 1$, so by Example 2 the series diverges.

3. This is a p-series with $p = 1.01 > 1$, so by Example 2 the series

converges.

4. This is a p-series with $p = 0.99 < 1$, so it diverges.

5. Let $f(x) = 1/(2x-1)$. Then f is continuous, positive, and decreasing for
$x \geq 1$, and $f(n) = 1/(2n-1)$ is the typical term of the series. Since

$$\int_1^\infty \frac{dx}{2x-1} = \lim_{b\to\infty} \tfrac{1}{2}\ln(2b-1) = \infty$$

the series diverges.

6. The function $f(x) = 1/(2x-1)^2$ satisfies the hypotheses of the Integral

Test. Since $\int_1^\infty f(x)dx = \lim\limits_{b\to\infty}[\tfrac{1}{2} - \frac{1}{2(2b-1)}] = \tfrac{1}{2}$, the series converges.

7. Let $f(x) = \frac{x}{x^2+1}$. Since $f'(x) = \frac{(x^2+1) - x(2x)}{(x^2+1)^2} = \frac{1-x^2}{(x^2+1)^2} > 0$ for $x > 1$, f is decreasing for $x \geq 1$. Since

$$\int_1^\infty f(x)dx = \lim_{b \to \infty} [\tfrac{1}{2}\ell n(b^2+1) - \tfrac{1}{2}\ell n\, 2] = \infty$$

the series diverges.

8. Since $\int_1^\infty \frac{dx}{x^2+1} = \lim_{b \to \infty} (\tan^{-1}b - \pi/4) = \pi/4$, the series converges.

9. Since $\int_1^\infty \frac{dx}{\sqrt{x^2+1}} = \lim_{b \to \infty} [\ell n\,(b+\sqrt{b^2+1}) - \ell n\,(1+\sqrt{2})] = \infty$, the series diverges.

10. Let $f(x) = xe^{-x^2}$. Since $f'(x) = x(-2xe^{-x^2}) + e^{-x^2} = e^{-x^2}(1 - 2x^2) < 0$ for $x > 1/\sqrt{2}$, f is decreasing for $x \geq 1$. Since

$$\int_1^\infty f(x)dx = \lim_{b \to \infty} \tfrac{1}{2}(e^{-1} - e^{-b^2}) = \tfrac{1}{2}e^{-1}$$

the series converges.

11. Let $f(x) = xe^{-x}$. Since $f'(x) = x(-e^{-x}) + e^{-x} = e^{-x}(1-x) < 0$ for $x > 1$, f is decreasing for $x \geq 1$. Since

$$\int_1^\infty f(x)dx = \lim_{b \to \infty} [2e^{-1} - (b+1)e^{-b}] = 2e^{-1}$$

the series converges.

12. Let $f(x) = \frac{\ell n\, x}{x}$. Since $f'(x) = \frac{1 - \ell n\, x}{x^2} < 0$ for $x > e$, f is decreasing for $x \geq 3$. Since

$$\int_3^\infty f(x)dx = \lim_{b \to \infty} [\tfrac{1}{2}(\ell n\, b)^2 - \tfrac{1}{2}(\ell n\, 3)^2] = \infty$$

the series diverges.

13. Since $\lim_{n \to \infty} \frac{n}{\ell n\, n} = \lim_{n \to \infty} \frac{1}{1/n} = \infty$, the typical term of the series does not approach 0, so the series diverges.

14. Since $\int_2^\infty \frac{dx}{x\,\ell n\, x} = \lim_{b \to \infty} [\ell n(\ell n\, b) - \ell n(\ell n\, 2)] = \infty$, the series diverges.

15. Since $f(x) = \text{sech}^2 x$ is decreasing for $x \geq 0$ and since

$$\int_1^\infty f(x)dx = \lim_{b \to \infty} (\tanh b - \tanh 1) = 1 - \tanh 1$$

the series converges.

16. The error in the approximation is $\leq a_{N+1} = 1/(N+1)^2$. To obtain one-place accuracy, we choose N satisfying $1/(N+1)^2 < 0.05 \Rightarrow (N+1)^2 > 20 \Rightarrow$

$N + 1 > \sqrt{20} \implies N > \sqrt{20} - 1 \approx 3.5$. Hence we choose $N = 4$. Then

$$\sum_{n=1}^{\infty} \frac{1}{n^2} \approx 1 + \frac{1}{4} + \frac{1}{9} + \frac{1}{16} + \int_5^{\infty} \frac{dx}{x^2}$$

Since $\int_5^{\infty} \frac{dx}{x^2} = \lim_{b \to \infty} \left(\frac{1}{5} - \frac{1}{b} \right) = \frac{1}{5}$, we have $\sum_{n=1}^{\infty} \frac{1}{n^2} \approx 1.6$ (correct to one place). To obtain five-place accuracy, we need

$$1/(N+1)^2 < \tfrac{1}{2} \times 10^{-5} \implies (N+1)^2 > 2 \times 10^5 = 20 \times 10^4 \implies N + 1 > \sqrt{20} \times 10^2$$
$$\implies N > \sqrt{20} \times 10^2 - 1 \approx 446.2$$

Hence N should be at least 447.

17. The error is $\leq a_{N+1} = \dfrac{1}{(N+1)^2 + 1}$. To obtain two-place accuracy, we need

$$\frac{1}{(N+1)^2 + 1} < 0.005 \implies (N+1)^2 + 1 > 200 \implies (N+1)^2 > 199$$
$$\implies N + 1 > \sqrt{199} \implies N > \sqrt{199} - 1 \approx 13.1$$

Hence N should be 14. Then

$$\sum_{n=1}^{\infty} \frac{1}{n^2 + 1} \approx \frac{1}{2} + \frac{1}{5} + \cdots + \frac{1}{197} + \int_{15}^{\infty} \frac{dx}{x^2 + 1}$$

Since the integral is $\pi/2 - \tan^{-1} 15$, we find $\sum_{n=1}^{\infty} \frac{1}{n^2 + 1} \approx 1.07$ (correct to two places).

18. The error is $\leq a_{N+1} = \operatorname{sech}^2(N+1)$. To obtain four-place accuracy, we need

$$\operatorname{sech}^2(N+1) < \tfrac{1}{2} \times 10^{-4} \implies \cosh^2(N+1) > 2 \times 10^4 \implies \cosh(N+1) > \sqrt{2} \times 10^2$$
$$\implies N + 1 > \cosh^{-1}(\sqrt{2} \times 10^2)$$
$$\implies N > \cosh^{-1}(\sqrt{2} \times 10^2) - 1 \approx 4.6$$

Hence N should be 5. Then

$$\sum_{n=1}^{\infty} \operatorname{sech}^2 n \approx \operatorname{sech}^2 1 + \operatorname{sech}^2 2 + \cdots + \operatorname{sech}^2 5 + \int_6^{\infty} \operatorname{sech}^2 x \, dx$$

Since the integral is $\lim_{b \to \infty} (\tanh b - \tanh 6) = 1 - \tanh 6$, $\sum_{n=1}^{\infty} \operatorname{sech}^2 n \approx 0.5020$ (correct to four places).

19. Apply Figure 1 with $f(x) = 1/x$. The shaded area is $\int_1^n \frac{dx}{x} = \ln n$, so

$$\frac{1}{2} + \frac{1}{3} + \cdots + \frac{1}{n} < \ln n < 1 + \frac{1}{2} + \frac{1}{3} + \cdots + \frac{1}{n-1}$$

Add 1 to each side of the first of these inequalities to obtain

$$1 + \frac{1}{2} + \frac{1}{3} + \cdots + \frac{1}{n} < 1 + \ln n$$

Replace n by $n+1$ in the second inequality to obtain

$$\ell n \, (n+1) < 1 + \frac{1}{2} + \frac{1}{3} + \cdots + \frac{1}{n}$$

These combine to produce $\ell n \, (n+1) < 1 + \frac{1}{2} + \frac{1}{3} + \cdots + \frac{1}{n} < 1 + \ell n \, n$.

20. Let $S_n = 1 + \frac{1}{2} + \frac{1}{3} + \cdots + \frac{1}{n}$. Since $1 + \ell n \, n > S_n$, we have

$$S_n > 10 \Longrightarrow 1 + \ell n \, n > 10 \Longrightarrow \ell n \, n > 9 \Longrightarrow n > e^9 \approx 8103.1$$

Hence n must be at least 8104. (This does not guarantee $S_n > 10$, but is simply a necessary condition.) Since $S_n > \ell n \, (n+1)$, a sufficient condition for $S_n > 10$ is $\ell n \, (n+1) \geq 10 \Longleftrightarrow n+1 \geq e^{10} \Longleftrightarrow n \geq e^{10} - 1 \approx 22{,}025.5$. Hence if n is 22,026 or larger, we can guarantee $S_n > 10$. In other words, we <u>must</u> use at least 8104 terms and <u>need not</u> use more than 22,026. The proper choice of n is therefore between 8103 and 22,027.

Similarly, $S_n > 100 \Longrightarrow 1 + \ell n \, n > 100 \Longrightarrow \ell n \, n > 99 \Longrightarrow n > e^{99} \approx 9.9 \times 10^{42}$, so we must use at least this many terms. A sufficient condition for $S_n > 100$ is $\ell n \, (n+1) \geq 100 \Longleftrightarrow n+1 \geq e^{100} \Longleftrightarrow n \geq e^{100} - 1 \approx 2.7 \times 10^{43}$, so we need not use more than this many terms.

21. The inequalities $\int_1^n f(x)dx \leq S_n \leq a_1 + \int_1^n f(x)dx$ derived at the beginning of this section lead to

$$\int_1^\infty f(x)dx \leq S \leq a_1 + \int_1^\infty f(x)dx$$

when we let $n \to \infty$. Subtract the integral from each side to obtain

$$0 \leq S - \int_1^\infty f(x)dx \leq a_1$$

Hence the approximation $S \approx \int_1^\infty f(x)dx$ may involve an error as large as a_1, the first term of the series.

22. If the series converges, both $\lim_{n \to \infty} S_n$ and $\int_1^\infty f(x)dx$ exist. Hence $\lim_{n \to \infty} d_n = \lim_{n \to \infty} S_n - \int_1^\infty f(x)dx$ exists.

23. (a) The inequality $\int_1^n f(x)dx \leq S_n$ derived at the beginning of this section shows that $d_n \geq 0$.

(b) $d_n - d_{n+1} = [S_n - \int_1^n f(x)dx] - [S_{n+1} - \int_1^{n+1} f(x)dx]$

$$= \int_1^{n+1} f(x)dx - \int_1^n f(x)dx - (S_{n+1} - S_n) = \int_n^{n+1} f(x)dx - a_{n+1}$$

Figure 1 in the text (with n replaced by $n+1$) shows that the shaded area between n and $n+1$ is greater than or equal to the area of the rectangle of height a_{n+1} and base 1. Hence $\int_n^{n+1} f(x)dx \geq a_{n+1}$, that is, $d_n - d_{n+1} \geq 0$.

(c) Since $d_{n+1} \leq d_n$ for $n = 1, 2, 3, \ldots$, the sequence is decreasing (more precisely, nonincreasing). It is bounded because $d_n \geq 0$ for all n.

24. $d_n = S_n - \int_1^n \frac{dx}{x} = (1 + \frac{1}{2} + \frac{1}{3} + \cdots + \frac{1}{n}) - \ln n$

25.(a) If $S_n \leq S - \epsilon$ for every n, then $S - \epsilon$ is an upper bound, contradicting the fact that S is the least upper bound. Hence there must be a term S_N of the sequence such that $S_N > S - \epsilon$. Since the sequence is increasing, $S_n \geq S_N > S - \epsilon$ for all $n > N$. Since $S_n \leq S$ for every n, it is obvious that $S_n < S + \epsilon$ for every n.

(b) $n > N \Longrightarrow S - \epsilon < S_n < S + \epsilon \Longrightarrow -\epsilon < S_n - S < \epsilon \Longrightarrow |S_n - S| < \epsilon$. This is the definition of $\lim_{n \to \infty} S_n = S$.

26. Suppose that $S_1, S_2, S_3, \ldots$ is a bounded decreasing sequence, and let S be its greatest lower bound. Given $\epsilon > 0$, we cannot have $S_n \geq S + \epsilon$ for all n, for then $S + \epsilon$ would be a lower bound greater than S. Hence there must be a term S_N such that $S_N < S + \epsilon$. Since the sequence is decreasing, $S_n \leq S_N < S + \epsilon$ for all $n > N$. Since $S_n \geq S$ for every n, we also have $S_n > S - \epsilon$ for all n. Hence $n > N \Longrightarrow S - \epsilon < S_n < S + \epsilon \Longrightarrow -\epsilon < S_n - S < \epsilon \Longrightarrow |S_n - S| < \epsilon$. This proves that $\lim_{n \to \infty} S_n = S$.

27. Let $S_1, S_2, S_3, \ldots$ be a sequence with limit L, and consider the interval $(L - 1, L + 1)$. Since $S_n \to L$ as $n \to \infty$, all the terms of the sequence with sufficiently large index (say $n > N$) are in this interval; only a finite number of terms $(S_1, S_2, \ldots, S_N)$ can be outside it. The largest term in this finite list (or $L + 1$, whichever is larger) serves as an upper bound of the sequence. The smallest term in the list (or $L - 1$, whichever is smaller) serves as a lower bound. Hence the sequence is bounded.

Section 12.3   COMPARISON TESTS

1. Since $\frac{1}{2n - 1} \approx \frac{1}{2}(\frac{1}{n})$ for large n, we compare the series with the divergent harmonic series $\sum \frac{1}{n}$: $\lim \frac{1/(2n - 1)}{1/n} = \lim \frac{n}{2n - 1} = \frac{1}{2} > 0$. This proves that the series diverges.

2. Compare with the convergent p-series $\sum \frac{1}{n^2}$: $\lim \frac{1/(2n - 1)^2}{1/n^2} = \lim (\frac{n}{2n - 1})^2$ $= \frac{1}{4} > 0$. The series converges.

3. Compare with the divergent series $\sum \frac{1}{n}$: $\lim \frac{n/(n^2+1)}{1/n} = \lim \frac{n^2}{n^2+1} = 1 > 0$. The series diverges.

4. $\frac{1}{n^2+1} < \frac{1}{n^2}$, so the series converges because $\sum \frac{1}{n^2}$ does.

5. Compare with the divergent series $\sum \frac{1}{n}$: $\lim \frac{1/\sqrt{n^2+1}}{1/n} = \lim \sqrt{\frac{n^2}{n^2+1}} = 1 > 0$. The series diverges.

6. $\frac{1}{n^2+n} < \frac{1}{n^2}$, so the series converges because $\sum \frac{1}{n^2}$ does.

7. Compare with the divergent series $\sum \frac{1}{n}$: $\lim \frac{1/\sqrt{n^2+n}}{1/n} = \lim \sqrt{\frac{n^2}{n^2+n}} = 1 > 0$. The series diverges.

8. $\frac{1}{\sqrt{n}(n+2)} < \frac{1}{n^{3/2}}$, so the series converges because $\sum 1/n^{3/2}$ does (a p-series with $p = 3/2 > 1$).

9. Compare with the divergent p-series $\sum 1/n^{2/3}$:
$$\lim \frac{1/(n^2+1)^{1/3}}{1/n^{2/3}} = \lim \left(\frac{n^2}{n^2+1}\right)^{1/3} = 1 > 0$$
The series diverges.

10. Compare with the divergent series $\sum 1/n$:
$$\lim \frac{(n-1)/(n^2+n+1)}{1/n} = \lim \frac{n^2-n}{n^2+n+1} = 1 > 0$$
The series diverges.

11. Compare with the convergent p-series $\sum 1/n^2$: $\lim \frac{1/(n^2-8)}{1/n^2} = \lim \frac{n^2}{n^2-8} = 1 > 0$. The series converges.

12. $1/\sqrt{n^2-8} > 1/n$, so the series diverges because $\sum 1/n$ does.

13. $\frac{\sin^2 n}{n^2} < \frac{1}{n^2}$, so the series converges because $\sum 1/n^2$ does.

14. Since $0 < \ell n\, x < x$ for all $x > 1$, we have $1/\ell n\, n > 1/n$ for $n \geq 2$. Hence the series diverges because $\sum 1/n$ does.

15. $1/(2^n+n) < 1/2^n$, so the series converges because $\sum 1/2^n$ does (geometric, with $x = \frac{1}{2} < 1$).

16. Compare with the convergent geometric series $\sum (1/e)^n$:
$$\lim \frac{1/(e^n-n)}{1/e^n} = \lim \frac{e^n}{e^n-n} = 1 > 0$$
The series converges.

17. Compare with the convergent geometric series $\sum (2/3)^n$:
$$\lim \frac{2^n/(3^n-1000)}{2^n/3^n} = \lim \frac{2^n \cdot 3^n}{2^n(3^n-1000)} = 1 > 0$$

The series converges.

18. Since 2^n overwhelms n^2 for large n, it may seem reasonable to use the convergent geometric series $\Sigma \, 1/2^n$ for comparison:

$$\lim \frac{n^2/2^n}{1/2^n} = \lim n^2 = \infty$$

This leads to no conclusion, however, as you can see by reading Statement (3) of the Limit Comparison Test. Let's try a geometric series with a little more clout, namely $\Sigma \, (1.9/2)^n$. Since $n^2/2^n < (1.9)^n/2^n$ for $n \geq 6$, our series converges because $\Sigma \, (1.9/2)^n$ does.

19. $\mathrm{sech}\, n = 2/(e^n + e^{-n}) < 2/e^n$, so the series converges because $2\Sigma \, (1/e)^n$ does.

20. $\left(\dfrac{n+1}{2n}\right)^n \approx \left(\dfrac{1}{2}\right)^n$ for large n, so we compare with the convergent geometric series $\Sigma \, (1/2)^n$: $\lim \dfrac{[(n+1)/(2n)]^n}{(1/2)^n} = \lim \left(\dfrac{n+1}{n}\right)^n = \lim \left(1 + \dfrac{1}{n}\right)^n = e > 0$. The series converges.

21. $e^n \sin 2^{-n} = \dfrac{e^n}{2^n} \cdot \dfrac{\sin 2^{-n}}{2^{-n}} \approx \left(\dfrac{e}{2}\right)^n$ for large n, because

$$\lim_{n \to \infty} \frac{\sin 2^{-n}}{2^{-n}} = \lim_{h \to 0} \frac{\sin h}{h} = 1 \quad (h = 2^{-n})$$

Hence we compare with the divergent geometric series $\Sigma \, (e/2)^n$:

$$\lim \frac{e^n \sin 2^{-n}}{(e/2)^n} = \lim \frac{\sin 2^{-n}}{2^{-n}} = 1 > 0$$

The series diverges.

22. $2^n \sin e^{-n} = \dfrac{2^n}{e^n} \cdot \dfrac{\sin e^{-n}}{e^{-n}} \approx \left(\dfrac{2}{e}\right)^n$ for large n, because

$$\lim_{n \to \infty} \frac{\sin e^{-n}}{e^{-n}} = \lim_{h \to 0} \frac{\sin h}{h} = 1 \quad (h = e^{-n})$$

Hence we compare with the convergent geometric series $\Sigma \, (2/e)^n$:

$$\lim \frac{2^n \sin e^{-n}}{(2/e)^n} = \lim \frac{\sin e^{-n}}{e^{-n}} = 1 > 0$$

The series converges.

23. If $p < 1$, $n^p < n$ for all n, so $1/n^p > 1/n$. Hence $\Sigma \, 1/n^p$ diverges because $\Sigma \, 1/n$ does.

24. $\dfrac{1}{n!} = \dfrac{1}{1} \cdot \dfrac{1}{2} \cdot \dfrac{1}{3} \cdot \dfrac{1}{4} \cdots \dfrac{1}{n} < \dfrac{1}{1} \cdot \dfrac{1}{2} \cdot \dfrac{1}{2} \cdot \dfrac{1}{2} \cdots \dfrac{1}{2} = 1/2^{n-1} = (1/2)^{n-1}$. Since $\Sigma \, (1/2)^{n-1}$ is a convergent geometric series, the given series converges.

25. If $n \geq 3$, $\dfrac{1 \cdot 2 \cdot 3 \cdots n}{n \cdot n \cdot n \cdots n} = \left(\dfrac{1}{n} \cdot \dfrac{2}{n}\right)\left(\dfrac{3}{n} \cdots \dfrac{n}{n}\right) \leq \dfrac{2}{n^2}$ because $\dfrac{3}{n} \cdots \dfrac{n}{n} \leq 1$.   Hence $\sum n!/n^n$ converges because $2\sum 1/n^2$ does.

26. The typical term of a convergent series must approach 0 as $n \to \infty$.

27.(a) If $n \geq 2$, $n < n^{3/2} < n^2$.   Hence $1/n^2 < 1/n^{3/2} < 1/n$ and (since $\ell n\, n > 0$)

$$\frac{\ell n\, n}{n^2} < \frac{\ell n\, n}{n^{3/2}} < \frac{\ell n\, n}{n}$$

(b) Since $\sum \dfrac{\ell n\, n}{n^2}$ converges, the first inequality tells us nothing about $\sum \dfrac{\ell n\, n}{n^{3/2}}$.   The second inequality tells us nothing because $\sum \dfrac{\ell n\, n}{n}$ diverges.

(c) Compare $\sum \dfrac{\ell n\, n}{n^{3/2}}$ with $\sum n^{0.4}/n^{1.5} = \sum 1/n^{1.1}$ (a convergent p-series):

$$\lim \frac{(\ell n\, n)/n^{1.5}}{1/n^{1.1}} = \lim \frac{\ell n\, n}{n^{0.4}} = \lim \frac{1/n}{0.4n^{-0.6}} \quad \text{(L'Hôpital's Rule)}$$

$$= \lim \frac{1}{0.4n^{0.4}} = 0$$

Our series converges by Statement (2) of the Limit Comparison Test.

28. Since $\sum a_n$ converges, $\lim a_n = 0$.   Hence $\lim a_n^2/a_n = \lim a_n = 0$ and by Statement (2) of the Limit Comparison Test, $\sum a_n^2$ converges.

29. The idea is that $0 < \ell n\,(1 + a_n) < a_n$ for all n.   For if this is true, then $\sum \ell n\,(1 + a_n)$ converges because $\sum a_n$ does.   To prove that the inequality is correct, we need only show that $0 < \ell n\,(1 + x) < x$ for all $x > 0$.   This may be done in several ways; one proof has been given before (in Problem 43, Sec. 8.1), where we showed that $1 - 1/x < \ell n\, x < x - 1$ for all $x > 1$.   Replace x by $x + 1$ to obtain $1 - \dfrac{1}{x+1} < \ell n\,(x+1) < x$ for all $x > 0$ (and observe that $1 - \dfrac{1}{x+1}$ is positive for $x > 0$).

30. Since $a_n > 0$, $\lim\limits_{n \to \infty} n a_n = L > 0$.   Then $\lim\limits_{n \to \infty} \dfrac{a_n}{1/n} = L > 0$, so $\sum a_n$ diverges because $\sum 1/n$ does.

31.(a) The interval $(\tfrac{1}{2}L, \tfrac{3}{2}L)$ is a neighborhood of L.   Since $\lim\limits_{n \to \infty} a_n/b_n = L$, we can force a_n/b_n into this neighborhood by making n large, say $n > N$.   In other words, $\tfrac{1}{2}L < a_n/b_n < \tfrac{3}{2}L$ for $n > N$.

(b) Since $b_n > 0$ for all n, we can multiply by b_n to obtain

$$\tfrac{1}{2}Lb_n < a_n < \tfrac{3}{2}Lb_n \quad \text{for } n > N$$

If $\sum b_n$ converges, so does $\sum \tfrac{3}{2}Lb_n$, so the inequality $a_n < \tfrac{3}{2}Lb_n$ implies that

$\Sigma\, a_n$ converges. If $\Sigma\, a_n$ converges, the inequality $\frac{1}{2}Lb_n < a_n$ implies that $\Sigma\, \frac{1}{2}Lb_n$ converges. Since $L \neq 0$, we can write $\Sigma\, b_n = \Sigma\, \frac{2}{L}\cdot\frac{1}{2}Lb_n$, so $\Sigma\, b_n$ also converges.

32. If $\lim\limits_{n\to\infty} a_n/b_n = 0$, the argument in Problem 31 breaks down at the start, because the "interval" $(\frac{1}{2}L, \frac{3}{2}L)$ is $(0,0)$, which is the empty set. However, we can force a_n/b_n into the interval $(0,1)$ by making n large, that is, $0 < a_n/b_n < 1$ for $n > N$. Then $0 < a_n < b_n$ for $n > N$ and hence $\Sigma\, a_n$ converges if $\Sigma\, b_n$ does.

33. If $\lim\limits_{n\to\infty} a_n/b_n = \infty$, then $\lim\limits_{n\to\infty} b_n/a_n = 0$. By Statement (2), convergence of $\Sigma\, a_n$ implies convergence of $\Sigma\, b_n$.

Section 12.4   ALTERNATING SERIES

1. The series converges absolutely because $1 + \frac{1}{3} + \frac{1}{9} + \frac{1}{27} + \cdots$ is geometric with $x = 1/3 < 1$.

2. Absolutely convergent because $1 + \frac{1}{2} + \frac{1}{4} + \frac{1}{8} + \frac{1}{16} + \cdots$ is geometric with $x = \frac{1}{2}$.

3. Divergent because it is the negative of the harmonic series.

4. Conditionally convergent because it is a convergent alternating series but $1 + 1/3 + 1/5 + 1/7 + \cdots$ diverges (by comparison with the harmonic series).

5. Conditionally convergent because it is a convergent alternating series but $1 + 1/\sqrt{2} + 1/\sqrt{3} + 1/\sqrt{4} + \cdots$ is a divergent p-series ($p = \frac{1}{2} < 1$).

6. Divergent because the typical term $\dfrac{(-1)^{n+1}(n+1)}{\ln(n+1)}$ does not approach 0 as $n \to \infty$. (L'Hôpital's Rule shows that the absolute value becomes infinite.)

7. Absolutely convergent because $0 < \dfrac{\left|\sin n^2\right|}{n^2} < \dfrac{1}{n^2}$ and $\Sigma\, 1/n^2$ converges.

8. The absolute value of the typical term is $a_n = n/(n^2+1)$, which approaches 0 as $n \to \infty$. Moreover, the function $f(x) = x/(x^2+1)$ is decreasing for $x \geq 1$ because $f'(x) = \dfrac{(x^2+1) - x(2x)}{(x^2+1)^2} = \dfrac{1-x^2}{(x^2+1)^2} < 0$ for $x > 1$. Hence the series converges by the Alternating Series Test. The series of absolute values, $\Sigma\, n/(n^2+1)$, diverges (by comparison with $\Sigma\, 1/n$). Hence we have conditional convergence.

9. The series of absolute values is $\Sigma\, \dfrac{\ln n}{n}$, which diverges. (See Example 5, Sec. 12.3.) Hence the original series does not converge absolutely.

10. $a_n = n/(n^2 - 2) \to 0$ as $n \to \infty$. Moreover, if $f(x) = x/(x^2 - 2)$, then

$$f'(x) = \frac{(x^2 - 2) - x(2x)}{(x^2 - 2)^2} = \frac{-(x^2 + 2)}{(x^2 - 2)^2} < 0 \text{ for } x > \sqrt{2}$$

Hence $a_{n+1} < a_n$ for $n = 2, 3, 4, \ldots$ and the series converges by the Alternating Series Test.

11. The series is $-1 + 1/2 - 1/3 + 1/4 - \cdots$, which converges by the Alternating Series Test.

12. The typical term $\frac{(-1)^{n-1}n}{n+1}$ does not approach 0 as $n \to \infty$, so the series diverges.

13. The typical term $(-1)^{n-1}\ell n\,(1/n)$ does not approach 0 as $n \to \infty$, so the series diverges.

14. Let $f(x) = x/e^x$. Then $f(x) \to 0$ as $x \to \infty$. Since

$$f'(x) = \frac{e^x - xe^x}{e^{2x}} = \frac{e^x(1-x)}{e^{2x}} < 0 \quad \text{for } x > 1$$

f is decreasing for $x \geq 1$. Hence the series converges by the Alternating Series Test.

15. $a_n = \sin\left(\frac{\pi}{n+1}\right)$ decreases to 0 as $n \to \infty$, so the series converges.

16. The typical term $(-1)^{n+1}\cos\left(\frac{\pi}{n+1}\right)$ does not approach 0 as $n \to \infty$, so the series diverges.

17. The typical term $a_n = \frac{\sin n}{n^2}$ does not alternate in sign as n takes on the values $1, 2, 3, \cdots$. (For example, $a_1 > 0$, $a_2 > 0$, $a_3 > 0$, $a_4 < 0$, $a_5 < 0$, $a_6 < 0$, $\cdots$.) Neither is the series positive (or even "ultimately positive"). As $n \to \infty$, $\sin n$ takes on both positive and negative values infinitely often. The series converges absolutely because $0 < |\sin n|/n^2 < 1/n^2$ and $\sum 1/n^2$ converges.

18. If $p > 0$, then $a_n = 1/n^p$ decreases to 0 as $n \to \infty$. Hence the series converges by the Alternating Series Test. It diverges when $p \leq 0$ because $(-1)^{n-1}/n^p$ does not approach 0 when $n \to \infty$. The series of absolute values is $\sum 1/n^p$, which converges if $p > 1$ and diverges if $p \leq 1$. Thus the original series is absolutely convergent if $p > 1$, conditionally convergent if $0 < p \leq 1$, and divergent if $p \leq 0$.

19. The series is geometric (with $x = -1/2$), its sum being $\frac{1}{1-x} = \frac{1}{1+1/2} = \frac{2}{3}$.

20. We know that the series diverges if $|x| \geq 1$, so the question is what kind of convergence it displays when $|x| < 1$. The series of absolute values is $1 + |x| + |x|^2 + \cdots$, which converges because $|x| < 1$. Hence the original series

converges absolutely or diverges; it is never conditionally convergent.

21. The error in the approximation $S \approx S_n$ is $\leq a_{n+1} = 1/\sqrt{n+1}$. For three-place accuracy we need

$$1/\sqrt{n+1} < 0.0005 \implies \sqrt{n+1} > 2000 \implies n+1 > 2000^2 \implies n > 3,999,999$$

Hence four million terms are sufficient. The series converges slowly!

22. The series converges by the Alternating Series Test. To obtain five-place accuracy from $S \approx S_n$, we need $a_{n+1} = 1/(n+1)! < 0.000005$. A little experimenting with a calculator shows that $1/8!$ is not small enough, but $1/9!$ is. Hence we choose $n+1 = 9$, that is, $n = 8$:

$$S \approx 1 - \frac{1}{3!} + \frac{1}{5!} - \frac{1}{7!} + \frac{1}{9!} - \frac{1}{11!} + \frac{1}{13!} - \frac{1}{15!} \approx 0.84147 \quad \text{(correct to five places)}$$

Note that $\sin 1 = 0.8414709\cdots$.

23. The series converges by the Alternating Series Test. To obtain five-place accuracy, we need $a_{n+1} = \dfrac{1}{(2n+1)(n+1)!} < 0.000005$. A calculator shows that we may choose $n = 7$, so

$$S \approx 1 - \frac{1}{3 \cdot 2!} + \frac{1}{5 \cdot 3!} - \frac{1}{7 \cdot 4!} + \frac{1}{9 \cdot 5!} - \frac{1}{11 \cdot 6!} + \frac{1}{13 \cdot 7!} \approx 0.86153$$

(correct to five places).

24. The typical partial sum with even index is

$$S_{2n} = (1 + \frac{1}{2} + \frac{1}{3} + \cdots + \frac{1}{n}) - (1 + \frac{1}{2} + \frac{1}{4} + \cdots + \frac{1}{2^{n-1}}), \quad n = 1, 2, 3, \ldots$$

The expression in the first parenthesis is the nth partial sum of the harmonic series, which increases without bound as $n \to \infty$. The expression in the second parenthesis is the nth partial sum of the geometric series $1 + \frac{1}{2} + \frac{1}{4} + \frac{1}{8} + \cdots$, which approaches $1/(1 - \frac{1}{2}) = 2$ as $n \to \infty$. Hence $\lim S_{2n} = \infty$, which shows that the original series diverges. This does not contradict Theorem 2 (which requires that the nth term <u>decreases</u> to zero, not merely approaches zero). The terms of the given series do not decrease to zero.

25. The first partial sum is $S_1 = a_1$ and the second is $S_2 = a_1 - a_2$. The limit of the partial sums (the sum of the series) is always between consecutive partial sums. (See the argument for Theorem 2 in the text.)

26. This statement is equivalent to Theorem 1. For if $\sum |a_n|$ converges, so does $\sum a_n$.

27. Take $a_n = b_n = (-1)^n/\sqrt{n}$. Then $\sum a_n$ and $\sum b_n$ are convergent alternating series, but $\sum a_n b_n = \sum 1/n$ is the divergent harmonic series.

28. $\cosh 1 = \frac{1}{2}(e + e^{-1}) = \frac{1}{2}\left(\sum_{n=0}^{\infty} \frac{1}{n!} + \sum_{n=0}^{\infty} \frac{(-1)^n}{n!}\right) = \frac{1}{2} \sum_{n=0}^{\infty} \left(\frac{1}{n!} + \frac{(-1)^n}{n!}\right)$ (Problem 45,

Sec. 12.1). Thus $\cosh 1 = \frac{1}{2}[(\frac{1}{0!}+\frac{1}{0!})+(\frac{1}{1!}-\frac{1}{1!})+(\frac{1}{2!}+\frac{1}{2!})+\cdots] = \frac{1}{0!}+\frac{1}{2!}+\frac{1}{4!}$ $+\cdots$.

29. $\cosh 1 \approx 1+\frac{1}{2}+\frac{1}{24}+\frac{1}{720}+\frac{1}{40,320} = 1.54308035\cdots$. A calculator gives

$\cosh 1 = 1.54308063\cdots$. Hence $\cosh 1 = 1.54308$ correct to five places.

30. Theorem 2 is not involved at all; the series for $\cosh 1$ is not alternating.

31. The series on the left is a (conditionally) convergent alternating series. Each series on the right diverges (by comparison with the divergent p-series with $p = \frac{1}{2}$). This is another example of how rearrangement of the terms of a conditionally convergent series can lead to nonsense.

32. The series on the left is absolutely convergent (because the p-series with $p = 2$ converges). Rearrangement of the terms of such a series affects neither convergence nor the sum.

33.(a) The series $1+1/3+1/5+1/7+\cdots$ diverges (by comparison with the harmonic series). Since it is a positive series, its partial sums must increase without bound. Hence a partial sum exceeding π must exist.

   (b) The series $-1/2-1/4-1/6-\cdots$ diverges (because it is the negative of $1/2+1/4+1/6+\cdots$, which diverges by comparison with the harmonic series). Its partial sums (negatives of the partial sums of $1/2+1/4+1/6+\cdots$) decrease without bound, so there must be one that, added to the sum in (a), produces a number less than π.

   (c) We do not run out of positive terms because $1+1/3+1/5+1/7+\cdots$ is an _infinite_ series. Similarly, we do not run out of negative terms because $-1/2-1/4-1/6-\cdots$ is an infinite series. Every term of the original series is used because the process never hits π. (If it did, π would be a rational number.) Hence we have to keep it going indefinitely; every term of the original series is eventually included in one or another sum. The sums converge to π because the typical term of the original series approaches 0. Hence we box in π more closely with every step of the process.

34.(a) Same reasoning as in Problem 33, with π replaced by 10 in the first step and by 10^{-2} in the second step.

   (b) Same reasoning as in Problem 33, except that the sums do not approach a limit; they oscillate more and more wildly without positive or negative bound.

35.(a) $\frac{1}{2}(|a_n|+a_n)-\frac{1}{2}(|a_n|-a_n) = \frac{1}{2}a_n+\frac{1}{2}a_n = a_n$. The first inequality reads $0 \le \frac{1}{2}(2a_n) \le a_n$ if $a_n \ge 0$ and $0 \le \frac{1}{2}(0) \le -a_n$ if $a_n < 0$. Both statements are correct. The second inequality reads $0 \le \frac{1}{2}(0) \le a_n$ if $a_n \ge 0$ and $0 \le \frac{1}{2}(-2a_n)$

$\leq -a_n$ if $a_n < 0$. Both statements are correct.

(b) Convergence of the first series follows from the first inequality by the ordinary Comparison Test (because $\sum |a_n|$ converges). Convergence of the second series follows from the second inequality in the same way. The sum of the two series is convergent, and is equal to $\sum a_n$ by the formula in (a).

Section 12.5   THE RATIO TEST AND ROOT TEST

1. $a_{n+1}/a_n = n!/(n+1)! = 1/(n+1) \to 0$ as $n \to \infty$. Hence the series converges.

2. $a_{n+1}/a_n = \dfrac{3^{n+1}}{(n+1)!} \cdot \dfrac{n!}{3^n} = \dfrac{3}{n+1} \to 0$ as $n \to \infty$. The series converges.

3. $a_{n+1}/a_n = \dfrac{2^{n+1}}{(2n+1)!} \cdot \dfrac{(2n-1)!}{2^n} = \dfrac{2}{(2n+1)(2n)} \to 0$ as $n \to \infty$. The series converges.

4. $|a_{n+1}/a_n| = \dfrac{2^{n+1}}{(2n+2)!} \cdot \dfrac{(2n)!}{2^n} = \dfrac{2}{(2n+2)(2n+1)} \to 0$ as $n \to \infty$. The series converges.

5. $a_{n+1}/a_n = \dfrac{(n+1)^2}{2^{n+1}} \cdot \dfrac{2^n}{n^2} = \dfrac{1}{2}\left(\dfrac{n+1}{n}\right)^2 \to \dfrac{1}{2}$ as $n \to \infty$. The series converges.

6. Neither test applies. The series converges, however, by comparison with $\sum 1/n^2$.

7. $\sqrt[n]{a_n} = 1/n \to 0$ as $n \to \infty$. The series converges.

8. $\sqrt[n]{a_n} = e^{-n} \to 0$ as $n \to \infty$. The series converges.

9. $\sqrt[n]{a_n} = 1/\ln n \to 0$ as $n \to \infty$. The series converges.

10. $a_{n+1}/a_n = \dfrac{(n+1)!}{(n+1)^{n+1}} \cdot \dfrac{n^n}{n!} = \dfrac{(n+1)n^n}{(n+1)^{n+1}} = \dfrac{n^n}{(n+1)^n} = \left(\dfrac{n}{n+1}\right)^n = \left(\dfrac{n+1}{n}\right)^{-n}$

$= \left(1 + \dfrac{1}{n}\right)^{-n} = (1+h)^{-1/h}$ $(h = 1/n)$

$= [(1+h)^{1/h}]^{-1} \to e^{-1}$ as $n \to \infty$ (and $h \to 0$)

Since $e^{-1} < 1$, the series converges.

11. Neither test applies. The series diverges, however, because its nth term approaches e as $n \to \infty$.

12. Neither test applies. The series diverges, however, because $\left(\dfrac{n}{n+1}\right)^n \to e^{-1}$ as $n \to \infty$. (See the solution of Problem 10.)

13. The series converges when $x = 0$, so assume that $x \neq 0$. Then

$$a_{n+1}/a_n = \frac{x^{2n+2}}{(2n+2)!} \cdot \frac{(2n)!}{x^{2n}} = \frac{x^2}{(2n+2)(2n+1)} \to 0 \text{ as } n \to \infty$$

The series converges (absolutely) for all x.

14. The series converges when x = 0, so assume that $x \neq 0$. Then

$$|a_{n+1}/a_n| = \frac{|x|^{2n+1}}{(2n+1)!} \cdot \frac{(2n-1)!}{|x|^{2n-1}} = \frac{x^2}{(2n+1)(2n)} \to 0 \text{ as } n \to \infty$$

The series converges (absolutely) for all x.

15. Same reasoning as in Problem 14. The factor $(-1)^{n-1}$ does not affect absolute value.

16. The series converges when x = 0, so assume that $x \neq 0$. Then

$$|a_{n+1}/a_n| = \frac{(n+1)! \, |x|^{n+1}}{n! \, |x|^n} = (n+1)|x| \to \infty \text{ as } n \to \infty$$

The series diverges for all $x \neq 0$.

17. $\sqrt[n]{|a_n|} = |x|$, with limit $\rho = |x|$ as $n \to \infty$. This is less than 1 when $-1 < x < 1$, so the series converges (absolutely) when $-1 < x < 1$ and diverges when x > 1 or x < -1. It also diverges when $x = \pm 1$, as shown in Example 5, Sec. 12.1.

18. The series converges when x = 0, so assume that $x \neq 0$. Then

$$|a_{n+1}/a_n| = \frac{(n+1)|x|^n}{n|x|^{n-1}} = |x|(\frac{n+1}{n}) \to |x| \text{ as } n \to \infty$$

The series converges (absolutely) when $-1 < x < 1$ and diverges when x > 1 or x < -1. When x = 1 the series is $\sum n$, which diverges because its typical term does not approach 0. When x = -1 the series is $\sum (-1)^{n-1}n$, which diverges for the same reason.

19. The series converges when x = 0, so assume that $x \neq 0$. Then

$$|a_{n+1}/a_n| = \frac{(n+1)(n)|x|^{n-1}}{n(n-1)|x|^{n-2}} = |x|(\frac{n+1}{n-1}) \to |x| \text{ as } n \to \infty$$

The series converges (absolutely) when $-1 < x < 1$ and diverges when x > 1 or x < -1. It also diverges when $x = \pm 1$ because the typical term does not approach 0.

20. $\sqrt[n]{|a_n|} = |x-1|$, with limit $\rho = |x-1|$ as $n \to \infty$. The series converges (absolutely) when $-1 < x-1 < 1$, that is, when $0 < x < 2$. It diverges when x > 2 or x < 0. When x = 2 the series is $\sum 1$, which diverges. When x = 0 the series is $\sum (-1)^n$, which also diverges. An easier solution is to recognize the series as geometric, converging absolutely when $|x-1| < 1$ and diverging otherwise.

21. The series converges when $x = 0$, so assume that $x \neq 0$. Then

$$\left| a_{n+1} / a_n \right| = \frac{|x|^{n+1}}{n+1} \cdot \frac{n}{|x|^n} = |x|\left(\frac{n}{n+1}\right) \to |x| \text{ as } n \to \infty$$

The series converges (absolutely) when $-1 < x < 1$ and diverges when $x > 1$ or $x < -1$. When $x = 1$ the series is $\Sigma\, 1/n$, the divergent harmonic series. When $x = -1$ the series is $\Sigma\, (-1)^n/n$, which converges (conditionally) by the Alternating Series Test.

22. The series converges when $x = 0$, so assume that $x \neq 0$. Then

$$\left| a_{n+1} / a_n \right| = \frac{|x|^{2n+1}}{2n+1} \cdot \frac{2n-1}{|x|^{2n-1}} = x^2\left(\frac{2n-1}{2n+1}\right) \to x^2 \text{ as } n \to \infty$$

The series converges (absolutely) when $-1 < x < 1$ and diverges when $x > 1$ or $x < -1$. When $x = 1$ the series is $\Sigma\, (-1)^{n-1}/(2n-1)$, which converges by the Alternating Series Test. When $x = -1$ the series is $\Sigma\, (-1)^{n-1}(-1)^{2n-1}/(2n-1)$. Since $(-1)^{2n-1} = -1$ (because $2n-1$ is odd), the series is $-\Sigma\, (-1)^{n-1}/(2n-1)$, the negative of the series when $x = 1$. Hence it converges. In both cases the convergence is conditional because $\Sigma\, 1/(2n-1)$ diverges by comparison with $\Sigma\, 1/n$.

23. The series converges when $x = 2$, so assume that $x \neq 2$. Then

$$\left| a_{n+1} / a_n \right| = \frac{|x-2|^{n+1}}{(n+1)^2} \cdot \frac{n^2}{|x-2|^n} = |x-2|\left(\frac{n}{n+1}\right)^2 \to |x-2| \text{ as } n \to \infty$$

The series converges (absolutely) when $-1 < x - 2 < 1$, that is, when $1 < x < 3$. It diverges when $x > 3$ or $x < 1$. When $x = 3$ the series is $\Sigma\, 1/n^2$, which converges. When $x = 1$ the series is $\Sigma\, (-1)^n/n^2$, which also converges. In both cases the convergence is absolute.

24. $\sqrt[n]{|a_n|} = \frac{1}{2}|x+2|$, with limit $\rho = \frac{1}{2}|x+2|$ as $n \to \infty$. The series converges (absolutely) when $-1 < \frac{1}{2}(x+2) < 1$, that is, when $-4 < x < 0$. It diverges when $x > 0$ or $x < -4$. When $x = 0$ the series is $\Sigma\, 1$, which diverges. When $x = -4$ the series is $\Sigma\, (-1)^n$, which also diverges.

25. $\sqrt[n]{|a_n|} = |2x|$, with limit $\rho = |2x|$ as $n \to \infty$. The series converges (absolutely) when $-1 < 2x < 1$, that is, when $-\frac{1}{2} < x < \frac{1}{2}$. It diverges when $x > \frac{1}{2}$ or $x < -\frac{1}{2}$. When $x = \frac{1}{2}$ the series is $\Sigma\, 1$, which diverges. When $x = -\frac{1}{2}$ the series is $\Sigma\, (-1)^n$, which also diverges.

26. The series converges when $x = -1$, so assume that $x \neq -1$. Then

$$\left| a_{n+1} / a_n \right| = \frac{|x+1|^{n+1}}{\sqrt{n+1}} \cdot \frac{\sqrt{n}}{|x+1|^n} = |x+1|\left(\frac{n}{n+1}\right)^{1/2} \to |x+1| \text{ as } n \to \infty$$

The series converges (absolutely) when $-1 < x + 1 < 1$, that is, when $-2 < x < 0$.

It diverges when $x > 0$ or $x < -2$. When $x = 0$ the series is $\sum 1/\sqrt{n}$, which is a divergent p-series with $p = \frac{1}{2}$. When $x = -2$ the series is $\sum (-1)^n/\sqrt{n}$, which converges (conditionally) by the Alternating Series Test.

27. $\sqrt[n]{|a_n|} = |x|/n \to 0$ as $n \to \infty$. The series converges (absolutely) for all x.

28. The series converges when $x = 0$, so assume that $x \neq 0$. Then

$$\left| a_{n+1}/a_n \right| = \frac{(n+1)! \, |x|^{n+1}}{(n+1)^{n+1}} \cdot \frac{n^n}{n! \, |x|^n} = \frac{|x|(n+1)n^n}{(n+1)^{n+1}} = |x| \left(\frac{n}{n+1} \right)^n \to |x|/e$$

as $n \to \infty$. (See the solution of Problem 10.) The series converges (absolutely) when $-1 < x/e < 1$, that is, when $-e < x < e$. It diverges when $x > e$ or $x < -e$. When $x = e$ the series is $\sum n! e^n/n^n$, the behavior of which is not obvious. One way to discuss it is to use Stirling's Formula (Problem 35, Sec. 8.3), which says that $n! \approx \sqrt{2\pi n}(n/e)^n$ for large n. Then the typical term of the series is $n! e^n/n^n \approx \sqrt{2\pi n} \to \infty$ as $n \to \infty$, which implies that the series diverges. When $x = -e$ the series is $\sum (-1)^n n! e^n/n^n$, which diverges for the same reason. (If you thought of using Stirling's Formula, you should get some kind of award for remembering obscure facts!)

29. $\sqrt[n]{|a_n|} = |x^2 - 1|$, with limit $\rho = |x^2 - 1|$ as $n \to \infty$. The series converges (absolutely) when $-1 < x^2 - 1 < 1 \iff 0 < x^2 < 2 \iff -\sqrt{2} < x < \sqrt{2}$ and $x \neq 0$. It diverges when $x > \sqrt{2}$ or $x < -\sqrt{2}$. The doubtful cases (when $\rho = 1$) are $x = 0$ and $x = \pm\sqrt{2}$, which yield the series $\sum (-1)^n$ and $\sum 1$, respectively. These diverge.

30.(a) The series converges when $x = 1$, so assume that $x \neq 1$. Then

$$\left| a_{n+1}/a_n \right| = \frac{|x-1|^{n+1}}{n+1} \cdot \frac{n}{|x-1|^n} = |x-1| \left(\frac{n}{n+1} \right) \to |x-1| \text{ as } n \to \infty$$

The series converges when $-1 < x - 1 < 1$ (or $0 < x < 2$) and diverges when $x > 2$ or $x < 0$. When $x = 2$ the series is $\sum (-1)^{n-1}/n$, which converges by the Alternating Series Test. When $x = 0$ the series is $\sum (-1)^{n-1}(-1)^n/n = -\sum 1/n$, which diverges because it is the negative of the harmonic series. Thus $f(x)$ is defined when $0 < x \leq 2$, that is, the domain is $(0,2]$.

(b) Since $f(x) = (x-1) - \frac{(x-1)^2}{2} + \frac{(x-1)^3}{3} - \cdots$, term-by-term differentiation (as if the series were a polynomial) yields

$$f'(x) = 1 - (x-1) + (x-1)^2 - \cdots = \sum_{n=0}^{\infty} (-1)^n (x-1)^n$$

The Root Test applied to this series yields $\rho = |x-1|$, so the domain of f' is at least $(0,2)$, as in part (a). When $x = 2$ the series is $\sum (-1)^n$ and when $x = 0$ it is $\sum 1$, so it diverges in both cases. Thus the domain of f' is $(0,2)$.

(c) From part (b) we have

$$f'(x) = 1 - (x-1) + (x-1)^2 - \cdots = 1 + (1-x) + (1-x)^2 + \cdots$$
$$= \sum_{n=1}^{\infty} (1-x)^{n-1} = \sum_{n=0}^{\infty} (1-x)^n$$

(The two sums look different, but in fact they represent the same series, as you can see by writing them out. The index of summation has been changed, although it is labeled n in both cases.) More directly, we can obtain this result from the summation in part (b) by writing

$$f'(x) = \sum_{n=0}^{\infty} (-1)^n (x-1)^n = \sum_{n=0}^{\infty} (1-x)^n$$

(d) Replace t by 1 - x to obtain $\sum_{n=0}^{\infty} (1-x)^n = \dfrac{1}{1-(1-x)} = \dfrac{1}{x}$. The inequality -1 < t < 1 becomes -1 < 1 - x < 1, or 0 < x < 2. Hence $f'(x) = 1/x$ (0 < x < 2) the domain being the same as in part (b).

(e) $f(x) = (x-1) - \dfrac{(x-1)^2}{2} + \dfrac{(x-1)^3}{3} - \cdots$, so f(1) = 0. Since $\dfrac{dy}{dx} = \dfrac{1}{x} \Rightarrow$ y = ℓn x + C, and y = 0 when x = 1, we have y = f(x) = ℓn x.

(f) The series for f(x) yields f(2) = 1 - 1/2 + 1/3 - 1/4 + $\cdots$. Assuming that the formula f(x) = ℓn x applies at x = 2, we have ℓn 2 = 1 - 1/2 + 1/3 - 1/4 + $\cdots$.

(g) ℓn x is easy to find on a calculator, but of course the calculator itself must have been programmed by somebody with a practical formula for computing ℓn x. Why not regard the series $(x-1) - \dfrac{(x-1)^2}{2} + \dfrac{(x-1)^3}{3} - \cdots$ as such a formula? The actual formula used in calculators is not important; the point is that the discovery that f(x) = ℓn x, while impressive, really puts us no closer than we were to computation of f(x).

31. Since the given limit is less than 1, the Ratio Test says that the series $a_1 + a_2 + a_3 + \cdots$ converges. The typical term of a convergent series must approach 0, so $\lim_{n\to\infty} a_n = 0$, that is, the limit of the sequence a_1, a_2, a_3, $\cdots$ is 0.

32. $a_{n+1}/a_n = \dfrac{10^{n+1}}{(n+1)^{10}} \cdot \dfrac{n^{10}}{10^n} = 10\left(\dfrac{n}{n+1}\right)^{10} \to 10$ as $n \to \infty$. Hence the sequence does not approach 0.

33. (a) If $\rho = \lim_{n\to\infty} \sqrt[n]{|a_n|} > 1$ (or if $\rho = \infty$), then $\sqrt[n]{|a_n|} > 1$ for large n. This implies $|a_n| > 1$ for large n, so the typical term of $\sum a_n$ does not approach 0. Hence the series diverges.

(b) If $\rho < r < 1$, then (since $\sqrt[n]{|a_n|} \to \rho$ as $n \to \infty$) we have $\sqrt[n]{|a_n|} < r$ for large

n. This implies $|a_n| < r^n$ for large n. Since $\sum r^n$ is a convergent geometric series (because $r < 1$), the series $\sum |a_n|$ converges by the ordinary Comparison Test. Hence $\sum a_n$ converges absolutely.

(c) The series $1 - 1/2 + 1/3 - 1/4 + \cdots$ converges (by the Alternating Series Test), while the harmonic series $1 + 1/2 + 1/3 + 1/4 + \cdots$ does not. In each case $\sqrt[n]{|a_n|} = 1/n^{1/n} = n^{-1/n}$. To find the limit as $n \to \infty$, let $y = n^{-1/n}$. Then

$$\ell n \, y = -\frac{1}{n} \ell n \, n \quad \text{and (by L'Hôpital's Rule)} \quad \lim_{n \to \infty} \ell n \, y = \lim_{n \to \infty} (-1/n) = 0$$

Hence $\rho = \lim_{n \to \infty} y = 1$.

34. If $\rho = 1$, there is no point between ρ and 1. (Or, if we interpret "between" to allow equality, we must choose $r = 1$. But then the series $\sum r^n$ does not converge.)

35. The statement in part (a) is correct. But it does not follow that $|a_n|$ is close to 1 because $\sqrt[n]{|a_n|}$ is. If $a_n = (-1)^n/n$, for example, then $\sqrt[n]{|a_n|} \to 1$ as $n \to \infty$ (as shown in Problem 33). But $|a_n| = 1/n \to 0$, not 1. The series $\sum a_n$ converges even though $\rho = 1$.

Chapter 12   TRUE-FALSE QUIZ

1. False. $\sum_{n=0}^{\infty} (-1)^n$ diverges, but its sequence of partial sums is 1, 0, 1, 0, 1, ..., which is bounded.

2. False. The typical term is $(-1)^{n-1} \cos(1/n)$, which does not approach 0 as $n \to \infty$.

3. False. The typical term of $\sum 1/n$ approaches 0, but the series diverges.

4. False. The series is geometric, with $x = 1.02 > 1$, so it diverges.

5. False. The series is a p-series with $p = \frac{1}{4} < 1$, so it diverges.

6. False. The series diverges by comparison with $\sum 1/n$.

7. False. The series converges by comparison with the convergent p-series $\sum 1/n^2$.

8. False. If $\sum b_n$ were <u>convergent</u>, the inequalities would imply that $\sum a_n$ is convergent. As it is, no conclusion is implied. For example, $0 \le 1/n^2 \le 1/n$ for all n and $\sum 1/n$ diverges. But $\sum 1/n^2$ converges.

9. False. $\sum 1/n^2$ converges, but $\sum 1/n$ does not.

10. False. The series $1 + 1/2 + 1/3 + 1/4 + \cdots$ diverges.

11. False. The series converges by the Alternating Series Test.

12. False. The series converges absolutely because $\sum 1/n^2$ converges.

154

13. False.   The Ratio Test yields $\rho = 1$, which is inconclusive.

14. False. $a_{n+1}/a_n = \dfrac{(n+1)!}{2^{n+1}} \cdot \dfrac{2^n}{n!} = \frac{1}{2}(n+1) \to \infty$ as $n \to \infty$, so the series diverges by the Ratio Test.

15. False. $\sum 1/n^2$ converges, but $\dfrac{1/(n+1)^2}{1/n^2} = \left(\dfrac{n}{n+1}\right)^2 \to 1$ as $n \to \infty$.

Chapter 12   ADDITIONAL PROBLEMS

1. The partial sums are $S_1 = 1$, $S_2 = 0$, $S_3 = 1/2$, $S_4 = 0$, $S_5 = 1/3$, $S_6 = 0$, and so on.   These have limit 0, so the sum of the series is 0.

2. Decompose $\dfrac{1}{k^2 - 1}$ by writing $\dfrac{1}{k^2 - 1} = \dfrac{1}{(k-1)(k+1)} = \dfrac{A}{k-1} + \dfrac{B}{k+1} \Longrightarrow 1 = A(k+1) + B(k-1)$.   Put $k = 1$ to find $A = \frac{1}{2}$ and $k = -1$ to find $B = -\frac{1}{2}$.   Then $\dfrac{1}{k^2 - 1} = \dfrac{1}{2}\left(\dfrac{1}{k-1} - \dfrac{1}{k+1}\right)$ and the typical partial sum of the series is

$$\frac{1}{2}\left[(1 - \tfrac{1}{3}) + (\tfrac{1}{2} - \tfrac{1}{4}) + (\tfrac{1}{3} - \tfrac{1}{5}) + \cdots + (\tfrac{1}{n-1} - \tfrac{1}{n+1})\right] =$$

$$\frac{1}{2}\left[(1 + \tfrac{1}{2} + \tfrac{1}{3} + \cdots + \tfrac{1}{n-1}) - (\tfrac{1}{3} + \tfrac{1}{4} + \tfrac{1}{5} + \cdots + \tfrac{1}{n+1})\right] = \frac{1}{2}(1 + \tfrac{1}{2} - \tfrac{1}{n} - \tfrac{1}{n+1})$$

This has limit $\frac{1}{2}(1 + \frac{1}{2}) = \frac{3}{4}$ as $n \to \infty$, so the sum of the series is 3/4.

3. The typical term is $n/(2n+2)$, which approaches $\frac{1}{2}$ (not 0) as $n \to \infty$.   Hence the series diverges.

4. This is a geometric series $a + ar + ar^2 + \cdots$ with $a = \frac{1}{2}$ and $r = -\frac{1}{2}$.   Hence its sum is $\dfrac{a}{1-r} = \dfrac{1/2}{1 + 1/2} = \dfrac{1}{3}$.

5. $0.999\cdots$ means $0.9 + 0.09 + 0.009 + \cdots$, which is geometric with $a = 0.9$ and $r = 0.1$.   Its sum is $\dfrac{a}{1-r} = \dfrac{0.9}{1 - 0.1} = 1$.

6. $f(x) = 1/(1-x)$ if $-1 < x < 1$, so $f(2/5) = 5/3$.

7. $\displaystyle\sum_{n=1}^{\infty} x^n = x + x^2 + x^3 + \cdots$, which is geometric with $a = x$ and $r = x$.   Its sum is $\dfrac{a}{1-r} = \dfrac{x}{1-x}$ if $|x| < 1$.

8. In the geometric series $1 + t + t^2 + t^3 + \cdots = \dfrac{1}{1-t}$ $(|t| < 1)$ replace t by x^3.   Then $\dfrac{1}{1-x^3} = 1 + x^3 + x^6 + x^9 + \cdots$.   Since $|t| < 1 \Longleftrightarrow |x^3| < 1 \Longleftrightarrow |x| < 1$, the domain is $-1 < x < 1$.

9. The ball falls 3 ft, rebounds $3(1/3)$ ft and falls, rebounds $3(1/3)^2$ ft and falls, and so on.   The distance traveled is

$$3 + 2 \cdot 3(\tfrac{1}{3}) + 2 \cdot 3(\tfrac{1}{3})^2 + \cdots = 3 + 2(1 + \tfrac{1}{3} + \tfrac{1}{3^2} + \cdots) = 3 + \frac{2}{1 - 1/3} = 6 \text{ ft}$$

More directly, we may use Problem 37, Sec. 12.1, to find the distance

$$\frac{a(1 + r)}{1 - r} = \frac{3(1 + 1/3)}{1 - 1/3} = 6 \text{ ft.}$$

10. The series converges by comparison with the convergent p-series $\sum 1/n^2$:

$$\frac{1/(2n - 1)^2}{1/n^2} = \left(\frac{n}{2n - 1}\right)^2 \to \frac{1}{4} > 0 \text{ as } n \to \infty$$

The error in the approximation formula is $\leq a_{N+1} = 1/(2N + 1)^2$; for two-place accuracy we need $1/(2N + 1)^2 < 0.005 \implies (2N + 1)^2 > 200 \implies 2N + 1 > 10\sqrt{2} \implies N > \tfrac{1}{2}(10\sqrt{2} - 1) \approx 6.6$. We choose $N = 7$. Then

$$S \approx 1 + \frac{1}{9} + \frac{1}{25} + \frac{1}{49} + \frac{1}{81} + \frac{1}{121} + \frac{1}{169} + \int_8^\infty \frac{dx}{(2x - 1)^2}$$

The integral is $\lim_{b \to \infty} \tfrac{1}{2}\left(\frac{1}{15} - \frac{1}{2b - 1}\right) = \frac{1}{30}$, so $S \approx 1.23$ correct to two places.

11.(a) $f(x) = 1/(x^2 + 4)$ satisfies the hypotheses of the test; since

$$\int_1^\infty \frac{dx}{x^2 + 4} = \lim_{b \to \infty} \tfrac{1}{2}\left(\tan^{-1}\frac{b}{2} - \tan^{-1}\frac{1}{2}\right) = \tfrac{1}{2}\left(\frac{\pi}{2} - \tan^{-1}\frac{1}{2}\right)$$

the series converges.

(b) $\frac{1}{n^2 + 4} < \frac{1}{n^2}$, so the series converges by comparison with $\sum 1/n^2$.

(c) Compare with $\sum 1/n^2$: $\frac{1/(n^2 + 4)}{1/n^2} = \frac{n^2}{n^2 + 4} \to 1 > 0$ as $n \to \infty$. Hence the series converges.

(d) $a_{n+1}/a_n = \frac{1}{(n + 1)^2 + 4} \cdot \frac{n^2 + 4}{1} = \frac{n^2 + 4}{(n + 1)^2 + 4} \to 1$ as $n \to \infty$. The test does not apply.

12. Let $f(x) = x/(x^2 + 4)$. Then $f'(x) = \frac{(x^2 + 4) - x(2x)}{(x^2 + 4)^2} = \frac{4 - x^2}{(x^2 + 4)^2} < 0$ if $x > 2$. Hence f is decreasing for $x \geq 2$ and the series converges by the Alternating Series Test. The series of absolute values is $\sum n/(n^2 + 4)$, which diverges by comparison with $\sum 1/n$. Hence the original series is conditionally convergent.

13. The series converges by the Alternating Series Test. The error in the approximation $S \approx S_n$ is $\leq a_{n+1} = 1/(n + 1)^2$. Hence we choose n satisfying $1/(n + 1)^2 < 0.005 \implies (n + 1)^2 > 200 \implies n + 1 > \sqrt{200} \implies n > \sqrt{200} - 1 \approx 13.1$. Thus 14 terms will suffice.

14. The series converges by the Alternating Series Test. Since $a_n = 1/(2n - 2)!$, $n = 1, 2, 3, \ldots$, the error in the approximation $S \approx S_n$ is $\leq a_{n+1} = 1/(2n)!$. For five-place accuracy we need $1/(2n)! < 0.000005$. The smallest n

satisfying this is n = 5, so $S \approx 1 - \frac{1}{2!} + \frac{1}{4!} - \frac{1}{6!} + \frac{1}{8!} \approx 0.54030$ (correct to five places). A calculator gives $\cos 1 = 0.540302 \cdots$.

15. Use the Ratio Test: $a_{n+1}/a_n = \frac{(n+1)^3}{e^{n+1}} \cdot \frac{e^n}{n^3} = \frac{1}{e}\left(\frac{n+1}{n}\right)^3 \to \frac{1}{e} < 1$ as $n \to \infty$. The series converges.

16. The series converges when x = 2, so assume that $x \neq 2$. Then

$$\left| a_{n+1}/a_n \right| = \frac{|x-2|^{n+1}}{n+1} \cdot \frac{n}{|x-2|^n} = |x-2|\left(\frac{n}{n+1}\right) \to |x-2| \text{ as } n \to \infty$$

The series converges (absolutely) when $-1 < x - 2 < 1$, that is, when $1 < x < 3$. It diverges when $x > 3$ or $x < 1$. When x = 3 the series is $\sum 1/n$, which diverges. When x = 1 the series is $\sum (-1)^n/n$, which converges (conditionally) by the Alternating Series Test.

CHAPTER 13   POWER SERIES

Section 13.1   FUNCTIONS DEFINED BY POWER SERIES

1. Writing $f(x) = \sum_{n=0}^{\infty} \frac{(-1)^n x^{2n}}{(2n)!}$, we observe that the series converges when x = 0. If $x \neq 0$, we compute

$$\left| a_{n+1}/a_n \right| = \frac{|x|^{2n+2}}{(2n+2)!} \cdot \frac{(2n)!}{|x|^{2n}} = \frac{x^2}{(2n+2)(2n+1)} \to 0 \text{ as } n \to \infty$$

Hence the series converges for all x.

2. See the solution of Additional Problem 14, Chap. 12, where we found f(1) = 0.54030 correct to five places. A calculator gives $\cos 1 = 0.540302 \cdots$

3. The series is geometric, with a = 1 and r = x - 2. Hence

$$f(x) = \frac{a}{1-r} = \frac{1}{1-(x-2)} = \frac{1}{3-x}$$

The domain is $-1 < x - 2 < 1$, that is, $1 < x < 3$.

4. The domain is symmetric about the base point a = 1. If it includes x = -1 (which is two units from the base point), it automatically includes x = 2 (which is only one unit from the base point). It extends as far as x = 3, but since it may be an open interval, x = 3 is not necessarily included.

5. Differentiate each side (using the Chain Rule on the left) to obtain

$$\frac{1}{(1-x)^2} = 1 + 2x + 3x^2 + \cdots$$

The domain of the given series is (-1,1), so the domain of the derivative is at least (-1,1). It cannot contain x = 1 (because the left side is undefined and the right side diverges). Since the right side also diverges when $x = -1$, the domain cannot be enlarged. Note that if we substitute $x = -1$, we obtain the "equation" $\frac{1}{4} = 1 - 2 + 3 - 4 + \cdots$. This kind of thing was commonly done in the early days of calculus, with results that were sometimes brilliant and sometimes preposterous.

6. Substitute $x = \frac{1}{2}$ in the given equation to obtain $4 = \sum_{n=1}^{\infty} n/2^{n-1}$. Then divide each side by 2 to derive the required result.

7.(a) Writing $f(x) = \sum_{n=1}^{\infty} \frac{(-1)^{n-1} x^n}{n}$, observe that the series converges when $x = 0$. If $x \neq 0$, we compute

$$|a_{n+1}/a_n| = \frac{|x|^{n+1}}{n+1} \cdot \frac{n}{|x|^n} = |x|(\frac{n}{n+1}) \to |x| \text{ as } n \to \infty$$

The series converges when $-1 < x < 1$ and diverges when $x > 1$ or $x < -1$. When $x = 1$ the series is $\sum (-1)^{n-1}/n$, which converges by the Alternating Series Test. When $x = -1$ the series is $-\sum 1/n$, which diverges because it is the negative of the harmonic series. Hence the domain of f is $(-1,1]$.

(b) In the domain $(-1,1)$ we know that $f'(x) = 1 - x + x^2 - x^3 + \cdots$. This is a geometric series with $a = 1$ and $r = -x$, so $f'(x) = 1/(1 + x)$. The series diverges when $x = \pm 1$, so the domain cannot be enlarged; it is simply $(-1,1)$. Thus it does not include the point $x = 1$ in the domain of f.

(c) Since $y = x - \frac{x^2}{2} + \frac{x^3}{3} - \frac{x^4}{4} + \cdots$, $y = 0$ when $x = 0$. In the domain $(-1,1)$ $\frac{dy}{dx} = \frac{1}{1 + x} \implies y = \ell n\,(1 + x) + C$. Since $y = 0$ when $x = 0$, we find $C = 0$ and hence $y = \ell n\,(1 + x)$. The result holds at $x = 1$ because $y = f(x)$ is continuous at 1: $\lim_{x \uparrow 1} \ell n\,(1 + x) = \lim_{x \uparrow 1} f(x) = f(1)$. In other words $\ell n\,2 = 1 - \frac{1}{2} + \frac{1}{3} - \frac{1}{4} + \cdots$ (as already shown in Example 7 by different means).

8. $\int_0^x \frac{dt}{1 + t} = (t - \frac{t^2}{2} + \frac{t^3}{3} - \frac{t^4}{4} + \cdots)\Big|_0^x$, that is, $\ell n\,(1 + x) = x - \frac{x^2}{2} + \frac{x^3}{3} - \frac{x^4}{4} + \cdots$ $(-1 < x < 1)$. The result also holds at $x = 1$ because of continuity at $x = 1$.

9. If x is replaced by $1 + x$ in the given formula, we have

$$\ell n\,(1 + x) = x - \frac{x^2}{2} + \frac{x^3}{3} - \frac{x^4}{4} + \cdots$$

The domain $0 < x \leq 2$ of the given formula becomes $0 < 1 + x \leq 2$, or $-1 < x \leq 1$.

10. Differentiation yields $1/x = 1 - (x - 1) + (x - 1)^2 - (x - 1)^3 + \cdots$ in the domain $(0,2)$ at least. There is no guarantee that the domain can be enlarged; we cannot let $x = 2$ unless the series converges.

11.(a) Replacing x by -x in the series $\ln(1+x) = x - \frac{x^2}{2} + \frac{x^3}{3} - \frac{x^4}{4} + \cdots$, we have

$\ln(1-x) = -x - \frac{x^2}{2} - \frac{x^3}{3} - \frac{x^4}{4} - \cdots$. The domain $-1 < x \le 1$ in Problem 7 becomes

$-1 < -x \le 1$, or $-1 \le x < 1$.

    (b) $\ln(1+x) - \ln(1-x) = (x - \frac{x^2}{2} + \frac{x^3}{3} - \frac{x^4}{4} + \cdots) + (x + \frac{x^2}{2} + \frac{x^3}{3} + \frac{x^4}{4} + \cdots)$, or

$\ln\frac{1+x}{1-x} = 2(x + \frac{x^3}{3} + \frac{x^5}{5} + \cdots)$. Divide by 2 to obtain the required formula. The

result holds in the common domain of the series for $\ln(1+x)$ and $\ln(1-x)$,

namely $(-1,1)$. This excludes $x = 1$. (Note that each side of the equation is

undefined at $x = 1$.)

12. The result follows from the formula $\tanh^{-1}x = \frac{1}{2}\ln\frac{1+x}{1-x}$ $(|x| < 1)$ in

Sec. 9.4.

13.(a) $\frac{1}{1-t^2} = 1 + t^2 + t^4 + \cdots$ $(-1 < t < 1)$, so for each $x \in (-1,1)$ we have

$$\int_0^x \frac{dt}{1-t^2} = (t + \frac{t^3}{3} + \frac{t^5}{5} + \cdots)\Big|_0^x \implies \frac{1}{2}\ln\frac{1+x}{1-x} = x + \frac{x^3}{3} + \frac{x^5}{5} + \cdots$$

$$\implies \tanh^{-1}x = x + \frac{x^3}{3} + \frac{x^5}{5} + \cdots$$

    (b) Using the given formula, we have $\int_0^x \frac{dt}{1-t^2} = \tanh^{-1}x = x + \frac{x^3}{3} + \frac{x^5}{5} + \cdots$.

14. The domain of $f(x) = x - \frac{x^3}{3} + \frac{x^5}{5} - \frac{x^7}{7} + \cdots$ is $(-1,1]$, and we know that

$\tan^{-1}x = f(x)$ in $(-1,1)$. Since f is continuous at $x = 1$, we have

$$\lim_{x\uparrow1}\tan^{-1}x = \lim_{x\uparrow1}f(x) = f(1) \quad \text{or} \quad \frac{\pi}{4} = 1 - \frac{1}{3} + \frac{1}{5} - \frac{1}{7} + \cdots$$

Gregory's series does not hold at $x = -1$ because $-1 - \frac{1}{3} - \frac{1}{5} - \frac{1}{7} - \cdots$ is the

negative of $\sum 1/(2n-1)$, which diverges by comparison with $\sum 1/n$.

15.(a) $t = \tan^{-1}\frac{1}{5} \implies \tan t = \frac{1}{5} \implies \tan 2t = \frac{2\tan t}{1 - \tan^2 t} = \frac{2/5}{1 - 1/25} = \frac{5}{12} \implies$

$\tan 4t = \frac{2\tan 2t}{1 - \tan^2 2t} = \frac{5/6}{1 - 25/144} = \frac{120}{119} \implies \tan(4t - \frac{\pi}{4}) = \frac{\tan 4t - \tan(\pi/4)}{1 + \tan 4t \tan(\pi/4)} =$

$\frac{\tan 4t - 1}{1 + \tan 4t} = \frac{(120/119) - 1}{1 + (120/119)} = \frac{1}{239}$

    (b) Since $t = \tan^{-1}\frac{1}{5}$, we have $0 < t < \pi/8 \implies 0 < 4t < \pi/2 \implies -\pi/4 <$

$4t - \pi/4 < \pi/4$. In this domain $\tan(4t - \frac{\pi}{4}) = \frac{1}{239} \implies 4t - \frac{\pi}{4} = \tan^{-1}\frac{1}{239} \implies$

$\frac{\pi}{4} = 4\tan^{-1}\frac{1}{5} - \tan^{-1}\frac{1}{239}$.

16. From Problem 15, $\pi = 16\tan^{-1}\frac{1}{5} - 4\tan^{-1}\frac{1}{239}$. Gregory's series gives

$$16\tan^{-1}\frac{1}{5} = 16\left(\frac{1}{5} - \frac{1}{3\cdot5^3} + \frac{1}{5\cdot5^5} - \frac{1}{7\cdot5^7} + \frac{1}{9\cdot5^9} - \frac{1}{11\cdot5^{11}} + \cdots\right)$$

$$4\tan^{-1}\frac{1}{239} = 4\left(\frac{1}{239} - \frac{1}{3\cdot239^3} + \frac{1}{5\cdot239^5} - \cdots\right)$$

Since $\frac{16}{11\cdot5^{11}} < 3\times10^{-8}$ and $\frac{4}{5\cdot239^5} < 2\times10^{-12}$, we can be sure of seven-place accuracy by writing

$$\pi \approx 16\left(\frac{1}{5} - \frac{1}{3\cdot5^3} + \frac{1}{5\cdot5^5} - \frac{1}{7\cdot5^7} + \frac{1}{9\cdot5^9}\right) - 4\left(\frac{1}{239} - \frac{1}{3\cdot239^3}\right) \approx 3.141\,5927$$

17. $f(x) = c_0 + c_1(x-a) + c_2(x-a)^2 + c_3(x-a)^3 + \cdots = 0 \implies f(a) = c_0 = 0$,

$f'(x) = c_1 + 2c_2(x-a) + 3c_3(x-a)^2 + \cdots = 0 \implies f'(a) = c_1 = 0$,

$f''(x) = 2c_2 + 3!c_3(x-a) + \cdots = 0 \implies f''(a) = 2c_2 = 0 \implies c_2 = 0$,

$f'''(x) = 3!c_3 + \cdots = 0 \implies f'''(a) = 3!c_3 = 0 \implies c_3 = 0$,

and so on.

18. $\sum_{n=0}^{\infty} a_n(x-a)^n = \sum_{n=0}^{\infty} b_n(x-a)^n \implies \sum_{n=0}^{\infty}(a_n - b_n)(x-a)^n = 0 \implies a_n - b_n = 0$ for

all n (Problem 17) $\implies a_n = b_n$ for all n.

19. If $f(x)$ were equal to "another" series, say $f(x) = \sum_{n=0}^{\infty} a_n(x-a)^n$, then by

Problem 18 we have $a_n = c_n$ for all n. Hence this "other" series is the same as the one given.

20. $f(-x) = f(x) \implies c_0 - c_1 x + c_2 x^2 - c_3 x^3 + \cdots = c_0 + c_1 x + c_2 x^2 + c_3 x^3 + \cdots \implies$

$2(c_1 x + c_3 x^3 + \cdots) = 0 \implies c_1 = 0, c_3 = 0, \ldots$ (Problem 17). Hence $f(x) = c_0 + c_2 x^2 + c_4 x^4 + \cdots$.

21. $f(-x) = -f(x) \implies c_0 - c_1 x + c_2 x^2 - c_3 x^3 + \cdots = -(c_0 + c_1 x + c_2 x^2 + c_3 x^3 + \cdots)$

$\implies 2(c_0 + c_2 x^2 + \cdots) = 0 \implies c_0 = 0, c_2 = 0, \ldots$. Hence $f(x) = c_1 x + c_3 x^3 + c_5 x^5 + \cdots$.

22.(a) $\frac{1}{1-1/x} = 1 + \frac{1}{x} + \frac{1}{x^2} + \frac{1}{x^3} + \cdots$. Since $\frac{1}{1-1/x} - 1 = \frac{x}{x-1} - 1 = \frac{1}{x-1}$, we have

$$\frac{1}{x-1} = \frac{1}{x} + \frac{1}{x^2} + \frac{1}{x^3} + \cdots$$

(b) $\frac{1}{1-x} + \frac{1}{x-1} = 0$, so $\cdots + \frac{1}{x^3} + \frac{1}{x^2} + \frac{1}{x} + 1 + x + x^2 + x^3 + \cdots = 0$. The equation

is preposterous because whatever the left side may mean, it cannot be 0. The proof is defective because the domain of $1/(1-x) = 1 + x + x^2 + x^3 + \cdots$ is $|x| < 1$, while the domain of $1/(x-1) = 1/x + 1/x^2 + 1/x^3 + \cdots$ is $|x| > 1$ (because we replaced x by $1/x$). There is no value of x for which both series converge. Hence they cannot be added.

Section 13.2   TAYLOR SERIES

1. $e^x = 1 + x + \dfrac{x^2}{2!} + \dfrac{x^3}{3!} + \cdots \implies e^{-x} = 1 - x + \dfrac{x^2}{2!} - \dfrac{x^3}{3!} + \cdots$. This is the Maclaurin series for e^{-x} because only one power series (with base point 0) representing e^{-x} exists.

2.(a) The values of f and its successive derivatives at $x = 0$ are $f(x) = e^{-x} = 1$, $f'(x) = -e^{-x} = -1$, $f''(x) = e^{-x} = 1$, and so on. Hence the series is $1 - x + x^2/2! - x^3/3! + \cdots$.

(b) Since every derivative is $\pm e^{-x}$,

$$|R_n(x)| = \frac{e^{-c}}{(n+1)!} |x|^{n+1} \text{ for some c between 0 and x}$$

Since $0 < |c| < |x|$, $e^{-c} \le e^{|c|} \le e^{|x|}$, so $|R_n(x)| \le \dfrac{e^{|x|}}{(n+1)!} |x|^{n+1}$. This approaches 0 as $n \to \infty$ because the series $\sum x^n/n!$ is absolutely convergent for all x. (See Example 4, Sec. 12.5.) Hence $R_n(x) \to 0$ as $n \to \infty$, which proves that the series is equal to $f(x) = e^{-x}$.

3. $\cosh x = \frac{1}{2}e^x + \frac{1}{2}e^{-x} = \frac{1}{2}(1 + x + \dfrac{x^2}{2!} + \dfrac{x^3}{3!} + \cdots) + \frac{1}{2}(1 - x + \dfrac{x^2}{2!} - \dfrac{x^3}{3!} + \cdots)$

$$= 1 + \frac{x^2}{2!} + \frac{x^4}{4!} + \cdots$$

4. $\sinh x = \frac{1}{2}e^x - \frac{1}{2}e^{-x} = \frac{1}{2}(1 + x + \dfrac{x^2}{2!} + \dfrac{x^3}{3!} + \cdots) - \frac{1}{2}(1 - x + \dfrac{x^2}{2!} - \dfrac{x^3}{3!} + \cdots)$

$$= x + \frac{x^3}{3!} + \frac{x^5}{5!} + \cdots$$

5. $\dfrac{d}{dx}(\cosh x) = \dfrac{d}{dx}(1 + \dfrac{x^2}{2!} + \dfrac{x^4}{4!} + \dfrac{x^6}{6!} + \cdots) \implies \sinh x = 0 + \dfrac{2x}{2!} + \dfrac{4x^3}{4!} + \dfrac{6x^5}{6!} + \cdots =$

$x + \dfrac{x^3}{3!} + \dfrac{x^5}{5!} + \cdots$.

6. $\cosh t = 1 + \dfrac{t^2}{2!} + \dfrac{t^4}{4!} + \cdots$, so $\displaystyle\int_0^x \cosh t\, dt = (t + \dfrac{t^3}{3!} + \dfrac{t^5}{5!} + \cdots)\Big|_0^x$, that is,

$\sinh x = x + \dfrac{x^3}{3!} + \dfrac{x^5}{5!} + \cdots$.

7. The values of f and its successive derivatives at $x = 0$ are $f(x) = \sinh x = 0$, $f'(x) = \cosh x = 1$, $f''(x) = \sinh x = 0$, and so on. Hence the series is

$$0 + x + 0x^2 + \frac{x^3}{3!} + 0x^4 + \frac{x^5}{5!} + \cdots = x + \frac{x^3}{3!} + \frac{x^5}{5!} + \cdots$$

Since every derivative is $\sinh x$ or $\cosh x$ and since $|\sinh x| \le \cosh x$ for all x, we have $|f^{(n+1)}(c)| \le \cosh c \le \cosh x$ for c between 0 and x. Hence

$$|R_n(x)| \le (\cosh x)\frac{|x|^{n+1}}{(n+1)!} \to 0 \text{ as } n \to \infty.$$

Thus $R_n(x) \to 0$ as $n \to \infty$ and the series is equal to $f(x) = \sinh x$.

8. $\sin t = t - \frac{t^3}{3!} + \frac{t^5}{5!} - \cdots$, so $\int_0^x \sin t\, dt = \left(\frac{t^2}{2!} - \frac{t^4}{4!} + \frac{t^6}{6!} - \cdots\right)\Big|_0^x$, that is,

$1 - \cos x = \frac{x^2}{2!} - \frac{x^4}{4!} + \frac{x^6}{6!} - \cdots$ and hence $\cos x = 1 - \frac{x^2}{2!} + \frac{x^4}{4!} - \frac{x^6}{6!} + \cdots$.

9. The values of f and its successive derivatives at $x = 0$ are $f(x) = \cos x$ $= 1$, $f'(x) = -\sin x = 0$, $f''(x) = -\cos x = -1$, $f'''(x) = \sin x = 0$, $f^{(4)}(x) = \cos x = 1$, and so on. Hence the series is

$$1 + 0x - \frac{x^2}{2!} + 0x^3 + \frac{x^4}{4!} + 0x^5 - \frac{x^6}{6!} + \cdots = 1 - \frac{x^2}{2!} + \frac{x^4}{4!} - \frac{x^6}{6!} + \cdots$$

Since every derivative is $\pm\sin x$ or $\pm\cos x$, we have $|f^{(n+1)}(c)| \le 1$ for any c, so $|R_n(x)| \le |x|^{n+1}/(n+1)! \to 0$ as $n \to \infty$. Hence $R_n(x) \to 0$ as $n \to \infty$ and the series is equal to $f(x) = \cos x$.

10.(a) $S'(x) = 1 - \frac{x^2}{2!} + \frac{x^4}{4!} - \frac{x^6}{6!} + \cdots$ and $S''(x) = -x + \frac{x^3}{3!} - \frac{x^5}{5!} + \cdots$, so

$$y'' + y = S''(x) + S(x) = \left(-x + \frac{x^3}{3!} - \frac{x^5}{5!} + \cdots\right) + \left(x - \frac{x^3}{3!} + \frac{x^5}{5!} - \cdots\right) = 0$$

Put $x = 0$ in the series $S(x)$ and $S'(x)$ to obtain $S(0) = 0$ and $S'(0) = 1$.

(b) If $f(x) = \sin x$, then $f'(x) = \cos x$ and $f''(x) = -\sin x$, so $f''(x) + f(x)$ $= 0$. Moreover, $f(0) = \sin 0 = 0$ and $f'(0) = \cos 0 = 1$.

11. $S(x) = 1 - \frac{x^2}{2!} + \frac{x^4}{4!} - \frac{x^6}{6!} + \cdots$, so $S'(x) = -x + \frac{x^3}{3!} - \frac{x^5}{5!} + \cdots$ and $S''(x) = -1 + \frac{x^2}{2!} - \frac{x^4}{4!} + \cdots$. Hence $y'' + y = \left(-1 + \frac{x^2}{2!} - \frac{x^4}{4!} + \cdots\right) + \left(1 - \frac{x^2}{2!} + \frac{x^4}{4!} - \cdots\right) = 0$. Put $x = 0$ in the series $S(x)$ and $S'(x)$ to obtain $y = S(0) = 1$ and $y' = S'(0) = 0$. If $f(x)$ $= \cos x$, then $f'(x) = -\sin x$ and $f''(x) = -\cos x$, so $f''(x) + f(x) = 0$. Moreover, $f(0) = \cos 0 = 1$ and $f'(0) = -\sin 0 = 0$.

12. The values of f and its successive derivatives at $x = 1$ are $f(x) = x^{-2}$ $= 1$, $f'(x) = -2x^{-3} = -2$, $f''(x) = 3!x^{-4} = 3!$, $f'''(x) = -4!x^{-5} = -4!$, and so on. Hence the series is

$$1 - 2(x-1) + \frac{3!}{2!}(x-1)^2 - \frac{4!}{3!}(x-1)^3 + \cdots = 1 - 2(x-1) + 3(x-1)^2 - 4(x-1)^3$$
$$+ \cdots$$

13. Differentiation yields $-1/x^2 = -1 + 2(x-1) - 3(x-1)^2 + \cdots$ or $1/x^2 = 1 - 2(x-1) + 3(x-1)^2 - \cdots$ $(0 < x < 2)$.

14. $e^x = e^a e^{x-a} = e^a[1 + (x-a) + \frac{(x-a)^2}{2!} + \frac{(x-a)^3}{3!} + \cdots]$

$\qquad = e^a + e^a(x-a) + \frac{e^a}{2!}(x-a)^2 + \frac{e^a}{3!}(x-a)^3 + \cdots$

15. $2^x = e^{x\ln 2} = 1 + x\ln 2 + \frac{(x\ln 2)^2}{2!} + \frac{(x\ln 2)^3}{3!} + \cdots$

$\qquad = 1 + x(\ln 2) + \frac{x^2}{2!}(\ln 2)^2 + \frac{x^3}{3!}(\ln 2)^3 + \cdots$

16. See the solution of Problem 24, Sec. 11.5. The Maclaurin series for $\tan x$ is $x + \frac{1}{3}x^3 + \frac{2}{15}x^5 + \cdots$.

17. At $x = 0$ we have $f(x) = e^x \cos x = 1$, $f'(x) = e^x(-\sin x) + e^x \cos x = e^x(\cos x - \sin x) = 1$, $f''(x) = e^x(-\sin x - \cos x) + e^x(\cos x - \sin x) = -2e^x \sin x = 0$, $f'''(x) = -2e^x \cos x - 2e^x \sin x = -2e^x(\cos x + \sin x) = -2$, $f^{(4)}(x) = -2e^x(-\sin x + \cos x) - 2e^x(\cos x + \sin x) = -4e^x \cos x = -4$, and so on. Hence the series is

$\qquad 1 + x + 0x^2 - \frac{2}{3!}x^3 - \frac{4}{4!}x^4 + \cdots = 1 + x - \frac{1}{3}x^3 - \frac{1}{6}x^4 + \cdots$

18. If $f(x) = c_0 + c_1 x + c_2 x^2 + \cdots$, then $c_n = \frac{f^{(n)}(0)}{n!}$. Hence $f^{(4)}(0) = 4!c_4 = 0$ and $f^{(5)}(0) = 5!c_5 = \frac{5!}{5} = 4! = 24$.

19.(a) $e^{ix} = 1 + (ix) + \frac{(ix)^2}{2!} + \frac{(ix)^3}{3!} + \frac{(ix)^4}{4!} + \frac{(ix)^5}{5!} + \cdots$. Since $i^2 = -1$, $i^3 = -i$, $i^4 = 1$, $i^5 = i$, and so on, we have

$\qquad e^{ix} = 1 + ix - \frac{x^2}{2!} - \frac{ix^3}{3!} + \frac{x^4}{4!} + \frac{ix^5}{5!} - \frac{x^6}{6!} - \frac{ix^7}{7!} + \cdots$

$\qquad = (1 - \frac{x^2}{2!} + \frac{x^4}{4!} - \frac{x^6}{6!} + \cdots) + i(x - \frac{x^3}{3!} + \frac{x^5}{5!} - \frac{x^7}{7!} + \cdots)$

(b) The two series in parentheses represent $\cos x$ and $\sin x$, respectively.

Section 13.3   MORE ABOUT POWER SERIES

1.(a) Replacing t by x^2 in $1/(1-t) = 1 + t + t^2 + t^3 + \cdots$ $(|t| < 1)$ gives $1/(1-x^2) = 1 + x^2 + x^4 + x^6 + \cdots$ $(|x| < 1)$.

(b) $\frac{d}{dx}(\tanh^{-1}x) = \frac{d}{dx}(x + \frac{x^3}{3} + \frac{x^5}{5} + \frac{x^7}{7} + \cdots)$, or $\frac{1}{1-x^2} = 1 + x^2 + x^4 + x^6 + \cdots$ $(-1 < x < 1)$.

(c) $\frac{1}{1-x^2} = \frac{1}{1-x} \cdot \frac{1}{1+x} = (1 + x + x^2 + x^3 + \cdots)(1 - x + x^2 - x^3 + \cdots)$. The coefficients of these series are $a_n = 1$ and $b_n = (-1)^n$, respectively, so

$\qquad \frac{1}{1-x^2} = 1 + (-1+1)x + (1-1+1)x^2 + (-1+1-1+1)x^3 + (1-1+1-1+1)x^4 + \cdots$

$$= 1 + x^2 + x^4 + \cdots$$

Each series converges in $(-1,1)$, so the product does, too.

(d)

$$
1 - x^2 \overline{\left)1\right.}
$$
$$
\frac{1 + x^2 + x^4 + \cdots}{}
$$
$$
\underline{1 - x^2}
$$
$$
x^2
$$
$$
\underline{x^2 - x^4}
$$
$$
x^4
$$
$$
\underline{x^4 - x^6}
$$
$$
\vdots
$$

2. When x is replaced by $2 - x$, $x - 1$ becomes $(2 - x) - 1 = 1 - x$. Hence

$$\frac{1}{2 - x} = 1 - (1 - x) + (1 - x)^2 - (1 - x)^3 + \cdots = 1 + (x - 1) + (x - 1)^2 + (x - 1)^3 + \cdots$$

The original domain $0 < x < 2$ becomes $0 < 2 - x < 2$, or $0 < x < 2$ again.

3.(a) $\dfrac{1}{x(2 - x)} = \dfrac{1}{x} \cdot \dfrac{1}{2 - x} = [1 - (x - 1) + (x - 1)^2 - (x - 1)^3 + \cdots][1 + (x - 1) +$

$$(x - 1)^2 + (x - 1)^3 + \cdots]$$

The coefficients of these series are $a_n = (-1)^n$ and $b_n = 1$, respectively, so

$$\frac{1}{x(2 - x)} = 1 + (1 - 1)(x - 1) + (1 - 1 + 1)(x - 1)^2 + (1 - 1 + 1 - 1)(x - 1)^3 +$$

$$(1 - 1 + 1 - 1 + 1)(x - 1)^4 + \cdots$$

$$= 1 + (x - 1)^2 + (x - 1)^4 + \cdots$$

Each series converges in $(0,2)$, so the product does, too.

(b) $\dfrac{1}{x(2 - x)} = \dfrac{A}{x} + \dfrac{B}{2 - x} \Longrightarrow 1 = A(2 - x) + Bx$. Put $x = 0$ to find $A = \frac{1}{2}$ and

$x = 2$ to find $B = \frac{1}{2}$. Then

$$\frac{1}{x(2 - x)} = \frac{1}{2} \cdot \frac{1}{x} + \frac{1}{2} \cdot \frac{1}{2 - x} = \frac{1}{2}[1 - (x - 1) + (x - 1)^2 - (x - 1)^3 + \cdots] +$$

$$\frac{1}{2}[1 + (x - 1) + (x - 1)^2 + (x - 1)^3 + \cdots]$$

$$= 1 + (x - 1)^2 + (x - 1)^4 + \cdots \quad (0 < x < 2)$$

(c)

$$
1 - (x - 1)^2 \overline{\left)1\right.}
$$
$$
\frac{1 + (x - 1)^2 + (x - 1)^4 + \cdots}{}
$$
$$
\underline{1 - (x - 1)^2}
$$
$$
(x - 1)^2
$$
$$
\underline{(x - 1)^2 - (x - 1)^4}
$$
$$
(x - 1)^4
$$
$$
\underline{(x - 1)^4 - (x - 1)^6}
$$
$$
\vdots
$$

4. $\sin^2 \dfrac{x}{2} = \dfrac{1}{2}\left[1 - \left(1 - \dfrac{x^2}{2!} + \dfrac{x^4}{4!} - \dfrac{x^6}{6!} + \cdots\right)\right] = \dfrac{1}{2}\left(\dfrac{x^2}{2!} - \dfrac{x^4}{4!} + \dfrac{x^6}{6!} - \cdots\right)$

5. Replace x by $2x$ in Problem 4 to obtain

$$\sin^2 x = \frac{1}{2}\left[\frac{(2x)^2}{2!} - \frac{(2x)^4}{4!} + \frac{(2x)^6}{6!} - \cdots\right] = \frac{2x^2}{2!} - \frac{2^3 x^4}{4!} + \frac{2^5 x^6}{6!} - \cdots$$

$$= \sum_{n=1}^{\infty} \frac{(-1)^{n-1} 2^{2n-1} x^{2n}}{(2n)!}$$

6. At $x = 0$ we have $f(x) = \sin(x + c) = \sin c$, $f'(x) = \cos(x + c) = \cos c$, $f''(x) = -\sin(x + c) = -\sin c$, $f'''(x) = -\cos(x + c) = -\cos c$, $f^{(4)}(x) = \sin(x + c)$ $= \sin c$, and so on. Hence the series for $\sin(x + c)$ is

$$\sin c + (\cos c)x - (\sin c)\frac{x^2}{2!} - (\cos c)\frac{x^3}{3!} + (\sin c)\frac{x^4}{4!} + \cdots$$

Since every derivative is $\pm\sin(x + c)$ or $\pm\cos(x + c)$,

$$|R_n(x)| \le \frac{|x|^{n+1}}{(n+1)!} \to 0 \text{ as } n \to \infty$$

Hence $R_n(x) \to 0$ as $n \to \infty$ and the series is equal to $f(x) = \sin(x + c)$.

7. $\sin(x + c) = \sin c \left(1 - \frac{x^2}{2!} + \frac{x^4}{4!} - \cdots\right) + \cos c \left(x - \frac{x^3}{3!} + \frac{x^5}{5!} - \cdots\right)$

$$= \sin c \cos x + \cos c \sin x = \sin x \cos c + \cos x \sin c$$

8. Replace x by $-t^2$ in the Maclaurin series for e^x to obtain

$$e^{-t^2} = 1 - t^2 + \frac{t^4}{2!} - \frac{t^6}{3!} + \frac{t^8}{4!} - \cdots$$

Then $\int_0^x e^{-t^2} dt = x - \frac{x^3}{3} + \frac{x^5}{5 \cdot 2!} - \frac{x^7}{7 \cdot 3!} + \frac{x^9}{9 \cdot 4!} - \cdots = \sum_{n=0}^{\infty} \frac{(-1)^n x^{2n+1}}{(2n+1)n!}$

9. $e^x \cos x = \left(1 + x + \frac{x^2}{2!} + \frac{x^3}{3!} + \frac{x^4}{4!} + \cdots\right)\left(1 - \frac{x^2}{2!} + \frac{x^4}{4!} - \cdots\right)$. The coefficients of these series are

$$a_0 = 1, \quad a_1 = 1, \quad a_2 = 1/2, \quad a_3 = 1/6, \quad a_4 = 1/24, \quad \ldots$$

$$b_0 = 1, \quad b_1 = 0, \quad b_2 = -1/2, \quad b_3 = 0, \quad b_4 = 1/24, \quad \ldots$$

so $e^x \cos x = 1 + (0 + 1)x + (-1/2 + 0 + 1/2)x^2 + (0 - 1/2 + 0 + 1/6)x^3 +$

$$(1/24 + 0 - 1/4 + 0 + 1/24)x^4 + \cdots$$

$$= 1 + x - \frac{1}{3}x^3 - \frac{1}{6}x^4 + \cdots$$

10.(a) Integration by parts (Problem 37, Sec. 10.1) gives

$$\int_0^{0.5} e^x \cos x \, dx = \frac{1}{2}e^x(\sin x + \cos x)\Big|_0^{0.5} = \frac{1}{2}e^{0.5}(\sin 0.5 + \cos 0.5) - \frac{1}{2}$$

$$= 0.618664\cdots$$

(b) $\int_0^{0.5} e^x \cos x \, dx = \int_0^{0.5}\left(1 + x - \frac{1}{3}x^3 - \frac{1}{6}x^4 + \cdots\right)dx = \left(x + \frac{x^2}{2} - \frac{x^4}{12} - \frac{x^5}{30} + \cdots\right)\Big|_0^{0.5}$

$$= 0.5 + \frac{(0.5)^2}{2} - \frac{(0.5)^4}{12} - \frac{(0.5)^5}{30} + \cdots \approx 0.61875$$

(c) The partition is $\{0, 0.125, 0.25, 0.375, 0.5\}$, with $\Delta x = 0.125$. Hence

$$\int_0^{0.5} e^x \cos x\, dx \approx \frac{0.125}{3}(1 + 4e^{0.125}\cos 0.125 + 2e^{0.25}\cos 0.25 +$$
$$4e^{0.375}\cos 0.375 + e^{0.5}\cos 0.5)$$
$$= 0.618660\cdots$$

11.

$$1 - \frac{x^2}{2} + \frac{x^4}{24} - \frac{x^6}{720} + \cdots \overline{\bigg)\,1}$$

with quotient

$$1 + \frac{x^2}{2} + \frac{5x^4}{24} + \frac{61x^6}{720} + \cdots$$

$$1 - \frac{x^2}{2} + \frac{x^4}{24} - \frac{x^6}{720} + \cdots$$

$$\frac{x^2}{2} - \frac{x^4}{24} + \frac{x^6}{720} - \cdots$$

$$\frac{x^2}{2} - \frac{x^4}{4} + \frac{x^6}{48} - \cdots$$

$$\frac{5x^4}{24} - \frac{7x^6}{360} + \cdots$$

$$\frac{5x^4}{24} - \frac{5x^6}{48} + \cdots$$

$$\frac{61x^6}{720} + \cdots$$

The series is $1 + \frac{1}{2}x^2 + \frac{5}{24}x^4 + \frac{61}{720}x^6 + \cdots$.

12.(a) $\sec^2 t = (1 + \frac{1}{2}t^2 + \frac{5}{24}t^4 + \frac{61}{720}t^6 + \cdots)^2$

$$= 1 + (\frac{1}{2} + \frac{1}{2})t^2 + (\frac{5}{24} + \frac{1}{4} + \frac{5}{24})t^4 + (\frac{61}{720} + \frac{5}{48} + \frac{5}{48} + \frac{61}{720})t^6 + \cdots$$

$$= 1 + t^2 + \frac{2}{3}t^4 + \frac{17}{45}t^6 + \cdots$$

(b) $\int_0^x \sec^2 t\, dt = \int_0^x (1 + t^2 + \frac{2}{3}t^4 + \frac{17}{45}t^6 + \cdots)dt$, or

$$\tan x = x + \frac{1}{3}x^3 + \frac{2}{15}x^5 + \frac{17}{315}x^7 + \cdots$$

13. Replace x by $-x^2$ in the Maclaurin series for e^x to obtain

$$e^{-x^2} = 1 - x^2 + \frac{x^4}{2!} - \frac{x^6}{3!} + \cdots$$

Then $\int_0^1 e^{-x^2} dx = (x - \frac{x^3}{3} + \frac{x^5}{5\cdot 2!} - \frac{x^7}{7\cdot 3!} + \cdots)\Big|_0^1 = 1 - \frac{1}{3} + \frac{1}{5\cdot 2!} - \frac{1}{7\cdot 3!} + \frac{1}{9\cdot 4!} - \frac{1}{11\cdot 5!} + \cdots$

Since $1/(11\cdot 5!) < 0.001$, we can achieve two-place accuracy by writing

$$\int_0^1 e^{-x^2} dx \approx 1 - \frac{1}{3} + \frac{1}{10} - \frac{1}{42} + \frac{1}{216} \approx 0.75$$

14. Replace x by $x^{1/2}$ in the Maclaurin series for $\sin x$ to obtain

$$\sin \sqrt{x} = x^{1/2} - \frac{x^{3/2}}{3!} + \frac{x^{5/2}}{5!} - \frac{x^{7/2}}{7!} + \cdots$$

Then $\int_0^1 \sin \sqrt{x}\, dx = \left(\frac{2x^{3/2}}{3} - \frac{2x^{5/2}}{5\cdot 3!} + \frac{2x^{7/2}}{7\cdot 5!} - \frac{2x^{9/2}}{9\cdot 7!} + \cdots\right)\Big|_0^1$

166

$$= 2\left(\frac{1}{3} - \frac{1}{5\cdot 3!} + \frac{1}{7\cdot 5!} - \frac{1}{9\cdot 7!} + \cdots\right)$$

Since $2/(9\cdot 7!) < 0.0001$, we can achieve three-place accuracy by writing

$$\int_0^1 \sin\sqrt{x}\, dx \approx 2\left(\frac{1}{3} - \frac{1}{30} + \frac{1}{840}\right) \approx 0.602$$

15. Replace t by $-x^4$ in the series $1/(1-t) = 1 + t + t^2 + t^3 + \cdots$ to obtain $1/(1+x^4) = 1 - x^4 + x^8 - x^{12} + \cdots$. Then

$$\int_0^{0.5} \frac{dx}{1+x^4} = \left.\left(x - \frac{x^5}{5} + \frac{x^9}{9} - \frac{x^{13}}{13} + \cdots\right)\right|_0^{0.5} = 0.5 - \frac{(0.5)^5}{5} + \frac{(0.5)^9}{9} - \frac{(0.5)^{13}}{13} + \cdots$$

Since $(0.5)^{13}/13 < 0.00001$, we can achieve four-place accuracy by writing

$$\int_0^{0.5} \frac{dx}{1+x^4} \approx 0.5 - \frac{(0.5)^5}{5} + \frac{(0.5)^9}{9} \approx 0.4940$$

16. Following the hint, we have $N = (1+x)/(1-x) \iff N - Nx = 1 + x \iff N - 1 = (N+1)x \iff x = (N-1)/(N+1)$. Since $N-1 < N+1$ and $N+1 > 0$, we have $(N-1)/(N+1) < 1$. Moreover, if $(N-1)/(N+1) \le -1$, then $N - 1 \le -N - 1$, $2N \le 0$, and $N \le 0$, contradicting the fact that $N > 0$. Hence $(N-1)/(N+1) > -1$. In other words, $-1 < x < 1$. Thus we can find $\ln N = \ln\frac{1+x}{1-x}$ by using the given series with x replaced by $(N-1)/(N+1)$.

17. Taking $N = 2$ in Problem 16, we have $x = (N-1)/(N+1) = 1/3$. Hence

$$\ln 2 = 2\left[\frac{1}{3} + \frac{1}{3}\left(\frac{1}{3}\right)^3 + \frac{1}{5}\left(\frac{1}{3}\right)^5 + \frac{1}{7}\left(\frac{1}{3}\right)^7 + \cdots\right] \approx 0.6931$$

18.(a) $\displaystyle\lim_{x\to 0} \frac{\sin x - x + x^3/6}{x^5} = \lim_{x\to 0} \frac{\cos x - 1 + x^2/2}{5x^4} = \lim_{x\to 0} \frac{-\sin x + x}{20x^3} = \lim_{x\to 0} \frac{-\cos x + 1}{60x^2}$

$\displaystyle\qquad\qquad = \lim_{x\to 0} \frac{\sin x}{120x} = \frac{1}{120}$ (because $\frac{\sin x}{x} \to 1$ as $x\to 0$)

(b) Since $\sin x = x - x^3/3! + x^5/5! - x^7/7! + \cdots$, we have

$$\sin x - x + x^3/6 = x^5/5! - x^7/7! + \cdots$$

$$\frac{\sin x - x + x^3/6}{x^5} = \frac{1}{5!} - \frac{x^2}{7!} + \cdots \to \frac{1}{5!} \text{ as } x\to 0$$

Section 13.4   THE BINOMIAL SERIES

1. Replace x by $-x$ and take $p = -1$ in the binomial series for $(1+x)^p$:

$$(1-x)^{-1} = 1 + x + \frac{(-1)(-2)}{2!}x^2 - \frac{(-1)(-2)(-3)}{3!}x^3 + \cdots$$

$$= 1 + x + x^2 + x^3 + \cdots \quad (-1 < x < 1)$$

2. Take $p = 1/5$ in the binomial series for $(1+x)^p$:

$$(1+x)^{1/5} = 1 + \frac{1}{5}x + \frac{(1/5)(-4/5)}{2!}x^2 + \frac{(1/5)(-4/5)(-9/5)}{3!}x^3 + \cdots$$

Since this is an alternating series after the first term, we may write

167

$(1 + x)^{1/5} \approx 1 + \frac{1}{5}x$ with an error no larger than the next term, $\frac{2}{25}x^2 = 0.08x^2$.

3. $\sqrt[5]{35} = (32 + 3)^{1/5} = 2(1 + \frac{3}{32})^{1/5} \approx 2(1 + \frac{1}{5} \cdot \frac{3}{32}) = 2.0375$, with error $\leq$ $2[0.08(\frac{3}{32})^2] < 0.002$. Hence $\sqrt[5]{35} \approx 2.04$ correct to two places.

4.(a) The binomial series yields $(1 - v^2/c^2)^{-1/2} \approx 1 + (-1/2)(-v^2/c^2) = 1 + \frac{v^2}{2c^2}$. Hence $mc^2 = m_0 c^2 (1 - v^2/c^2)^{-1/2} \approx m_0 c^2 + \frac{1}{2}m_0 v^2$.

(b) The left side, mc^2, is the energy of a body of mass m. The right side, $m_0 c^2 + \frac{1}{2}m_0 v^2$, is the energy due to its rest mass plus the kinetic energy due to its motion.

5. $(1 + x)^{2/3} = 1 + \frac{2}{3}x + \frac{(2/3)(-1/3)}{2!}x^2 + \frac{(2/3)(-1/3)(-4/3)}{3!}x^3 +$

$\qquad \frac{(2/3)(-1/3)(-4/3)(-7/3)}{4!}x^4 + \frac{(2/3)(-1/3)(-4/3)(-7/3)(-10/3)}{5!}x^5 + \cdots$

$\qquad = 1 + \frac{2}{3}x - \frac{2}{3^2 \cdot 2!}x^2 + \frac{2 \cdot 4}{3^3 \cdot 3!}x^3 - \frac{2 \cdot 4 \cdot 7}{3^4 \cdot 4!}x^4 + \frac{2 \cdot 4 \cdot 7 \cdot 10}{3^5 \cdot 5!}x^5 - \cdots \quad (-1 < x < 1)$

6. $(1 - x^3)^{1/2} = 1 - \frac{1}{2}x^3 + \frac{(1/2)(-1/2)}{2!}x^6 - \frac{(1/2)(-1/2)(-3/2)}{3!}x^9 +$

$\qquad\qquad\qquad\qquad \frac{(1/2)(-1/2)(-3/2)(-5/2)}{4!}x^{12} - \cdots$

$\qquad = 1 - \frac{1}{2}x^3 - \frac{1}{8}x^6 - \frac{1}{16}x^9 - \frac{5}{128}x^{12} - \cdots$

Hence $\int_0^{0.5} \sqrt{1 - x^3}\, dx \approx (x - \frac{x^4}{8} - \frac{x^7}{56} - \frac{x^{10}}{160}) \Big|_0^{0.5} = 0.5 - \frac{(0.5)^4}{8} - \frac{(0.5)^7}{56} - \frac{(0.5)^{10}}{160}$

$\qquad\qquad \approx 0.49204$

7. $\sin^{-1}\frac{1}{2} = \frac{\pi}{6}$, so

$\qquad \pi = 6\sin^{-1} 0.5 \approx 6[0.5 + \frac{1}{2} \cdot \frac{(0.5)^3}{3} + \frac{1 \cdot 3}{2 \cdot 4} \cdot \frac{(0.5)^5}{5} + \frac{1 \cdot 3 \cdot 5}{2 \cdot 4 \cdot 6} \cdot \frac{(0.5)^7}{7}] \approx 3.141$

8. As in Example 3, the binomial series gives

$\qquad (1 + t^2)^{-1/2} = 1 - \frac{1}{2}t^2 + \frac{(-1/2)(-3/2)}{2!}t^4 + \frac{(-1/2)(-3/2)(-5/2)}{3!}t^6 + \cdots$

$\qquad\qquad\qquad = 1 - \frac{1}{2}t^2 + \frac{1 \cdot 3}{2 \cdot 4}t^4 - \frac{1 \cdot 3 \cdot 5}{2 \cdot 4 \cdot 6}t^6 + \cdots \quad (-1 < t < 1)$

Integrating from 0 to x, we find

$\qquad \sinh^{-1}x = x - \frac{1}{2} \cdot \frac{x^3}{3} + \frac{1 \cdot 3}{2 \cdot 4} \cdot \frac{x^5}{5} - \frac{1 \cdot 3 \cdot 5}{2 \cdot 4 \cdot 6} \cdot \frac{x^7}{7} + \cdots \quad (-1 < x < 1)$

9.(a) At $x = 1$ we have $f(x) = x^{1/2} = 1$, $f'(x) = \frac{1}{2}x^{-1/2} = \frac{1}{2}$, $f''(x) = \frac{-1}{2^2}x^{-3/2} = \frac{-1}{2^2}$, $f'''(x) = \frac{1 \cdot 3}{2^3}x^{-5/2} = \frac{1 \cdot 3}{2^3}$, and so on. Hence the desired series is

$$1+\frac{1}{2}(x-1)-\frac{1}{2^2\cdot 2!}(x-1)^2+\frac{1\cdot 3}{2^3\cdot 3!}(x-1)^3-\cdots = 1+\frac{1}{2}(x-1)-\frac{1}{2\cdot 4}(x-1)^2+$$

$$\frac{1\cdot 3}{2\cdot 4\cdot 6}(x-1)^3-\cdots,\ 0<x<2$$

(b) Following the hint, we have

$$\sqrt{x}=[1+(x-1)]^{1/2}=1+\frac{1}{2}(x-1)+\frac{(1/2)(-1/2)}{2!}(x-1)^2+$$

$$\frac{(1/2)(-1/2)(-3/2)}{3!}(x-1)^3+\cdots$$

$$=1+\frac{1}{2}(x-1)-\frac{1}{2\cdot 4}(x-1)^2+\frac{1\cdot 3}{2\cdot 4\cdot 6}(x-1)^3-\cdots,\ 0<x<2$$

10. $\sqrt{10}=3\sqrt{10/9}=3[1+\frac{1}{2}(\frac{1}{9})-\frac{1}{2\cdot 4}(\frac{1}{9})^2+\frac{1\cdot 3}{2\cdot 4\cdot 6}(\frac{1}{9})^3-\cdots].$ Since

$$3(\frac{1\cdot 3\cdot 5}{2\cdot 4\cdot 6\cdot 8})(\frac{1}{9})^4<0.00002$$

we obtain four-place accuracy by using four terms of the series, $\sqrt{10}\approx 3.1623$.

11.(a) $(1+x)^5=1+5x+\frac{(5)(4)}{2!}x^2+\frac{(5)(4)(3)}{3!}x^3+\frac{(5)(4)(3)(2)}{4!}x^4+$

$$\frac{(5)(4)(3)(2)(1)}{5!}x^5$$

$$=1+5x+10x^2+10x^3+5x^4+x^5$$

(b) $(a+b)^5=a^5(1+\frac{b}{a})^5=a^5(1+\frac{5b}{a}+\frac{10b^2}{a^2}+\frac{10b^3}{a^3}+\frac{5b^4}{a^4}+\frac{b^5}{a^5})$

$$=a^5+5a^4b+10a^3b^2+10a^2b^3+5ab^4+b^5$$

12. $(1+h)^{1/h}=1+\frac{1}{h}h+\frac{(1/h)(1/h-1)}{2!}h^2+\frac{(1/h)(1/h-1)(1/h-2)}{3!}h^3+\cdots$

$$=1+1+\frac{1-h}{2!}+\frac{(1-h)(1-2h)}{3!}+\cdots$$

The series converges when $-1<h<1$ (provided that $h\neq 0$). When $h\to 0$ we have

$\lim\limits_{h\to 0}(1+h)^{1/h}=1+1+\frac{1}{2!}+\frac{1}{3!}+\cdots.$ Each side is e.

13. $\sqrt{4+x^2}=2[1+(\frac{x}{2})^2]^{1/2}=2[1+\frac{1}{2}(\frac{x}{2})^2+\frac{(1/2)(-1/2)}{2!}(\frac{x}{2})^4+$

$$\frac{(1/2)(-1/2)(-3/2)}{3!}(\frac{x}{2})^6+\frac{(1/2)(-1/2)(-3/2)(-5/2)}{4!}(\frac{x}{2})^8+\cdots]$$

$$=2(1+\frac{1}{8}x^2-\frac{1}{8^2\cdot 2!}x^4+\frac{1\cdot 3}{8^3\cdot 3!}x^6-\frac{1\cdot 3\cdot 5}{8^4\cdot 4!}x^8+\cdots)$$

The neighborhood of 0 in which the series converges is given by $(\frac{x}{2})^2<1$, that is, $-2<x<2$.

14.(a) $\int_0^1\sqrt{4+x^2}\,dx=[\frac{1}{2}x\sqrt{x^2+4}+2\ln(x+\sqrt{x^2+4})]\Big|_0^1=\frac{1}{2}\sqrt{5}+2\ln(1+\sqrt{5})-2\ln 2$

$$=\frac{1}{2}\sqrt{5}+2\ln\frac{1}{2}(1+\sqrt{5})\approx 2.0805$$

(b) Integration of the series from 0 to 1 yields

$$\int_0^1 \sqrt{4+x^2}\,dx = 2(1 + \frac{1}{8}\cdot\frac{1}{3} - \frac{1}{8^2\cdot 2!}\cdot\frac{1}{5} + \frac{1\cdot 3}{8^3\cdot 3!}\cdot\frac{1}{7} - \frac{1\cdot 3\cdot 5}{8^4\cdot 4!}\cdot\frac{1}{9} + \cdots)$$

Since $2(\frac{1\cdot 3\cdot 5}{8^4\cdot 4!}\cdot\frac{1}{9}) < 0.00004$, we obtain four-place accuracy by using four terms

of the series, $\int_0^1 \sqrt{4+x^2}\,dx \approx 2.0805$.

15.(a) The multiplication called for yields $(1+x)^p S'(x) = p(1+x)^{p-1} S(x)$.
Since $f(x) = (1+x)^p$ and $f'(x) = p(1+x)^{p-1}$, we have $f(x)S'(x) - f'(x)S(x) = 0$.
The Quotient Rule says that

$$\frac{d}{dx}[\frac{S(x)}{f(x)}] = \frac{f(x)S'(x) - S(x)f'(x)}{f(x)^2}$$

so the above equation implies that this derivative is 0.

(b) Since the derivative of $S(x)/f(x)$ is 0, we have $S(x)/f(x) = C$, or
$S(x) = Cf(x)$ for some constant C. Since $f(0) = 1$ and $S(0) = 1$, we find $C = 1$
and hence $S(x) = f(x)$.

Chapter 13   TRUE-FALSE QUIZ

1. False. A power series is of the form $c_0 + c_1(x-a) + c_2(x-a)^2 + \cdots$.

2. True. The domain in which the series converges is an interval symmetric
about the base point $a = 0$. If this interval does not contain 1/3, it cannot
contain $x = -2/3$.

3. True. The Ratio Test shows that the interval of convergence (not counting
endpoints) is given by $|x-3| < 1$.

4. False. The series for $f'(x)$ is formally correct, but the series for $f(x)$
converges only at $x = 0$ (by the Ratio Test). The domain of f consists of only
the one point $x = 0$ and f cannot be differentiated.

5. True. If $-1 < x < 1$, then $\phi(x) = (1-x)^{-1}$ and $\phi'(x) = (1-x)^{-2} = \phi(x)^2$.

6. True. The coefficients of the series are $c_n = f^{(n)}(0)/n!$, $n = 0, 1, 2, \cdots$.
Hence $f'''(0)/3! = 4$, from which $f'''(0) = 4!$.

7. False. See Example 3, Sec. 13.2.

8. True. Put $x = 1$ in the Maclaurin series for e^x.

9. False. Such a series has base point $a = 0$; the derivatives of f are
undefined at 0.

10. True. The binomial series yields the (ultimately) alternating series

$$(1+x^2)^{1/2} = 1 + \frac{1}{2}x^2 + \frac{(1/2)(-1/2)}{2!}x^4 + \cdots = 1 + \frac{1}{2}x^2 - \frac{1}{8}x^4 + \cdots \quad (-1 < x < 1)$$

Chapter 13   ADDITIONAL PROBLEMS

1. The series is $\sum_{n=1}^{\infty} \frac{(2x)^n}{n}$, which converges at $x = 0$. Assuming that $x \neq 0$,
we have

$$|a_{n+1}/a_n| = \frac{|2x|^{n+1}}{n+1} \cdot \frac{n}{|2x|^n} = |2x|\left(\frac{n}{n+1}\right) \to |2x| \text{ as } n \to \infty$$

The series converges when $-1 < 2x < 1$, that is, when $-\frac{1}{2} < x < \frac{1}{2}$. When $x = \frac{1}{2}$
the series is $\sum 1/n$, which diverges. When $x = -\frac{1}{2}$ the series is $\sum (-1)^n/n$,
which converges. Hence the domain is $[-\frac{1}{2}, \frac{1}{2})$.

2.(a) Since $|a_{n+1}/a_n| = \frac{|x|^{n+1}}{(n+1)!} \cdot \frac{n!}{|x|^n} = \frac{|x|}{n+1} \to 0$ as $n \to \infty$, the series converges
for all x.

   (b) Differentiating the series for S(x) term-by-term, we have

$$S'(x) = -1 + x - \frac{x^2}{2!} + \frac{x^3}{3!} - \cdots = -S(x)$$

   (c) Since $y = 1$ when $x = 0$, we can separate the variables by dividing by y:
$dy/dx = -y \implies dy/y = -dx \implies \ell n\, y = -x + A$. (No absolute value needed because
$y > 0$ near $x = 0$.) Hence $y = e^{-x+A} = e^A e^{-x} = Ce^{-x}$, where $C = e^A$.

   (d) The series for S(x) shows that $S(0) = 1$. This gives $C = 1$ and hence
$y = S(x) = e^{-x}$.

3.(a) When x is replaced by $1 - t$ the series $1/(1 - x) = 1 + x + x^2 + x^3 + \cdots$
becomes $1/t = 1 + (1 - t) + (1 - t)^2 + (1 - t)^3 + \cdots$. The domain $-1 < x < 1$ becomes
$-1 < 1 - t < 1$, or $0 < t < 2$.

   (b) Rewrite the series in part (a) in the form $1/t = 1 - (t - 1) + (t - 1)^2 - (t - 1)^3 + \cdots$. Then

$$\int_1^x \frac{dt}{t} = \left[t - \frac{(t-1)^2}{2} + \frac{(t-1)^3}{3} - \frac{(t-1)^4}{4} + \cdots\right]\Big|_1^x$$

$$\ell n\, x = (x - 1) - \frac{(x-1)^2}{2} + \frac{(x-1)^3}{3} - \frac{(x-1)^4}{4} + \cdots$$

where $0 < x < 2$. The domain can be enlarged to $0 < x \leq 2$ by continuity.

4.(a) When t is replaced by $-x^2$ the series $1/(1 - t) = 1 + t + t^2 + t^3 + \cdots$
becomes $1/(1 + x^2) = 1 - x^2 + x^4 - x^6 + \cdots$. The domain $|t| < 1$ becomes $|-x^2| < 1$,
or $-1 < x < 1$.

   (b) Since $\tan^{-1} x = x - \frac{x^3}{3} + \frac{x^5}{5} - \frac{x^7}{7} + \cdots$ ($-1 < x \leq 1$), differentiation yields
$1/(1 + x^2) = 1 - x^2 + x^4 - x^6 + \cdots$ in at least the domain $(-1,1)$.

171

(c)

$$1 + x^2 \overline{\left| \begin{array}{l} 1 - x^2 + x^4 - x^6 + \cdots \\ 1 \\ \underline{1 + x^2} \\ \quad -x^2 \\ \quad \underline{-x^2 - x^4} \\ \qquad x^4 \\ \qquad \underline{x^4 + x^6} \\ \qquad\quad -x^6 \\ \qquad\qquad \vdots \end{array} \right.}$$

5.(a) At $x = 0$ we have

$f(x) = e^x \sin x = 0$

$f'(x) = e^x \cos x + e^x \sin x = e^x(\cos x + \sin x) = 1$

$f''(x) = e^x(-\sin x + \cos x) + e^x(\cos x + \sin x) = 2e^x \cos x = 2$

$f'''(x) = 2e^x(-\sin x) + 2e^x \cos x = 2e^x(\cos x - \sin x) = 2$

and so on. Hence the series is

$$0 + x + \frac{2x^2}{2!} + \frac{2x^3}{3!} + \cdots = x + x^2 + \frac{1}{3}x^3 + \cdots$$

(b) $e^x \sin x = \left(1 + x + \frac{x^2}{2!} + \frac{x^3}{3!} + \cdots\right)\left(x - \frac{x^3}{3!} + \cdots\right)$

$$= 0 + (1 + 0)x + (0 + 1 + 0)x^2 + (-1/6 + 0 + 1/2 + 0)x^3 + \cdots$$

$$= x + x^2 + \frac{1}{3}x^3 + \cdots$$

6.(a) Integration by parts (Problem 36, Sec. 10.1) gives

$$\int_0^{0.5} e^x \sin x\, dx = \tfrac{1}{2}e^x(\sin x - \cos x)\Big|_0^{0.5} = \tfrac{1}{2}e^{0.5}(\sin 0.5 - \cos 0.5) + \tfrac{1}{2}$$

$$\approx 0.171775\cdots$$

(b) $\displaystyle\int_0^{0.5} e^x \sin x\, dx \approx \left(\frac{x^2}{2} + \frac{x^3}{3} + \frac{x^4}{12}\right)\Big|_0^{0.5} = \frac{(0.5)^2}{2} + \frac{(0.5)^3}{3} + \frac{(0.5)^4}{12} \approx 0.1719$

(c) The partition is $\{0, 0.125, 0.25, 0.375, 0.5\}$, with $\Delta x = 0.125$. Hence

$$\int_0^{0.5} e^x \sin x\, dx \approx \frac{0.125}{3}(0 + 4e^{0.125}\sin 0.125 + 2e^{0.25}\sin 0.25 +$$

$$4e^{0.375}\sin 0.375 + e^{0.5}\sin 0.5) \approx 0.171774$$

7. Since $x\cos x = x\left(1 - \frac{x^2}{2!} + \frac{x^4}{4!} - \frac{x^6}{6!} + \cdots\right) = x - \frac{x^3}{2} + \frac{x^5}{24} - \frac{x^7}{720} + \cdots$, we have

$$\int_0^1 x\cos x\, dx = \frac{1}{2} - \frac{1}{8} + \frac{1}{144} - \frac{1}{5760} + \cdots$$

The fourth term is less than 0.0002, so we obtain three-place accuracy by using three terms, $\displaystyle\int_0^1 x\cos x\, dx \approx 0.382$. Integration by parts (with $u = x$, $dv = \cos x\, dx$, $du = dx$, $v = \sin x$) gives

$$\int_0^1 x\cos x\,dx = x\sin x\Big|_0^1 - \int_0^1 \sin x\,dx = (x\sin x + \cos x)\Big|_0^1 = \sin 1 + \cos 1 - 1$$

$$= 0.38177\cdots$$

8. Put $x = -1$ in the Maclaurin series for e^x to obtain

$$e^{-1} = 1 - 1 + \frac{1}{2!} - \frac{1}{3!} + \frac{1}{4!} - \cdots$$

Since $1/7! < 0.0002$, we obtain three-place accuracy by using seven terms, $e^{-1} \approx 0.368$.

9. Since $a^x = e^{x\ln a}$, we put $x\ln a$ in the Maclaurin series for e^x, obtaining the given series.

10. It is not obvious where the series comes from, so let's work backwards to a known result (if possible). If $t = (x-1)/x$, then $tx = x - 1$ and $x = \frac{1}{1-t}$. The given series then reads $-\ln(1-t) = t + \frac{1}{2}t^2 + \frac{1}{3}t^3 + \cdots$. The formula

$$\ln(1+t) = t - \frac{t^2}{2} + \frac{t^3}{3} - \frac{t^4}{4} + \cdots \quad (-1 < t \le 1)$$

is listed in Sec. 13.2; if t is replaced by $-t$, we have

$$\ln(1-t) = -t - \frac{t^2}{2} - \frac{t^3}{3} - \frac{t^4}{4} - \cdots \quad (-1 \le t < 1)$$

This looks promising; rewrite it in the form $-\ln(1-t) = t + \frac{1}{2}t^2 + \frac{1}{3}t^3 + \cdots$ and replace t by $(x-1)/x$ to obtain the desired series. The domain $-1 \le t < 1$ becomes $-1 \le (x-1)/x < 1$, which is equivalent to $x \ge 1/2$.

11.(a) At $x = 0$ we have $f(x) = e^{\sin x} = 1$, $f'(x) = e^{\sin x}\cos x = 1$, $f''(x) = e^{\sin x}(-\sin x) + e^{\sin x}\cos^2 x = e^{\sin x}(\cos^2 x - \sin x) = 1$. Hence the series is $1 + x + \frac{1}{2}x^2 + \cdots$.

(b) $e^{\sin x} = 1 + \sin x + \frac{\sin^2 x}{2!} + \cdots$

$$= 1 + (x - \frac{1}{6}x^3 + \cdots) + \frac{1}{2}(x^2 - \frac{1}{3}x^4 + \cdots) + \cdots \text{(Problem 5, Sec. 13.3)}$$

$$= 1 + x + \frac{1}{2}x^2 + \cdots$$

12. At $x = 0$ we have $f(x) = \cos(x+c) = \cos c$, $f'(x) = -\sin(x+c) = -\sin c$, $f''(x) = -\cos(x+c) = -\cos c$, $f'''(x) = \sin(x+c) = \sin c$, $f^{(4)}(x) = \cos(x+c) = \cos c$, and so on. Hence the Maclaurin series associated with f is the right side of the required formula. Since every derivative of f is $\pm\sin(x+c)$ or $\pm\cos(x+c)$, we have $|R_n(x)| \le |x|^{n+1}/(n+1)! \to 0$ as $n \to \infty$, so the series is equal to $f(x)$. Rewriting it in the form

$$cos(x+c) = \cos c \left(1 - \frac{x^2}{2!} + \frac{x^4}{4!} - \cdots\right) - \sin c \left(x - \frac{x^3}{3!} + \frac{x^5}{5!} - \cdots\right)$$

we find $\cos(x+c) = \cos c \cos x - \sin c \sin x = \cos x \cos c - \sin x \sin c$.

13. (a) Replace x by $-x$ in the geometric series for $1/(1-x)$ to obtain

$1/(1+x) = 1 - x + x^2 - x^3 + \cdots$ $(-1 < x < 1)$. Then differentiation yields

$-1/(1+x)^2 = -1 + 2x - 3x^2 + \cdots$, or $1/(1+x)^2 = 1 - 2x + 3x^2 - \cdots$ $(-1 < x < 1)$.

(b) $\dfrac{1}{(1+x)^2} = (1+x)^{-2} = 1 - 2x + \dfrac{(-2)(-3)}{2!}x^2 + \dfrac{(-2)(-3)(-4)}{3!}x^3 + \cdots$

$$= 1 - 2x + 3x^2 - 4x^3 + \cdots$$

The domain is $(-1,1)$.

14. The binomial series gives

$$(1+x)^{1/4} = 1 + \frac{1}{4}x + \frac{(1/4)(-3/4)}{2!}x^2 + \frac{(1/4)(-3/4)(-7/4)}{3!}x^3 + \cdots$$

$$= 1 + \frac{1}{4}x - \frac{3}{32}x^2 + \frac{7}{128}x^3 - \cdots \quad (-1 < x < 1)$$

Since this is alternating (after the first term), we may use the first three terms with an error no larger than the absolute value of the fourth. To find $\sqrt[4]{15}$, we write

$$\sqrt[4]{15} = (16-1)^{1/4} = 2\left(1 - \frac{1}{16}\right)^{1/4} \approx 2\left(1 - \frac{1}{4}\cdot\frac{1}{16} - \frac{3}{32}\cdot\frac{1}{16^2}\right) = 1.9680175\cdots$$

The error is $\leq 2\cdot\dfrac{7}{128}\cdot\dfrac{1}{16^3} < 0.00003$, so $\sqrt[4]{15} \approx 1.9680$ correct to four places.

15. (a) Since $\phi'(x) = 1 + \phi(x)$ and $\phi(0) = 1$, we have $\phi'(0) = 1 + \phi(0) = 2$.
Repeated differentiation yields $\phi''(x) = \phi'(x)$, $\phi'''(x) = \phi''(x)$, ..., so
$\phi''(0) = 2$, $\phi'''(0) = 2$, $\cdots$.

(b) $\phi(x) = \phi(0) + \phi'(0)x + \dfrac{\phi''(0)}{2!}x^2 + \dfrac{\phi'''(0)}{3!}x^3 + \cdots$

$$= 1 + 2\left(x + \frac{x^2}{2!} + \frac{x^3}{3!} + \cdots\right) = 1 + 2(e^x - 1) = 2e^x - 1$$

(c) Since $y = 1$ when $x = 0$, we can divide by $1+y$ to separate the

variables: $\dfrac{dy}{dx} = 1 + y \implies \dfrac{dy}{1+y} = dx \implies \ln(1+y) = x + C = x + \ln 2 \implies$

$\ln\dfrac{1+y}{2} = x \implies \dfrac{1+y}{2} = e^x \implies y = 2e^x - 1$.

16. (a) Since $\phi'(x) = x + \phi(x)$ and $\phi(0) = 0$, we have $\phi'(0) = \phi(0) = 0$.
Differentiation yields $\phi''(x) = 1 + \phi'(x)$, $\phi'''(x) = \phi''(x)$, $\phi^{(4)}(x) = \phi'''(x)$, $\cdots$
so $\phi''(0) = 1 + \phi'(0) = 1$, $\phi'''(0) = 1$, $\phi^{(4)}(0) = 1$, $\cdots$.

(b) $\phi(x) = 0 + 0x + \dfrac{x^2}{2!} + \dfrac{x^3}{3!} + \dfrac{x^4}{4!} + \cdots = e^x - x - 1$

(c) $y' - y = x \implies e^{-x}y' - e^{-x}y = xe^{-x} \implies (ye^{-x})' = xe^{-x} \implies ye^{-x} = \int xe^{-x}dx$

$= -xe^{-x} - e^{-x} + C \implies y = -x - 1 + Ce^{x}$. Since $y = 0$ when $x = 0$, we find $C = 1$ and hence $y = \phi(x) = e^{x} - x - 1$.

17. Let $\phi(x)$ be the solution satisfying the conditions $\phi(0) = 0$ and $\phi'(0) = 1$. (According to the existence and uniqueness theorem mentioned at the end of Sec. 7.7, such a solution exists and is unique.) Then $\phi''(x) + \phi'(x) = 0$ and hence $\phi''(0) = -\phi'(0) = -1$. Differentiation yields $\phi'''(x) = -\phi''(x)$, $\phi^{(4)}(x) = -\phi'''(x)$, $\cdots$, so $\phi'''(0) = 1$, $\phi^{(4)}(0) = -1$, $\cdots$. The Maclaurin series is
$$\phi(x) = 0 + x - \frac{x^2}{2!} + \frac{x^3}{3!} - \frac{x^4}{4!} + \cdots = 1 - e^{-x}.$$

CHAPTER 14   GEOMETRY IN THE PLANE

Section 14.1   POLAR COORDINATES

1. $x = 3 \cos \pi = -3$, $y = 3 \sin \pi = 0$.

2. $x = 1 \cos (\pi/2) = 0$, $y = 1 \sin (\pi/2) = 1$.

3. $x = -1 \cos 3\pi = 1$, $y = -1 \sin 3\pi = 0$.

4. $x = 0 \cos \pi = 0$, $y = 0 \sin \pi = 0$.

5. $x = 2 \cos 135° = -\sqrt{2}$, $y = 2 \sin 135° = \sqrt{2}$.

6. $x = 4 \cos 30° = 2\sqrt{3}$, $y = 4 \sin 30° = 2$.

7. $x = 4 \cos (-30°) = 2\sqrt{3}$, $y = 4 \sin (-30°) = -2$.

8. $x = 2 \cos (\pi/3) = 1$, $y = 2 \sin (\pi/3) = \sqrt{3}$.

9. $x = -2 \cos (4\pi/3) = 1$, $y = -2 \sin (4\pi/3) = \sqrt{3}$.

10. $r^2 = 3^2 + 0^2 = 9$, $\tan \theta = 0/3 = 0$, so one choice of polar coordinates is $r = 3$, $\theta = 0$.

11. $r^2 = 4$ and $\tan \theta$ is undefined, so one choice is $r = 2$, $\theta = \pi/2$.

12. $r^2 = 2$, $\tan \theta = 1$, so one choice is $r = \sqrt{2}$, $\theta = \pi/4$.

13. $r^2 = 2$, $\tan \theta = -1$, so one choice is $r = \sqrt{2}$, $\theta = -\pi/4$.

14. $r^2 = 4$, $\tan \theta = -1/\sqrt{3}$, so one choice is $r = 2$, $\theta = -\pi/6$.

15. $r^2 = 4$, $\tan \theta = -\sqrt{3}$, so one choice is $r = 2$, $\theta = 2\pi/3$.

16. $r = 2$ represents the circle of center $(0,0)$ and radius 2, with equation $x^2 + y^2 = 4$ in rectangular coordinates.

17. $\theta = 3\pi/4$ represents the line through $(0,0)$ with slope -1 and equation $y = -x$.

18. If $x \neq 0$, $\tan \theta = 2 \iff y/x = 2 \iff y = 2x$. The origin, while not a point of the graph of $y/x = 2$, satisfies $\tan \theta = 2$ in the polar form $(0, \tan^{-1} 2)$ and satisfies $y = 2x$ in the rectangular form $(0,0)$. Hence the graph is the straight line $y = 2x$.

20. $r = 1/(\sin\theta + \cos\theta) \iff r\sin\theta + r\cos\theta = 1 \iff x + y = 1$, the line with intercepts $(1,0)$ and $(0,1)$.

21. If $r \neq 0$, $r = 2\sin\theta \iff r^2 = 2r\sin\theta \iff x^2 + y^2 = 2y \iff x^2 + (y-1)^2 = 1$. Since the origin satisfies both equations, we may drop the restriction $r \neq 0$; the graph is the circle of center $(0,1)$ and radius 1.

22. If $r \neq 0$, $r = 2\sin\theta + 4\cos\theta \iff r^2 = 2r\sin\theta + 4r\cos\theta \iff x^2 + y^2 = 2y + 4x \iff (x-2)^2 + (y-1)^2 = 5$. Since the origin satisfies the first equation in the polar form $(0, \tan^{-1}(-2))$ and the second in the rectangular form $(0,0)$, we may drop the restriction $r \neq 0$. The graph is the circle of center $(2,1)$ and radius $\sqrt{5}$.

23. $r^2 = 2\csc 2\theta \iff r^2 \sin 2\theta = 2 \iff r^2(2\sin\theta\cos\theta) = 2 \iff (r\cos\theta)(r\sin\theta) = 1 \iff xy = 1$ (a hyperbola).

24. $r^2 = \sec 2\theta \iff r^2 \cos 2\theta = 1 \iff r^2(\cos^2\theta - \sin^2\theta) = 1 \iff r^2\cos^2\theta - r^2\sin^2\theta = 1 \iff x^2 - y^2 = 1$ (a hyperbola).

25. $r = 1/(1 - \cos\theta) \iff r(1 - \cos\theta) = 1 \iff r = r\cos\theta + 1 \iff r = x + 1$. Now square both sides (which may introduce points not previously present) to obtain $r^2 = (x+1)^2 \iff x^2 + y^2 = (x+1)^2 \iff y^2 = 1 + 2x$. This is a parabola, but does it contain any points not on the graph of the original polar equation? To find out, replace r by $-r$ and θ by $\theta + \pi$ in the original equation (which does not affect the graph) to obtain

$$-r = \frac{1}{1 - \cos(\theta + \pi)} \iff -r = \frac{1}{1 + \cos\theta} \iff -r(1 + \cos\theta) = 1$$

$$\iff -r = r\cos\theta + 1 \iff -r = x + 1$$

At this point it is clear that since the squared equation $r^2 = (x+1)^2$ is equivalent to $\pm r = x + 1$, the graph is indeed the whole parabola.

26. $r = \sin 2\theta \iff r = 2\sin\theta\cos\theta \implies r^2 = 4\sin^2\theta\cos^2\theta \implies r^6 = 4(r^2\sin^2\theta)(r^2\cos^2\theta) \iff (x^2 + y^2)^3 = 4x^2y^2$. (We don't bother to check the reverse implications; the rectangular form of the equation is too complicated to be of much help.)

27. When $\theta = 0$, $r = 2a$. As θ increases from 0 to $\pi/2$, r goes from $2a$ to a, then from a to 0 as θ goes from $\pi/2$ to π. This gives the top half of Fig. 1; the rest is obtained by symmetry about the x axis (as in Example 5).

28. If θ is replaced by $\pi - \theta$, the equation is unchanged, which implies symmetry about the y axis. Start with $\theta = -\pi/2$, $r = 2a$, and let θ increase to $\pi/2$, which causes r to decrease to a (at $\theta = 0$) and then to 0 (at $\theta = \pi/2$). This gives the right-hand half of Figure 2; the rest is sketched by symmetry.

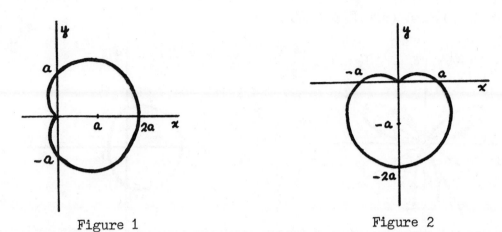

Figure 1   Figure 2

29. As in Problem 28, we have symmetry about the y axis. As θ goes from -π/2 to π/2, r goes from 0 to a (at θ = 0) to 2a (at θ = π/2). This gives the right-hand half of Figure 3.

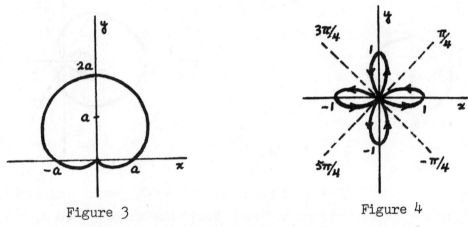

Figure 3   Figure 4

30. r = -1 has the same graph as r = 1, namely the unit circle.

31. The graph is the x axis.

32. When θ increases from -π/4 to π/4, r goes from 0 to 1 (at θ = 0) back to 0, generating one loop of the graph. The rest of the graph is generated as indicated by the arrows in Figure 4.

33. When θ increases from 0 to π/3, r goes from 0 to 1 (at θ = π/6) back to 0, generating one loop of the graph. The rest of the graph is generated as indicated by the arrows in Figure 5.

34. The graph is symmetric about the x axis because cos(-θ) = cos θ. As θ increases from 0 to π, r goes from its smallest value 1 to 2 (at θ = π/2) to its largest value 3. See Figure 6.

35. The graph is symmetric about the y axis because sin(π - θ) = sin θ. As θ

increases from -π/2 to π/2, r goes from its largest value 3 to 2 (at θ = 0) to its smallest value 1. See Figure 7.

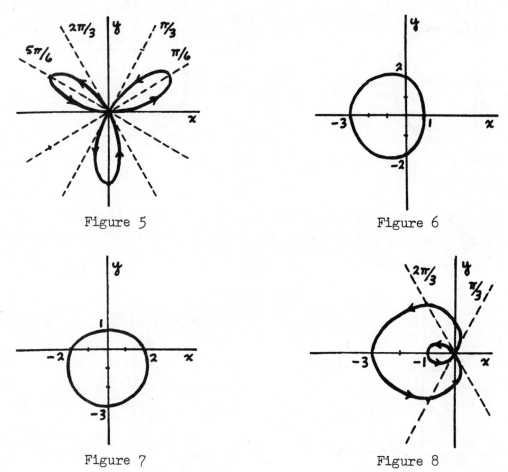

Figure 5   Figure 6

Figure 7   Figure 8

36. As θ increases from 0 to π/3, r goes from -1 to 0, generating the lower half of the inside loop in Figure 8. As θ increases from π/3 to π, r goes from 0 to 1 (at θ = π/2) to 3. The graph is symmetric about the x axis because cos(-θ) = cos θ.

37. Since sin θ = cos(θ - π/2), the graph may be obtained by rotating the graph in Problem 36 through 90°. See Figure 9. (Note that we could have done Problem 29 this way, using Problem 27; Problem 28 follows in the same way from Example 5; and Problem 35 follows from Problem 34.)

38. Since r increases with θ, the graph is simply a spiral starting at the origin. See Figure 10.

39. Since r = 1/θ ⟹ r sin θ = (sin θ)/θ, y = r sin θ is close to 1 when θ is small. As θ increases, r→0, so the graph spirals in toward the origin. See Figure 11.

40. When θ is negatively large, r is close to 0; as θ increases, so does r.

The graph spirals away from the origin (which is not, however, a point of the graph).   See Figure 12.

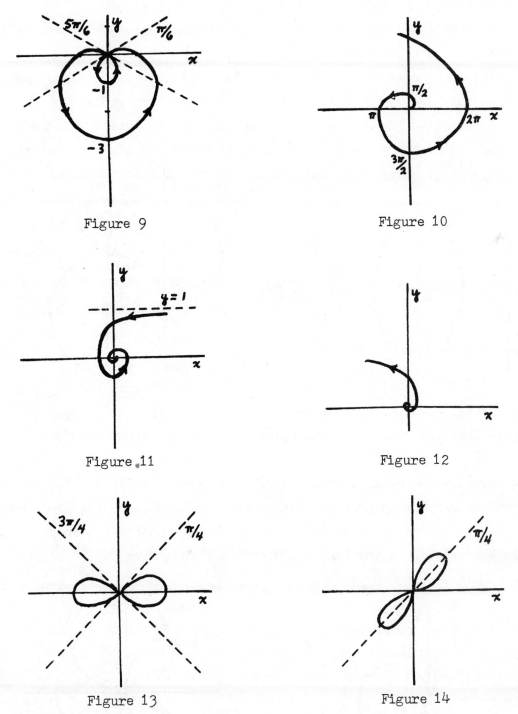

Figure 9

Figure 10

Figure 11

Figure 12

Figure 13

Figure 14

41. Since the equation is unchanged when r is replaced by -r, the graph is symmetric about the origin.   It is also symmetric about the x axis because θ may be replaced by -θ without affecting the equation.   Assuming that r ≥ 0, we obtain the first-quadrant portion of the graph by letting θ run from 0 to π/4;

the rest is obtained by symmetry. See Figure 13.

42. Since $\sin 2\theta = \cos(2\theta - \pi/2) = \cos 2(\theta - \pi/4)$, the graph may be obtained by rotating the graph in Problem 41 through $45°$. See Figure 14.

43. The graph is symmetric about the x axis because $\sec(-\theta) = \sec\theta$. In the domain $0 \le \theta < \pi/2$ we have $r = 2\sec\theta - 1 \iff r\cos\theta = 2 - \cos\theta \iff x = 2 - \cos\theta$. Hence x increases from 1 at $\theta = 0$ toward the limiting value 2 as $\theta \to \pi/2$. Hence the line $x = 2$ is a vertical asymptote. The reflection of this part of the graph in the line $x = 2$ corresponds to the domain $\pi/2 < \theta \le \pi$. The rest of the graph is sketched by symmetry about the x axis. See Fig. 15.

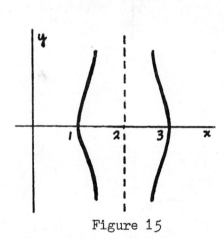

Figure 15

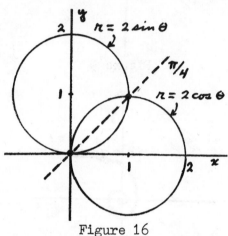

Figure 16

44. The curves are both circles, as shown in Figure 16. It is apparent from the figure that the origin and the point $(\sqrt{2}, \pi/4)$ are the points of intersection.

45. The curves are a cardioid and a circle, as shown in Figure 17. Solving the equations simultaneously, we have $1 + \cos\theta = 2\cos\theta \implies \cos\theta = 1 \implies \theta = 0$ (plus multiples of 2π). Hence $(2,0)$ is one point of intersection. The other is the origin, in the form $(0,\pi)$ on the first curve and $(0,\pi/2)$ on the second.

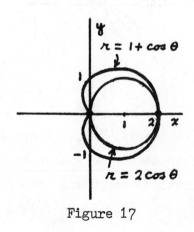

Figure 17

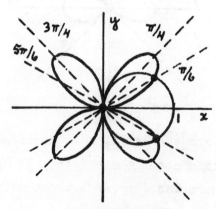

Figure 18

46. Figure 18 indicates three points of intersection. Solving the equations simultaneously, we have $\cos\theta = \sin 2\theta \implies \cos\theta = 2\sin\theta\cos\theta \implies \cos\theta(2\sin\theta - 1) = 0 \implies \cos\theta = 0$ or $\sin\theta = 1/2 \implies \theta = \pi/2$ or $\theta = \pi/6,\ 5\pi/6$ (in the interval $0 \le \theta \le \pi$, which is sufficient here). Hence the points of intersection are $(0, \pi/2)$, $(\sqrt{3}/2, \pi/6)$, and $(-\sqrt{3}/2, 5\pi/6)$.

47. Figure 19 indicates four points of intersection. Solving the equations simultaneously, we have $\sin\theta = \cos 2\theta \implies \sin\theta = 1 - 2\sin^2\theta \implies 2\sin^2\theta + \sin\theta - 1 = 0 \implies (2\sin\theta - 1)(\sin\theta + 1) = 0 \implies \sin\theta = 1/2$ or $\sin\theta = -1 \implies \theta = \pi/6,\ 5\pi/6$ or $\theta = 3\pi/2$ (in the interval $0 \le \theta \le 2\pi$). This yields the points $(1/2, \pi/6)$, $(1/2, 5\pi/6)$, and $(-1, 3\pi/2)$, the latter being the same as $(1, \pi/2)$. The origin is also a point of intersection, in the form $(0,0)$ on the first curve and $(0, \pi/4)$ on the second.

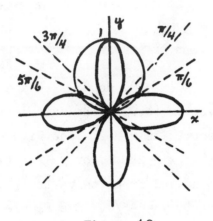

Figure 19

48. Figure 10 shows that the spiral $r = \theta$ intersects the line $\theta = \pi/2$ (the y axis) infinitely many times. Solving the equations simultaneously, we have $r = \theta = \pi/2$, which yields only the one point $(\pi/2, \pi/2)$. Of course the others may be obtained by representing the y axis in the form $\theta = \pi/2 + n\pi$ ($n = 0, \pm 1, \pm 2, \ldots$).

49. If (x_1, y_1) and (x_2, y_2) are rectangular coordinates of the points, the square of the distance is

$$(x_2 - x_1)^2 + (y_2 - y_1)^2 = (r_2\cos\theta_2 - r_1\cos\theta_1)^2 + (r_2\sin\theta_2 - r_1\sin\theta_1)^2 =$$

$$r_2^2\cos^2\theta_2 - 2r_1r_2\cos\theta_1\cos\theta_2 + r_1^2\cos^2\theta_1 + r_2^2\sin^2\theta_2 - 2r_1r_2\sin\theta_1\sin\theta_2 + r_1^2\sin^2\theta_1 =$$

$$r_1^2(\sin^2\theta_1 + \cos^2\theta_1) + r_2^2(\sin^2\theta_2 + \cos^2\theta_2) - 2r_1r_2(\cos\theta_1\cos\theta_2 + \sin\theta_1\sin\theta_2) =$$

$$r_1^2 + r_2^2 - 2r_1r_2\cos(\theta_1 - \theta_2)$$

Hence the distance is as stated in the problem.

Section 14.2   CONICS: THE PARABOLA

1. The standard form is $x^2 = -(y-4)$, from which we have $4c = -1$ and $c = -1/4$. Thus the parabola opens downward from its vertex $(0,4)$. The axis is $x = 0$ (the y axis), the focus is $(0,15/4)$, and the directrix is $x = 17/4$. See Figure 1.

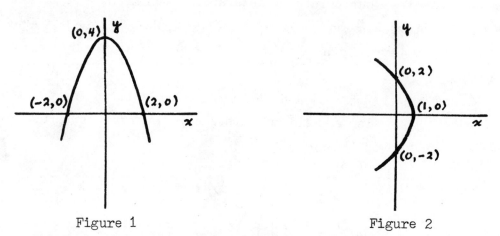

Figure 1   Figure 2

2. The standard form is $y^2 = -4(x-1)$, so $4c = -4$ and $c = -1$. The parabola opens to the left from its vertex $(1,0)$. The axis is $y = 0$ (the x axis), the focus is $(0,0)$, and the directrix is $x = 2$. See Figure 2.

3. Complete the square: $y+1 = x^2 - 2x + 1$, or $y+1 = (x-1)^2$. Then $4c = 1$ and $c = 1/4$. The parabola opens upward from its vertex $(1,-1)$. The axis is $x = 1$, focus $(1,-3/4)$, directrix $y = -5/4$. See Figure 3.

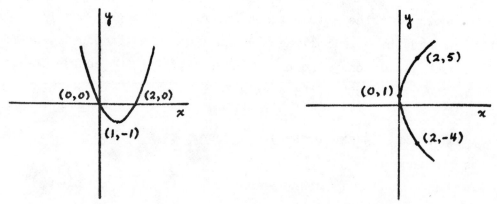

Figure 3   Figure 4

4. $y^2 - 2y - 8x + 1 = 0 \iff (y-1)^2 = 8x$, so $4c = 8$ and $c = 2$. Vertex $(0,1)$, axis $y = 1$, focus $(2,1)$, directrix $x = -2$. See Figure 4.

5. $x^2 - 4x + 4y - 8 = 0 \iff x^2 - 4x + 4 = -4y + 8 + 4 \iff (x-2)^2 = -4(y-3)$, so $4c = -4$ and $c = -1$. Vertex $(2,3)$, axis $x = 2$, focus $(2,2)$, directrix $y = 4$. See Figure 5.

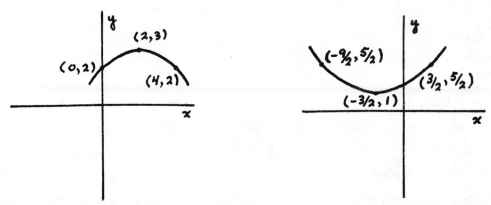

Figure 5   Figure 6

6. $4x^2 + 12x - 24y + 33 = 0 \iff 4(x^2 + 3x + 9/4) = 24y - 33 + 9 \iff 4(x + 3/2)^2 =$
$24y - 24 \iff (x + 3/2)^2 = 6(y - 1)$, so $4c = 6$ and $c = 3/2$. Vertex $(-3/2, 1)$,
axis $x = -3/2$, focus $(-3/2, 5/2)$, directrix $y = -1/2$. See Figure 6.

7. The vertex is halfway between the focus and directrix, so it is $(1,1)$.
Since $c = 1$ and the parabola opens upward, the standard form is $4(y - 1) =$
$(x - 1)^2$.

8. The vertex is $(1,0)$, $c = 1$, and the parabola opens to the right. Hence
the standard form is $4(x - 1) = y^2$.

9. Since $c = -1/2$ and the parabola opens downward, the standard form is
$-2(y - 1) = x^2$.

10. Since $c = 3/2$ and the parabola opens to the right, the standard form is
$6(x + 1) = (y - 1)^2$.

11. Since the axis is horizontal, the standard form is $4cx = y^2$. Put $(1,4)$ in
the equation to find $4c = 16$. The equation is $16x = y^2$.

12. The points $(0,1)$ and $(2,1)$ are symmetrically located about the axis, which
must therefore be $x = 1$. The vertex is of the form $(1,k)$. Hence the standard
form is $4c(y - k) = (x - 1)^2$. Put $(0,1)$ and $(4,-1)$ in the equation to find
$4c(1 - k) = 1$ and $4c(-1 - k) = 9$. Solving for $4c$, we have

$$\frac{1}{1 - k} = \frac{-9}{1 + k} \implies k + 1 = 9k - 9 \implies 8k = 10 \implies k = 5/4$$

Then $4c = 1/(1 - k) = -4$ and the standard form becomes $-4(y - 5/4) = (x - 1)^2$.

13. Let F be the focus and L the directrix. Then $P \in S \iff d(P,F) = d(P,L)$
$\iff d(P,F)^2 = d(P,L)^2 \iff x^2 + (y - c)^2 = (y + c)^2 \iff x^2 + y^2 - 2cy + c^2 = y^2 +$
$2cy + c^2 \iff x^2 = 4cy$.

14. Let F be the focus, L the directrix, and $P(x,y)$ any point of the plane.
If S is the parabola, then $P \in S \iff d(P,F) = d(P,L) \iff d(P,F)^2 = d(P,L)^2$

183

$\iff [x-(h+c)]^2 + (y-k)^2 = [x-(h-c)]^2 \iff x^2 - 2(h+c)x + (h+c)^2 + (y-k)^2$

$= x^2 - 2(h-c)x + (h-c)^2 \iff -2hx - 2cx + h^2 + 2ch + c^2 + (y-k)^2 = -2hx + 2cx + h^2 -$

$2ch + c^2 \iff (y-k)^2 = 4c(x-h)$.

15. The axis is the line $y = -x$ with slope -1. Hence the directrix (which is perpendicular to the axis) has slope 1. An equation of the directrix is $y = x + b$, where b is its y intercept. The distance between the origin and this line is the same as the distance between the origin and the focus, namely $\sqrt{2}$. Using the formula $d = |Ax_0 + By_0 + C|/\sqrt{A^2 + B^2}$ for the distance between the point (x_0, y_0) and the line $Ax + By + C = 0$ (Problem 50, Sec. 1.2), we have $\sqrt{2} = |b|/\sqrt{2}$, from which b = 2 (because b > 0). Thus the directrix is $y = x + 2$. (You can avoid the above distance formula by drawing a picture and using similar triangles.)

16. Let F be the focus, L the directrix, and $P(x,y)$ any point of the plane. If S is the parabola, then $P \in S \iff d(P,F) = d(P,L) \iff \sqrt{(x-1)^2 + (y-1)^2} = |x+y+2|/\sqrt{2} \iff (x-1)^2 + (y-1)^2 = (x+y+2)^2/2 \iff 2(x^2 - 2x + 1 + y^2 - 2y + 1) = x^2 + y^2 + 4 + 2xy + 4x + 4y \iff x^2 - 2xy + y^2 - 8x - 8y - 2 = 0$. Note that this equation is still second-degree in x and y (like the standard forms in this section). The presence of an xy term, however, signals a "tilted" parabola.

17. As explained in the text, the equation represents a parabola with focus at the origin. The curve is swept out as θ runs through the interval $(0, 2\pi)$, with r = 4 at $\theta = \pi/2$, r = 2 at $\theta = \pi$, and r = 4 at $\theta = 3\pi/2$. In rectangular coordinates the vertex is $(-2,0)$, the axis is $y = 0$, and the directrix is $x = -4$. See Figure 7.

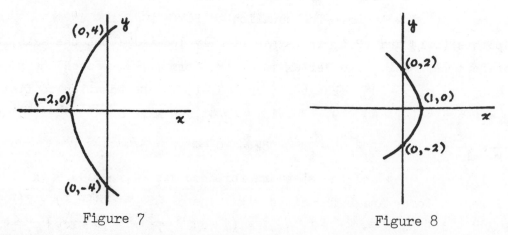

Figure 7   Figure 8

18. The equation represents a parabola with focus at the origin, swept out as θ runs through the interval $(-\pi, \pi)$. We find r = 2 at $\theta = -\pi/2$, r = 1 at $\theta = 0$, and r = 2 at $\theta = \pi/2$. Vertex $(1,0)$, axis $y = 0$, directrix $x = 2$. See Fig. 8.

19. The parabola has focus at the origin, and is swept out as θ runs through the interval $(-3\pi/2, \pi/2)$. We find $r = 1$ at $\theta = -\pi$, $r = 1/2$ at $\theta = -\pi/2$, and $r = 1$ at $\theta = 0$. Vertex $(0, -1/2)$, axis $x = 0$, directrix $y = -1$. See Fig. 9.

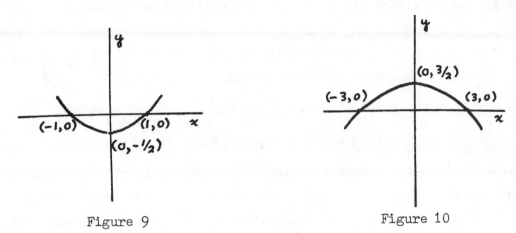

Figure 9   Figure 10

20. The parabola has focus at the origin, and is swept out as θ runs through the interval $(-\pi/2, 3\pi/2)$. We find $r = 3$ at $\theta = 0$, $r = 3/2$ at $\theta = \pi/2$, and $r = 3$ at $\theta = \pi$. Vertex $(0, 3/2)$, axis $x = 0$, directrix $y = 3$. See Figure 10.

21. Since $\sin^2\frac{1}{2}\theta = \frac{1}{2}(1 - \cos\theta)$, we have

$$r = \frac{p}{2} \cdot \frac{2}{1 - \cos\theta} = \frac{p}{1 - \cos\theta}$$

This represents a parabola with focus at the origin.

22. Let F be the focus, L the directrix, and $P(r, \theta)$ any point of the plane (with rectangular coordinates x and y). If S is the parabola, then $P \in S \iff d(P, F) = d(P, L) \iff |r| = |y + p| \iff r = \pm(y + p) \iff r = \pm(r\sin\theta + p) \iff r \mp r\sin\theta = \pm p \iff r(1 \mp \sin\theta) = \pm p \iff r = \pm p/(1 \mp \sin\theta)$. Since $r = p/(1 - \sin\theta)$ and $r = -p/(1 + \sin\theta)$ represent the same graph (replace r by $-r$ and θ by $\theta + \pi$ to obtain one from the other), we conclude that the parabola may be represented by $r = p/(1 - \sin\theta)$.

23. See the solution of Problem 25, Sec. 3.4.

24. Choose the coordinate system so that the parabola is $y^2 = 4cx$, where $c > 0$. Then the focus is $(c, 0)$ and the endpoints of the latus rectum are $(c, \pm 2c)$ (because $y^2 = 4c^2$ when $x = c$). The distance between the endpoints is $4c$.

25. With the same coordinate system as in Problem 24, we use Problem 23 to write the tangents at $(c, \pm 2c)$ in the form $\pm 2cy = 2c(x + c)$, or $\pm y = x + c$. Solving these equations simultaneously, we have $x + c = -(x + c)$, or $x = -c$, so the points of intersection of the tangents lie on the directrix $x = -c$. The

slopes of the tangents are ± 1, so the angle between them is $90°$.

26. The endpoints of the latus rectum (Problem 24) are $(c, \pm 2c)$ and the vertex is $(0,0)$. Hence the center of the circle is $(c,0)$ and the radius is $|c|$. An equation of the circle is $(x - c)^2 + y^2 = c^2$, or (in polar coordinates) $r = 2c \cos \theta$.

27. The focus is $F = (c,0)$ and the directrix is $L: x = -c$. If $P_1 = (x_1, y_1)$ and $P_2 = (x_2, y_2)$, the length of the chord is

$$d(P_1, F) + d(P_2, F) = d(P_1, L) + d(P_2, L) \quad \text{(definition of parabola)}$$

$$= (x_1 + c) + (x_2 + c) = x_1 + x_2 + 2c$$

28. Choose the coordinate system so that the parabola is $y^2 = 4cx$, where $c > 0$, and suppose that $P = (x_0, y_0)$. Since P is not the vertex, we have $x_0 > 0$ and $y_0 \neq 0$. Implicit differentiation in $y^2 = 4cx$ yields $2yy' = 4c$, so the slope of the tangent at P is $2c/y_0$. The slope of the normal is $-y_0/2c$ and hence an equation of the normal is

$$y - y_0 = \frac{-y_0}{2c}(x - x_0) \iff 2cy - 2cy_0 = -y_0 x + x_0 y_0$$

This line intersects the axis of the parabola (the x axis) when $y = 0$, so $Q = (x,0)$, where $-2cy_0 = -y_0 x + x_0 y_0$, that is, $x = x_0 + 2c$. The focus is $F = (c,0)$, so $d(Q,F) = (x_0 + 2c) - c = x_0 + c$. By definition of the parabola, $d(P,F) = d(P,L)$, where L is the directrix $x = -c$. Hence $d(P,F) = x_0 + c = d(Q,F)$.

29. Choose the coordinate system as in Figure 6 in the text. Then the focus of the parabola is at the origin and its equation in polar coordinates is $r = p/(1 - \cos \theta)$. If $P(r, \theta)$ is any point of the parabola, then $d(P,F) = |r|$, which has its minimum value when $1 - \cos \theta$ is largest, that is, when $\cos \theta = -1$. This occurs when $\theta = \pi$, which places P at the vertex, with polar coordinates $(p/2, \pi)$.

30. As in Problem 29, use Figure 6 in the text. We are told that $r = 8 \times 10^7$ when $\theta = \pi/3$, so the equation $r = p/(1 - \cos \theta)$ yields $p = 8 \times 10^7 (1 - \frac{1}{2}) = 4 \times 10^7$. The comet is closest to the sun when it is at the vertex $(p/2, \pi)$. (See Problem 29.) Its distance from the sun at that point is $p/2 = 2 \times 10^7 = 20,000,000$ km.

Section 14.3   CONICS: THE ELLIPSE AND HYPERBOLA

1. The standard form is $x^2/9 + y^2/4 = 1$, so $a = 3$, $b = 2$, and $c = \sqrt{a^2 - b^2} =$

$\sqrt{5}$. The center is $(0,0)$, the endpoints of the major diameter (on the x axis) are $(\pm 3,0)$, the endpoints of the minor diameter (on the y axis) are $(0,\pm 2)$, the foci (on the x axis) are $(\pm\sqrt{5},0)$, the eccentricity is $e = c/a = \sqrt{5}/3$, and the directrices (vertical lines $a/e = a^2/c$ units from the center) are $x = \pm 9/\sqrt{5}$. See Figure 1.

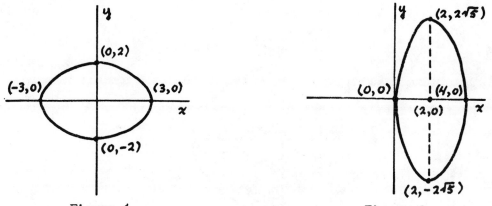

Figure 1   Figure 2

2. Complete the square: $5x^2 + y^2 - 20x = 0 \iff 5(x^2 - 4x + 4) + y^2 = 20 \iff 5(x - 2)^2 + y^2 = 20 \iff y^2/20 + (x - 2)^2/4 = 1$. We have $a = 2\sqrt{5}$, $b = 2$, $c = \sqrt{20 - 4} = 4$, center and endpoints of major and minor diameters shown in Figure 2, foci $(2,\pm 4)$, directrices $y = \pm a/e = \pm a^2/c = \pm 5$, and eccentricity $e = c/a = 2/\sqrt{5}$.

3. $x^2 + 4y^2 - 4x - 8y - 8 = 0 \iff (x^2 - 4x + 4) + 4(y^2 - 2y + 1) = 8 + 4 + 4 \iff (x - 2)^2 + 4(y - 1)^2 = 16 \iff (x - 2)^2/16 + (y - 1)^2/4 = 1$. We have $a = 4$, $b = 2$, $c = 2\sqrt{3}$, center and endpoints shown in Figure 3, foci $(2 \pm 2\sqrt{3},1)$, directrices $x = 2 \pm a^2/c = 2 \pm 8/\sqrt{3}$, and eccentricity $e = \frac{1}{2}\sqrt{3}$.

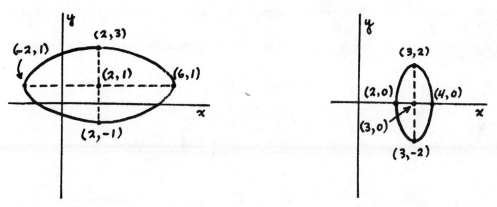

Figure 3   Figure 4

4. $4x^2 + y^2 - 24x + 32 = 0 \iff 4(x^2 - 6x + 9) + y^2 = -32 + 36 \iff 4(x - 3)^2 + y^2 = 4 \iff y^2/4 + (x - 3)^2/1 = 1$. We have $a = 2$, $b = 1$, $c = \sqrt{3}$, center and endpoints

shown in Figure 4, foci $(3, \pm\sqrt{3})$, directrices $y = \pm a^2/c = \pm 4/\sqrt{3}$, and eccentricity $e = \frac{1}{2}\sqrt{3}$.

5. $16x^2 + 25y^2 - 64x + 50y - 311 = 0 \iff 16(x^2 - 4x + 4) + 25(y^2 + 2y + 1) = 311 + 64 + 25 \iff 16(x - 2)^2 + 25(y + 1)^2 = 400 \iff (x - 2)^2/25 + (y + 1)^2/16 = 1$. We have $a = 5$, $b = 4$, $c = 3$, center, endpoints, and foci shown in Figure 5, directrices $x = 2 \pm a^2/c = 2 \pm 25/3$, and eccentricity $e = 3/5$.

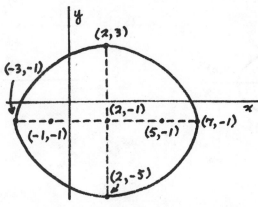

Figure 5

6. Since $x^2 + 4y^2 - 24y + 36 = 0 \iff x^2 + 4(y^2 - 6y + 9) = -36 + 36 \iff x^2 + 4(y - 3)^2 = 0$, the graph consists of the single point $(0,3)$.

7. The center is $(0,0)$, $a = 4$, and $c = 2$. Hence $b^2 = a^2 - c^2 = 12$ and the standard form is $y^2/16 + x^2/12 = 1$.

8. The center is $(1,1)$, $a = 2$, and $e = c/a = c/2 = 2/3$. Hence $c = 4/3$ and $b^2 = a^2 - c^2 = 20/9$. The standard form is

$$\frac{(x - 1)^2}{4} + \frac{(y - 1)^2}{20/9} = 1$$

9. The center is $(2,0)$ and $c = 1$, so the standard form is

$$\frac{(x - 2)^2}{a^2} + \frac{y^2}{a^2 - 1} = 1$$

Put $(1, 3/2)$ in the equation to obtain

$$\frac{1}{a^2} + \frac{9}{4(a^2 - 1)} = 1 \iff 4(a^2 - 1) + 9a^2 = 4a^2(a^2 - 1) \iff 4a^4 - 17a^2 + 4 = 0$$

$$\iff (4a^2 - 1)(a^2 - 4) = 0 \iff a^2 = 1/4 \text{ or } a^2 = 4$$

Since $a > c$, we reject $a^2 = 1/4$. Hence $a^2 = 4$ and the equation is $(x - 2)^2/4 + y^2/3 = 1$.

10. We have $c = 2$ and directrix $x = -3 - a^2/c = -7$, so $a^2 = 8$ and $b^2 = a^2 - c^2 = 4$. The standard form is $(x + 3)^2/8 + (y - 5)^2/4 = 1$.

11. The center is $(-1,2)$ and $b = 2$. The first directrix is $y = 2 + a^2/c = 7$, so $a^2 = 5c$. Since $b^2 = a^2 - c^2 = 4$, we have $5c - c^2 = 4 \iff c^2 - 5c + 4 = 0 \iff$

$(c-1)(c-4) = 0 \iff c = 1$ or $c = 4$. Hence $a^2 = 5$ or $a^2 = 20$ and the two answers are $(y-2)^2/5 + (x+1)^2/4 = 1$ or $(y-2)^2/20 + (x+1)^2/4 = 1$.

12. Since $\cos t = \frac{1}{3}(x-1)$ and $\sin t = \frac{1}{5}(y+2)$, we have $(y+2)^2/25 + (x-1)^2/9 = 1$, which represents an ellipse with center $(1,-2)$ and vertical major diameter, traversed counterclockwise from the initial point $(4,-2)$.

13. The standard form is $x^2/9 - y^2/16 = 1$, so $a = 3$, $b = 4$, $c = \sqrt{a^2 + b^2} = 5$. The center is $(0,0)$, the vertices are $(\pm 3, 0)$, the foci are $(\pm 5, 0)$, the directrices are $x = \pm a^2/c = \pm 9/5$, and the eccentricity is $e = c/a = 5/3$. See Figure 6.

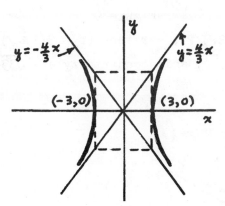

Figure 6

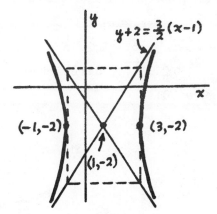

Figure 7

14. $9x^2 - 4y^2 - 18x - 16y - 43 = 0 \iff 9(x^2 - 2x + 1) - 4(y^2 + 4y + 4) = 43 + 9 - 16 \iff 9(x-1)^2 - 4(y+2)^2 = 36 \iff (x-1)^2/4 - (y+2)^2/9 = 1$. We have $a = 2$, $b = 3$, $c = \sqrt{13}$, center and vertices shown in Figure 7, foci $(1 \pm \sqrt{13}, -2)$, directrices $x = 1 \pm a^2/c = 1 \pm 4/\sqrt{13}$, and eccentricity $e = \frac{1}{2}\sqrt{13}$.

15. $16x^2 - 9y^2 - 96x + 128 = 0 \iff 16(x^2 - 6x + 9) - 9y^2 = -128 + 144 \iff 16(x-3)^2 - 9y^2 = 16 \iff$

$$\frac{(x-3)^2}{1} - \frac{y^2}{16/9} = 1$$

We have $a = 1$, $b = 4/3$, $c = 5/3$, center and vertices shown in Figure 8, foci $(3 \pm 5/3, 0)$, directrices $x = 3 \pm a^2/c = 3 \pm 3/5$, and eccentricity $e = 5/3$.

16. $9x^2 - 4y^2 + 36x - 8y + 68 = 0 \iff 9(x^2 + 4x + 4) - 4(y^2 + 2y + 1) = -68 + 36 - 4$
$9(x+2)^2 - 4(y+1)^2 = -36 \iff (y+1)^2/9 - (x+2)^2/4 = 1$. We have $a = 3$, $b = 2$, $c = \sqrt{13}$, center and vertices shown in Figure 9, foci $(-2, -1 \pm \sqrt{13})$, directrices $y = -1 \pm a^2/c = -1 \pm 9/\sqrt{13}$, and eccentricity $e = \sqrt{13}/3$.

17. $12x^2 - 32y^2 - 12x + 96y + 27 = 0 \iff 12(x^2 - x + 1/4) - 32(y^2 - 3y + 9/4) = -27 + 3 - 72 \iff 12(x-1/2)^2 - 32(y-3/2)^2 = -96 \iff$

$$\frac{(y-3/2)^2}{3} - \frac{(x-1/2)^2}{8} = 1$$

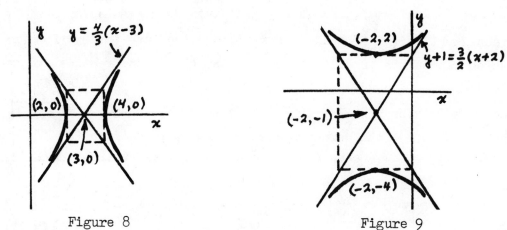

Figure 8   Figure 9

We have a = $\sqrt{3}$, b = $2\sqrt{2}$, c = $\sqrt{11}$, center (1/2,3/2), vertices (1/2,3/2 ± $\sqrt{3}$), foci (1/2,3/2 ± $\sqrt{11}$), directrices y = 3/2 ± 3/$\sqrt{11}$, and eccentricity e = $\sqrt{33}$/3. See Figure 10.

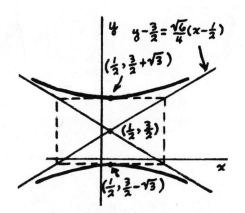

Figure 10

18. $9x^2 - 4y^2 - 18x + 8y + 5 = 0$ $\Leftrightarrow$ $9(x^2 - 2x + 1) - 4(y^2 - 2y + 1) = -5 + 9 - 4$ $\Leftrightarrow$ $9(x - 1)^2 - 4(y - 1)^2 = 0$ $\Leftrightarrow$ $y - 1 = \pm\frac{3}{2}(x - 1)$. The graph is a pair of intersecting straight lines.

19. The center is $(0,0)$ and a = 2. The asymptote y = $\frac{1}{2}x$ has slope a/b = 1/2, so b = 2a = 4. The standard form is $y^2/4 - x^2/16 = 1$.

20. The center is $(-1,2)$ and a = 2. Since e = c/a = $\sqrt{2}$, we have c = a$\sqrt{2}$ = $2\sqrt{2}$. Hence $b^2 = c^2 - a^2 = 8 - 4 = 4$ and the standard form is $(x + 1)^2/4 - (y - 2)^2/4 = 1$.

21. The center is $(3,0)$ and c = 4. The standard form is

$$\frac{(x - 3)^2}{a^2} - \frac{y^2}{16 - a^2} = 1$$

Put $(6,\sqrt{15})$ in the equation to obtain

$$\frac{9}{a^2} - \frac{15}{16 - a^2} = 1 \iff 9(16 - a^2) - 15a^2 = a^2(16 - a^2) \iff a^4 - 40a^2 + 144 = 0$$

$$\iff (a^2 - 4)(a^2 - 36) = 0 \iff a^2 = 4 \text{ or } a^2 = 36$$

Since $a < c$, we reject $a^2 = 36$. Hence $a^2 = 4$ and the standard form is $(x - 3)^2/4 - y^2/12 = 1$.

22. We have $c = 3$ and directrix $y = a^2/c = 2$, so $a^2 = 2c = 6$. Hence $b^2 = c^2 - a^2 = 3$ and the standard form is $y^2/6 - x^2/3 = 1$.

23. Since $\cosh t = x/2$ and $\sinh t = (y - 2)/3$, we have $x^2/4 - (y - 2)^2/9 = 1$. The path is the right branch of this hyperbola, traversed upward.

24. Each hyperbola has $a = b = 1$. The asymptotes of $x^2 - y^2 = 1$ are $y = \pm\frac{b}{a}x = \pm x$ and the asymptotes of $y^2 - x^2 = 1$ are $y = \pm\frac{a}{b}x = \pm x$. See Figure 11.

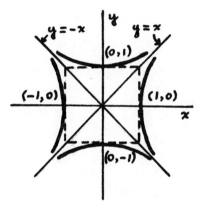

Figure 11

25. Choose a coordinate system so that the hyperbola is $x^2/a^2 - y^2/b^2 = 1$. The slopes of the asymptotes are b/a and $-b/a$; if the asymptotes are perpendicular, we have $-b^2/a^2 = -1$ or $a^2 = b^2$. Hence $c = \sqrt{a^2 + b^2} = a\sqrt{2}$ and the eccentricity is $e = c/a = a\sqrt{2}/a = \sqrt{2}$.

26. For an ellipse, the distance from center to directrix is $a/e > a$ because $0 < e < 1$. Since a is the distance from center to vertex, the directrices are outside the ellipse. For a hyperbola, $a/e < a$ because $e > 1$. Hence the directrices are between the vertices.

27. Since $d(P,F)/d(P,L) = e = 1/2$, the curve is an ellipse.

28.(a) When $k < 0$ the curve is an ellipse with vertical major diameter (because $1 - k > 1$). As $k \uparrow 0$ the ellipse becomes more like a circle. When $k = 0$ the curve <u>is</u> a circle.

   (b) When $0 < k < 1$ the curve is an ellipse with horizontal major diameter (because $0 < 1 - k < 1$). As $k \uparrow 1$ the curve becomes more like the line segment joining $(1,0)$ and $(-1,0)$.

(c) When k > 1 the curve is a hyperbola with horizontal transverse diameter (because 1 - k < 0).

29. Put the equation in the standard form $r = ep/(1 - e \cos \theta)$ by writing

$$r = \frac{16/5}{1 - (3/5) \cos \theta}$$

Then e = 3/5 and p = 16/3, so the curve is an ellipse with focus (0,0) and corresponding directrix x = -16/3. The vertices (corresponding to θ = 0 and θ = π) have rectangular coordinates (8,0) and (-2,0), so the center is (3,0) and a = 5. Hence c = 3 and the other focus is (6,0). The corresponding directrix is x = 3 + a^2/c = 34/3. The points (3,±4) in Figure 12 are obtained from b = $\sqrt{a^2 - c^2}$ = 4.

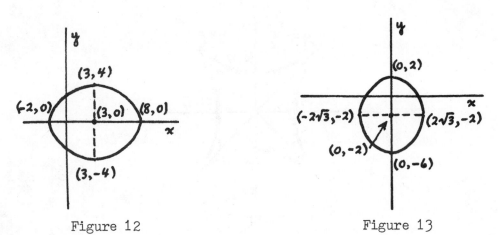

Figure 12   Figure 13

30. Put the equation in the standard form $r = ep/(1 + e \sin \theta)$ by writing

$$r = \frac{3}{1 + (1/2) \sin \theta}$$

Then e = 1/2 and p = 6, so the curve is an ellipse with focus (0,0) and corresponding directrix y = 6. The vertices (corresponding to θ = ±π/2) are (0,2) and (0,-6), so the center is (0,-2) and a = 4. Hence c = 2 and the other focus is (0,-4). The corresponding directrix is y = -2 - a^2/c = -10. The points (±2$\sqrt{3}$,-2) in Figure 13 are obtained from b = 2$\sqrt{3}$.

31. This is in the standard form $r = ep/(1 + e \sin \theta)$ with e = 2 and p = 3/2, so the curve is a hyperbola with focus (0,0) and corresponding directrix y = 3/2. The vertices (corresponding to θ = ±π/2) are (0,1) and (0,3), so the center is (0,2) and a = 1. Hence c = 2 and the other focus is (0,4). The corresponding directrix is y = 2 + a^2/c = 5/2. See Figure 14.

32. This is in the standard form $r = ep/(1 - e \cos \theta)$ with e = 2 and p = 3, so the curve is a hyperbola with focus (0,0) and corresponding directrix x = -3.

The vertices (corresponding to $\theta = 0$ and $\theta = \pi$) are $(-6,0)$ and $(-2,0)$, so the center is $(-4,0)$ and $a = 2$. Hence $c = 4$ and the other focus is $(-8,0)$. The corresponding directrix is $x = -4 - a^2/c = -5$. See Figure 15.

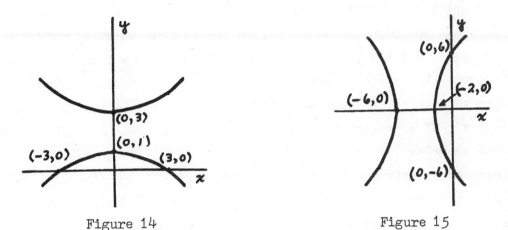

Figure 14   Figure 15

33. One focus is at the origin. The endpoints of the latus rectum through this focus correspond to $\theta = \pm\pi/2$ and are $(0,\pm ep)$ in rectangular coordinates. Hence the length of the latus rectum is $2ep$.

34. Choose the coordinate system so that the ellipse or hyperbola is $x^2/a^2 \pm y^2/b^2 = 1$. Then one focus is $(c,0)$. In the case of the ellipse we have $y = \pm\dfrac{b}{a}\sqrt{a^2 - x^2}$, so the y coordinates of the endpoints of the latus rectum through $(c,0)$ are $\pm\dfrac{b}{a}\sqrt{a^2 - c^2} = \pm\dfrac{b}{a}\cdot b = \pm b^2/a$ (because $b^2 = a^2 - c^2$). Hence the length of the latus rectum is $2b^2/a$. In the case of the hyperbola, $y = \pm\dfrac{b}{a}\sqrt{c^2 - a^2} = \pm b^2/a$ (because $b^2 = c^2 - a^2$). Again the length is $2b^2/a$.

35. Choose the coordinate system so that the ellipse is $x^2/a^2 + y^2/b^2 = 1$, that is, $b^2x^2 + a^2y^2 = a^2b^2$. Implicit differentiation yields $2b^2x + 2a^2yy' = 0$, or $y' = -b^2x/(a^2y)$. In Problem 34 we found the endpoints of the latus rectum through $(c,0)$ to be $(c,\pm b^2/a)$, so the tangents at these points have slopes $\mp b^2c/(ab^2) = \mp c/a$. Equations of the tangents are

$$y - \frac{b^2}{a} = \frac{-c}{a}(x - c) \quad \text{and} \quad y + \frac{b^2}{a} = \frac{c}{a}(x - c)$$

so the tangents intersect when

$$\frac{b^2}{a} - \frac{c}{a}(x - c) = \frac{-b^2}{a} + \frac{c}{a}(x - c) \implies \frac{2c}{a}(x - c) = \frac{2b^2}{a} \implies c(x - c) = b^2$$

$$\implies x = \frac{b^2 + c^2}{c} = \frac{a^2}{c}$$

Thus the tangents intersect on the directrix $x = a^2/c$ corresponding to the focus $(c,0)$. By symmetry we conclude that the tangents at the endpoints of the latus rectum through $(-c,0)$ intersect on the directrix $x = -a^2/c$.   A similar argument (with appropriate changes in sign) applies to the hyperbola.

36. See the solution of Problem 26, Sec. 3.4.

37. See the solution of Problem 27, Sec. 3.4.

38. The focus of the parabola is $(c,0)$, so the ellipse is $y^2/a^2 + x^2/c^2 = 1$. It is tempting to end the problem right here by using the formula $c^2 = a^2 - b^2 = a^2 - c^2$, from which $2c^2 = a^2$ and $e = c/a = 1/\sqrt{2}$.   The trouble is that c for the ellipse may not be the same as c for the parabola!   So let us be careful and call it c'.   The problem is to find a relation between c' and a so that we can compute $e = c'/a$.

Implicit differentiation in $y^2 = 4cx$ gives $2yy' = 4c$ or $y' = 2c/y$, while in $c^2y^2 + a^2x^2 = a^2c^2$ it gives $2c^2yy' + 2a^2x = 0$ or $y' = -a^2x/(c^2y)$.   Since the parabola and ellipse intersect at right angles, we have

$$\frac{2c}{y}\left(\frac{-a^2 x}{c^2 y}\right) = -1 \quad \text{or} \quad 2a^2 x = cy^2$$

at each point of intersection (x,y).   Since (x,y) satisfies $y^2 = 4cx$, we find $2a^2x = 4c^2x$, from which $a^2 = 2c^2$.   Hence the equation of the ellipse becomes $y^2/(2c^2) + x^2/c^2 = 1$ and we have $c'^2 = a^2 - b^2 = 2c^2 - c^2 = c^2$.   In other words, $c' = c$ after all, and $e = 1/\sqrt{2}$.   (This is a good example of a problem in which we can get the right answer by more luck than skill, making an assumption we have no right to make.)

39. The vertex and focus of the right-hand branch of the hyperbola are $(a,0)$ and $(c,0)$, respectively, where $c = \sqrt{a^2 + b^2}$.   The distance between them is $c - a$, so the parabola (which opens to the right) is $y^2 = 4(c - a)(x - a)$.

40.(a) The ratio is $\dfrac{(b^2/a^2)(x^2 - a^2)}{4(c - a)(x - a)} = \dfrac{b^2(x + a)}{4a^2(c - a)} = \dfrac{(c^2 - a^2)(x + a)}{4a^2(c - a)} = \dfrac{(c + a)(x + a)}{4a^2}$.   Since $e = c/a$, we divide numerator and denominator by a to obtain $\dfrac{(1 + e)(x + a)}{4a}$.

(b) Since $e > 1$ and $x > a$, the ratio is $\dfrac{(1 + e)(x + a)}{4a} > \dfrac{(2)(2a)}{4a} = 1$.   Hence each point (x,y) on the hyperbola is farther from the x axis than the corresponding point (with first coordinate x) on the parabola.   Thus the parabola is "inside" the hyperbola.

41. The vertex and focus of the right-hand half of the ellipse are $(a,0)$ and $(c,0)$, respectively, where $c = \sqrt{a^2 - b^2}$.   The distance between them is $a - c$, so the parabola (which opens to the left) is $y^2 = -4(a - c)(x - a) =$

$4(c-a)(x-a)$. The ratio of y^2 for the ellipse to y^2 for the parabola is

$$\frac{(b^2/a^2)(a^2-x^2)}{4(c-a)(x-a)} = \frac{-b^2(x+a)}{4a^2(c-a)} = \frac{(c^2-a^2)(x+a)}{4a^2(c-a)} = \frac{(c+a)(x+a)}{4a^2}$$

$$= \frac{(1+e)(x+a)}{4a}$$

Since $e < 1$ and $x < a$, we have $\dfrac{(1+e)(x+a)}{4a} < \dfrac{(2)(2a)}{4a} = 1$, so the parabola is outside the ellipse.

42. Choose the coordinate system so that the focus F is at the origin and the polar equation is $r = ep/(1 - e\cos\theta)$. If $P(r,\theta)$ is any point of the curve, then $d(P,F) = |r|$, which has its minimum value when $\cos\theta = -1$. This occurs when $\theta = \pi$, which places P at the nearest vertex, with polar coordinates $ep/(1+e)$ and π.

43. As in Problem 42, use the equation $r = ep/(1 - e\cos\theta)$, with the sun at the origin. The point nearest the sun has polar coordinates $(\frac{ep}{1+e}, \pi)$, so the distance is $r = ep/(1+e)$. Since $p = a/e - c = (a-ce)/e$, we have

$$r = \frac{a-ce}{1+e} = \frac{a-ae^2}{1+e} = a(1-e) \quad \text{(because } c = ae\text{)}$$

We are told that $e = 0.0167$ and $2a = 185.8$, so $r = 92.9(1 - 0.0167) \approx 91.35$ million miles. The point farthest from the sun is the other end of the major diameter, with polar coordinates $(\frac{ep}{1-e}, 0)$. The distance is

$$r = \frac{ep}{1-e} = \frac{a-ce}{1-e} = \frac{a-ae^2}{1-e} = a(1+e) = 92.9(1 + 0.0167) \approx 94.45$$

million miles. The average of these distances is $\frac{1}{2}[a(1-e) + a(1+e)] = a =$ 92.9 million miles.

44. Place the gun at $F_1 = (-c,0)$ and the target at $F_2 = (c,0)$, and suppose that the observer is at $P = (x,y)$. Let v be the speed of the bullet and r the speed of sound, where $r < v$. The time for the sound of the gun to reach P is $d(P,F_1)/r$, while the time for the bullet to reach the target and for the sound of its striking the target to reach P is $d(F_1,F_2)/v + d(P,F_2)/r = 2c/v + d(P,F_2)/r$. These times are equal, so

$$d(P,F_1)/r = 2c/v + d(P,F_2)/r$$

$$d(P,F_1) = 2cr/v + d(P,F_2) = 2a + d(P,F_2) \quad (a = cr/v < c)$$

$$\sqrt{(x+c)^2+y^2} = 2a + \sqrt{(x-c)^2+y^2}$$

$$(x+c)^2+y^2 = 4a^2 + 4a\sqrt{(x-c)^2+y^2} + (x-c)^2+y^2$$

$$cx - a^2 = a\sqrt{(x-c)^2+y^2}$$

$$c^2x^2 - 2a^2cx + a^4 = a^2[(x-c)^2+y^2]$$

195

$$(c^2 - a^2)x^2 - a^2y^2 = a^2(c^2 - a^2)$$

Since $a < c$, we can let $b = \sqrt{c^2 - a^2}$, so our equation becomes $b^2x^2 - a^2y^2 = a^2b^2$ or $x^2/a^2 - y^2/b^2 = 1$. Since the equation leading to this hyperbola was $d(P,F_1) = 2a + d(P,F_2) > d(P,F_2)$, we are dealing only with the right branch. (The left branch got included when we squared to eliminate the radicals.) Thus the observer is somewhere on the right branch of the hyperbola having the gun and target as foci.

Section 14.4   AREA AND LENGTH IN POLAR COORDINATES

1. $A = \frac{1}{2} \int_0^{2\pi} \theta^2 d\theta = \frac{4}{3}\pi^3$

2. $A = \frac{1}{2} \int_0^{2\pi} e^{2\theta} d\theta = \frac{1}{4}(e^{4\pi} - 1)$

3. $A = \frac{1}{2} \int_0^{2\pi} \frac{d\theta}{1 + \theta} = \frac{1}{2}\ell n(1 + 2\pi)$

4. $A = \frac{1}{2} \int_0^{\pi/4} 4\sec^2\theta \, d\theta = 2\tan\theta \Big|_0^{\pi/4} = 2$. Since $r = 2\sec\theta \iff r\cos\theta = 2$ $\iff x = 2$, the region is the right triangle with vertices $(0,0)$, $(2,0)$, and $(2,2)$. Hence $A = \frac{1}{2}(2)(2) = 2$.

5. The curve is a cardioid like that shown in the solution of Problem 27, Sec. 14.1. We have

$$A = \frac{1}{2} \int_0^{2\pi} 4(1 + \cos\theta)^2 d\theta = 2\int_0^{2\pi}(1 + 2\cos\theta + \cos^2\theta)d\theta$$

$$= 2\int_0^{2\pi}[1 + 2\cos\theta + \tfrac{1}{2}(1 + \cos 2\theta)]d\theta = 2\int_0^{2\pi}(\tfrac{3}{2} + 2\cos\theta + \tfrac{1}{2}\cos 2\theta)d\theta$$

$$= (3\theta + 4\sin\theta + \tfrac{1}{2}\sin 2\theta)\Big|_0^{2\pi} = 6\pi$$

This checks with $A = \frac{3}{2}\pi a^2$ in Example 1, because $a = 2$. (The cardioids are oriented differently, but that doesn't affect the area.)

6. The curve is a cardioid like that shown in the solution of Problem 29, Sec. 14.1. We have

$$A = \frac{1}{2} \int_0^{2\pi} 9(1 + \sin\theta)^2 d\theta = \frac{9}{2}\int_0^{2\pi}(1 + 2\sin\theta + \sin^2\theta)d\theta$$

$$= \frac{9}{2}\int_0^{2\pi}[1 + 2\sin\theta - \tfrac{1}{2}(1 - \cos 2\theta)]d\theta = \frac{9}{2}\int_0^{2\pi}(\tfrac{3}{2} + 2\sin\theta - \tfrac{1}{2}\cos 2\theta)d\theta$$

$$= (\tfrac{27}{4}\theta - 9\cos\theta - \tfrac{9}{8}\sin 2\theta)\Big|_0^{2\pi} = \frac{27}{2}\pi$$

This checks with $A = \frac{3}{2}\pi a^2$ in Example 1, because $a = 3$.

7. The graph is the circle with center $(0,1)$ and radius 1. It is generated as θ runs from 0 to π, so

$$A = \frac{1}{2}\int_0^\pi 4\sin^2\theta\, d\theta = 2\cdot\frac{1}{2}\cdot\pi = \pi \quad \begin{array}{l}\text{(See the reduction formula in Example 8,}\\ \text{Sec. 10.1.)}\end{array}$$

By geometry, $A = \pi\cdot 1^2 = \pi$.

8. The graph is shown in the solution of Problem 32, Sec. 14.1. One of the four loops is generated as θ runs from $-\pi/4$ to $\pi/4$, the upper half as θ runs from 0 to $\pi/4$. Hence

$$A = 8\cdot\frac{1}{2}\int_0^{\pi/4}\cos^2 2\theta\, d\theta = 2\int_0^{\pi/4}(1 + \cos 4\theta)d\theta = \left.(2\theta + \tfrac{1}{2}\sin 4\theta)\right|_0^{\pi/4} = \pi/2$$

9. The graph is shown in the solution of Problem 33, Sec. 14.1. One of the three loops is generated as θ runs from 0 to $\pi/3$, so

$$A = 3\cdot\frac{1}{2}\int_0^{\pi/3}\sin^2 3\theta\, d\theta = \frac{3}{4}\int_0^{\pi/3}(1 - \cos 6\theta)d\theta = \left.(\tfrac{3}{4}\theta - \tfrac{1}{8}\sin 6\theta)\right|_0^{\pi/3} = \pi/4$$

10. The graph is shown in the solution of Problem 41, Sec. 14.1. The first-quadrant portion is generated as θ runs from 0 to $\pi/4$, so

$$A = 4\cdot\frac{1}{2}\int_0^{\pi/4}\cos 2\theta\, d\theta = 1$$

11. Multiply by r^2 to obtain $r^4\cos^4\theta - 2r^2\cos^2\theta + r^2 = 0 \iff x^4 - 2x^2 + x^2 + y^2 = 0 \iff y^2 = x^2(1 - x^2) \iff y = \pm x\sqrt{1 - x^2}$. The graph is shown in Figure 1. In rectangular coordinates we have

$$A = 4\int_0^1 x\sqrt{1 - x^2}\, dx = \left.-2\cdot\frac{2}{3}(1 - x^2)^{3/2}\right|_0^1 = \frac{4}{3}$$

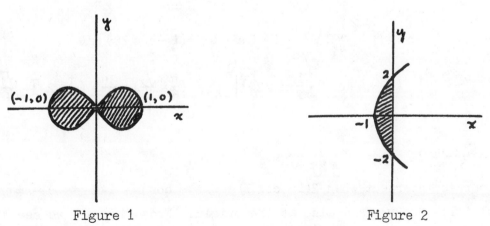

| Figure 1 | Figure 2 |

It is interesting to check by using polar coordinates. Since

$$r^2 = \frac{2\cos^2\theta - 1}{\cos^4\theta} = 2\sec^2\theta - \sec^4\theta$$

and since the first-quadrant portion of the graph is generated as θ runs from

0 to $\pi/4$, we have

$$A = 4 \cdot \frac{1}{2} \int_0^{\pi/4} (2 \sec^2 \theta - \sec^4 \theta) d\theta = 2 \int_0^{\pi/4} (2 - \sec^2 \theta) \sec^2 \theta \, d\theta$$

$$= 2 \int_0^{\pi/4} (1 - \tan^2 \theta) \sec^2 \theta \, d\theta = \left. \left(2 \tan \theta - \frac{2}{3} \tan^3 \theta \right) \right|_0^{\pi/4} = \frac{4}{3}$$

12. The region is shown in Figure 2. (The curve is a parabola and $\theta = \pi/2$ is the y axis.) The area is

$$A = 2 \cdot \frac{1}{2} \int_{\pi/2}^{\pi} \frac{4 \, d\theta}{(1 - \cos \theta)^2} = \int_{\pi/2}^{\pi} \csc^4 \tfrac{1}{2} \theta \, d\theta \quad [\text{because } \sin^2 \tfrac{1}{2} \theta = \tfrac{1}{2}(1 - \cos \theta)]$$

$$= \int_{\pi/2}^{\pi} (\cot^2 \tfrac{1}{2} \theta + 1) \csc^2 \tfrac{1}{2} \theta \, d\theta = \left. \left(-\frac{2}{3} \cot^3 \tfrac{1}{2} \theta - 2 \cot \tfrac{1}{2} \theta \right) \right|_{\pi/2}^{\pi} = \frac{8}{3}$$

13. The graphs are as shown in the solution of Problem 44, Sec. 14.1 (except that each circle has radius a instead of 1). Half the area is generated by the radial line from the origin to the circle $r = 2a \sin \theta$, $0 \le \theta \le \pi/4$. Hence

$$A = 2 \cdot \frac{1}{2} \int_0^{\pi/4} 4a^2 \sin^2 \theta \, d\theta = 2a^2 \int_0^{\pi/4} (1 - \cos 2\theta) d\theta = \left. 2a^2 \left(\theta - \frac{1}{2} \sin 2\theta \right) \right|_0^{\pi/4}$$

$$= 2a^2 \left(\frac{\pi}{4} - \frac{1}{2} \right) = \frac{1}{2} a^2 (\pi - 2)$$

14. The curves intersect when $2 \sin \theta = 2(1 - \sin \theta) \Longrightarrow \sin \theta = 1/2 \Longrightarrow \theta = \pi/6$ or $5\pi/6$ (plus multiples of 2π), and also at the origin. From Figure 3 we conclude that

$$\frac{1}{2} A = \frac{1}{2} \int_0^{\pi/6} 4 \sin^2 \theta \, d\theta + \frac{1}{2} \int_{\pi/6}^{\pi/2} 4(1 - \sin \theta)^2 d\theta$$

$$= \int_0^{\pi/6} (1 - \cos 2\theta) d\theta + 2 \int_{\pi/6}^{\pi/2} (1 - 2 \sin \theta + \sin^2 \theta) d\theta$$

$$= \left. \left(\theta - \frac{1}{2} \sin 2\theta \right) \right|_0^{\pi/6} + 2 \int_{\pi/6}^{\pi/2} \left[1 - 2 \sin \theta + \frac{1}{2}(1 - \cos 2\theta) \right] d\theta$$

$$= \left(\frac{\pi}{6} - \frac{\sqrt{3}}{4} \right) + \left. \left(3\theta + 4 \cos \theta - \frac{1}{2} \sin 2\theta \right) \right|_{\pi/6}^{\pi/2} = \left(\frac{\pi}{6} - \frac{\sqrt{3}}{4} \right) + \frac{3\pi}{2} - \left(\frac{\pi}{2} + 2\sqrt{3} - \frac{\sqrt{3}}{4} \right)$$

$$= \frac{7\pi}{6} - 2\sqrt{3}$$

Hence $A = \frac{7\pi}{3} - 4\sqrt{3}$.

15. The curves intersect when $2(1 + \cos \theta) = 3 \Longrightarrow \cos \theta = 1/2 \Longrightarrow \theta = \pm \pi/3$ (plus multiples of 2π), and also at the origin. From Figure 4 we see that A_1 is the area of a circular sector of radius 3 and central angle $\pi/3$, so

$$A_1 = \frac{1}{2}(3^2) \left(\frac{\pi}{3} \right) = \frac{3\pi}{2}$$

(See Problem 5, Sec. 2.3.) Also,

$$A_2 = \frac{1}{2}\int_{\pi/3}^{\pi} 4(1 + \cos\theta)^2 d\theta = 2\int_{\pi/3}^{\pi}(1 + 2\cos\theta + \cos^2\theta)d\theta$$

$$= 2\int_{\pi/3}^{\pi}[1 + 2\cos\theta + \frac{1}{2}(1 + \cos 2\theta)]d\theta = (3\theta + 4\sin\theta + \frac{1}{2}\sin 2\theta)\Big|_{\pi/3}^{\pi}$$

$$= 3\pi - (\pi + 2\sqrt{3} + \sqrt{3}/4) = 2\pi - 9\sqrt{3}/4$$

Hence $A = 2(A_1 + A_2) = 7\pi - 9\sqrt{3}/2$.

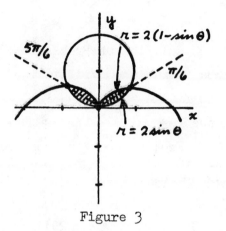

Figure 3

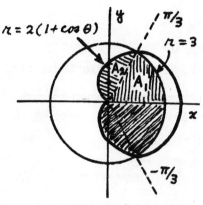

Figure 4

16. The lower half of the loop (Figure 5) is generated as θ runs from $2\pi/3$ to π. Hence

$$A = 2\cdot\frac{1}{2}\int_{2\pi/3}^{\pi}(1 + 2\cos\theta)^2 d\theta = \int_{2\pi/3}^{\pi}(1 + 4\cos\theta + 4\cos^2\theta)d\theta$$

$$= \int_{2\pi/3}^{\pi}[1 + 4\cos\theta + 2(1 + \cos 2\theta)]d\theta = (3\theta + 4\sin\theta + \sin 2\theta)\Big|_{2\pi/3}^{\pi}$$

$$= 3\pi - (2\pi + 2\sqrt{3} - \sqrt{3}/2) = \pi - 3\sqrt{3}/2$$

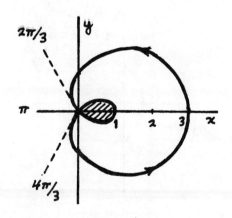

Figure 5

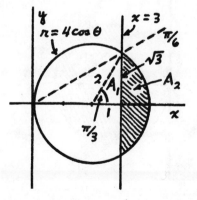

Figure 6

17. The curves intersect when $4\cos\theta = 3\sec\theta \Longrightarrow \cos^2\theta = 3/4 \Longrightarrow \cos\theta = \pm\sqrt{3}/2 \Longrightarrow \theta = \pm\pi/6$ (plus multiples of 2π). ($\theta = \pm 5\pi/6$ yield the same points.) The easiest procedure is ordinary geometry. From Figure 6 we

have $A_1 = \frac{1}{2}(1)(\sqrt{3}) = \frac{1}{2}\sqrt{3}$ and $A_1 + A_2 = \frac{1}{2}(2^2)(\frac{\pi}{3}) = \frac{2}{3}\pi$. Hence $A_2 = \frac{2}{3}\pi - \frac{1}{2}\sqrt{3}$ and

$A = 2A_2 = \frac{4}{3}\pi - \sqrt{3}$. Checking by integration, we have

$$\frac{1}{2}A = \frac{1}{2}\int_0^{\pi/6} 16\cos^2\theta\,d\theta - \frac{1}{2}\int_0^{\pi/6} 9\sec^2\theta\,d\theta = 4\int_0^{\pi/6}(1+\cos 2\theta)d\theta - \frac{9}{2}\tan\theta\Big|_0^{\pi/6}$$

$$= (4\theta + 2\sin 2\theta)\Big|_0^{\pi/6} - \frac{3}{2}\sqrt{3} = \frac{2}{3}\pi + \sqrt{3} - \frac{3}{2}\sqrt{3} = \frac{2}{3}\pi - \frac{1}{2}\sqrt{3}$$

Hence $A = \frac{4}{3}\pi - \sqrt{3}$.

18. The circle is inside the cardioid (as in the solution of Problem 45, Sec. 14.1). By Example 1 (with a = 1) the area inside the cardioid is $3\pi/2$. Subtract the area of the circle (which is π) to find $A = \pi/2$.

19. The curves intersect when $2(1+\cos\theta) = 6\cos\theta \Rightarrow \cos\theta = 1/2 \Rightarrow \theta = \pm\pi/3$ (plus multiples of 2π), and also at the origin. From Figure 7 we conclude that

$$A_1 = \frac{1}{2}\int_0^{\pi/3} 4(1+\cos\theta)^2 d\theta = 2\int_0^{\pi/3}(1+2\cos\theta+\cos^2\theta)d\theta$$

$$= 2\int_0^{\pi/3}[1+2\cos\theta+\tfrac{1}{2}(1+\cos 2\theta)]d\theta = (3\theta + 4\sin\theta + \tfrac{1}{2}\sin 2\theta)\Big|_0^{\pi/3}$$

$$= \pi + 2\sqrt{3} + \sqrt{3}/4 = \pi + 9\sqrt{3}/4$$

$$A_1 + A_2 = \frac{1}{2}\int_0^{\pi/3} 36\cos^2\theta\,d\theta = 9\int_0^{\pi/3}(1+\cos 2\theta)d\theta = (9\theta + \frac{9}{2}\sin 2\theta)\Big|_0^{\pi/3}$$

$$= 3\pi + 9\sqrt{3}/4$$

Hence $A_2 = (3\pi + 9\sqrt{3}/4) - (\pi + 9\sqrt{3}/4) = 2\pi$ and $A = 2A_2 = 4\pi$.

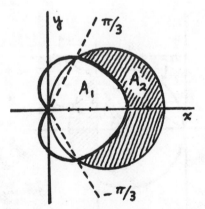

Figure 7

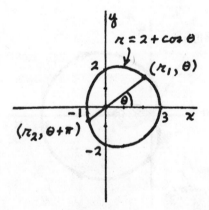

Figure 8

20. (a) From Figure 8 we conclude that the segment has length

$$r_1 + r_2 = 2 + \cos\theta + 2 + \cos(\theta + \pi) = 4 + \cos\theta - \cos\theta = 4$$

(b) $A = \frac{1}{2}\int_0^{2\pi}(2+\cos\theta)^2 d\theta = \frac{1}{2}\int_0^{2\pi}(4 + 4\cos\theta + \cos^2\theta)d\theta$

$$= \frac{1}{2}\int_0^{2\pi}[4+4\cos\theta+\tfrac{1}{2}(1+\cos 2\theta)]\,d\theta = 9\pi/2$$

The area of the circle, on the other hand, is $\pi(2^2) = 4\pi$.

(c) The answer is evidently "No." It sounds like a reasonable proposition, but it is false.

21. Since $dr/d\theta = 6\cos\theta$, we have $r^2 + (dr/d\theta)^2 = 36\sin^2\theta + 36\cos^2\theta = 36$. The curve is generated as θ runs from 0 to π (not 0 to 2π), so

$$s = \int_0^{\pi} 6\,d\theta = 6\pi$$

By geometry the length is the circumference of a circle of radius 3, namely $2\pi(3) = 6\pi$.

22. Since $r' = 2\sec\theta\tan\theta$, $r^2 + r'^2 = 4\sec^2\theta + 4\sec^2\theta\tan^2\theta = 4\sec^2\theta(1 + \tan^2\theta)$ $= 4\sec^4\theta$. Hence

$$s = \int_0^{\pi/4} 2\sec^2\theta\,d\theta = 2\tan\theta\Big|_0^{\pi/4} = 2$$

Since $r = 2\sec\theta \iff r\cos\theta = 2 \iff x = 2$, the curve is the segment of the vertical line $x = 2$ between $(2,0)$ and $(2,2)$, which has length 2.

23. Since $r' = e^\theta$, $r^2 + r'^2 = e^{2\theta} + e^{2\theta} = 2e^{2\theta}$ and

$$s = \int_0^{2\pi} \sqrt{2}\,e^\theta\,d\theta = \sqrt{2}\,e^\theta\Big|_0^{2\pi} = \sqrt{2}(e^{2\pi} - 1)$$

24. Since $r' = 2\theta$, $r^2 + r'^2 = \theta^4 + 4\theta^2 = \theta^2(\theta^2 + 4)$ and

$$s = \int_0^{2\pi} \theta\sqrt{\theta^2 + 4}\,d\theta = \frac{1}{2}\cdot\frac{2}{3}(\theta^2 + 4)^{3/2}\Big|_0^{2\pi} = \frac{1}{3}(4\pi^2 + 4)^{3/2} - \frac{1}{3}(8)$$

$$= \frac{8}{3}[(\pi^2 + 1)^{3/2} - 1]$$

25. Since $r' = -\cos\theta$, $r^2 + r'^2 = (1 - \sin\theta)^2 + \cos^2\theta = 1 - 2\sin\theta + \sin^2\theta + \cos^2\theta$ $= 2(1 - \sin\theta)$. The square root of this is hard to integrate as it stands, so we write $2(1 - \sin\theta) = \dfrac{2(1 - \sin\theta)(1 + \sin\theta)}{1 + \sin\theta} = \dfrac{2\cos^2\theta}{1 + \sin\theta}$. If we choose the domain of integration so that $\cos\theta \geq 0$, then

$$\int \sqrt{2(1 - \sin\theta)}\,d\theta = \sqrt{2}\int \frac{\cos\theta\,d\theta}{\sqrt{1 + \sin\theta}} = \sqrt{2}\int u^{-1/2}\,du \quad (u = 1 + \sin\theta,\ du = \cos\theta\,d\theta)$$

$$= 2\sqrt{2}\,u^{1/2} + C = 2\sqrt{2(1 + \sin\theta)} + C$$

The curve is a cardioid like that shown in the solution of Problem 28, Sec. 14.1. To avoid the cusp and to keep $\cos\theta \geq 0$, we integrate from $-\pi/2$ to $\pi/2$ (which generates the right-hand part of the curve):

$$s = 2 \int_{-\pi/2}^{\pi/2} \sqrt{2(1 - \sin \theta)} \, d\theta = 4\sqrt{2(1 + \sin \theta)} \Big|_{-\pi/2}^{\pi/2} = 8$$

We can check by Example 5 (with a = 1), obtaining s = 8a = 8. (The cardioids are differently oriented, but that doesn't affect the length.)

26. Use Example 5 with a = 2 to obtain s = 8a = 16. To do the problem independently, we compute $r' = -2 \sin \theta$ and $r^2 + r'^2 = 4(1 + \cos \theta)^2 + 4 \sin^2 \theta = 4(1 + 2 \cos \theta + \cos^2 \theta) + 4 \sin^2 \theta = 8(1 + \cos \theta) = 16 \cos^2 \frac{1}{2}\theta$. Then (integrating from cusp back to cusp) we have

$$s = \int_{-\pi}^{\pi} 4 \cos \tfrac{1}{2}\theta \, d\theta \quad (\cos \tfrac{1}{2}\theta \geq 0 \text{ because } -\pi/2 \leq \tfrac{1}{2}\theta \leq \pi/2)$$

$$= 8 \sin \tfrac{1}{2}\theta \Big|_{-\pi}^{\pi} = 8(1 + 1) = 16$$

27. Since $r' = -e^{-\theta}$, $r^2 + r'^2 = e^{-2\theta} + e^{-2\theta} = 2e^{-2\theta}$ and

$$s = \int_0^\infty \sqrt{2} \, e^{-\theta} \, d\theta = \lim_{b \to \infty} \sqrt{2}(1 - e^{-b}) = \sqrt{2}$$

28. The spiral is shown in the solution of Problem 39, Sec. 14.1. It hits the unit circle (r = 1) when $1/\theta = 1$, or $\theta = 1$. Since $r' = -1/\theta^2$, $r^2 + r'^2 = 1/\theta^2 + 1/\theta^4 = (\theta^2 + 1)/\theta^4$ and we have

$$s = \int_1^\infty \frac{\sqrt{\theta^2 + 1}}{\theta^2} \, d\theta \quad \text{(provided that the integral exists)}.$$

A way to find the integral is shown in the solution of Problem 12, Sec. 10.2. It is easier, however, to observe that

$$\frac{\sqrt{\theta^2 + 1}}{\theta^2} > \frac{\sqrt{\theta^2}}{\theta^2} = \frac{1}{\theta} \quad (\text{if } \theta > 0)$$

Hence $\int_1^b \frac{\sqrt{\theta^2 + 1}}{\theta^2} \, d\theta > \int_1^b \frac{d\theta}{\theta} = \ell n \, b \to \infty$ as $b \to \infty$. Thus the integral diverges, which means that the part of the curve inside the unit circle does not have finite length.

Section 14.5   VECTORS IN THE PLANE

Note: In this section and throughout the rest of the solutions manual the typed symbol $\vec{x}$ means boldface x.

1. $\vec{x}_1 + \vec{x}_2 = (6,-8) + (-9,12) = (-3,4)$

2. $\vec{x}_1 - \vec{x}_2 = (6,-8) - (-9,12) = (21,-20)$

3. $3\vec{x}_1 + 2\vec{x}_2 = 3(6,-8) + 2(-9,12) = (18,-24) + (-18,24) = (0,0)$

4. $|\vec{x}_1| = \sqrt{36+64} = 10$ and $|\vec{x}_2| = \sqrt{81+144} = 15$.

5. $\vec{x}_1 \cdot \vec{x}_2 = (6)(-9) + (-8)(12) = -150$

6. $\cos\theta = \dfrac{\vec{x}_1 \cdot \vec{x}_2}{|\vec{x}_1||\vec{x}_2|} = \dfrac{-150}{(10)(15)} = -1$, so $\theta = \pi$.

7. $\vec{P_1 P_2} = (6-3, -5-4) = (3, -9)$

8. $\vec{P_2 P_1} = (3-6, 4+5) = (-3, 9) = -\vec{P_1 P_2}$

9. $\vec{P_1 P_2} + \vec{P_2 P_1} = \vec{P_1 P_1} = \vec{0}$. Check by writing $(3,-9) + (-3,9) = (0,0)$.

10. $|\vec{P_1 P_2}| = \sqrt{9+81} = 3\sqrt{10}$

11. $\cos\theta = \dfrac{\vec{P_1 P_2} \cdot \vec{i}}{|\vec{P_1 P_2}||\vec{i}|} = \dfrac{(3)(1) + (-9)(0)}{(3\sqrt{10})(1)} = 1/\sqrt{10}$

12. $\cos\theta = \dfrac{\vec{P_1 P_2} \cdot \vec{j}}{|\vec{P_1 P_2}||\vec{j}|} = \dfrac{(3)(0) + (-9)(1)}{(3\sqrt{10})(1)} = -3/\sqrt{10}$

13. If $P = (x,y)$ is the point, then $\vec{P_1 P} = \frac{2}{3}(\vec{P_1 P_2})$, that is,

$$(x-3, y-4) = \frac{2}{3}(3,-9) = (2,-6)$$

Hence $x - 3 = 2$, $y - 4 = -6$, and $P = (5,-2)$.

14. Since $(3,0) = 3\vec{i}$, the answer is $\vec{i}$.

15. The answer is $-\vec{j}$.

16. The length of $(4,-3)$ is 5, so the required unit vector is $\vec{u} = \frac{1}{5}(4,-3) = (4/5, -3/5)$.

17. The length of $5\vec{i} - 12\vec{j} = (5,-12)$ is 13, so $\vec{u} = \frac{1}{13}(5,-12) = (\frac{5}{13}, -\frac{12}{13}) = \frac{5}{13}\vec{i} - \frac{12}{13}\vec{j}$.

18. Since $(\pi,\pi) = \pi(1,1)$, a vector in the same direction is $(1,1)$, with length $\sqrt{2}$. Hence $\vec{u} = \frac{1}{\sqrt{2}}(1,1)$.

19. $\vec{u}_1 \cdot \vec{u}_2 = -\sqrt{3}/4 + \sqrt{3}/4 = 0$, so the vectors are perpendicular. Moreover, $|\vec{u}_1|^2 = 1/4 + 3/4 = 1$ and $|\vec{u}_2|^2 = 3/4 + 1/4 = 1$, so each has unit length.

20. Let $\vec{u} = (u,v)$ be a unit vector perpendicular to $\vec{x} = (2,1)$. Then $u^2 + v^2 = 1$ and $\vec{u} \cdot \vec{x} = 2u + v = 0$. Put $v = -2u$ into $u^2 + v^2 = 1$ to obtain $u^2 + 4u^2 = 1 \iff 5u^2 = 1 \iff u = \pm 1/\sqrt{5}$. Then $v = \mp 2/\sqrt{5}$, so $\vec{u} = \frac{1}{\sqrt{5}}(1,-2)$ or $\vec{u} = \frac{1}{\sqrt{5}}(-1,2)$.

Two answers (opposite in direction) are what a picture leads us to expect.

21. $\vec{a} \cdot \vec{x} = 0 \iff ax + by = 0$, so the path is the straight line $ax + by = 0$.

Since $\vec{x}$ lies in the line, $\vec{a}$ is perpendicular to the line.

22. Let $P_0 = (x_0, y_0)$ be any point of the line and $P = (x, y)$ any other point. Then the vector $\overrightarrow{P_0 P} = (x - x_0, y - y_0)$ is parallel to the line. Since

$$(a, b) \cdot \overrightarrow{P_0 P} = a(x - x_0) + b(y - y_0) = (ax + by) - (ax_0 + by_0)$$
$$= (ax + by + c) - (ax_0 + by_0 + c) = 0 - 0 = 0$$

(a, b) is perpendicular to $\overrightarrow{P_0 P}$, hence perpendicular to the line.

23. From Figure 1 we have

$$\cos \alpha = \frac{\overrightarrow{AB} \cdot \overrightarrow{AC}}{|\overrightarrow{AB}| \, |\overrightarrow{AC}|} = \frac{(3, 3) \cdot (2, 0)}{(3\sqrt{2})(2)} = 1/\sqrt{2}, \text{ so } \alpha = 45°.$$

Similarly, $\cos \beta = \dfrac{\overrightarrow{BA} \cdot \overrightarrow{BC}}{|\overrightarrow{BA}| \, |\overrightarrow{BC}|} = \dfrac{(-3, -3) \cdot (-1, -3)}{(3\sqrt{2})(\sqrt{10})} = 4/\sqrt{20} = 2/\sqrt{5},$ so $\beta = $

$\cos^{-1}(2/\sqrt{5}) \approx 26.6°.$ Finally,

$$\cos \gamma = \frac{\overrightarrow{CA} \cdot \overrightarrow{CB}}{|\overrightarrow{CA}| \, |\overrightarrow{CB}|} = \frac{(-2, 0) \cdot (1, 3)}{(2)(\sqrt{10})} = -1/\sqrt{10}$$

so $\gamma = \cos^{-1}(-1/\sqrt{10}) \approx 108.4°.$ (We can also find γ from $\alpha + \beta + \gamma = 180°$.)

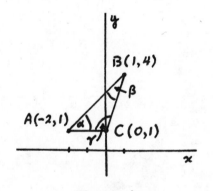

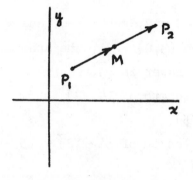

Figure 1   Figure 2

24. (a) It is clear from Figure 2 that $\overrightarrow{P_1 M}$ and $\overrightarrow{MP_2}$ have the same length and direction, so they are equal.

(b) $\overrightarrow{P_1 M} = \overrightarrow{MP_2} \implies (x - x_1, y - y_1) = (x_2 - x, y_2 - y) \implies x - x_1 = x_2 - x$ and $y - y_1 = y_2 - y \implies x = \frac{1}{2}(x_1 + x_2)$ and $y = \frac{1}{2}(y_1 + y_2)$.

25. Choose the coordinate system as shown in Figure 3. Then

$$\overrightarrow{AC} \cdot \overrightarrow{BC} = (x + a, y) \cdot (x - a, y) = x^2 - a^2 + y^2 = 0$$

(because $x^2 + y^2 = a^2$). Hence $\overrightarrow{AC}$ and $\overrightarrow{BC}$ are perpendicular and angle ACB is a right angle.

26. (a) See Figure 4. Showing that $\overrightarrow{M_1 M_2} = \frac{1}{2} \overrightarrow{P_1 P_3}$ will accomplish two things simultaneously; it will prove that $\overrightarrow{M_1 M_2}$ and $\overrightarrow{P_1 P_3}$ are parallel and it will show

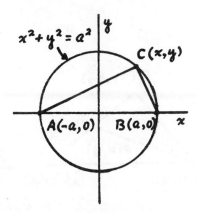

Figure 3   Figure 4

that the length of $\overrightarrow{M_1 M_2}$ is half the length of $\overrightarrow{P_1 P_3}$. To confirm the given
equation, write $\overrightarrow{P_1 M_1} + \overrightarrow{M_1 M_2} = \overrightarrow{P_1 M_2}$ (true for any points). Then the equation
reads $\overrightarrow{P_1 M_2} + \overrightarrow{M_2 P_3} = \overrightarrow{P_1 P_3}$ (also true for any points).

   (b) These equations follow from the fact that M_1 is the midpoint of $P_1 P_2$
and M_2 is the midpoint of $P_2 P_3$. Substituting in part (a), we have

$$\tfrac{1}{2}\overrightarrow{P_1 P_2} + \overrightarrow{M_1 M_2} + \tfrac{1}{2}\overrightarrow{P_2 P_3} = \overrightarrow{P_1 P_3} \implies \overrightarrow{M_1 M_2} + \tfrac{1}{2}(\overrightarrow{P_1 P_2} + \overrightarrow{P_2 P_3}) = \overrightarrow{P_1 P_3}$$

$$\implies \overrightarrow{M_1 M_2} + \tfrac{1}{2}\overrightarrow{P_1 P_3} = \overrightarrow{P_1 P_3} \implies \overrightarrow{M_1 M_2} = \tfrac{1}{2}\overrightarrow{P_1 P_3}$$

27. The problem (see Figure 5) is to prove that $\overrightarrow{M_1 M_2} = \overrightarrow{M_4 M_3}$ and $\overrightarrow{M_2 M_3} = \overrightarrow{M_1 M_4}$.
We begin by using the general principle $\overrightarrow{P_1 P_2} = \overrightarrow{P_1 P_3} + \overrightarrow{P_3 P_2}$ repeatedly to write

$$\overrightarrow{M_1 P_2} + \overrightarrow{P_2 M_2} + \overrightarrow{M_2 P_3} + \overrightarrow{P_3 M_3} + \overrightarrow{M_3 P_4} + \overrightarrow{P_4 M_4} + \overrightarrow{M_4 P_1} + \overrightarrow{P_1 M_1} = \vec{0}$$

(This does not depend on the figure, but is simply an identity. Recombining
the terms two at a time, you can see that it says nothing more than $\overrightarrow{M_1 M_1} = \vec{0}$.)
Now use the midpoint properties of M_1, M_2, M_3, M_4 to obtain

$$\overrightarrow{P_1 M_1} = \overrightarrow{M_1 P_2}, \;\; \overrightarrow{M_2 P_3} = \overrightarrow{P_2 M_2}, \;\; \overrightarrow{P_3 M_3} = \overrightarrow{M_3 P_4}, \;\; \overrightarrow{M_4 P_1} = \overrightarrow{P_4 M_4}$$

Substituting in the above identity, we have

$$2\overrightarrow{M_1 P_2} + 2\overrightarrow{P_2 M_2} + 2\overrightarrow{M_3 P_4} + 2\overrightarrow{P_4 M_4} = \vec{0} \implies (\overrightarrow{M_1 P_2} + \overrightarrow{P_2 M_2}) + (\overrightarrow{M_3 P_4} + \overrightarrow{P_4 M_4}) = \vec{0}$$

$$\implies \overrightarrow{M_1 M_2} + \overrightarrow{M_3 M_4} = \vec{0} \implies \overrightarrow{M_1 M_2} = -\overrightarrow{M_3 M_4} = \overrightarrow{M_4 M_3}$$

This proves the first of our desired equations; the other one is equivalent.

28.(a) From Figure 6 we have $M = (\tfrac{1}{2}(x_2 + x_3), \tfrac{1}{2}(y_2 + y_3))$. Since $\overrightarrow{P_1 P} = \tfrac{2}{3}\overrightarrow{P_1 M}$, we
have $(x - x_1, y - y_1) = \tfrac{2}{3}(\tfrac{1}{2}(x_2 + x_3) - x_1, \tfrac{1}{2}(y_2 + y_3) - y_1)$

$$= \tfrac{1}{3}(x_2 + x_3 - 2x_1, y_2 + y_3 - 2y_1)$$

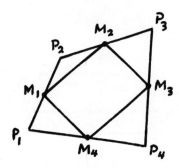

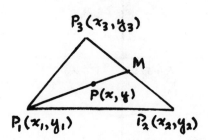

Figure 5   Figure 6

Hence $x - x_1 = \frac{1}{3}(x_2 + x_3 - 2x_1)$ and $y - y_1 = \frac{1}{3}(y_2 + y_3 - 2y_1)$, from which

$$x = \frac{1}{3}(x_1 + x_2 + x_3) \text{ and } y = \frac{1}{3}(y_1 + y_2 + y_3)$$

(b) If a different vertex had been used in part (a), the result would have been the same (because of the symmetry in the formulas for x and y). Hence each median passes through P.

29. Using Properties 1 through 4 of the dot product stated in the text (but omitting a few nit-picking steps), we have

$$(\vec{x}_1 + \vec{x}_2) \cdot (\vec{x}_1 - \vec{x}_2) = (\vec{x}_1 + \vec{x}_2) \cdot \vec{x}_1 - (\vec{x}_1 + \vec{x}_2) \cdot \vec{x}_2$$

$$= \vec{x}_1 \cdot \vec{x}_1 + \vec{x}_2 \cdot \vec{x}_1 - \vec{x}_1 \cdot \vec{x}_2 - \vec{x}_2 \cdot \vec{x}_2 = |\vec{x}_1|^2 - |\vec{x}_2|^2$$

If $\vec{x}_1$ and $\vec{x}_2$ are sides of a square (Figure 7), the right side of the above equation is 0. Hence $\vec{x}_1 + \vec{x}_2$ and $\vec{x}_1 - \vec{x}_2$ (the diagonals of the square) are perpendicular because their dot product is 0.

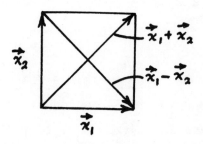

Figure 7

30. If $\vec{x} = (x,y)$, then $a(b\vec{x}) = a(bx, by) = ab(x,y) = (ab)\vec{x}$.

31. If $\vec{x}_1 = (x_1, y_1)$ and $\vec{x}_2 = (x_2, y_2)$, then

$$c(\vec{x}_1 + \vec{x}_2) = c(x_1 + x_2, y_1 + y_2) = (cx_1 + cx_2, cy_1 + cy_2) = (cx_1, cy_1) + (cx_2, cy_2)$$

$$= c(x_1, y_1) + c(x_2, y_2) = c\vec{x}_1 + c\vec{x}_2$$

32. If $\vec{x} = (x, y)$, then $c\vec{x} = \vec{0} \iff (cx, cy) = (0, 0) \iff cx = 0$ and $cy = 0 \iff$
$c = 0$ or $x = y = 0 \iff c = 0$ or $\vec{x} = \vec{0}$.

33. If $\vec{x} = (x, y)$, then $\vec{x} \cdot \vec{x} = (x, y) \cdot (x, y) = x^2 + y^2 = |\vec{x}|^2$.

34. If $\vec{x} = (x, y)$, then $\vec{x} \cdot \vec{x} = 0 \iff |\vec{x}|^2 = 0 \iff x^2 + y^2 = 0 \iff x = y = 0$
$\iff \vec{x} = \vec{0}$.

35. If $\vec{x}_1 = (x_1, y_1)$ and $\vec{x}_2 = (x_2, y_2)$, then $\vec{x}_1 \cdot \vec{x}_2 = x_1 x_2 + y_1 y_2$. If $\vec{x}_1 = \vec{0}$ or
$\vec{x}_2 = \vec{0}$, this product is 0, so the implication from right to left is correct.
The implication from left to right is false; for example, $\vec{i} \cdot \vec{j} = 0$ but $\vec{i} \neq \vec{0}$
and $\vec{j} \neq \vec{0}$.

36. If $\vec{x}_1 = (x_1, y_1)$ and $\vec{x}_2 = (x_2, y_2)$, then $\vec{x}_1 \cdot \vec{x}_2 = x_1 x_2 + y_1 y_2 = x_2 x_1 + y_2 y_1 =$
$\vec{x}_2 \cdot \vec{x}_1$.

37. If $\vec{x}_1 = (x_1, y_1)$, $\vec{x}_2 = (x_2, y_2)$, and $\vec{x}_3 = (x_3, y_3)$, then

$$\vec{x}_1 \cdot (\vec{x}_2 + \vec{x}_3) = (x_1, y_1) \cdot (x_2 + x_3, y_2 + y_3) = x_1(x_2 + x_3) + y_1(y_2 + y_3)$$

$$= (x_1 x_2 + x_1 x_3) + (y_1 y_2 + y_1 y_3) = (x_1 x_2 + y_1 y_2) + (x_1 x_3 + y_1 y_3)$$

$$= \vec{x}_1 \cdot \vec{x}_2 + \vec{x}_1 \cdot \vec{x}_3$$

38. If $\vec{x}_1 = (x_1, y_1)$ and $\vec{x}_2 = (x_2, y_2)$, then

$$(c\vec{x}_1) \cdot \vec{x}_2 = (cx_1, cy_1) \cdot (x_2, y_2) = cx_1 x_2 + cy_1 y_2 = c(x_1 x_2 + y_1 y_2) = c(\vec{x}_1 \cdot \vec{x}_2)$$

Similarly, $\vec{x}_1 \cdot (c\vec{x}_2) = c(\vec{x}_1 \cdot \vec{x}_2)$.

39. Neither side of the "equation" makes sense. The left side, for example,
is the dot product of the <u>number</u> $\vec{x}_1 \cdot \vec{x}_2$ and the <u>vector</u> $\vec{x}_3$, which is undefined.

40. This is geometrically apparent. Our technical definition of "same
direction," however, is that the angle between (nonzero) vectors is $\theta = 0$,
whereas "opposite directions" means $\theta = \pi$. Hence assume that $\vec{x} \neq \vec{0}$ and $c \neq 0$.
Then the angle between $\vec{x}$ and $c\vec{x}$ satisfies

$$\cos \theta = \frac{\vec{x} \cdot (c\vec{x})}{|\vec{x}| \, |c\vec{x}|} = \frac{c(\vec{x} \cdot \vec{x})}{|c| \, |\vec{x}| \, |\vec{x}|} = \frac{c}{|c|}$$

This is ± 1 (that is, $\theta = 0$ or $\theta = \pi$) depending on whether $c > 0$ or $c < 0$.
The only case left out by this argument is $\vec{x} = \vec{0}$ or $c = 0$. But then $\vec{x}$ or $c\vec{x}$
is $\vec{0}$ and the statements are trivial (because we have adopted the convention

that $\vec{0}$ has any direction).

41.(a) The right side reduces to $1 - \dfrac{(\vec{x}_1 \cdot \vec{x}_2)^2}{|\vec{x}_1|^2 |\vec{x}_2|^2} = 1 - \cos^2\theta = \sin^2\theta$.

(b) "Parallel" means $\theta = 0$ or $\theta = \pi$, so

$\vec{x}_1$ and $\vec{x}_2$ are parallel $\iff$ $\sin\theta = 0$ $\iff$ $\sin^2\theta = 0$

$\iff |\vec{x}_1|^2 |\vec{x}_2|^2 = (\vec{x}_1 \cdot \vec{x}_2)^2$ (from part (a))

$\iff |\vec{x}_1 \cdot \vec{x}_2| = |\vec{x}_1| |\vec{x}_2|$

42. If $\vec{x}_1$ or $\vec{x}_2$ is $\vec{0}$, the "inequality" reduces to $0 = 0$. If $\vec{x}_1 \neq \vec{0}$ and $\vec{x}_2 \neq \vec{0}$, then

$|\vec{x}_1 \cdot \vec{x}_2| = |\vec{x}_1| |\vec{x}_2| |\cos\theta|$ (where θ is the angle between $\vec{x}_1$ and $\vec{x}_2$)

$\leq |\vec{x}_1| |\vec{x}_2|$ (because $|\cos\theta| \leq 1$)

43. Geometrically (Figure 8) the inequality says that the sum of the lengths of two sides of a triangle is never less than the length of the third side. To prove it, use the hint to write

$$|\vec{x}_1 + \vec{x}_2|^2 = (\vec{x}_1 + \vec{x}_2) \cdot (\vec{x}_1 + \vec{x}_2) = \vec{x}_1 \cdot \vec{x}_1 + 2\vec{x}_1 \cdot \vec{x}_2 + \vec{x}_2 \cdot \vec{x}_2$$

$$= |\vec{x}_1|^2 + 2\vec{x}_1 \cdot \vec{x}_2 + |\vec{x}_2|^2$$

Since $\vec{x}_1 \cdot \vec{x}_2 \leq |\vec{x}_1 \cdot \vec{x}_2| \leq |\vec{x}_1| |\vec{x}_2|$ (by the Cauchy-Schwarz Inequality), we have

$$|\vec{x}_1 + \vec{x}_2|^2 \leq |\vec{x}_1|^2 + 2|\vec{x}_1| |\vec{x}_2| + |\vec{x}_2|^2 = (|\vec{x}_1| + |\vec{x}_2|)^2$$

The Triangle Inequality follows by taking (positive) square roots.

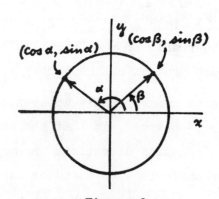

Figure 8   Figure 9

44.(a) $|\vec{u}|^2 = \cos^2\alpha + \sin^2\alpha = 1$ and $|\vec{v}|^2 = \cos^2\beta + \sin^2\beta = 1$.

(b) If the initial points of $\vec{u}$ and $\vec{v}$ (as arrows) are placed at the origin, their terminal points $(\cos\alpha, \sin\alpha)$ and $(\cos\beta, \sin\beta)$ are on the unit circle. The angle between them (in the special case shown in Figure 9) is $\alpha - \beta$; in general it is $\theta = \pm(\alpha - \beta) + 2\pi m$.

(c) $\cos\theta = \cos[\pm(\alpha - \beta) + 2\pi m] = \cos(\alpha - \beta) \implies \dfrac{\vec{u} \cdot \vec{v}}{|\vec{u}| \, |\vec{v}|} = \cos(\alpha - \beta) \implies$

$\vec{u} \cdot \vec{v} = \cos(\alpha - \beta)$ (because $|\vec{u}| = |\vec{v}| = 1$) $\implies \cos\alpha \cos\beta + \sin\alpha \sin\beta = \cos(\alpha - \beta)$.

45.(a) Place the initial points of the vectors at the origin. Then their terminal points are on the unit circle; since the vectors are perpendicular, one terminal point can be reached from the other by proceeding $\pi/2$ units counterclockwise along the circle. Hence one of the vectors is $(\cos\theta, \sin\theta)$ for some θ and the other is $(\cos(\theta + \pi/2), \sin(\theta + \pi/2)) = (-\sin\theta, \cos\theta)$. It is merely a matter of labeling to call $\vec{u}_1 = (\cos\theta, \sin\theta)$ and $\vec{u}_2 = (-\sin\theta, \cos\theta)$.

(b) If $\vec{x} = (x,y)$, then $c_1 = \vec{x} \cdot \vec{u}_1 = x\cos\theta + y\sin\theta$ and $c_2 = \vec{x} \cdot \vec{u}_2 = -x\sin\theta + y\cos\theta$. Hence

$$c_1\vec{u}_1 + c_2\vec{u}_2 = (x\cos^2\theta + y\sin\theta\cos\theta, x\sin\theta\cos\theta + y\sin^2\theta) +$$
$$(x\sin^2\theta - y\sin\theta\cos\theta, -x\sin\theta\cos\theta + y\cos^2\theta)$$
$$= (x\cos^2\theta + x\sin^2\theta, y\sin^2\theta + y\cos^2\theta) = (x,y) = \vec{x}$$

The reader may legitimately object that the coefficients $c_1 = \vec{x} \cdot \vec{u}_1$ and $c_2 = \vec{x} \cdot \vec{u}_2$ came from out of the blue. They work, but where did we get them? The answer is to regard c_1 and c_2 in the expression $\vec{x} = c_1\vec{u}_1 + c_2\vec{u}_2$ as unknown.

Then $\vec{x} \cdot \vec{u}_1 = (c_1\vec{u}_1 + c_2\vec{u}_2) \cdot \vec{u}_1 = c_1(\vec{u}_1 \cdot \vec{u}_1) + c_2(\vec{u}_1 \cdot \vec{u}_2) = c_1|\vec{u}_1|^2 + c_2(0) = c_1$

(because $\vec{u}_1$ and $\vec{u}_2$ are perpendicular and $\vec{u}_1$ is a unit vector). Similarly, $\vec{x} \cdot \vec{u}_2 = c_2$. Hence if $\vec{x}$ can be expressed in the form $c_1\vec{u}_1 + c_2\vec{u}_2$, c_1 and c_2 must necessarily be $\vec{x} \cdot \vec{u}_1$ and $\vec{x} \cdot \vec{u}_2$, respectively. They didn't come from out of the blue! We had no other choice but to give them as stated in the problem.

Section 14.6 VECTOR FUNCTIONS

1. $x = 2t \implies t = x/2$, so $y = 3t + 1 = \frac{3}{2}x + 1$. The vector derivative is $\vec{F}'(t) = (2,3)$, that is, $dx/dt = 2$ and $dy/dt = 3$ for all t. Hence x and y increase with the parameter t and the direction is as indicated in Figure 1.

2. $y = t \implies x = t^2 = y^2$. Since $\vec{F}'(t) = (2t, 1)$, y increases with t; the direction is indicated in Figure 2.

3. $x = t \implies y = t^3 = x^3$. Since $\vec{F}'(t) = (1, 3t^2)$, x and y increase with t; the direction is shown in Figure 3.

4. $x^2 + y^2 = \cos^2 t^2 + \sin^2 t^2 = 1$. We compute
$$\vec{F}'(t) = (-2t\sin t^2, 2t\cos t^2) = 2t(-\sin t^2, \cos t^2)$$

$$= 2t(\cos(t^2 + \pi/2), \sin(t^2 + \pi/2))$$

Since $t \geq 0$, the direction of $\vec{F}'(t)$ is always $90°$ counterclockwise from the direction of $\vec{F}(t)$. Hence the curve is traversed as shown in Figure 4, the initial position of (x,y) being $(1,0)$.

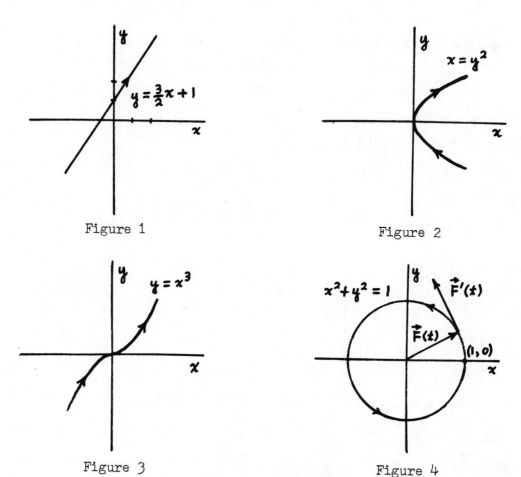

Figure 1   Figure 2

Figure 3   Figure 4

5. $x^2/a^2 + y^2/b^2 = \cos^2 t + \sin^2 t = 1$. We have $\vec{F}'(t) = (-a \sin t, b \cos t)$, so x decreases and y increases for $0 \leq t \leq \pi/2$, x and y both decrease for $\pi/2 \leq t \leq \pi$, and so on. Hence the curve (Figure 5) is traversed counterclockwise.

6. $x^2 - y^2 = \cosh^2 t - \sinh^2 t = 1$. Since $x = \cosh t \geq 1$, the graph is the right-hand branch of the hyperbola $x^2 - y^2 = 1$. We have $\vec{F}'(t) = (\sinh t, \cosh t)$ so y is always increasing, while x is decreasing when $t \leq 0$ and increasing when $t \geq 0$. See Figure 6.

7. $y = e^{-t} = 1/x$. Since e^t and e^{-t} are always positive, the graph is the first-quadrant branch of the hyperbola $xy = 1$. We have $\vec{F}'(t) = (e^t, -e^{-t})$, so x is increasing and y is decreasing for all t. See Figure 7.

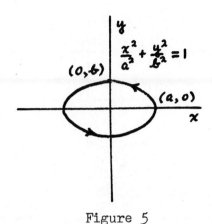

Figure 5

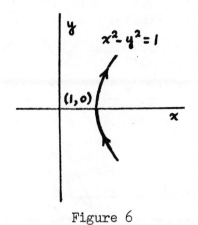

Figure 6

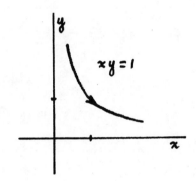

Figure 7

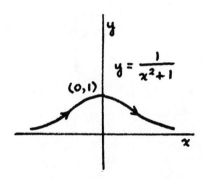

Figure 8

8. $y = \cos^2 t = \dfrac{1}{\sec^2 t} = \dfrac{1}{\tan^2 t + 1} = \dfrac{1}{x^2 + 1}$. Since $x = \tan t$ increases in

$(-\pi/2, \pi/2)$, the curve is traversed as shown in Figure 8.

9. $x^2 + y^2 = \dfrac{1}{1 + t^2} + \dfrac{t^2}{1 + t^2} = \dfrac{1 + t^2}{1 + t^2} = 1$. Since $x = 1/\sqrt{1 + t^2} > 0$, the graph is

the right-hand half of the unit circle (excluding the endpoints). It is

traversed in the clockwise direction because x is increasing when $t \le 0$ and

decreasing when $t \ge 0$.

10. If $(x, y) = (t \cos t, t \sin t)$, then $x^2 + y^2 = t^2 \cos^2 t + t^2 \sin^2 t = t^2$ and (for

$t > 0$) $\dfrac{y}{x} = \dfrac{t \sin t}{t \cos t} = \tan t$. One set of polar coordinates of (x, y) is therefore

(r, θ), where $r = t$ and $\theta = t$. Thus $r = \theta$, which also holds at $t = 0$ because

(x, y) is the origin in that case.

11. If $(x, y) = (e^t \cos t, e^t \sin t)$, then $x^2 + y^2 = e^{2t} \cos^2 t + e^{2t} \sin^2 t = e^{2t}$ and

$\dfrac{y}{x} = \dfrac{e^t \sin t}{e^t \cos t} = \tan t$. One set of polar coordinates of (x, y) is therefore (r, θ), where $r = e^t$ and $\theta = t$. Thus $r = e^\theta$.

12. $\vec{F}'(t) = (\cos t, 2\cos 2t)$, so we obtain the following table.

t	0	$\pi/4$	$\pi/2$	$3\pi/4$	π	$5\pi/4$	$3\pi/2$	$7\pi/4$	2π
$\vec{F}(t)$	$(0,0)$	$(\sqrt{2}/2,1)$	$(1,0)$	$(\sqrt{2}/2,-1)$	$(0,0)$	$(-\sqrt{2}/2,1)$	$(-1,0)$	$(-\sqrt{2}/2,-1)$	$(0,0)$
$\vec{F}'(t)$	$(1,2)$	$(\sqrt{2}/2,0)$	$(0,-2)$	$(-\sqrt{2}/2,0)$	$(-1,2)$	$(-\sqrt{2}/2,0)$	$(0,-2)$	$(\sqrt{2}/2,0)$	$(1,2)$

The graph is shown in Figure 9.

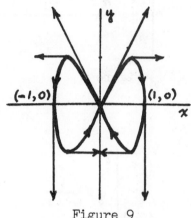

Figure 9

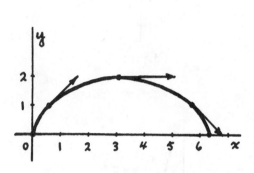

Figure 10

13.(a) If $\vec{F}(\theta) = (x,y)$, then $\vec{F}'(\theta) = (dx/d\theta, dy/d\theta)$, where $dx/d\theta = a(1 - \cos\theta)$ and $dy/d\theta = a\sin\theta$. We construct the following table, taking $a = 1$ so as to have concrete numerical data.

θ	0	$\pi/2$	π	$3\pi/2$	2π
$\vec{F}(\theta)$	$(0,0)$	$(\pi/2-1,1)$	$(\pi,2)$	$(3\pi/2+1,1)$	$(2\pi,0)$
$\vec{F}'(\theta)$	$(0,0)$	$(1,1)$	$(2,0)$	$(1,-1)$	$(0,0)$

(b) $\dfrac{dy}{dx} = \dfrac{dy/d\theta}{dx/d\theta} = \dfrac{a\sin\theta}{a(1-\cos\theta)} = \dfrac{\sin\theta}{1-\cos\theta} = \dfrac{1}{\tan\frac{1}{2}\theta} = \cot\frac{1}{2}\theta$. When θ is near 0, 2π, 4π, ..., dy/dx is numerically large. The tangent line at the corresponding points of the graph is vertical. See Figure 10.

14.(a) From Figure 11 we conclude that $P(x,y) \in L \iff \vec{P_0 P} = t\vec{m}$ for some $t \iff \vec{x} - \vec{x_0} = t\vec{m}$ for some t.

(b) $\vec{x} - \vec{x_0} = t\vec{m} \iff (x - x_0, y - y_0) = t(a,b) \iff x - x_0 = at$ and $y - y_0 = bt$ $\iff x = at + x_0$ and $y = bt + y_0$.

(c) Since $\vec{x} = (at + x_0, bt + y_0)$, we have $d\vec{x}/dt = (a,b) = \vec{m}$. In other words, the tangent vector at each point (the derivative) is the same as the vector $\vec{m}$ that gives the direction of the line.

15. If $\vec{x} = (x,y)$, then $\vec{F}'(t) = (dx/dt, dy/dt)$. Letting $\vec{m} = (a,b)$, we write $\vec{F}'(t) = \vec{m} \implies (dx/dt, dy/dt) = (a,b) \implies dx/dt = a$ and $dy/dt = b \implies x = at + x_0$

and $y = bt + y_0$ (where x_0 and y_0 are constants) $\Rightarrow \vec{x} = (at + x_0, bt + y_0) =$
$t(a,b) + (x_0, y_0) = t\vec{m} + \vec{x}_0$, where $\vec{x}_0 = (x_0, y_0)$. Hence $\vec{x} = \vec{F}(t) = t\vec{m} + \vec{x}_0$, which
is a vector equation of the line through (x_0, y_0) parallel to $\vec{m}$.

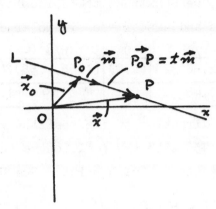

Figure 11

16. If $a \neq 0$, the slope of the vector (a,b) is b/a. Hence the slope of $\vec{F}'(t)$
is $g'(t)/f'(t) = dy/dx$. Since $\vec{F}'(t)$ is a tangent vector and dy/dx is the
slope of the tangent, this equation is what we should expect.

17. If $\vec{x} = (x,y)$, then $|\vec{x}|^2 = x^2 + y^2$. Hence
$$\frac{d}{dt}|\vec{x}|^2 = 2x\frac{dx}{dt} + 2y\frac{dy}{dt} = (2x, 2y) \cdot \left(\frac{dx}{dt}, \frac{dy}{dt}\right) = 2\vec{x} \cdot \frac{d\vec{x}}{dt}$$

18. (a) The vector $\vec{x}$ has constant length a, but may have any direction. Hence
the point (x,y) is any point of the circle $x^2 + y^2 = a^2$.

(b) $|\vec{x}| = a \Rightarrow |\vec{x}|^2 = a^2 \Rightarrow \frac{d}{dt}|\vec{x}|^2 = 0 \Rightarrow 2\vec{x} \cdot \frac{d\vec{x}}{dt} = 0$ (Problem 17) $\Rightarrow$
$\vec{x} \cdot \frac{d\vec{x}}{dt} = 0$. This says that the position vector $\vec{x}$ and the tangent vector $d\vec{x}/dt$
are always perpendicular, which is characteristic of a circle.

19. The distance between the origin and a point $\vec{x} = (x,y)$ of the graph is $|\vec{x}|$.
When this has its minimum value, so does $|\vec{x}|^2$, and hence $\frac{d}{dt}|\vec{x}|^2 = 0$. By
Problem 17 this means that $\vec{x} \cdot (d\vec{x}/dt) = 0$. Hence $\vec{x}$ and $d\vec{x}/dt$ are perpendicular
at (x_0, y_0).

20. (a) A tangent vector is $\vec{F}'(t) = (-e^t \sin t + e^t \cos t, e^t \cos t + e^t \sin t) =$
$e^t(\cos t - \sin t, \cos t + \sin t)$. The angle between $\vec{F}(t)$ and $\vec{F}'(t)$ satisfies
$$\cos \theta = \frac{\vec{F}(t) \cdot \vec{F}'(t)}{|\vec{F}(t)||\vec{F}'(t)|}$$
Since $\vec{F}(t) = e^t(\cos t, \sin t)$, we have
$$\vec{F}(t) \cdot \vec{F}'(t) = e^{2t}(\cos^2 t - \sin t \cos t + \sin t \cos t + \sin^2 t) = e^{2t}$$
Moreover, $|\vec{F}(t)| = e^t\sqrt{\cos^2 t + \sin^2 t} = e^t$ and

213

$$|\vec{F}'(t)| = e^t\sqrt{\cos^2 t - 2\sin t \cos t + \sin^2 t + \cos^2 t + 2\sin t \cos t + \sin^2 t} = \sqrt{2}\,e^t$$

Hence $\cos\theta = \dfrac{e^{2t}}{(e^t)(\sqrt{2}\,e^t)} = 1/\sqrt{2}$ and $\theta = 45°$.

(b) Using a calculator, we construct the following table, which gives $\vec{F}(t)$ in rectangular coordinates and also $r = e^{\theta}$ in polar coordinates.

$t = \theta$	$-\pi/2$	$-\pi/4$	0	$\pi/4$	$\pi/2$
$\vec{F}(t)$	$(0,-0.21)$	$(0.32,-0.32)$	$(1,0)$	$(1.55,1.55)$	$(0,4.81)$
r	0.21	0.46	1	2.19	4.81

At each point we note the direction of the position vector and draw a tangent vector making an angle of $45°$ with the position vector. This helps sketch the curve with the proper direction at each point. See Figure 12.

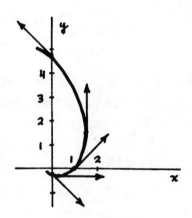

Figure 12

21. Since $\vec{x} = (t, t^3)$, $d\vec{x}/dt = (1, 3t^2)$. Or, using the Product Rule on $\vec{x} = t(1, t^2)$, we have $d\vec{x}/dt = t(0, 2t) + (1, t^2) = (1, 3t^2)$.

22. Since $\vec{x} = (t\cos t, t\sin t)$, $d\vec{x}/dt = (-t\sin t + \cos t, t\cos t + \sin t)$. Or, using the Product Rule on $\vec{x} = t(\cos t, \sin t)$, we have

$$d\vec{x}/dt = t(-\sin t, \cos t) + (\cos t, \sin t) = (-t\sin t + \cos t, t\cos t + \sin t)$$

23. Since $\vec{x} = (e^t \cos t, e^t \sin t)$, $d\vec{x}/dt = e^t(\cos t - \sin t, \cos t + \sin t)$, as shown in the solution of Problem 20. Or, using the Product Rule on $\vec{x} = e^t(\cos t, \sin t)$, we have

$$d\vec{x}/dt = e^t(-\sin t, \cos t) + e^t(\cos t, \sin t) = e^t(\cos t - \sin t, \cos t + \sin t)$$

24. Since $\vec{x} = (t, t^{3/2})$, $d\vec{x}/dt = (1, \frac{3}{2}\sqrt{t})$. Or, using the Chain Rule on $\vec{x} = (u^2, u^3)$ with $u = \sqrt{t}$, we have

$$\frac{d\vec{x}}{dt} = \frac{d\vec{x}}{du}\frac{du}{dt} = (2u, 3u^2)\frac{1}{2\sqrt{t}} = \frac{1}{2\sqrt{t}}(2\sqrt{t}, 3t) = (1, \frac{3}{2}\sqrt{t})$$

25. Since $\vec{x} = (\cos t^2, \sin t^2)$, $d\vec{x}/dt = (-2t \sin t^2, 2t \cos t^2) = 2t(-\sin t^2, \cos t^2)$. Or, using the Chain Rule,

$$\frac{d\vec{x}}{dt} = \frac{d\vec{x}}{du}\frac{du}{dt} = (-\sin u, \cos u)(2t) = 2t(-\sin t^2, \cos t^2)$$

26. Since $f(t) = e^t e^{-t} + e^{-t} e^t = 2$, $f'(t) = 0$. Or, using the Product Rule, we have $f'(t) = (e^t, e^{-t}) \cdot (-e^{-t}, e^t) + (e^t, -e^{-t}) \cdot (e^{-t}, e^t) = (-1+1) + (1-1) = 0$.

27. Since $f(t) = t^3 \cos t + t^2 \sin t$, $f'(t) = -t^3 \sin t + 3t^2 \cos t + t^2 \cos t + 2t \sin t$
$= -t^3 \sin t + 4t^2 \cos t + 2t \sin t$. Or, using the Product Rule, we have

$$f'(t) = (t^3, t^2) \cdot (-\sin t, \cos t) + (3t^2, 2t) \cdot (\cos t, \sin t)$$
$$= (-t^3 \sin t + t^2 \cos t) + (3t^2 \cos t + 2t \sin t)$$
$$= -t^3 \sin t + 4t^2 \cos t + 2t \sin t$$

28. $\dfrac{\vec{F}(z) - \vec{F}(t)}{z - t} = \dfrac{1}{z - t}[(f(z), g(z)) - (f(t), g(t))] = \left(\dfrac{f(z) - f(t)}{z - t}, \dfrac{g(z) - g(t)}{z - t}\right)$.

Hence $\vec{F}'(t) = \left(\lim\limits_{z \to t} \dfrac{f(z) - f(t)}{z - t}, \lim\limits_{z \to t} \dfrac{g(z) - g(t)}{z - t}\right) = (f'(t), g'(t))$.

29. If $\vec{F} = (f_1, f_2)$ and $\vec{G} = (g_1, g_2)$, then $\vec{F} + \vec{G} = (f_1 + g_1, f_2 + g_2)$ and hence
$(\vec{F} + \vec{G})' = (f_1' + g_1', f_2' + g_2') = (f_1', f_2') + (g_1', g_2') = \vec{F}' + \vec{G}'$

30. If $\vec{F} = (F, G)$, then $f\vec{F} = (fF, fG)$ and hence
$(f\vec{F})' = (fF' + f'F, fG' + f'G) = (fF', fG') + (f'F, f'G) = f(F', G') + f'(F, G)$
$= f\vec{F}' + f'\vec{F}$

31. If $\vec{F} = (f_1, f_2)$ and $\vec{G} = (g_1, g_2)$, then $\vec{F} \cdot \vec{G} = f_1 g_1 + f_2 g_2$ and hence
$(\vec{F} \cdot \vec{G})' = (f_1 g_1' + f_1' g_1) + (f_2 g_2' + f_2' g_2) = (f_1 g_1' + f_2 g_2') + (f_1' g_1 + f_2' g_2)$
$= (f_1, f_2) \cdot (g_1', g_2') + (f_1', f_2') \cdot (g_1, g_2) = \vec{F} \cdot \vec{G}' + \vec{F}' \cdot \vec{G}$

32. If $\vec{x} = \vec{F}(u) = (F(u), G(u))$ and $u = f(t)$, then
$$\frac{d\vec{x}}{dt} = \left(\frac{d}{dt}F(u), \frac{d}{dt}G(u)\right) = \left(F'(u)\frac{du}{dt}, G'(u)\frac{du}{dt}\right) = \frac{du}{dt}(F'(u), G'(u))$$
$$= \frac{du}{dt}\frac{d\vec{x}}{du} = \frac{d\vec{x}}{du}\frac{du}{dt}$$

Section 14.7   MOTION IN THE PLANE

1. $\vec{v} = \vec{F}'(t) = (2, 3)$, $|\vec{v}| = \sqrt{13}$, $\vec{a} = d\vec{v}/dt = (0, 0)$.

2. $\vec{v} = (2t, 1)$, $|\vec{v}| = \sqrt{4t^2 + 1}$, $\vec{a} = (2, 0)$.

3. $\vec{v} = (1, 3t^2)$, $|\vec{v}| = \sqrt{1 + 9t^4}$, $\vec{a} = (0, 6t)$.

4. $\vec{v} = (-2t \sin t^2, 2t \cos t^2) = 2t(-\sin t^2, \cos t^2)$, $|\vec{v}| = |2t|\sqrt{\sin^2 t^2 + \cos^2 t^2} =$

$|2t| = 2t$ (because $t \geq 0$), $\vec{a} = 2t(-2t\cos t^2, -2t\sin t^2) + 2(-\sin t^2, \cos t^2) = 2(-2t^2\cos t^2 - \sin t^2, -2t^2\sin t^2 + \cos t^2)$.

5. $\vec{v} = (-a\sin t, b\cos t)$, $|\vec{v}| = \sqrt{a^2\sin^2 t + b^2\cos^2 t}$, $\vec{a} = (-a\cos t, -b\sin t) = -\vec{F}(t)$.

6. $\vec{v} = (\sinh t, \cosh t)$, $|\vec{v}| = \sqrt{\sinh^2 t + \cosh^2 t}$, $\vec{a} = (\cosh t, \sinh t) = \vec{F}(t)$.

7. $\vec{v} = (e^t, -e^{-t})$, $|\vec{v}| = (e^{2t} + e^{-2t})^{1/2}$, $\vec{a} = (e^t, e^{-t}) = \vec{F}(t)$.

8.(a) The path is $y = \sin x$, $-\pi \leq x \leq \pi$, traversed from left to right.

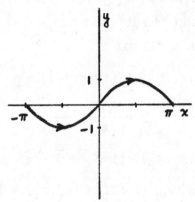

Figure 1

(b) Since $\vec{v} = (1, \cos t)$, the speed is $|\vec{v}| = ds/dt = \sqrt{1 + \cos^2 t}$. Its maximum value is $\sqrt{2}$, occurring when $\cos^2 t = 1$, that is, when $t = 0$ or $t = \pm\pi$. Its minimum value is 1, occurring when $\cos^2 t = 0$, that is, when $t = \pm\pi/2$.

(c) Force is $m\vec{a} = m(0, -\sin t)$, where m is mass. This is the zero vector when $\sin t = 0$, that is, when $t = 0$ or $t = \pm\pi$.

(d) Since $\vec{a} = a_T\vec{T} + a_N\vec{N}$, the force $m\vec{a}$ is entirely normal when $a_T = d^2s/dt^2 = 0$. Since $\dfrac{d^2s}{dt^2} = \dfrac{-\sin t \cos t}{\sqrt{1 + \cos^2 t}}$, $a_T = 0$ when $\sin t = 0$ or $\cos t = 0$, that is, when $t = 0, \pm\pi/2, \pm\pi$. We construct the following table, using $\vec{a} = (0, -\sin t)$:

t	$-\pi$	$-\pi/2$	0	$\pi/2$	π
$\vec{a}$	$(0,0)$	$(0,1)$	$(0,0)$	$(0,-1)$	$(0,0)$
$|\vec{a}|$	0	1	0	1	0

Of course when $\vec{a} = (0,0)$ the statement that "the force is entirely normal" does not mean much, since the force is zero. (It could also be characterized as "entirely tangential!") But at $t = \pm\pi/2$ the marble experiences a nonzero force which is perpendicular to the direction of motion.

9. $\vec{v} = (\cos t, 2\cos 2t)$ and $\vec{a} = (-\sin t, -4\sin 2t)$. The force is zero when $\sin t = 0$ and $\sin 2t = 0$, that is, when $t = 0, \pi, 2\pi$. (See the solution of

Problem 12, Sec. 14.6. The force is zero when the moving point is at the origin.)

The force is directed from the point (x,y) toward the origin when $\vec{a} = -k\vec{x}$ (where $k > 0$). This means that $(-\sin t, -4 \sin 2t) = -k(\sin t, \sin 2t) \Longrightarrow \sin t = k \sin t$ and $4 \sin 2t = k \sin 2t \Longrightarrow (k-1)\sin t = 0$ and $(k-4)\sin 2t = 0$. These equations hold when $\sin t = 0$ and $\sin 2t = 0$, but then the force is zero and its direction is of no interest. They also hold when $k = 1$, $\sin t \neq 0$, and $\sin 2t = 0$, or when $k = 4$, $\sin 2t \neq 0$, and $\sin t = 0$. The first of these conditions occurs when $t = \pi/2$ or $3\pi/2$, which puts us at the points $(\pm 1, 0)$ on the figure eight. The second condition is impossible (because $\sin t = 0 \Longrightarrow \sin 2t = 2 \sin t \cos t = 0$). Hence the force is directed toward the origin when the moving point is at $(\pm 1, 0)$.

10.(a) $\vec{v} = (1, 3t^2)$ and $|\vec{v}| = ds/dt = \sqrt{1 + 9t^4}$. Hence

$$a_T = \frac{d^2s}{dt^2} = \frac{18t^3}{\sqrt{1 + 9t^4}}$$

(b) Since $\vec{a} = (0, 6t)$, we have $|\vec{a}|^2 = 36t^2$ and hence

$$a_N^2 = |\vec{a}|^2 - a_T^2 = 36t^2 - \frac{324t^6}{1 + 9t^4} = \frac{36t^2}{1 + 9t^4}$$

Since $a_N \geq 0$, we find

$$a_N = \frac{|6t|}{\sqrt{1 + 9t^4}}$$

(c) Since $a_N = \varkappa(ds/dt)^2 = \varkappa(1 + 9t^4)$, we find $\varkappa = \frac{a_N}{1 + 9t^4} = \frac{|6t|}{(1 + 9t^4)^{3/2}}$.

11.(a) $\vec{v} = (e^t, -e^{-t})$ and $\vec{a} = (e^t, e^{-t}) = \vec{F}(t)$. Since $\vec{F}(t)$ points from $(0,0)$ to (x,y), the force $m\vec{a}$ points in the same direction; if its initial point is considered to be (x,y), then it is directed from the particle away from the origin.

(b) Since $|\vec{v}|^2 = e^{2t} + e^{-2t} = 2 \cosh 2t$, $ds/dt = |\vec{v}| = \sqrt{2 \cosh 2t}$. Since $\cosh 2t \geq 1$ for all t (and is equal to 1 when $t = 0$), the minimum speed is $\sqrt{2}$ at $(1,1)$.

(c) $a_T = \frac{d^2s}{dt^2} = \frac{2 \sinh 2t}{\sqrt{2 \cosh 2t}}$. The particle is slowing down when $a_T < 0$, that is, when $t < 0$. It is speeding up when $a_T > 0$, that is, when $t > 0$. Thus it is slowing down before it reaches $(1,1)$ and speeding up afterwards. (See the figure in the solution of Problem 7, Sec. 14.6.)

(d) Since $|\vec{a}|^2 = e^{2t} + e^{-2t} = 2 \cosh 2t$, we have

$$a_N^2 = |\vec{a}|^2 - a_T^2 = 2 \cosh 2t - \frac{4 \sinh^2 2t}{2 \cosh 2t} = \frac{4(\cosh^2 2t - \sinh^2 2t)}{2 \cosh 2t} = \frac{2}{\cosh 2t} =$$

2 sech 2t.   Hence $a_N = \sqrt{2}\,\text{sech}\,2t$.

(e) $\varkappa = \dfrac{a_N}{(ds/dt)^2} = \dfrac{\sqrt{2}\,\text{sech}\,2t}{2\cosh 2t} = \dfrac{\sqrt{2}}{2}(\text{sech}\,2t)^{3/2}$

12.(a) $\vec{v} = (-\sin t + t\cos t + \sin t, \cos t + t\sin t - \cos t) = t(\cos t, \sin t)$, so $ds/dt = |\vec{v}| = |t|\sqrt{\cos^2 t + \sin^2 t} = |t| = t$ (because $t \geq 0$).

(b) $s = \displaystyle\int_0^t u\,du = \tfrac{1}{2}t^2$

(c) $a_T = d^2s/dt^2 = 1$. Since $\vec{a} = t(-\sin t, \cos t) + (\cos t, \sin t) = (\cos t - t\sin t, \sin t + t\cos t)$, we have

$|\vec{a}|^2 = \cos^2 t - 2t\sin t\cos t + t^2\sin^2 t + \sin^2 t + 2t\sin t\cos t + t^2\cos^2 t = 1 + t^2$

Hence $a_N^2 = |\vec{a}|^2 - a_T^2 = (1 + t^2) - 1 = t^2$ and $a_N = |t| = t$.

(d) $\varkappa = \dfrac{a_N}{(ds/dt)^2} = \dfrac{t}{t^2} = \dfrac{1}{t}$

13.(a) Since $\vec{v} = v\vec{T}$, we have $\vec{v}\cdot\vec{T} = (v\vec{T})\cdot\vec{T} = v(\vec{T}\cdot\vec{T}) = v|\vec{T}|^2 = v$ (because $\vec{T}$ is a unit vector). We also have $\vec{v}\cdot\vec{N} = (v\vec{T})\cdot\vec{N} = v(\vec{T}\cdot\vec{N}) = 0$ (because $\vec{T}$ and $\vec{N}$ are perpendicular).

(b) Since $\vec{a} = a_T\vec{T} + a_N\vec{N}$, we have

$\vec{a}\cdot\vec{T} = (a_T\vec{T} + a_N\vec{N})\cdot\vec{T} = a_T(\vec{T}\cdot\vec{T}) + a_N(\vec{N}\cdot\vec{T}) = a_T = d^2s/dt^2 = dv/dt$

Similarly, $\vec{a}\cdot\vec{N} = a_T(\vec{T}\cdot\vec{N}) + a_N(\vec{N}\cdot\vec{N}) = a_N = \varkappa(ds/dt)^2 = \varkappa v^2$.

(c) $\vec{a}\cdot\vec{v} = (a_T\vec{T} + a_N\vec{N})\cdot\vec{v} = a_T(\vec{T}\cdot\vec{v}) + a_N(\vec{N}\cdot\vec{v}) = a_T v$ (from part (a))

$= v\dfrac{dv}{dt}$

If the moving point is speeding up, then $dv/dt > 0$ and hence $\vec{a}\cdot\vec{v} > 0$ (because $v > 0$). If it is slowing down, then $dv/dt < 0$ and hence $\vec{a}\cdot\vec{v} < 0$. If the speed is constant, then $dv/dt = 0$ and hence $\vec{a}\cdot\vec{v} = 0$.

14. If the speed v is constant, then $a_T = d^2s/dt^2 = dv/dt = 0$, so $\vec{a} = a_N\vec{N}$ is entirely normal. Since $\vec{v} = v\vec{T}$ is entirely tangential, $\vec{a}$ and $\vec{v}$ are perpendicular. This is confirmed by $\vec{a}\cdot\vec{v} = (a_N\vec{N})\cdot(v\vec{T}) = va_N(\vec{N}\cdot\vec{T}) = 0$.

15. From Problem 13(c) and the perpendicularity of $\vec{a}$ and $\vec{v}$, we have $\vec{a}\cdot\vec{v} = v(dv/dt) = 0$. Since $v > 0$, it follows that $dv/dt = 0$ and hence v is constant.

16. Since $\vec{v} = v\vec{T}$, $\vec{a}$ and $\vec{v}$ are parallel when $\vec{a}$ is entirely tangential, that is, when $a_N = \varkappa v^2 = 0$. Since $v > 0$, this occurs when the curvature is 0.

17.(a) Use the Product Rule:

$\vec{F} = \dfrac{d}{dt}(m\vec{v}) = m\dfrac{d\vec{v}}{dt} + \dfrac{dm}{dt}\vec{v} = m\vec{a} + \dfrac{dm}{dt}\vec{v}$

(b) When m is constant, $dm/dt = 0$.

18.(a) $\vec{F} = m\vec{a} = \vec{0} \implies \vec{a} = \vec{F}''(t) = \vec{0}$

(b) Since $\vec{F}''(t) = (d^2x/dt^2, d^2y/dt^2)$, we have $\vec{F}''(t) = \vec{0} \implies d^2x/dt^2 = 0$ and $d^2y/dt^2 = 0 \implies dx/dt = a$ and $dy/dt = b$ (a and b constants) $\implies \vec{F}'(t) = (a,b)$ $= \vec{m}$. Since the motion is smooth, $|\vec{F}'(t)| \neq 0$ and hence $\vec{m} \neq \vec{0}$. The speed is $|\vec{m}|$, which is constant. According to Problem 14, Sec. 14.6, the path is a straight line.

(c) See the solutions of Problems 14 and 15, Sec. 14.6.

19.(a) $m\vec{a} = \vec{0} \implies \vec{a} = \vec{0} \implies a_T\vec{T} + a_N\vec{N} = \vec{0} \implies a_T = 0$ and $a_N = 0$.

(b) $a_T = 0 \implies d^2s/dt^2 = 0 \implies ds/dt = $ constant, while $a_N = 0 \implies \varkappa(ds/dt)^2 = 0 \implies \varkappa = 0$ (because $ds/dt > 0$).

20.(a) The only force is gravitational, with magnitude mg and direction opposite to the upward y axis. In other words, $\vec{F} = -mg\vec{j}$. Since $\vec{F} = m\vec{a}$, it follows that $\vec{a} = -g\vec{j}$.

(b) $d\vec{v}/dt = -g\vec{j} \implies \vec{v} = -gt\vec{j} + \vec{C}_1$, where $\vec{C}_1$ is a constant vector. (Check by differentiation.) Since $\vec{v} = \vec{v}_0 = v_0(\cos\alpha, \sin\alpha)$ when $t = 0$, we find $\vec{C}_1 = \vec{v}_0$ and hence $\vec{v} = -gt\vec{j} + \vec{v}_0$.

(c) $d\vec{x}/dt = -gt\vec{j} + \vec{v}_0 \implies \vec{x} = -\frac{1}{2}gt^2\vec{j} + t\vec{v}_0 + \vec{C}_2$. Since $\vec{x} = \vec{0}$ when $t = 0$, we find $\vec{C}_2 = \vec{0}$ and hence $\vec{x} = -\frac{1}{2}gt^2\vec{j} + t\vec{v}_0$.

(d) From part (c) we have $(x,y) = -\frac{1}{2}gt^2(0,1) + tv_0(\cos\alpha, \sin\alpha)$, which yields $x = (v_0\cos\alpha)t$ and $y = (v_0\sin\alpha)t - \frac{1}{2}gt^2$. Solve for t in the first equation and substitute in the second to obtain y as a quadratic function of x. This implies that the path is parabolic.

(e) See the solution of Problem 47, Sec. 1.3, where we showed that $R = (2v_0^2/g)\sin\alpha\cos\alpha$. Since $2\sin\alpha\cos\alpha = \sin 2\alpha$, the given formula follows. The maximum value of R occurs when $\sin 2\alpha = 1$, that is, when $2\alpha = \pi/2$ and $\alpha = \pi/4$.

(f) The maximum value of y occurs when $dy/dt = v_0\sin\alpha - gt = 0$, or $t = (v_0/g)\sin\alpha$. This yields

$$y = H = (v_0\sin\alpha)\left(\frac{v_0}{g}\sin\alpha\right) - \frac{1}{2}g\left(\frac{v_0}{g}\sin\alpha\right)^2 = \frac{v_0^2}{g}\sin^2\alpha - \frac{1}{2}\cdot\frac{v_0^2}{g}\sin^2\alpha = \frac{v_0^2}{2g}\sin^2\alpha$$

H is largest when $\sin\alpha = 1$, that is, when $\alpha = \pi/2$.

21.(a) The flight is over when $y = 0$, that is, when $(v_0\sin\alpha)t - \frac{1}{2}gt^2 = 0 \iff 80t - 16t^2 = 0 \iff 16t(5-t) = 0 \iff t = 0$ or $t = 5$. Since $t = 0$ corresponds to the beginning of the flight, the time of flight is $t = 5$ sec.

(b) $R = (v_0^2/g) \sin 2\alpha = \frac{160^2}{32} \cdot \frac{\sqrt{3}}{2} = 400\sqrt{3}$ ft

(c) $H = (v_0^2/2g)\sin^2\alpha = \frac{160^2}{64} \cdot \frac{1}{4} = 100$ ft

(d) Since $\vec{v} = -gt\vec{j} + \vec{v}_0 = -gt(0,1) + v_0(\cos\alpha, \sin\alpha) = (v_0 \cos\alpha, v_0 \sin\alpha - gt)$
$= (80\sqrt{3}, 80 - 32t)$, the velocity at impact $(t = 5)$ is $\vec{v} = (80\sqrt{3}, -80) = 80(\sqrt{3}, -1)$.
The speed is $|\vec{v}| = 80\sqrt{3+1} = 160$ ft/sec. The angle between $\vec{v}$ and $\vec{i}$ at impact
satisfies $\cos\theta = \frac{\vec{v} \cdot \vec{i}}{|\vec{v}||\vec{i}|} = \frac{80\sqrt{3}}{160} = \frac{\sqrt{3}}{2}$, so $\theta = 30°$.

(e) Since $x = (v_0 \cos\alpha)t = 80\sqrt{3}\,t$ and $y = (v_0 \sin\alpha)t - \frac{1}{2}gt^2 = 80t - 16t^2$, we
have $t = \frac{x}{80\sqrt{3}}$ and hence $y = 80\left(\frac{x}{80\sqrt{3}}\right) - 16\left(\frac{x^2}{6400 \cdot 3}\right) = \frac{x}{\sqrt{3}} - \frac{x^2}{1200}$.

22. Since $\vec{T} = (\cos\phi, \sin\phi)$, we have $\frac{d\vec{T}}{ds} = \frac{d\vec{T}}{d\phi}\frac{d\phi}{ds} = \frac{d\phi}{ds}(-\sin\phi, \cos\phi)$. Hence

$$|d\vec{T}/ds| = |d\phi/ds|\sqrt{\sin^2\phi + \cos^2\phi} = |d\phi/ds| = \varkappa$$

Section 14.8   MORE ON CURVATURE AND MOTION

1. If ϕ is constant, then $d\phi/ds = 0$, so $\varkappa = |d\phi/ds| = 0$.

2. $x' = a$, $x'' = 0$, $y' = b$, and $y'' = 0$, so
$$\varkappa = \frac{|x'y'' - y'x''|}{(x'^2 + y'^2)^{3/2}} = 0$$

3. $y' = m$ and $y'' = 0$, so $\varkappa = \frac{|y''|}{(1 + y'^2)^{3/2}} = 0$.

4. $\varkappa = 0 \implies d\phi/ds = 0 \implies \phi = $ constant. Hence the angle from $\vec{i}$ to $\vec{T}$ is
fixed and the path must be straight.

5. $x' = -r\sin t$, $x'' = -r\cos t$, $y' = r\cos t$, and $y'' = -r\sin t$, so
$$\varkappa = \frac{|r^2\sin^2 t + r^2\cos^2 t|}{(r^2\sin^2 t + r^2\cos^2 t)^{3/2}} = \frac{r^2}{r^3} = \frac{1}{r}$$

6. The curvature changes abruptly from $\varkappa = 0$ to $\varkappa = 1/r$, where r is the
radius of the circle. In other words, $\varkappa$ is discontinuous at the junction.

7. Since $x = t$ and $y = f(t)$, we have $x' = 1$, $x'' = 0$, $y' = f'(t) = f'(x)$, and
$y'' = f''(t) = f''(x)$. Hence
$$\varkappa = \frac{|y''|}{(1 + y'^2)^{3/2}}$$

8. This occurs when $1 + y'^2 = 1$, that is, when $y' = 0$. In other words, $\varkappa = |y''|$ at smooth critical points.

9. Since $y' = -\sin x$ and $y'' = -\cos x$, we have $\varkappa = |\cos x|/(1 + \sin^2 x)^{3/2} = 1$

at $(0,1)$. Hence the radius of the circle of curvature is $1/\varkappa = 1$. Since the circle is tangent to the curve at $(0,1)$, with its center in the direction of $\vec{N}$, it is the unit circle shown in Figure 1.

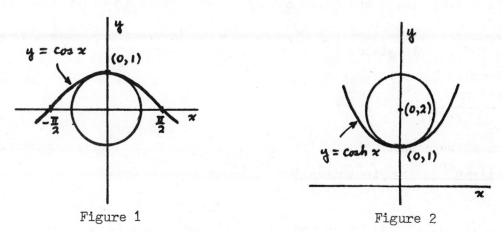

Figure 1   Figure 2

10. Since $y' = \sinh x$ and $y'' = \cosh x$, we have

$$\varkappa = \frac{|\cosh x|}{(1 + \sinh^2 x)^{3/2}} = \frac{\cosh x}{(\cosh^2 x)^{3/2}} = \frac{1}{\cosh^2 x} = \operatorname{sech}^2 x$$

Since $\varkappa = 1$ at $(0,1)$, the radius of the circle of curvature is $1/\varkappa = 1$. The center is in the direction of $\vec{N}$, so it is $(0,2)$. See Figure 2.

11. Since $y = x^{-1}$, $y' = -x^{-2}$, and $y'' = 2x^{-3}$, we have

$$\frac{1}{\varkappa} = \frac{(1 + x^{-4})^{3/2}}{|2x^{-3}|} = \sqrt{2}\ \text{ at } (1,1)$$

See Figure 3.

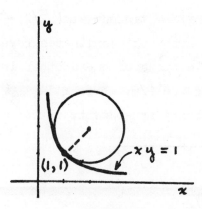

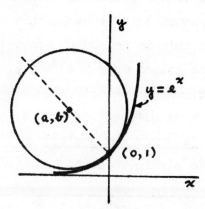

Figure 3   Figure 4

12. Since $y' = e^x$ and $y'' = e^x$, we have

$$\varkappa = \frac{e^x}{(1 + e^{2x})^{3/2}} = \frac{1}{2^{3/2}}\ \text{ at } (0,1)$$

Hence the radius of curvature is $1/\varkappa = 2\sqrt{2}$. The circle of curvature is as shown in Figure 4; if its center is (a,b), then (by the Distance Formula) $a^2 + (b-1)^2 = 8$. Since the slope of the tangent at (0,1) is $y' = e^x = 1$, the normal line through (a,b) and (0,1) has slope -1. Hence $(b-1)/a = -1$, from which $b - 1 = -a$. Therefore $a^2 + (-a)^2 = 8$, $2a^2 = 8$, $a^2 = 4$, and $a = -2$ (because a < 0). This yields $b = 1 - a = 3$, so the center is (-2,3).

13. From Problem 12 we have

$$\varkappa = \frac{e^x}{(1 + e^{2x})^{3/2}}$$

To maximize $\varkappa$, we compute

$$\frac{d\varkappa}{dx} = \frac{(1 + e^{2x})^{3/2} \cdot e^x - e^x(3/2)(1 + e^{2x})^{1/2} \cdot 2e^{2x}}{(1 + e^{2x})^3}$$

$$= \frac{e^x(1 + e^{2x})^{1/2}[(1 + e^{2x}) - 3e^{2x}]}{(1 + e^{2x})^3} = \frac{e^x(1 - 2e^{2x})}{(1 + e^{2x})^{5/2}} = 0$$

when $e^{2x} = \frac{1}{2} \iff 2x = \ell n \frac{1}{2} = -\ell n\, 2 \iff x = -\frac{1}{2}\ell n\, 2$. Since $d\varkappa/dx$ changes from plus to minus at the critical point, we have a maximum at $(-\frac{1}{2}\ell n\, 2, \sqrt{2}/2)$.

14. Since $y' = x^{-1}$ and $y'' = -x^{-2}$, we have

$$\varkappa = \frac{x^{-2}}{(1 + x^{-2})^{3/2}} = \frac{1/x^2}{(x^2 + 1)^{3/2}/|x|^3} = \frac{|x|}{(x^2 + 1)^{3/2}}$$

Since $\varkappa$ and $\varkappa^2 = x^2/(x^2 + 1)^3$ have maximum values at the same point, we compute

$$\frac{d(\varkappa^2)}{dx} = \frac{(x^2 + 1)^3 \cdot 2x - x^2 \cdot 3(x^2 + 1)^2 \cdot 2x}{(x^2 + 1)^6} = \frac{2x(x^2 + 1)^2[(x^2 + 1) - 3x^2]}{(x^2 + 1)^6} = \frac{2x(1 - 2x^2)}{(x^2 + 1)^4}$$

The domain is x > 0, so the only critical point is $x = \sqrt{2}/2$. The derivative changes from plus to minus at this point, so we have a maximum at $(\sqrt{2}/2, -\frac{1}{2}\ell n\, 2)$. The reason this is the point found in Problem 13 with its coordinates reversed is that the graphs of $y = e^x$ and $y = \ell n\, x$ are reflections of one another in the line y = x.

15.(a) $x' = -a\sin t$, $x'' = -a\cos t$, $y' = b\cos t$, and $y'' = -b\sin t$, so

$$\varkappa = \frac{|ab\sin^2 t + ab\cos^2 t|}{(a^2\sin^2 t + b^2\cos^2 t)^{3/2}} = \frac{ab}{[a^2\sin^2 t + b^2(1 - \sin^2 t)]^{3/2}}$$

$$= \frac{ab}{[b^2 + (a^2 - b^2)\sin^2 t]^{3/2}} = \frac{ab}{(b^2 + c^2\sin^2 t)^{3/2}}$$

If a = b, the graph is a circle with curvature $\varkappa = 1/a$. The next-to-last version of the above formula yields $\varkappa = ab/(b^2)^{3/2} = ab/b^3 = 1/a$ when a = b, so the formula applies.

(b) $\varkappa$ is greatest when $\sin t = 0$, which occurs at the points $(\pm a, 0)$ of the ellipse. The radius of curvature at these points is $1/\varkappa = (b^2)^{3/2}/(ab) = b^2/a$. $\varkappa$ is smallest when $\sin t = \pm 1$, which occurs at $(0, \pm b)$. The next-to-last version of the formula for $\varkappa$ in part (a) yields $1/\varkappa = (a^2)^{3/2}/(ab) = a^2/b$.

16.(a) $x' = a(1 - \cos\theta)$, $x'' = a\sin\theta$, $y' = a\sin\theta$, and $y'' = a\cos\theta$, so

$$\varkappa = \frac{|a^2\cos\theta(1 - \cos\theta) - a^2\sin^2\theta|}{[a^2(1 - \cos\theta)^2 + a^2\sin^2\theta]^{3/2}} = \frac{a^2|\cos\theta - (\cos^2\theta + \sin^2\theta)|}{a^3(1 - 2\cos\theta + \cos^2\theta + \sin^2\theta)^{3/2}}$$

$$= \frac{|\cos\theta - 1|}{a\sqrt{8}(1 - \cos\theta)^{3/2}} = \frac{1 - \cos\theta}{a\sqrt{8}(1 - \cos\theta)^{3/2}} = \frac{1}{a\sqrt{8}\sqrt{1 - \cos\theta}} = \frac{1}{\sqrt{8a^2(1 - \cos\theta)}}$$

$$= \frac{1}{\sqrt{8ay}}$$

(b) It is tempting to conclude from Figure 5 that the radius of curvature is the radius of the wheel, namely a.

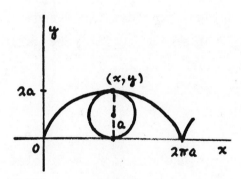

Figure 5

(c) From part (a) the radius of curvature when $y = 2a$ is $1/\varkappa = \sqrt{8ay} = 4a$.

17. $x' = -3a\cos^2 t\sin t$, $y' = 3a\sin^2 t\cos t$,

$x'' = -3a[\cos^2 t(\cos t) - 2\cos t\sin t\cdot\sin t] = -3a\cos t(\cos^2 t - 2\sin^2 t)$

$y'' = 3a[\sin^2 t(-\sin t) + 2\sin t\cos t\cdot\cos t] = 3a\sin t(2\cos^2 t - \sin^2 t)$

$$\varkappa = \frac{|9a^2\sin^2 t\cos^2 t(\sin^2 t - 2\cos^2 t) + 9a^2\sin^2 t\cos^2 t(\cos^2 t - 2\sin^2 t)|}{(9a^2\cos^4 t\sin^2 t + 9a^2\sin^4 t\cos^2 t)^{3/2}}$$

$$= \frac{|9a^2\sin^2 t\cos^2 t(-\sin^2 t - \cos^2 t)|}{27a^3[\sin^2 t\cos^2 t(\cos^2 t + \sin^2 t)]^{3/2}} = \frac{9a^2\sin^2 t\cos^2 t}{27a^3|\sin t|^3|\cos t|^3}$$

$$= \frac{1}{3a|\sin t\cos t|} = \frac{2}{3a|\sin 2t|} = \frac{2}{3a}|\csc 2t|$$

At the points corresponding to $t = 0$, $\pi/2$, π, $3\pi/2$, 2π the hypocycloid has a cusp. (See the figure in the solution of Problem 31, Sec. 3.4.)

18.(a) The force is $m\vec{a} = ma_T\vec{T} + ma_N\vec{N}$. Since the speed is constant, $a_T = dv/dt$

$= 0$. Hence $m\vec{a} = ma_N\vec{N}$ and the force is in the direction of $\vec{N}$ (toward the center of the circle).

(b) The magnitude of $m\vec{a} = ma_N\vec{N}$ is $ma_N = m\varkappa v^2 = m(\frac{1}{r})v^2 = \frac{mv^2}{r}$.

19. From Problem 18 the magnitude of the force on a car going 50 mph is mv^2/r $= 2500m/r$. On a track of radius $2r$ the force at v mph is $mv^2/(2r)$. Since the maximum force (to keep the car from rolling) is the same in both cases, we have $mv^2/(2r) = 2500m/r$, from which $v^2 = 5000$ and $v = 50\sqrt{2} \approx 71$ mph.

20. According to Example 3 the maximum curvature occurs at the vertex and is $\varkappa = 1/(2c)$. Since $a_N = \varkappa v^2 = v^2/(2c) \le c$, the maximum speed of the car as it passes the vertex is given by $v^2 = 2c^2$ or $v = c\sqrt{2}$.

22.(a) $a_T = dv/dt = 0$ (because $v = 2$ for all t).

(b) Since $y = x^2$ has the form $4cy = x^2$ with $c = 1/4$, the formula for curvature in Example 3 becomes $\varkappa = 2/(1 + 4x^2)^{3/2}$. Hence $a_N = \varkappa v^2 = 8/(1 + 4x^2)^{3/2}$.

23. Since the speed is constant, $a_T = dv/dt = 0$ and $|\vec{a}| = a_N = \varkappa v^2 = 9\varkappa$. Taking $a = 4$ and $b = 3$ in Problem 15, we find the maximum and minimum values of $|\vec{a}|$ to be $9a/b^2 = 4$ and $9b/a^2 = 27/16$, respectively.

24.(a) See the solution of Problem 4, Sec. 14.7.

(b) $s = \int_0^t 2u\,du = t^2$

(c) $a_T = d^2s/dt^2 = 2$. From the solution of Problem 4, Sec. 14.7 we have $\vec{a} = 2(-2t^2\cos t^2 - \sin t^2, -2t^2\sin t^2 + \cos t^2)$, so

$$|\vec{a}|^2 = 4(4t^4\cos^2 t^2 + 4t^2\sin t^2\cos t^2 + \sin^2 t^2 + 4t^4\sin^2 t^2 - 4t^2\sin t^2\cos t^2 + \cos^2 t^2)$$

$$= 4(4t^4 + 1)$$

Hence $a_N^2 = |\vec{a}|^2 - a_T^2 = 4(4t^4 + 1) - 4 = 16t^4$ and $a_N = 4t^2$.

(d) Since $a_N = \varkappa v^2$, we have $\varkappa = a_N/v^2 = \frac{4t^2}{4t^2} = 1$, so $\varkappa$ is, as it should be, the reciprocal of the radius.

25.(a) $x' = -3a\cos^2 t\sin t$ and $y' = 3a\sin^2 t\cos t$, so

$$x'^2 + y'^2 = 9a^2\cos^4 t\sin^2 t + 9a^2\sin^4 t\cos^2 t = 9a^2\sin^2 t\cos^2 t\,(\cos^2 t + \sin^2 t)$$

$$= 9a^2\sin^2 t\cos^2 t$$

Hence the speed is $ds/dt = |3a\sin t\cos t| = 3a\sin t\cos t$ (because $0 \le t \le \pi/2$) $= \frac{3}{2}a\sin 2t$. The distance is

$$s = \int_0^{\pi/2} \frac{3}{2}a\sin 2t\,dt = -\frac{3}{4}a\cos 2t \Big|_0^{\pi/2} = \frac{3}{2}a$$

(b) $a_T = d^2s/dt^2 = 3a\cos 2t$

(c) From Problem 17 we have $a_N = \varkappa v^2 = \frac{2}{3a}|\csc 2t|\cdot\frac{9}{4}a^2\sin^2 2t$. In the domain $0 < t < \pi/2$ (or $0 < 2t < \pi$) we can drop the absolute value, obtaining $a_N = \frac{3}{2}a\sin 2t$.

26. (a) $\vec{v} = (\sinh t, \cosh t)$ and $\vec{a} = (\cosh t, \sinh t) = \vec{F}(t)$, so the force $m\vec{a} = m\vec{F}(t)$ has the same direction as the position vector (which points from the origin to the particle). If we place its initial point at the particle, the force is directed from the particle away from the origin.

(b) $ds/dt = |\vec{v}| = \sqrt{\sinh^2 t + \cosh^2 t} = \sqrt{1 + 2\sinh^2 t}$. The minimum speed occurs when $\sinh t = 0$ (at $t = 0$) and is equal to 1. The corresponding point of the curve is $(1,0)$.

(c) $a_T = \dfrac{d^2s}{dt^2} = \dfrac{2\sinh t\cosh t}{\sqrt{1 + 2\sinh^2 t}}$

(d) $x' = \sinh t$, $x'' = \cosh t$, $y' = \cosh t$, and $y'' = \sinh t$, so

$$\varkappa = \frac{|\sinh^2 t - \cosh^2 t|}{(\sinh^2 t + \cosh^2 t)^{3/2}} = \frac{1}{(1 + 2\sinh^2 t)^{3/2}}$$

The curve is the right-hand branch of the hyperbola $x^2 - y^2 = \cosh^2 t - \sinh^2 t = 1$. The curvature is largest when $\sinh t = 0$ (at $t = 0$), which occurs at the point $(1,0)$. Its value at this point is $\varkappa = 1$, so the radius of curvature is $1/\varkappa = 1$. See Figure 6.

(e) $a_N = \varkappa\left(\dfrac{ds}{dt}\right)^2 = \dfrac{1 + 2\sinh^2 t}{(1 + 2\sinh^2 t)^{3/2}} = \dfrac{1}{\sqrt{1 + 2\sinh^2 t}}$

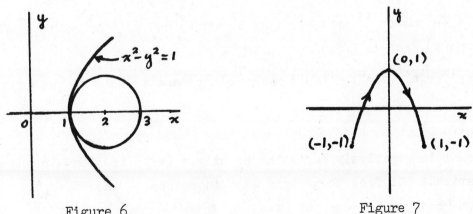

Figure 6   Figure 7

27. (a) $y = \cos 2t = \cos^2 t - \sin^2 t = 1 - 2\sin^2 t = 1 - 2x^2$. Since $x = \sin t$ increases in $(-\pi/2, \pi/2)$, the range of x is $-1 \le x \le 1$. See Figure 7.

(b) $x' = \cos t$ and $y' = -2\sin 2t = -4\sin t\cos t$, so

$$x'^2 + y'^2 = \cos^2 t + 16 \sin^2 t \cos^2 t = \cos^2 t \, (1 + 16 \sin^2 t)$$

Hence $ds/dt = |\cos t|\sqrt{1 + 16 \sin^2 t} = \cos t \sqrt{1 + 16 \sin^2 t}$ (because $-\pi/2 \le t \le \pi/2$).

(c) $s = 2\displaystyle\int_0^{\pi/2} \cos t \sqrt{1 + 16 \sin^2 t}\, dt = \frac{1}{2}\int_0^4 \sqrt{1 + u^2}\, du$ ($u = 4\sin t,\ du = 4\cos t\, dt$)

$$= \left[\tfrac{1}{4}u\sqrt{1 + u^2} + \tfrac{1}{4}\ell n\,(u + \sqrt{1 + u^2})\right]\Big|_0^4 = \sqrt{17} + \tfrac{1}{4}\ell n\,(4 + \sqrt{17})$$

(d) $y' = -4x$ and $y'' = -4$, so $\varkappa = 4/(1 + 16x^2)^{3/2}$. Hence

$$a_N = \varkappa\left(\frac{ds}{dt}\right)^2 = \frac{4\cos^2 t\,(1 + 16\sin^2 t)}{(1 + 16\sin^2 t)^{3/2}} = \frac{4\cos^2 t}{\sqrt{1 + 16\sin^2 t}}$$

28.(a) $x' = -t\sin t + \cos t$ and $y' = t\cos t + \sin t$, so

$$x'^2 + y'^2 = t^2\sin^2 t - 2t\sin t\cos t + \cos^2 t + t^2\cos^2 t + 2t\sin t\cos t + \sin^2 t$$
$$= t^2 + 1$$

Hence $ds/dt = \sqrt{t^2 + 1}$.

(b) $s = \displaystyle\int_0^t \sqrt{u^2 + 1}\, du = \tfrac{1}{2}t\sqrt{t^2 + 1} + \tfrac{1}{2}\ell n\,(t + \sqrt{t^2 + 1})$

(c) $x'' = -t\cos t - \sin t - \sin t = -t\cos t - 2\sin t$ and $y'' = -t\sin t + \cos t + \cos t = -t\sin t + 2\cos t$, so

$$\varkappa = \frac{|t^2\sin^2 t - 3t\sin t\cos t + 2\cos^2 t + t^2\cos^2 t + 3t\sin t\cos t + 2\sin^2 t|}{(t^2 + 1)^{3/2}}$$

$$= \frac{t^2 + 2}{(t^2 + 1)^{3/2}} \to 0 \text{ as } t \to \infty$$

The spiral $r = \theta$ gets more nearly straight as it recedes from the origin, so it is reasonable that $\varkappa \to 0$.

(d) $a_T = \dfrac{d^2 s}{dt^2} = \dfrac{t}{\sqrt{t^2 + 1}}$ and $a_N = \varkappa\left(\dfrac{ds}{dt}\right)^2 = \dfrac{(t^2 + 2)(t^2 + 1)}{(t^2 + 1)^{3/2}} = \dfrac{t^2 + 2}{\sqrt{t^2 + 1}}$.

29.(a) $x' = -e^t\sin t + e^t\cos t = e^t(\cos t - \sin t)$ and $y' = e^t\cos t + e^t\sin t = e^t(\cos t + \sin t)$, so

$$x'^2 + y'^2 = e^{2t}(\cos^2 t - 2\sin t\cos t + \sin^2 t + \cos^2 t + 2\sin t\cos t + \sin^2 t)$$
$$= 2e^{2t}$$

Hence $ds/dt = \sqrt{2}\, e^t$.

(b) When t is negatively large the point $\vec{x} = (x,y)$ is close to the origin; its path spirals out from the origin as t increases. Hence

$$s = \int_{-\infty}^t \sqrt{2}\, e^u\, du = \lim_{a \to -\infty} \sqrt{2}(e^t - e^a) = \sqrt{2}\, e^t$$

(c) $x'' = e^t(-\sin t - \cos t) + e^t(\cos t - \sin t) = -2e^t\sin t$ and $y'' = e^t(-\sin t + \cos t) + e^t(\cos t + \sin t) = 2e^t\cos t$, so

$$\varkappa = \frac{\left|2e^{2t}\cos t\,(\cos t - \sin t) + 2e^{2t}\sin t\,(\cos t + \sin t)\right|}{(2e^{2t})^{3/2}} = \frac{2e^{2t}}{2\sqrt{2}\,e^{3t}} = \frac{1}{\sqrt{2}\,e^t}$$

$$= \frac{1}{s}$$

When the particle is near the origin, t is negatively large and $s = \sqrt{2}\,e^t$ is small. Hence $\varkappa$ is large (which is consistent with the fact that the spiral is "tight" near the origin). When the particle is far away from the origin, t is large and s is large, so $\varkappa$ is small. (This is consistent with the fact that the spiral gets more nearly straight as it recedes from the origin.)

(d) $a_T = \dfrac{d^2 s}{dt^2} = \sqrt{2}\,e^t$ and $a_N = \varkappa\left(\dfrac{ds}{dt}\right)^2 = \dfrac{2e^{2t}}{\sqrt{2}\,e^t} = \sqrt{2}\,e^t$.

(e) From part (c) we have $\vec{a} = 2e^t(-\sin t, \cos t)$, while $\vec{x} = e^t(\cos t, \sin t)$. Hence $\vec{x}\cdot\vec{a} = 2e^{2t}(-\sin t\cos t + \sin t\cos t) = 0$. See Figure 8.

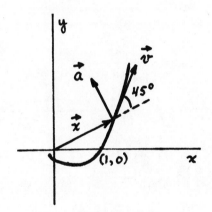

Figure 8

30.(a) $x' = -\dfrac{1}{2}(1 + t^2)^{-3/2}(2t) = \dfrac{-t}{(1 + t^2)^{3/2}}$ and

$$y' = \frac{\sqrt{1 + t^2} - t\,(t/\sqrt{1 + t^2})}{1 + t^2} = \frac{(1 + t^2) - t^2}{(1 + t^2)^{3/2}} = \frac{1}{(1 + t^2)^{3/2}}$$

Hence $x'^2 + y'^2 = \dfrac{t^2}{(1 + t^2)^3} + \dfrac{1}{(1 + t^2)^3} = \dfrac{1 + t^2}{(1 + t^2)^3} = \dfrac{1}{(1 + t^2)^2}$ and $\dfrac{ds}{dt} = \dfrac{1}{1 + t^2}$.

(b) When t is negatively large, x is close to 0 and y is close to -1. When t is positively large, x is close to 0 and y is close to 1. Hence the path is an arc with endpoints (0,-1) and (0,1). These points are not on the path, however, because x > 0 and -1 < y < 1 for all t. The particle traverses the path without stopping or changing direction because ds/dt > 0 for all t. When the particle is near (0,±1), t^2 is large and hence ds/dt is close to 0. The speed is largest when t = 0, the particle being at (1,0).

(c) Since $ds/dt = 1/(1+t^2)$, the part of the path corresponding to $-b \le t \le b$ (where b is arbitrary) has length $\int_{-b}^{b} \frac{dt}{1+t^2}$. Hence the whole path has length

$$\int_{-\infty}^{\infty} \frac{dt}{1+t^2} = 2 \int_{0}^{\infty} \frac{dt}{1+t^2} = 2 \lim_{b \to \infty} (\tan^{-1} b) = 2 \cdot \frac{\pi}{2} = \pi$$

(d) $a_T = \frac{d^2 s}{dt^2} = -(1+t^2)^{-2}(2t) = \frac{-2t}{(1+t^2)^2}$. The particle is speeding up when $a_T = dv/dt > 0$ (or $t < 0$), slowing down when $a_T < 0$ (or $t > 0$). Thus on the part of the path joining $(0,-1)$ and $(1,0)$ the particle is speeding up; it is slowing down on the part joining $(1,0)$ and $(0,1)$. Its speed is largest at $(1,0)$, as we saw in part (b).

(e) $x'' = \dfrac{(1+t^2)^{3/2}(-1) + t(3/2)(1+t^2)^{1/2}(2t)}{(1+t^2)^3} = \dfrac{(1+t^2)^{1/2}[-(1+t^2)+3t^2]}{(1+t^2)^3}$

$= \dfrac{2t^2 - 1}{(1+t^2)^{5/2}}$

$y'' = -\dfrac{3}{2}(1+t^2)^{-5/2}(2t) = \dfrac{-3t}{(1+t^2)^{5/2}}$

Hence $|\vec{a}|^2 = \dfrac{4t^4 - 4t^2 + 1 + 9t^2}{(1+t^2)^5} = \dfrac{(4t^2+1)(t^2+1)}{(1+t^2)^5} = \dfrac{4t^2+1}{(1+t^2)^4}$, from which

$a_N^2 = |\vec{a}|^2 - a_T^2 = \dfrac{4t^2+1}{(1+t^2)^4} - \dfrac{4t^2}{(1+t^2)^4} = \dfrac{1}{(1+t^2)^4}$ and $a_N = \dfrac{1}{(1+t^2)^2}$

It follows from $a_N = \varkappa (ds/dt)^2$ that $\varkappa = 1$.

(f) The length of half the unit circle is $\frac{1}{2}(2\pi \cdot 1) = \pi$ and the curvature is $\varkappa = 1/1 = 1$.

Chapter 14   TRUE-FALSE QUIZ

1. True. The terminal side of angle $\theta + \pi$ is the backward extension of the terminal side of angle θ.

2. True. $r\cos(\theta - \pi/2) = 3 \iff r\sin\theta = 3 \iff y = 3$.

3. True. If $r \ne 0$, $r = \cos\theta \iff r^2 = r\cos\theta \iff x^2 + y^2 = x$ (which is a circle), and the origin ($r = 0$) is on both curves.

4. True. Clockwise means θ is decreasing, so $r = e^\theta \to 0$.

5. False. The standard form $4cy = x^2$ shows that $c = 1$, so the distance between the focus and <u>vertex</u> (not directrix) is 1.

6. False. A circle is not a conic; its eccentricity is not even defined. Since an ellipse with small eccentricity is nearly circular, some textbooks adopt the convention that a circle has eccentricity 0, but even so the

statement is still false. A conic with eccentricity 1 is a parabola.

7. False. The asymptotes are $x^2 - 4y^2 = 0$, or $y = \pm\frac{1}{2}x$.

8. False. The standard form is $r = \dfrac{2/3}{1 - (2/3)\cos\theta}$, so the eccentricity is 2/3 and the curve is an ellipse.

9. False. The graph is the union of the lines $y = \pm x$.

10. True. $(1,-2)\cdot(4,2) = 4 - 4 = 0$.

11. True. $\cos\theta = \dfrac{\vec{u}\cdot\vec{v}}{|\vec{u}|\,|\vec{v}|} = \vec{u}\cdot\vec{v}$ because $|\vec{u}| = |\vec{v}| = 1$.

12. True. The path is the straight line $y = 2(x - 1)$.

13. True. The path is the circle $x^2 + y^2 = 4$, with radius 2 and curvature $\frac{1}{2}$.

14. False. $dv/dt = a_T$ is the tangential component of acceleration. Even in straight line motion (when $a_N = 0$) the statement should read that $|dv/dt|$ is the magnitude of the acceleration.

15. True. $a_T = dv/dt = 0$ when v has an extreme value.

Chapter 14   ADDITIONAL PROBLEMS

1. The graphs intersect when $6\cos\theta = 6\sin 2\theta \iff \cos\theta = 2\sin\theta\cos\theta \iff$ $\cos\theta(2\sin\theta - 1) = 0 \iff \cos\theta = 0$ or $\sin\theta = \frac{1}{2} \iff \theta = \pi/2$ or $\theta = \pi/6,\ 5\pi/6$ (in the domain $0 \le \theta \le \pi$, which generates the circle). The points of intersection are the origin, $(3\sqrt{3}, \pi/6)$, and $(-3\sqrt{3}, 5\pi/6)$, the latter point also being $(3\sqrt{3}, -\pi/6)$. See Figure 1.

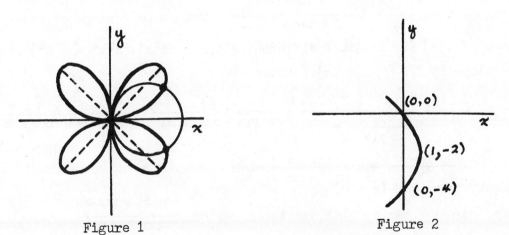

Figure 1   Figure 2

2. $y^2 + 4x + 4y = 0 \iff y^2 + 4y + 4 = -4x + 4 \iff (y + 2)^2 = -4(x - 1)$. The vertex is $(1,-2)$ and the axis is $y = -2$. Since $4c = -4$, $c = -1$; the focus is $(0,-2)$ and the directrix is $x = 2$. See Figure 2.

3. $4x^2 + 9y^2 - 40x + 64 = 0 \iff 4(x^2 - 10x + 25) + 9y^2 = -64 + 100 \iff$

$4(x-5)^2 + 9y^2 = 36 \iff (x-5)^2/9 + y^2/4 = 1$, so $a = 3$, $b = 2$, and $c = \sqrt{a^2-b^2}$ $= \sqrt{5}$.   Center and endpoints shown in Figure 3, foci $(5 \pm \sqrt{5}, 0)$, directrices $x = 5 \pm a^2/c = 5 \pm 9/\sqrt{5}$, $e = c/a = \sqrt{5}/3$.

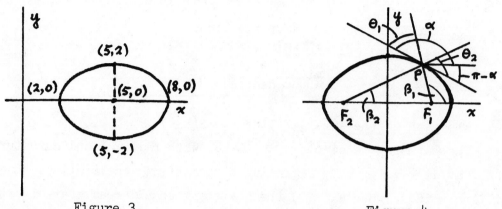

<table>
<tr><td>Figure 3</td><td>Figure 4</td></tr>
</table>

4. Choose the coordinate system so that the hyperbola is $x^2/a^2 - y^2/b^2 = 1$, and suppose that the line in question passes through the focus $(c, 0)$ perpendicular to the asymptote $y = \frac{b}{a}x$. Then the slope of the line is $-a/b$ and an equation is $y = -\frac{a}{b}(x - c)$. The line intersects the asymptote when

$$-\frac{a}{b}(x-c) = \frac{b}{a}x \iff -a^2(x-c) = b^2 x \iff a^2 c = (a^2 + b^2)x = c^2 x$$
$$\iff x = a^2/c$$

Since $x = a^2/c$ is a directrix, the stated property is correct.

5.(a) See Figure 4.

(b) $\tan \theta_1 = \tan(\alpha - \beta_1) = \dfrac{\tan\alpha - \tan\beta_1}{1 + \tan\alpha\tan\beta_1}$. But $\tan\alpha$ = slope of tangent = $dy/dx = -b^2 x/(a^2 y)$ (by implicit differentiation in $b^2 x^2 + a^2 y^2 = a^2 b^2$) and $\tan\beta_1$ = slope of $F_1 P = y/(x-c)$.   Hence

$$\tan\theta_1 = \frac{-b^2 x/(a^2 y) - y/(x-c)}{1 - \dfrac{b^2 xy}{a^2 y(x-c)}} = \frac{-b^2 x(x-c) - a^2 y^2}{a^2 y(x-c) - b^2 xy} = \frac{b^2 cx - (b^2 x^2 + a^2 y^2)}{y[(a^2 - b^2)x - a^2 c]}$$

$$= \frac{b^2 cx - a^2 b^2}{y(c^2 x - a^2 c)} = \frac{b^2(cx - a^2)}{cy(cx - a^2)} = \frac{b^2}{cy}$$

Similarly, $\tan\theta_2 = \tan(\pi - \alpha + \beta_2) = \tan(\beta_2 - \alpha) = \dfrac{\tan\beta_2 - \tan\alpha}{1 + \tan\beta_2 \tan\alpha}$

$$= \frac{y/(x+c) + b^2 x/(a^2 y)}{1 - \dfrac{b^2 xy}{a^2 y(x+c)}} = \frac{a^2 y^2 + b^2 x(x+c)}{a^2 y(x+c) - b^2 xy} = \frac{(b^2 x^2 + a^2 y^2) + b^2 cx}{y[(a^2 - b^2)x + a^2 c]}$$

$$= \frac{a^2 b^2 + b^2 cx}{y(c^2 x + a^2 c)} = \frac{b^2(a^2 + cx)}{cy(cx + a^2)} = \frac{b^2}{cy}$$

Thus $\tan \theta_1 = \tan \theta_2$; since θ_1 and θ_2 are acute angles, it follows that $\theta_1 = \theta_2$.

6. Choose the coordinate system so that the hyperbola is $x^2/a^2 - y^2/b^2 = 1$, with foci $F_1 = (c,0)$ and $F_2 = (-c,0)$, and let $P = (x,y)$ be a point of the hyperbola in the first quadrant. Then (see Figure 5) $\theta_1 = \beta_1 - \alpha$ and $\theta_2 = \alpha - \beta_2$, where θ_1, θ_2, α, β_1, β_2 have the same meaning as in Problem 5. Since $dy/dx = b^2x/(a^2y)$ (from implicit differentiation in $b^2x^2 - a^2y^2 = a^2b^2$), we find $\tan \theta_1 = \tan(\beta_1 - \alpha) = \dfrac{\tan \beta_1 - \tan \alpha}{1 + \tan \beta_1 \tan \alpha} = \dfrac{y/(x-c) - b^2x/(a^2y)}{1 + \dfrac{b^2xy}{a^2y(x-c)}}$

$$= \frac{a^2y^2 - b^2x(x-c)}{a^2y(x-c) + b^2xy} = \frac{b^2cx - (b^2x^2 - a^2y^2)}{y[(a^2 + b^2)x - a^2c]} = \frac{b^2cx - a^2b^2}{y(c^2x - a^2c)}$$

$$= \frac{b^2(cx - a^2)}{cy(cx - a^2)} = \frac{b^2}{cy}$$

Similarly, $\tan \theta_2 = b^2/(cy)$, so $\tan \theta_1 = \tan \theta_2$. Since θ_1 and θ_2 are acute, it follows that $\theta_1 = \theta_2$.

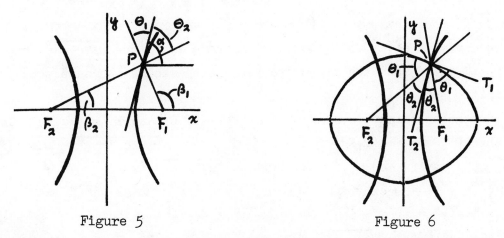

Figure 5   Figure 6

7. Let P be a point of intersection of an ellipse and hyperbola with common foci F_1 and F_2. (See Figure 6.) Then F_1P and F_2P make the same angle θ_1 with the tangent to the ellipse at P, and they make the same angle θ_2 with the tangent to the hyperbola at P. The angle between the tangents is $\theta_1 + \theta_2$; since $(\theta_1 + \theta_2) + (\theta_2 + \theta_1) = 180°$, we have $\theta_1 + \theta_2 = 90°$.

8. For the ellipse we have $c^2 = a^2 - b^2 = k^2 - (k^2 - 1) = 1$ and for the hyperbola $c^2 = a^2 + b^2 = \ell^2 + (1 - \ell^2) = 1$. Hence $c = 1$ in both cases and the common foci are $(\pm 1, 0)$. See Figure 7.

9. Let F be the focus and L the directrix, and suppose that $P = (x,y)$ is any point of the plane. If S is the ellipse, then $P \in S \iff d(P,F)/d(P,L) = 1/2$ $\iff 2d(P,F) = d(P,L) \iff 2\sqrt{(x-2)^2 + (y-1)^2} = |2x + y - 8|/\sqrt{5} \iff$

231

$4[(x-2)^2 + (y-1)^2] = (2x+y-8)^2/5 \iff 20(x^2-4x+4+y^2-2y+1) = 4x^2+y^2+$
$64+4xy-32x-16y \iff 16x^2-4xy+19y^2-48x-24y+36 = 0.$

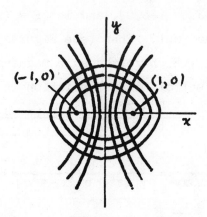

Figure 7

10. Choose the coordinate system so that $F_1 = (c,0)$ and $F_2 = (-c,0)$. If $P = (x,y)$, then $P \in S \iff d(P,F_1) = 2a - d(P,F_2) \iff \sqrt{(x-c)^2+y^2} = 2a - \sqrt{(x+c)^2+y^2} \iff (x-c)^2+y^2 = 4a^2 - 4a\sqrt{(x+c)^2+y^2} + (x+c)^2+y^2 \iff a\sqrt{(x+c)^2+y^2} = a^2+cx \iff a^2[(x+c)^2+y^2] = a^4 + 2a^2cx + c^2x^2 \iff (a^2-c^2)x^2 + a^2y^2 = a^2(a^2-c^2) \iff b^2x^2 + a^2y^2 = a^2b^2 \ (b = \sqrt{a^2-c^2}) \iff x^2/a^2 + y^2/b^2 = 1$. Thus the alternate definition yields the same equation as the definition of conic does.

11. Choose the coordinate system so that $F_1 = (c,0)$ and $F_2 = (-c,0)$. If $P = (x,y)$, then $P \in S \iff d(P,F_1) = \pm 2a + d(P,F_2) \iff \sqrt{(x-c)^2+y^2} = \pm 2a + \sqrt{(x+c)^2+y^2} \iff (x-c)^2+y^2 = 4a^2 \pm 4a\sqrt{(x+c)^2+y^2} + (x+c)^2+y^2 \iff \mp a\sqrt{(x+c)^2+y^2} = a^2+cx \iff a^2[(x+c)^2+y^2] = a^4 + 2a^2cx + c^2x^2 \iff (a^2-c^2)x^2 + a^2y^2 = a^2(a^2-c^2) \iff (c^2-a^2)x^2 - a^2y^2 = a^2(c^2-a^2) \iff b^2x^2 - a^2y^2 = a^2b^2 \ (b = \sqrt{c^2-a^2}) \iff x^2/a^2 - y^2/b^2 = 1$. Thus the alternate definition yields the same equation as the definition of conic does.

12.(a) This is apparent when P is as shown in Figure 1 in the text. In general it is a matter of observing that $d(0,P)$ is not affected by rotation and the polar angle is decreased by α when the axes are rotated counterclockwise through angle α.

(b) $\bar{x} = r\cos(\theta-\alpha) = r\cos\theta\cos\alpha + r\sin\theta\sin\alpha = x\cos\alpha + y\sin\alpha$

$\bar{y} = r\sin(\theta-\alpha) = r\sin\theta\cos\alpha - r\cos\theta\sin\alpha = -x\sin\alpha + y\cos\alpha$

Solve for x by eliminating y:

$\bar{x}\cos\alpha = x\cos^2\alpha + y\sin\alpha\cos\alpha$

$\bar{y}\sin\alpha = -x\sin^2\alpha + y\sin\alpha\cos\alpha$

$\bar{x}\cos\alpha - \bar{y}\sin\alpha = x(\cos^2\alpha + \sin^2\alpha) \iff x = \bar{x}\cos\alpha - \bar{y}\sin\alpha$

Similarly, solve for y by eliminating x:

$$\overline{x} \sin \alpha = x \sin \alpha \cos \alpha + y \sin^2 \alpha$$

$$\overline{y} \cos \alpha = -x \sin \alpha \cos \alpha + y \cos^2 \alpha$$

$$\overline{x} \sin \alpha + \overline{y} \cos \alpha = y(\sin^2 \alpha + \cos^2 \alpha) \iff y = \overline{x} \sin \alpha + \overline{y} \cos \alpha$$

13. Substitute $x = \overline{x} \cos \alpha - \overline{y} \sin \alpha$ and $y = \overline{x} \sin \alpha + \overline{y} \cos \alpha$ in the equation:

$A(\overline{x}^2 \cos^2 \alpha - 2\overline{x}\,\overline{y} \sin \alpha \cos \alpha + \overline{y}^2 \sin^2 \alpha) + B(\overline{x}^2 \sin \alpha \cos \alpha + \overline{x}\,\overline{y} \cos^2 \alpha - \overline{x}\,\overline{y} \sin^2 \alpha - \overline{y}^2 \sin \alpha \cos \alpha) + C(\overline{x}^2 \sin^2 \alpha + 2\overline{x}\,\overline{y} \sin \alpha \cos \alpha + \overline{y}^2 \cos^2 \alpha) + D(\overline{x} \cos \alpha - \overline{y} \sin \alpha) + E(\overline{x} \sin \alpha + \overline{y} \cos \alpha) + F = 0$, that is,

$(A \cos^2 \alpha + B \sin \alpha \cos \alpha + C \sin^2 \alpha)\overline{x}^2 + [B(\cos^2 \alpha - \sin^2 \alpha) - 2(A - C) \sin \alpha \cos \alpha]\overline{x}\,\overline{y} + (A \sin^2 \alpha - B \sin \alpha \cos \alpha + C \cos^2 \alpha)\overline{y}^2 + (D \cos \alpha + E \sin \alpha)\overline{x} + (-D \sin \alpha + E \cos \alpha)\overline{y} + F = 0$. The new coefficients are all as given in the problem except the coefficient of $\overline{x}\,\overline{y}$. The formulas $\cos^2 \alpha - \sin^2 \alpha = \cos 2\alpha$ and $2 \sin \alpha \cos \alpha = \sin 2\alpha$, however, change that one into the desired form as well.

14. We are assuming that $B \neq 0$ in the original equation. (Otherwise there would be no need to rotate the axes.) Moreover, $0 < \alpha < \pi/2$, that is, $0 < 2\alpha < \pi$. Hence $\sin 2\alpha \neq 0$ and we have $\overline{B} = 0 \iff B \cos 2\alpha = (A - C) \sin 2\alpha$ $\iff \cot 2\alpha = (A - C)/B$.

15. $\overline{A} + \overline{C} = A(\cos^2 \alpha + \sin^2 \alpha) + C(\sin^2 \alpha + \cos^2 \alpha) = A + C$.

16. $\overline{B}^2 - 4\overline{A}\,\overline{C} = B^2 \cos^2 2\alpha - 2B(A - C) \sin 2\alpha \cos 2\alpha + (A^2 - 2AC + C^2) \sin^2 2\alpha - 4[A^2 \sin^2 \alpha \cos^2 \alpha - AB \sin \alpha \cos^3 \alpha + AC \cos^4 \alpha + AB \sin^3 \alpha \cos \alpha - B^2 \sin^2 \alpha \cos^2 \alpha + BC \sin \alpha \cos^3 \alpha + AC \sin^4 \alpha - BC \sin^3 \alpha \cos \alpha + C^2 \sin^2 \alpha \cos^2 \alpha]$. The coefficient of B^2 on the right side is $\cos^2 2\alpha + 4 \sin^2 \alpha \cos^2 \alpha = \cos^2 2\alpha + \sin^2 2\alpha = 1$, while the coefficient of AC is

$$-2 \sin^2 2\alpha - 4 \cos^4 \alpha - 4 \sin^4 \alpha = -8 \sin^2 \alpha \cos^2 \alpha - 4(\cos^4 \alpha + \sin^4 \alpha)$$
$$= -4(\cos^4 \alpha + 2 \sin^2 \alpha \cos^2 \alpha + \sin^4 \alpha)$$
$$= -4(\cos^2 \alpha + \sin^2 \alpha)^2 = -4$$

Thus the right side includes the expression $B^2 - 4AC$; if the remaining terms add to 0, we are done. We'll check the coefficient of AB and leave the rest to you. (A dreary day should be shared!)

$$-2 \sin 2\alpha \cos 2\alpha + 4 \sin \alpha \cos^3 \alpha - 4 \sin^3 \alpha \cos \alpha = -2 \sin 2\alpha \cos 2\alpha +$$
$$4 \sin \alpha \cos \alpha (\cos^2 \alpha - \sin^2 \alpha) = -2 \sin 2\alpha \cos 2\alpha + 2 \sin 2\alpha \cos 2\alpha = 0$$

17. Assuming that $B \neq 0$, rotate the axes to eliminate the xy term, obtaining $\overline{A}\,\overline{x}^2 + \overline{C}\,\overline{y}^2 + \overline{D}\,\overline{x} + \overline{E}\,\overline{y} + \overline{F} = 0$. From Sec. 14.3 we know that (except for degenerate cases) the graph of this equation is an ellipse if $\overline{A}\,\overline{C} > 0$, a parabola if $\overline{A}\,\overline{C} = 0$, and a hyperbola if $\overline{A}\,\overline{C} < 0$. (A circle cannot occur because $B \neq 0$ in the original equation. See Problem 26.) Since $\overline{B} = 0$,

Problem 16 says that $B^2 - 4AC = -4\overline{A}\,\overline{C}$. Hence $B^2 - 4AC < 0 \Rightarrow \overline{A}\,\overline{C} > 0 \Rightarrow$ ellipse; $B^2 - 4AC = 0 \Rightarrow \overline{A}\,\overline{C} = 0 \Rightarrow$ parabola; and $B^2 - 4AC > 0 \Rightarrow \overline{A}\,\overline{C} < 0 \Rightarrow$ hyperbola. If $B = 0$ in the original equation, no rotation is needed; the discriminant reduces to $-4AC$ and we are back to Sec. 14.3. In that case a circle can occur; the statement of the problem (to be technically correct) should either specify that $B \neq 0$ or include the circle as a possibility when $B^2 - 4AC$ is negative.

18.(a) Since $A = B = C = 1$, we choose α satisfying $\cot 2\alpha = (A - C)/B = 0$, $0 < \alpha < \pi/2$. Hence $2\alpha = \pi/2$ and $\alpha = \pi/4$.

(b) $\overline{A} = \frac{1}{2} + \frac{1}{2} + \frac{1}{2} = 3/2$. Since $\overline{A} + \overline{C} = A + C = 2$, we have $\overline{C} = 2 - 3/2 = \frac{1}{2}$. $\overline{D}$ and $\overline{E}$ are zero because D and E are.

(c) The new equation is $\frac{3}{2}\overline{x}^2 + \frac{1}{2}\overline{y}^2 = 1 \iff \frac{\overline{x}^2}{2/3} + \frac{\overline{y}^2}{2} = 1$. With reference to the new coordinate system, this is a vertical ellipse with center at the origin.

19. $A = 1$, $B = -2$, $C = 1$, so $B^2 - 4AC = 0$ and the curve is a parabola (or a degenerate case). To eliminate the xy term, choose α satisfying $\cot 2\alpha = (A - C)/B = 0$, $0 < \alpha < \pi/2$, that is, $\alpha = \pi/4$. Then $\overline{A} = \frac{1}{2} - 2 \cdot \frac{1}{2} + \frac{1}{2} = 0$ and (since $\overline{A} + \overline{C} = A + C = 2$) $\overline{C} = 2$. Also, since $D = -2$ and $E = 0$, we find $\overline{D} = -\sqrt{2}$ and $\overline{E} = \sqrt{2}$. Hence the new equation is $2\overline{y}^2 - \sqrt{2}\,\overline{x} + \sqrt{2}\,\overline{y} + 5 = 0$, which represents a parabola.

20. $A = 4$, $B = -4$, $C = 1$, so $B^2 - 4AC = 0$ and the curve is a parabola (or a degenerate case). Choose α satisfying $\cot 2\alpha = (A - C)/B = -3/4$, $0 < \alpha < \pi/2$. Since $\pi/2 < 2\alpha < \pi$, we have $\cos 2\alpha = -3/5$ and

$$\sin^2\alpha = \frac{1}{2}\left(1 + \frac{3}{5}\right) = \frac{4}{5}, \quad \cos^2\alpha = \frac{1}{2}\left(1 - \frac{3}{5}\right) = \frac{1}{5}$$

Thus $\sin\alpha = 2/\sqrt{5}$ and $\cos\alpha = 1/\sqrt{5}$, from which $\overline{A} = 4 \cdot \frac{1}{5} - 4 \cdot \frac{2}{5} + \frac{4}{5} = 0$. Since $\overline{A} + \overline{C} = A + C = 5$, $\overline{C} = 5$ and the new equation is $5\overline{y}^2 = 5$ or $\overline{y} = \pm 1$. The "curve" is not a parabola, but a pair of horizontal lines (in the new coordinate system).

21. $A = 1$, $B = -1$, $C = 2$, so $B^2 - 4AC = 1 - 8 < 0$ and the curve is an ellipse (or a degenerate case). Choose α satisfying $\cot 2\alpha = (A - C)/B = 1$, $0 < \alpha < \pi/2$, that is, $2\alpha = \pi/4$ or $\alpha = \pi/8$. Since $\cos 2\alpha = \sqrt{2}/2$, we find

$$\sin^2\alpha = \frac{1}{2}\left(1 - \frac{\sqrt{2}}{2}\right) = \frac{1}{4}(2 - \sqrt{2}), \quad \cos^2\alpha = \frac{1}{2}\left(1 + \frac{\sqrt{2}}{2}\right) = \frac{1}{4}(2 + \sqrt{2})$$

Then $\sin\alpha = \frac{1}{2}(2 - \sqrt{2})^{1/2}$ and $\cos\alpha = \frac{1}{2}(2 + \sqrt{2})^{1/2}$, from which

$\overline{A} = \frac{1}{4}(2+\sqrt{2}) - \frac{\sqrt{2}}{4} + 2 \cdot \frac{1}{4}(2-\sqrt{2}) = \frac{1}{2}(3-\sqrt{2})$

Since $\overline{A} + \overline{C} = A + C = 3$, $\overline{C} = 3 - \frac{1}{2}(3-\sqrt{2}) = \frac{1}{2}(3+\sqrt{2})$ and the new equation is

$\frac{1}{2}(3-\sqrt{2})\overline{x}^2 + \frac{1}{2}(3+\sqrt{2})\overline{y}^2 = 1 \iff (3-\sqrt{2})\overline{x}^2 + (3+\sqrt{2})\overline{y}^2 = 2$. This represents an ellipse.

22. No formulas are needed to see that a rotation through $45°$ is required. Since $A = 0$, $B = 1$, $C = 0$, we find $\overline{A} = \frac{1}{2}$ and $\overline{C} = -\frac{1}{2}$, so the new equation is $\overline{x}^2/2 - \overline{y}^2/2 = 1$. This is a hyperbola with $a^2 = b^2 = 2$ and hence $c^2 = a^2 + b^2 = 4$, or $c = 2$. One focus (in the new coordinate system) is $(\overline{x}, \overline{y}) = (2, 0)$. The old coordinates (from Problem 12) are

$$x = \frac{\sqrt{2}}{2}(\overline{x} - \overline{y}) = \sqrt{2} \quad \text{and} \quad y = \frac{\sqrt{2}}{2}(\overline{x} + \overline{y}) = \sqrt{2}$$

The corresponding directrix is $\overline{x} = a^2/c = 1$. Since $\overline{x} = x\cos\alpha + y\sin\alpha$ (see the solution of Problem 12), this is the line $(1/\sqrt{2})(x+y) = 1$ in the old system, that is, $x + y = \sqrt{2}$. The eccentricity is $e = c/a = 2/\sqrt{2} = \sqrt{2}$. From Figure 8 we can see without further use of formulas that the center is $(0,0)$, the vertices are $(1,1)$ and $(-1,-1)$, and the asymptotes are the original coordinate axes.

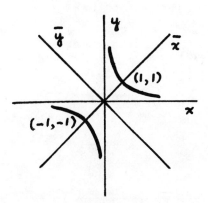

Figure 8

23. $A = 1$, $B = 0$, $C = 0$, so $B^2 - 4AC = 0$ and the graph is a "parabola." Since $x^2 - x - 6 = 0 \iff (x-3)(x+2) = 0 \iff x = 3$ or $x = -2$, the graph is actually the union of the vertical lines $x = 3$ and $x = -2$.

24. $A = 1$, $B = -1$, $C = -2$, so $B^2 - 4AC = 1 + 8 > 0$ and the graph is a "hyperbola." Since $x^2 - xy - 2y^2 = 0 \iff (x-2y)(x+y) = 0 \iff x - 2y = 0$ or $x + y = 0$, the graph is actually the union of the lines $y = \frac{1}{2}x$ and $y = -x$.

25. $A = 1$, $B = -2$, $C = 1$, so $B^2 - 4AC = 0$ and the graph is a "parabola." Since $x^2 - 2xy + y^2 - 1 = 0 \iff (x-y)^2 = 1 \iff x - y = \pm 1$, the graph is actually the

union of the lines $x - y = \pm 1$.

26. Rotate the axes to eliminate the xy term, obtaining $\overline{A}\overline{x}^2 + \overline{C}\overline{y}^2 + \overline{D}\overline{x} + \overline{E}\overline{y} + \overline{F} = 0$. If this represents a circle, then $\overline{A} = \overline{C}$, that is,

$$A\cos^2\alpha + B\sin\alpha\cos\alpha + C\sin^2\alpha = A\sin^2\alpha - B\sin\alpha\cos\alpha + C\cos^2\alpha$$

$$2B\sin\alpha\cos\alpha + (A - C)(\cos^2\alpha - \sin^2\alpha) = 0$$

$$B\sin 2\alpha + (A - C)\cos 2\alpha = 0$$

Since $\cot 2\alpha = (A - C)/B$, we have $A - C = B\cot 2\alpha$ and the preceding equation reads $B\sin 2\alpha + B\cot 2\alpha\cos 2\alpha = 0 \iff \sin 2\alpha + \cos^2 2\alpha/\sin 2\alpha = 0 \iff \sin^2 2\alpha + \cos^2 2\alpha = 0$. This is impossible; the original equation cannot represent a circle.

27. From Figure 9 we conclude that

$$A = \frac{1}{2}\int_0^\pi \frac{9\,d\theta}{(1 + \sin\theta)^2}$$

Since this is not easy to evaluate, we change to rectangular coordinates, $y = \frac{1}{6}(9 - x^2)$. Then

$$A = 2\int_0^3 \frac{1}{6}(9 - x^2)\,dx = \frac{1}{3}\left(9x - \frac{x^3}{3}\right)\Big|_0^3 = 6$$

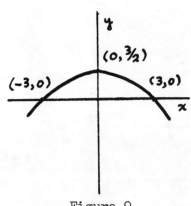

Figure 9

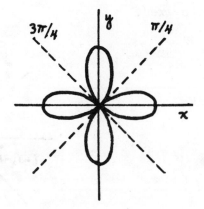

Figure 10

28. From Figure 10 we conclude that

$$A = 8\cdot\frac{1}{2}\int_0^{\pi/4} 9\cos^2 2\theta\,d\theta = 18\int_0^{\pi/4}(1 + \cos 4\theta)\,d\theta = \frac{9}{2}\pi$$

29. Since $r' = -a\sin\theta$, $r^2 + r'^2 = a^2(1 + \cos\theta)^2 + a^2\sin^2\theta = a^2(1 + 2\cos\theta + \cos^2\theta + \sin^2\theta) = 2a^2(1 + \cos\theta) = 4a^2\cos^2\frac{1}{2}\theta$. The curve is shown in the solution of Problem 27, Sec. 14.1; we integrate from cusp back to cusp:

$$s = \int_{-\pi}^\pi 2a\cos\tfrac{1}{2}\theta\,d\theta = 4a\sin\tfrac{1}{2}\theta\Big|_{-\pi}^\pi = 8a$$

(Check by Example 5, Sec. 14.4, which is a cardioid of the same length.)

236

30. Since $r' = -2e^{-2\theta}$, $r^2 + r'^2 = e^{-4\theta} + 4e^{-4\theta} = 5e^{-4\theta}$. Since the curve spirals toward the origin as $\theta \to \infty$, the length is

$$s = \int_0^\infty \sqrt{5}\, e^{-2\theta} d\theta = \lim_{b \to \infty} \tfrac{1}{2}\sqrt{5}(1 - e^{-2b}) = \tfrac{1}{2}\sqrt{5}$$

31. From Figure 11 we have

$$\cos\theta = \frac{\vec{AB}\cdot\vec{AC}}{|\vec{AB}||\vec{AC}|} = \frac{(-1,-2)\cdot(2,-6)}{\sqrt{5}\cdot 2\sqrt{10}} = \frac{-2+12}{10\sqrt{2}} = \frac{1}{\sqrt{2}}$$

Hence $\theta = 45°$.

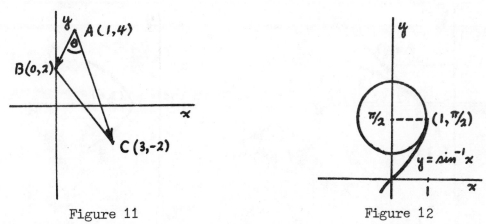

Figure 11   Figure 12

32. $y' = 1/\sqrt{1 - x^2}$ and $y'' = -\tfrac{1}{2}(1 - x^2)^{-3/2}(-2x) = x/(1 - x^2)^{3/2}$, so

$$\varkappa = \frac{|x|/(1 - x^2)^{3/2}}{\left(1 + \dfrac{1}{1 - x^2}\right)^{3/2}} = \frac{|x|}{(2 - x^2)^{3/2}} = \frac{x}{(2 - x^2)^{3/2}} \quad \text{if } 0 \le x \le 1$$

Since the numerator increases and the denominator decreases in $[0,1]$, $\varkappa$ increases. Its maximum and minimum values are $\varkappa = 1$ (at $x = 1$) and $\varkappa = 0$ (at $x = 0$). At $(1,\pi/2)$ we have $\varkappa = 1$, so the radius of the circle of curvature is $1/\varkappa = 1$. The tangent to the graph of $y = \sin^{-1}x$ at this point is vertical, so the radius from the center of the circle to $(1,\pi/2)$ is horizontal. The center is therefore $(0,\pi/2)$, as shown in Figure 12.

33. (a) Since $t = \ln x$, we have $y = \ln x$. The curve is traversed as indicated in Figure 13 because x and y increase with t.

(b) $\vec{v} = (e^t,1) = (1,1)$ when $t = 0$, and $v = ds/dt = (e^{2t} + 1)^{1/2} = \sqrt{2}$. If $P(x,y)$ is the position of the particle 1 sec after flying off on the tangent at $P_0(1,0)$, then $\vec{P_0P} = k(1,1)$, where k is a positive constant. Since $v = \sqrt{2}$, the distance traveled in 1 sec is $|\vec{P_0P}| = \sqrt{2}$, that is, $k\sqrt{2} = \sqrt{2}$. Hence $k = 1$ and $\vec{P_0P} = (1,1)$, from which $x - 1 = 1$ and $y = 1$. Thus $P = (2,1)$.

(c) $a_T = \dfrac{dv}{dt} = \dfrac{e^{2t}}{(e^{2t}+1)^{1/2}}$

(d) Referring to the equations $x = e^t$, $y = t$, we have $x' = e^t$, $x'' = e^t$, $y' = 1$, $y'' = 0$. Hence

$$\varkappa = \frac{\left|0 - e^t\right|}{(e^{2t}+1)^{3/2}} = \frac{e^t}{(e^{2t}+1)^{3/2}}$$

(e) $a_N = \varkappa v^2 = \dfrac{e^t(e^{2t}+1)}{(e^{2t}+1)^{3/2}} = \dfrac{e^t}{(e^{2t}+1)^{1/2}}$

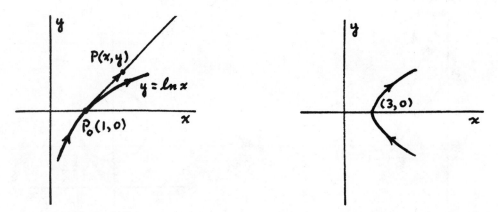

Figure 13   Figure 14

34.(a) Since $x = 3\cosh t$ and $y = 2\sinh t$, we have $x^2/9 - y^2/4 = \cosh^2 t - \sinh^2 t = 1$. This is the right-hand branch of a hyperbola (because $x = 3\cosh t \geq 3$), traversed upward because y increases with t. See Figure 14.

(b) $x' = 3\sinh t$ and $y' = 2\cosh t$, so $x'^2 + y'^2 = 9\sinh^2 t + 4\cosh^2 t = 13\sinh^2 t + 4$. Hence $v = ds/dt = \sqrt{13\sinh^2 t + 4}$, which is smallest when $\sinh t = 0$ (or $t = 0$). The minimum speed is 2 at $(3,0)$.

(c) $x'' = 3\cosh t$ and $y'' = 2\sinh t$, so

$$\varkappa = \frac{\left|6\sinh^2 t - 6\cosh^2 t\right|}{(13\sinh^2 t + 4)^{3/2}} = \frac{6}{(13\sinh^2 t + 4)^{3/2}}$$

This is largest when $\sinh t = 0$ (or $t = 0$). The maximum curvature is $3/4$ at $(3,0)$. When $t \to \infty$, $\varkappa \to 0$.

(d) $\vec{v} = (3\sinh t, 2\cosh t)$ and $\vec{a} = (3\cosh t, 2\sinh t) = \vec{F}(t)$, so $m\vec{a} = m\vec{F}(t)$, which is in the same direction as $\vec{x} = \vec{F}(t)$, namely away from the origin.

(e) $a_N = \varkappa v^2 = \dfrac{6(13\sinh^2 t + 4)}{(13\sinh^2 t + 4)^{3/2}} = \dfrac{6}{\sqrt{13\sinh^2 t + 4}} = \dfrac{6}{v}$

(f) $\dfrac{dv}{dt} = \dfrac{13\sinh t \cosh t}{\sqrt{13\sinh^2 t + 4}}$, which is negative when $t < 0$ and positive when $t > 0$. The particle slows down before reaching $(3,0)$, speeds up thereafter.

2 3 4 5 6 7 8 9 0